THE SHAPING OF SOCIAL
Social rule system theory with applications

scAsss

THE SWEDISH COLLEGIUM FOR ADVANCED STUDY IN THE SOCIAL SCIENCES

THE SHAPING OF
SOCIAL ORGANIZATION :
Social rule system theory with applications

by

Tom R. Burns and Helena Flam

with

Reinier de Man, Tormod Lunde, Atle Midttun, and Anders Olsson

Ⓢ SAGE Publications · London
Beverly Hills · Newbury Park · New Delhi

SAGE Publications Ltd
28 Banner Street
London EC1Y 8QE

SAGE Publications Inc
275 South Beverly Drive
Beverly Hills, California 90212
and 2111 West Hillcrest Drive
Newbury Park, California 91320

SAGE Publications India Pvt Ltd
C-236 Defence Colony
New Delhi 110 024

British Library Cataloguing in Publication Data

Burns, Tom R.
The shaping of social organization:
social rule system theory with applications
1. Social systems
I. Title   II. Flam, Helena
301   HM131

ISBN 0-8039-8027-2
ISBN 0-8039-8339-5 PBK.

Publishing services by Ponting–Green
London and Basingstoke
Photoset by Parker Typesetting Service, Leicester
Printed in Great Britain by J. W. Arrowsmith Ltd, Bristol

Contents

Acknowledgements

We are very grateful to and wish to thank the following persons for their comments, criticisms and suggestions relating to earlier drafts of parts, chapters or sections of this book: Hayward Alker, Jr, Bo Andersson, Maja Arnestad, Thomas Baumgartner, Walter Buckley, Mary Douglas, Amitai Etzioni, Jonathan Friedman, Rom Harré, Ulf Himmelstrand, Otto Keck, Les Johnson, John Robinson, Pablo Suarez, Ad Teulings, Rolf Torstendahl, Lars Udehn, Peter Wagner, Björn Wittrock.

This work has been carried out, in large part, in connection with the Social Science Theory/Methodology Programme of the Swedish Collegium for Advanced Study in the Social Sciences, Uppsala, Sweden.

Preface

> Though human animals are natural creatures subject to the laws of nature, human persons are creatures of culture, creatures whose distinctive mode of behavior must be specified in terms of the concepts of rules and norms and not merely of laws (of Nature).
>
> If language is, as it appears to be, essentially rulelike in nature, then it is impossible to reduce the phenomenon of language to any phenomenon that is explicable solely in terms of the laws of physical nature. Not merely the known laws of physical nature — any laws of physical nature, however comprehensive they may be.
>
> Rules or rulelike regularities are explicable only in terms of a peculiar set of conditions that include at least the following. Rules must be articulated in some recognizably social way; must be capable of being replaced in a viable way by alternative systems of rules; must be capable of being followed and violated by beings themselves capable of being conformed to and reformed or revised for reasons to which the beings affected subscribe.
>
> (Margolis, 1978:26)

Human activity — in all of its extraordinary variety and originality — is organized and governed largely by socially determined rules and rule systems. This is true whether the activities concern politics, economic production and exchange, science, art or everyday life. The organization of human activity, through social rule systems, is the subject of this book.

We take the position that a single theoretical/methodological framework — social rule system theory — can be used to describe and explain the formation and reformation of major types of social organization in contemporary society. The theory is used in the study of such organizations as government agencies and planning systems; inter-organizational networks and institutions including markets, negotiation systems and local government; and role relations including authority relationships between superiors and subordinates in work organizations.

1. From the perspective of our framework, human actors (individuals, groups, organizations, communities, and other collectivities) are seen as the producers and carriers of social rule systems. Rule systems structure and regulate social transactions and organization. At the same time, participating actors interpret, implement, and reformulate rules and systems of rules. On occasion, they struggle over the maintenance or reproduction of particular systems, such as an institutional framework for property rights or for

political authority or the basic laws and organizing principles governing such institutions as markets, local government, and collective bargaining systems.

2. Rule system theory assumes that different social actors often advance contradictory rule systems with which to structure and regulate social life, claiming ultimate legitimacy for their respective systems. They may also disagree about the interpretation and implementation of particular mutually shared rules and rule systems. Thus, norms, laws, organizing principles, and rule systems generally are considered — from the perspective of social rule system theory — to be linked as much to conflicts and struggle as to consensus and sharing.

In particular social rule systems are a major object of social struggle and social transformation. Social agents target upon them, some seeking to reform them while others try to maintain them. Through such processes, they give new or counter-interpretations to rules (as compared with the conventional interpretations), they create or adopt new rules and rule systems to bring to bear on the situation, and they activate and utilize meta-rules to resolve ambiguities and contradictions or to guide innovations and new developments in rule systems. In sum, social actors knowledgeably and actively use, interpret and implement rule systems. They also creatively reform and transform them. In such ways they bring about institutional innovation and transformation and shape the 'deep structures' of human history. *Indeed, major struggles in human history and contemporary society revolve around the formation and reformation of major rule systems, the core economic and political institutions of society.*

This approach to rules, norms, and normative orders differs substantially from that of Talcott Parsons (1951, 1960) and others who presume to a large extent consensus — or at least a lack of opposition — in social life. Even the study of deviance which has a long and distinguished history in sociology has tended to focus most attention on persons and groups who seek *to avoid following rules* rather than on agents and movements which *struggle to reform or to transform rule systems.*

3. Dominant rule systems, for example those organizing and regulating economic and political behaviour in modern society, give the behaviour recognizable, characteristic patterns. They also make it understandable and — in a limited, conditional sense — predictable for those sharing in rule knowledge. Human actors, as members of communities with certain established rule systems, are knowledgeable agents in the sense of 'knowing' how to utilize (and recognize) some or all of these systems. They possess also situa-

tional knowledge about concrete settings or conditions in which rule systems are implemented. In this sense, one may say *that a community or society consists of a human population which shares abstract as well as practical knowledge of major social rule systems:* language, norms and laws, codes of conduct, social institutions of family, community, economic organization and government, and social relationships. Languages, for instance, belong to particular communities whose members know and adhere to them, and whose communicative behaviour vis a vis one another is more or less reliable, because it is governed by a common language. (This applies not only to nations but to professions, status groups and social classes.)

Individuals, as partially socialized, knowledgeable agents have, in a certain sense, *internalized social structures in the form of social rule systems* which are shared among the members of a group, community or nation. Through implementing the systems, the members of such collectivities generate patterns of activity and outcomes which impact on the world. In a word, they objectify the systems, making a difference in the world.

4. Some of the central concepts of the theory are: rules, rule systems, the structure of rule systems; the social processes of making, interpreting and implementing rules; the maintenance, adaptation, and transformation of social rules and rule systems.

Rule system theory identifies several types of rules and specifies their place and relationships in rule systems, for example: classificatory and descriptive rules; evaluative rules and action rules; metarules; basic organizing principles; technical rules; formal, 'official' rules as opposed to informal and unwritten rules.

Typically, in any given action situation or sphere of social activity *multiple rule systems are activated and applied.* The theory examines some of the ways in which different rule systems may complement as well as contradict one another and the institutionalized and ad hoc ways in which social agents deal with rule and rule system contradictions.

5. The scope of rule system theory, as a framework with which to analyse and to explain patterns of social life, encompasses *those social phenomena where human agents have some element of choice, a choice within the constraints imposed by biological and physical forces and conditions.*

Not all regularities or patterns in social life are explainable solely in terms of social (as well as personal) rule systems. *Biological and physical constraints shape human possibilities.* The limits are not, however, fixed absolutely. They are subject to the availability of techniques and technologies which alter or transform the boundary between physical constraint and social possibility.

The studies and analyses presented in the book are particularly concerned with the interplay between social rule systems and the concrete interaction situations and activities in which social groups find themselves. Situational conditions enable or block the implementation of certain rules and rule systems. Successful enactment, however, usually has an impact on the physical, institutional, and cultural conditions of action. Conditions of action may be produced, often unintended, which make it difficult or impossible to implement and sustain the rule system in the future.

Seen at another level, rule system theory and its applications deal with the interplay between the world of human culture and institutions and the natural world of environment, resources, and technology. Such matters have only been peripherally treated in mainstream sociology. The use and development of uses of technology and energy resources (as well as other natural resources) can be understood only by examining them in relation to human action and its structuring through core institutions of modern, industrial society.[1]

6. Rule system theory redefines and develops a number of major social science concepts, among others:

(i) *social roles* as rule sets or sub-systems governing particular classes or categories of actors. The theory does not treat human agents as 'oversocialized beings' or 'cultural dopes' but expects them to advance innovative interpretations and reformulations of rules and person-specific rule systems (personality and personal styles).[2]

(ii) *social organizations and institutions* — such as markets, bureaucracy, and political systems — are defined and analysed as rule regimes.

(iii) *contradiction and certain conflicts* in social life are viewed as arising from multiple, intersecting rule systems (and changes in them) as well as from the concerted efforts of social agents to introduce, develop, or change rule systems.

(iv) *consensus and acceptance of legitimate rules and rule systems* are major but not the only bases for rule-governed behaviour.

Even when rules and norms effectively govern social action and societal development, they may not necessarily be shared by all or most members of the group, community or organization. In many instances, rules and systems of rules are accepted, and adhered to, on the basis of social sanctions, including the use or threat of force. In a word, rule system theory does not presuppose consensus about a social rule system within a group, community, or organization.

(v) *social power* is a major factor in the formation and reformation of social rule systems at the same time that rule systems structure the distribution of power resources and domination relations in any group, organization, or society.

(vi) *social order* is structured and regulated on the basis of systems of rules which have been instituted and to a greater or lesser extent enforced through human agency.

7. Social rule system theory is applied in the book to the analysis of concrete forms of social organization, with a particular stress on a few major economic and political/administrative formations in modern society:

• the organization of social domination and forms of interaction
• major institutions of modern society: markets, bureaucracy, and political-government systems
• collective bargaining systems
• technology and socio-technical systems
• science in relation to policy-making and politics

The macro-structural studies in the book, for example of government administration, collective bargaining, and planning systems entail historical studies of institutional formation and reformation. On the basis of rule system theory a number of special, partial theories are developed dealing with, for instance, markets, wage bargaining systems, technology and socio-technical systems, government organization and functioning, planning and forecasting activities.

The theory reveals the structure — a *universal social grammar underlying all social organization — and the particular forms of such grammar underlying different social institutions.* This provides the basis for describing and analysing comparatively different types of social institutions, for instance, markets, wage negotiation systems, bureaucracy, and democratic political systems.

8. Rule system theory, as a theory of social structure, is *a systematic alternative to such theories as structural functionalism and structuralism.* This is largely because of the central place it gives to human agency — the knowledgeability of human agents, their creative, active role in social rule formation and transformation processes, their strategic behaviour and struggles in the shaping and reshaping of social institutions and the forms of social life.[3] Rule system theory draws on the rich theoretical traditions of Marx and Weber, but is clearly distinct from them and goes beyond them in making use of the contributions of organizational theory, comparative institutional analysis, theories of social structuration, structural linguistics, and ethnomethodology as well as the theoretical works of a number of contemporary researchers who have developed rule

and rule system concepts, among others: Chomsky (1957, 1965), Cicourel (1974), Giddens (1976, 1984), Goffman (1974), Harre (1972, 1979a), Lindblom (1977) and Twining and Miers (1982). The book is divided into four parts. The first part outlines social rule system theory, its main concepts and tools for describing and analysing social organization. Parts II, III, and IV deal with several general types of social organization, their structural features, cases of their formation and reformation, and interactions between different modes of social organization. Part II focuses on market organization, including collective bargaining on labour markets. The chapters of Part III concern formal and informal organizations and, in particular, the structuration and dynamics of public bureaucracies. In Part IV we address the relationship between expert knowledge, science and technology, on the one hand, and social organization, on the other. Of particular interest is the organization of public policy processes. The final chapter discusses prevailing legitimate principles of social organization and their central role in the structuring of modern, Western societies. It is stressed that the core set of organizing principles are contradictory, generating tensions and pressures to restructure social organizations.

I
SOCIAL RULE SYSTEM THEORY

1
Actors, social action and systems[4]

Introduction: Actor-structure duality

Two fundamentally different conceptions of man and society underlie most approaches to the study of social behaviour and social
systems: one stresses the human agent while the other stresses
structure or system (Allardt, 1972; Burns et al., 1985; Etzioni, 1970;
Wallace, 1969).[5]

In the first, social actors are viewed as the essential sources of
social regularities and the forces that structure and restructure social
systems and the conditions of human activity. The individual, the
historic personality as exemplified by Schumpeter's entrepreneur or
by Weber's charismatic leader, enjoys an extensive freedom to act
within and upon social systems, and in this sense is independent of
them. In the other view, social actors are either not found or are
faceless automata following iron rules or given roles and functions
in social structures or systems which they cannot basically change.
Social action as a creative-destructive force — innovating, restructuring and transforming the conditions of human life — is absent.

Approaches to social phenomena stressing the human agent
(phenomenology, ethnomethodology, symbolic interactionism,
among others) achieved a limited breakthrough in the 1960s and
1970s, in the aftermath of the decline of structural functionalism as a
dominant paradigm (Wiley, 1985). Such approaches shared the
'marketplace of ideas' with an increasingly sophisticated causal
analysis and the re-emergence of historical sociology. This pluralism
certainly may have contributed to a sense of crisis, [6] but as Wiley
(1985) has stressed, it has also stimulated new creative efforts and
developments within sociology. Among these, we would include
attempts at new syntheses. In particular, Archer (1985; 1986),
Boudon (1979), Bourdieu (1977), Crozier (1980), Giddens (1976;
1984), among others, as well as our research associates and one of
us (Burns et al., 1985; 1986) have tried to systematically link 'actor
or agent conceptualizations' to 'structural or systemic approaches'.

In this brief introduction, we shall single out and discuss several

1

key elements of actor-system syntheses, indicating in some instances parallels or points of convergence between the work of Giddens and others and our own. The synthesizers, in their approach to the actor-system problem, make use of and develop linking or mediating concepts, such as social action, interaction, social process, social structuring and social rule formation. In Giddens, for instance, human action is pivotal. 'Structure' is viewed as both the product and medium of social action, a perspective conveyed by the notion of the duality of structure. Crozier (1980) employs, as do Alker et al. (1980; 1985) and Baumgartner et al. (1984), game theory as a vehicle to specify and analyse linkages between actors and larger structures and institutional frameworks. Archer (1985; 1986) focuses on social process where social structure conditions interactions among agents. The latter, through their interactions, elaborate and reform such structures. This is similar to the stress in Burns et al. (1985) on the process of strategic structuring: agents interact — struggle, form alliances, exercise power, negotiate, and cooperate — within the constraints and opportunities of existing structures, at the same time that they act upon and restructure these systems. The result is institutional change and development, but structurally conditioned. In the following section, these ideas are systematized in the theory of actor-system dynamics.

Introduction: Elements of the theory of actor-system dynamics
Human agents — individuals as well as organized groups, organizations and nations — are subject to material, political and cultural constraints on their actions. At the same time, they are active, often creative forces, shaping and reshaping social structures and institutions and their material circumstances. They thereby change, intentionally and unintentionally (often through mistakes and performance failures), the conditions of their own activities and transactions.

Having stated this general principle, we shall outline below a minimum set of concepts essential to dynamic description and model-building in social analysis.[7]

Levels of social systems
A *social system* consists of the set of relevant actors, their interrelationships, social activity and processes, their outcomes and effects, and the endogenous constraints and structuring processes which shape and reshape actors, cultural frames, social institutions. The theory identifies three levels of a social system: (1) actors, their roles and positions; (2) social action and interaction settings and processes; and (3) endogenous constraints: material, institutional

and cultural. Figures 1.1 and 1.2 represent these elements and their interrelationships in the structure of social systems.

Truly exogenous factors are those which conditionally structure actors, social action, and system development, but which are not influenced by them, *at least not in the short run.* In the long run, agents in the social system may gain control over them, thereby making them endogenous to the social system.

Fundamentally, social systems are dynamic because (1) exogenous factors invariably change and impact on them, causing internal restructuring, and (2) social activities within them often entail innovations and have unintended consequences. Through social interaction, endogenous structural factors and conditions as well as social agents are maintained and changed. These structuring effects of action are represented in Figure 1.2. Feedback loops, particularly multi-level feedback loops, make a social system potentially unstable. Stability depends on an extensive network of social controls and institutions. The institutional order of a social system may be viewed then as the macroscopic resultant of multiple, often contradictory structuring processes, including purposeful social action, a subject to which we shall return in later chapters.

Actors and social interaction

Social actors and agents. Human beings act purposefully. They take in and organize information, evaluate and make decisions.[8] They organize their behaviour and play out roles and interests in large part on the basis of social rule systems, including those organizing and regulating social domination. (Our treatment of social actors is conducted mainly in terms of their roles and relationships in social systems, not their actor unique characteristics or idiosyncrasies.)

Actors are the carriers of social rule systems and of practical knowledge essential to their implementation. At the same time, they give new and sometimes unexpected interpretations to social rules and action settings. More generally, they exhibit the capacity to innovate, demonstrating this through, for instance, the creation of new technologies and techniques as well as through reconstituting social norms and institutions. In this way, human agents through their actions transform the very conditions of their actions.

Collective actors — organized groups, enterprises, government agencies, parliamentary bodies, and political parties — make decisions, mobilize and allocate resources, and carry out collective actions. Such social agents have internal structures to organize the formulation and enforcement of internal rules, the making of various types of decisions and the execution of purposeful collective

FIGURE 1.1
General model of actor-system dynamics

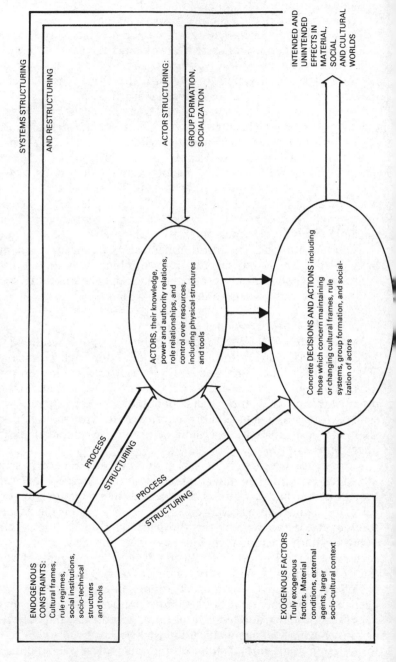

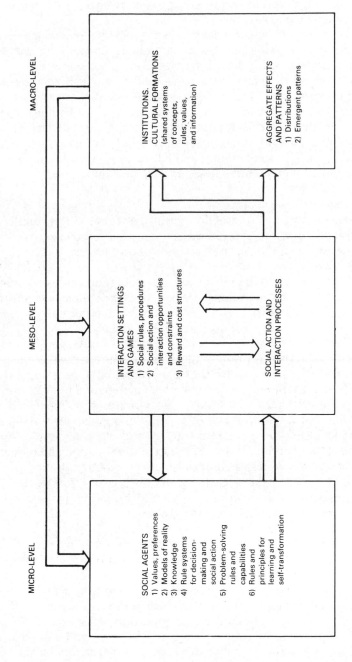

FIGURE 1.2
Model of multi-level social system

action. Such structures are constituted by social rule systems, as discussed in later chapters.

Social action and interaction. The concrete social activities of actors include loving and sharing, producing, cooperating, exercising power and struggling. These activities take place in concrete *transaction situations* in which the actors involved have unequal resources and opportunities to realize their purposes and interests. The distribution of action and interaction possibilities (including resource control) among actors not only determines their relative power in an ongoing situation but their capability of influencing future developments. Through their actions and interactions, social actors regulate and change their material, institutional and cultural worlds.

Constraints and opportunities

Concrete definable transaction settings or contexts structurally condition social action and interaction and their outcomes. We distinguish two general types of structural conditioning factors:

Institutions, cultural forms and social structure generally. Social rule systems, as found in, for instance, bureaucracy, economic and political systems and religion, structure and regulate social transactions. Cultural forms and institutionalized relationships are not reducible to the thoughts and acts of individuals.

Material and technological conditions. Physical conditions, climate, and the distribution of natural resources such as energy, as well as technologies (which are human creations) constrain as well as provide opportunities for certain social actions and interactions.

Cultural frames, institutions, and physical structures shape and regulate 'process-level' activities and conditions, such as those of production, exchange, conflict and the exercise of power. In particular, they condition: the definition of the situation and of relevant problems and issues, membership or participation in the activities, feasible or acceptable activities, relationships of actors or categories of actors to one another and to forms of property or resources, the outcomes of activities and the distribution of benefits and costs among different actors or categories of actors involved.

The structural conditioning of social action and interaction is not determining. In part, this is because it is often contradictory and problematic (Wardell and Benson, 1979), arising from the *multiple rule systems which converge on concrete interaction settings*. In part, social action and interaction are oriented not only to social rule systems but, as well, to the real conditions of action, such as the relative scarcity of certain strategic resources and the payoffs of action, and to the probable strategies of other actors insofar as the latter affect the same resources and payoffs (see note 23 on Weber).

Outcomes and developments
Social action and interaction have concrete outcomes and effects. These may be intended as well as unintended. They are the immediate payoffs and losses for those involved as well as more long-term consequences relating to the maintenance and transformation of social systems. The likely outcomes associated with human activity not only promote certain actions and discourage others, for instance promoting cooperation or competition and conflict. But they feed into the processes of resource distribution and accumulation which are important to future system development.[9]

Structuring activity. By structuring activity we mean that social action and its outcomes may be directed toward maintaining, modifying or transforming norms, institutions, and socio-cultural elements which regulate key societal processes such as production, socialization, conflict, and power processes.

Unintended and exogenous structuring of social systems. The structuring of social systems is not only the result of purposeful actions of social agents. Structuring also comes about as an unintended consequence of human activity.[10] In addition, exogenous material and social factors impinging on social systems have restructuring effects.

2
Social rule system theory

Introduction

In the previous chapter we suggested that concepts of social action and interaction are useful conceptual bridges between actor and structure. Another set of bridging or mediating concepts are those of 'social rules' and 'rule formation', which are closely related, as we shall see, to social action. These concepts can in many instances be traced to Weber, for whom rule concepts were central, particularly in his analyses of organizations. Albrow (1970:38–9) observes:

> Weber regarded the fact that human behavior was regularly oriented to a set of rules (*ordung*) as basic to sociological analysis. The existence of a distinctive set of rules governing behaviour was intrinsic to the concept of an organization. Without them it would not be possible to say what was and what was not organizational behavior... Commands and rules ranked as equally important in the structuring of social relationships. In an administrative order they were linked in that the rules regulated the scope and possession of authority.[11]

In this and the following chapters we develop *one limited approach* to tackling the actor-system problem in social theory and research, namely the theory of social rule systems.

The theory concerns the formation and implementation of social rule systems. *The rule systems governing transactions among agents in a defined sphere specify to a greater or lesser extent who participates (and who is excluded), who does what, when, where, and how, and in relation to whom.* In particular, they define possible rights and obligations, including rules of command and obedience, governing specified categories of actors or roles vis a vis one another. *The theory deals with the properties of social rule systems, their role in patterning social life, and the social and political processes whereby such systems are produced, maintained, and transformed as well as implemented* in social action and interaction. The main foci of the theory are:

- social agents as the formulators, carriers, and transformers of the rule systems
- social transactions among agents, conditioned but not determined by rule systems (which allow degrees of interpretive freedom, unregulated areas of action, as well as the intrusion of factors independent of the rule(s) in question, such as interests, antagon-

8

isms and alliances, structured elsewhere in society)
- processes of rule maintenance and reformation whereby social rule systems are reproduced, elaborated, and transformed through social transactions among agents
- major rule systems such as economic and political/administrative institutions, which shape the context and many of the conditions of social action in modern society

The theory addresses questions such as: (i) why do human actors create and maintain social rules, and why do they follow social rules? (ii) in any given social group, organization or sphere of action, which actors or groups are central to social rule formation, interpretation, and implementation? (iii) through what social processes are social rules produced and institutionalized, maintained and changed? (iv) under what conditions do actors and groups of actors try to change or transform social rule systems, how do they go about this and under what conditions do they succeed or fail? (v) in any given socio-political context, what are the structural opportunities and constraints defining different actors' capabilities to reform or transform specific social rule systems?

In the following sections, we outline a few of the main theoretical elements of social rule system theory.

Elements of rule system theory:
Actors, rule systems and social structuring
This section focuses on several of the major concepts and assumptions of social rule system theory. The concepts enable, at least in part, the bridging of actor and structure levels and the systematic analysis of the organization of social activity.[12]

Rule-making, rule-interpretation, and rule-implementation are basic, universal processes in human societies. The theory, as formulated here, focuses on two of the fundamental rule processes: (1) the formation and reformation of social rule systems, entailing the formulation, exclusion, selection and ordering of rules in relation to one another; (2) the implementation of social rules, which in many instances involves the mobilization of power and authority to enforce rules. In the course of producing and implementing social rule systems, human agents (individuals, groups, communities and organizations) cooperate, conflict, and carry on power struggles. In a word, *there is a politics and creative dynamics to rule processes.*

Our concepts of rule and rule system are considerably broader than that of 'norm', familiar to sociologists and found in every basic text in sociology. Various types of rules and rule systems can be identified and distinguished, for instance, in terms of their cognitive, behavioural and institutional status: norms and laws, moral principles, codes of conduct, rules of the game, administrative regulations and procedures, technical rules, conventions, customs and traditions. Norms then are only one type of rule. Different types of norms can be identified, as suggested by everyday distinctions between constitutional principles, legal, administrative, informal and local norms.

Organizational or administrative systems as well as modern economic and political institutions are special types of rules systems which we refer to as *rule regimes*. These are enforced through *networks of control in which sanctioning powers can be mobilized and applied.*

Rule system theory does not concern itself only or primarily with 'formal rules'. These may be important, particularly when backed by effective sanctions. On the other hand, many informal rules, unwritten and implicit rules play crucial roles in regulating social transactions and in the architecture of social structure. Hence, analytical focus must be broad enough to encompass both prescribed and operative rules, for example:

- Moral codes, which may be 'rewritten' or ignored in practice. There are varying degrees of pretention, hypocrisy and deviance from the theoretical or ideal code
- 'Constitutions', laws, and administrative regulations, both in theory and practice
- Administrative organizing principles and rules: division of functions, coordination and communication linkages, etc. (here one finds the well-established distinction between formal and informal rules)
- Institutional structures: the actual rules, including informal, unwritten or implicit ones relating to authority, power, and access to resources

Social rules and social action

The systematic linking of rule system concepts to those of social action is a major feature of the theory. Social interactions, such as those of exchange, conflict, and the exercise of power, have a *dual relation* to social rule systems. The latter organize and regulate social transactions, such as exchange or political competition, in terms of *who* is permitted to participate, *what transactions* are appropriate or legitimate, *where and when* may transactions be carried on, *how* are they to be carried out, and so forth. At the same time, transactional processes are essential to the formation and reformation of rule systems, as well as to their interpretation and implementation. Rules and systems of rules are manifested in the social activities which can be observed in everyday life. These transactions provide those involved with opportunities to modify or transform rules. In many instances rule formation and reformation occur through *strategic structuring*. Such *meta-processes* — entailing exchange, conflict and power struggles among the agents involved — are specifically oriented to maintaining or changing particular rules, sub-systems of rules, or entire rule systems. Such notions lead one in a natural way to look for the sources of 'institutional frameworks' and for those agents who consciously — as well as unwittingly — reproduce, adapt and change these systems: major companies, government policy centres, professional networks designing and developing substantially new technologies, etc.

Rules, freedom, and constraint
Rules as regulators of action — in contrast to most physical or biological constraints — can be transgressed or changed. Bennett (1964:17) stresses this point, 'For a creature to be correctly said to have a rule, it is necessary that it should be able to break the rule,' that is to make a decision not to follow the rule or to change it. Along similar lines, Harre and Secord (1972:17) emphasize the freedom of choice aspect:

> The mechanistic model is strongly deterministic; the role-rule model is not. Rules are not laws, they can be ignored or broken, if we admit that human beings are self-governing agents rather than objects controlled by external forces, aware of themselves only as helpless spectators of the flow of physical causality.

The existence of choice offers a spectrum of possible human responses, which are distinguishable within rule system theory: highly institutionalized rules such as laws and moral principles that may be deeply internalized or enforced by powerful sanctions; 'technical rules' which are adhered to because they result in effective or successful action (e.g., the operation of a machine or other technology); and those rules that are more or less open to sub-group or personal preference and choice (e.g. rules of dress in many settings in modern societies). The processes of rule formation and reformation as well as socialization differ substantially in these various cases, as argued and illustrated in this book.

Finally, not every action which is 'chosen' — as opposed to

externally determined or caused — is socially rule-guided or rule-governed. Acts may be personal, impulsive, psychically motivated, or ad hoc in character (even if strategically motivated). These actions are not, in a strict sense, governed by social rules. (On a meta-level, there may be a social principle defining the situation as one where social organizing principles and rules apply minimally.) To be sure, actors often crystallize or institutionalize what has been previously a pattern of ad hoc strategic responses. Such crystallization is observed in the formulation of rules of strategy in games, marketplaces, and war. In general, one distinguishes, at least analytically, between an isolated or ad hoc decision or activity and action governed by a social principle or rule. Along such lines, Lindblom (1977:22–3) has argued:

> Government officials sometimes issue individual orders, as ... when a judge declares at the conclusion of a civil trial that 'defendant must pay to plaintiff the sum of 5000 [dollars].' But authority usually operates through law and other prescriptive rules. Similarly, grants of governmental authority by those subject to it typically take the form of rules specifying who can exercise what kind of control over whom in what circumstances.

Rule-regulated action does not imply rule-determined action. Not all regularities or patterns in social life are rule determined. Biological, psychological and physical forces and constraints contribute to framing the contexts for human action and, in particular, the activities of rule-making, rule-interpretation and rule-implementation.

Certain actions are possible, others not, due to the constraints of the physical environment and of social ecology. Environmental conditions and developments also provide incentives and disincentives (payoff structures), thereby contributing to the patterning of social activities (see Figure 1.1). Of course, social agents may formulate rules in order to systematically exploit identifiable payoff structures. They also often establish normative rules to regulate payoffs, as in the case where attempts are made to correct the outcomes of market forces through the application of distributive norms. However, normative rules rarely succeed in fully regulating distributional outcomes, especially in complex, modern societies.

In sum, social rule systems do not fully *determine* patterns of social transactions among actors and their outcomes. Situational constraints, and actors' interpretations and evaluations of these result not only in 'local variation' in the implementation of social rule systems but may also lead to widespread deviance from social rules, including inappropriate or illegitimate behaviour.

Social rule systems
We refer to complex rule structures with terms such as rule systems,

social rule systems, rule regimes and social grammars.

Rule system is the most general concept. Rules are not simply autonomous entities that can be put together in purely ad hoc ways. They are organized into modules or rule systems. These consist of sets of context-dependent and time-specific rules organized for structuring and regulating social transactions, for carrying out certain activities, performing specific tasks, or interacting in socially defined forms with others. Rule systems may be purely *private rule or 'personality systems'* or they may be collectively shared systems. In the latter case we refer to *social rule systems*. A norm (complex) is an instance of a social rule or system of rules.

Social rule systems, which structure and regulate social transactions and which are backed to a greater or lesser extent by social sanctions and networks of power and control, are referred to as *rule regimes*. The organizing principles and core rules of these systems are authoritative, having behind them a high probability of organized social sanctioning (Friedman, 1977:4). Social institutions, such as private enterprises and government agencies, as well as complex institutional arrangements such as those lying at the core of, for instance, capitalism are rule regimes. For most individuals and groups these have an 'objective character'. A network of social controls maintains as well as depends to some extent on these regimes. For those who have the power and authority to assure the maintenance and/or partial restructuring of the system, the regime complex is not external or purely 'objective'. In other words, certain sub-sets of rules in a regime underlying the social order are not simply given for them but are subject to strategic structuring and reform.

Since social rule systems are collectively shared, they permit *supra-actor descriptions and analyses* of the patterning of social transactions and social structure in the sphere to which they apply (as stressed earlier, 'sharing' is not the same as consensus, since acceptance of or adherence to a particular social rule system may be imposed). A rule regime governing social transactions among agents in a defined sphere specifies to a greater or lesser extent *who participates (and who is excluded), who does what, when, where and how, and in relation to whom*. In particular, it defines the *rights and obligations, including possible rules of command and obedience, governing specified categories of actors or roles vis a vis one another*.[13] Social rule systems are then describable and analysable on an *institutional level,* for instance as regimes to which people are more or less compelled to adhere through social controls, including coercion (Allardt, 1972).

On the actor level, social rule systems function as grammars.

Participants in social transactions utilize the grammars *to structure and regulate their transactions* with one another in defined situations or spheres of activity. These are 'generative grammars' for social action. They provide a system for classifying different types of actors, interactions, and settings. They provide a set of rules which enable the actors involved to structure or order acts as sequential elements of social transactions.

Actors occupying different positions in a social structure are governed by role-specific grammars or role-sets. Such grammars are differentiated at the same time that they are more or less integrated into an institutional frame. The actors collectively produce *transaction sequences, the specific structuring of which is based on their respective and complementary social grammars.*[14] In sum, social rule systems organizing human transactions consist of a set of role grammars along with transaction norms and procedures, including 'rules of the game' that apply to all participants to a great extent irrespective of their roles.

Social institutions and spheres of social action
Institutionalized rule systems apply to — and indeed define — particular spheres of social activity. Examples are:

- Business enterprise and the organization of production are governed by civil law relating to property rights, company law, contract law, laws regulating employment and contracts negotiated with labour unions, legislation relating to work and natural environments, etc. as well as the 'work culture' prevailing in any region, branch or work organization
- Public administration is governed by public law, specific legislation for agency organization and programmes, laws governing civil service administration and employment, government policy and regulations
- Political settings where decisions about laws, policies, organizing principles, programmes, etc. are made are in Western countries governed by more or less democratic procedures. (Codified systems of procedure such as 'Robert's Rules of Order' or equivalent may apply)
- Criminal justice system is a complex of different rule systems (legal, administrative, informal, etc.) which govern the organization, decision rules and procedures of the police, courts, prisons and parole supervision in their dealings with criminals and juvenile delinquents

Markets, private and public production organizations, and democratic institutions can be specified and analysed in terms of abstract organizing principles and rule systems. Their enactment, however, is situationally conditioned. Participants usually have considerable concrete knowledge based on experience about how such rule systems are implemented in particular settings, how they function, what possibilities there are to adapt rules or to innovate in rule-making or rule interpretation. Thus, in the study of social institutions, we stress the importance of examining and analysing the *concrete action settings* to which rule system complexes apply and are implemented, i.e.:

- the specific social conditions, the configuration of actors and groups involved, their level of knowledge, the structure of commitments and loyalties they bring into the situation, including their level of predisposition to adhere to the relevant rule system complex and to prevail, if necessary, on other actors to do so as well, the relations of domination as well as the predispositions to cooperate and conflict among the actors and groups involved
- physical and spatial conditions of social action and interaction
- timing of events and developments which impact on action conditions and possibilities

In a certain sense, each and every enactment of a rule system is unique. And observable events and patterns are unique. (For many reasons — not least practical ones — we choose to ignore the infinite specificity of what can be observed in social activities.)

In sum, an institution or a social organization *in practice or in its implementation* is more than a social rule system. It entails particular groups of social actors, situational factors, situational analyses and interpretations as well as social controls whereby compliance with its core rules is more or less accomplished. Adherence to rules and their practical implementation are probabilistic. They shift as new situational analyses and rule interpretations emerge or as the institution loses legitimacy or power. In such a case, opposition actors successfully organize and mobilize resources while those with vested interests in, or strong ideological commitments to, the regime lose power or the capability to mobilize social control networks to defend and sustain the regime. This ultimately results in major reforms or possibly an entirely new order.

Basic rules in social rule systems
There are three general types of rules: descriptive rules, evaluative rules and prescriptive rules. *These enable human agents to make different types of choices relating to facts, evaluations or judgements, and actions,* respectively.[15]

The three general types of rules — descriptive, evaluative, and action rules — along with meta-rules (that is, rules about rules) make up *social paradigms* or *models*. These are the shared bases on which the members of any given group, organization, or community organize and regulate social action and transactions in defined spheres of activity.

In particular, *all established or institutionalized social relationships between individuals and groups are structured and regulated by social rule systems which are shared by those who participate in these relationships and which orient them to one another.*[16] The rule systems specify who participates in the relationship, how they should act, what is worthy of attainment and, in general, they organize and regulate transactions among participating agents. They consist of rules of classification and other descriptive rules (including beliefs), values and prescriptive rules or norms (see note 15). Such a conceptualization applied to social relationships can be extracted from Weber (1968), Blau and Scott (1962:5), and Haas and Drabek (1975), among others:

(a) *Classificatory and descriptive rules* distinguish different types of action situation, actors (types of participants and non-participants, status positions and roles among participants), actions and interactions, outcomes, events and so forth relevant to the relationship. They also include formulations about inter-relationships, including causal connections, among the different categories.

(b) *Evaluative rules or values* indicate the goals for which participants in the relationships should strive — their notions of what is desirable and suitable ideals — such as the value of egalitarian or democratic relations, the importance of being honest or working cooperatively, or the achievement of economic gain.

(c) *Prescriptive rules or norms* specify how actors in the relationships are to behave, including the legitimate or at least acceptable means to strive for what is defined as good or valuable in the action spheres to which the relationship applies. Aside from norms which all participants are expected to follow, the rule systems of social relationships specify complementary and asymmetrical roles. A superordinate, for instance in a work organization, has the designated rights vis a vis his subordinates to take initiatives, to give orders and to define tasks and standards of performance as well as to evaluate and sanction.

Human actors as rule creating and rule changing agents
Why do human actors and groups create and maintain social rules and rule systems? In general, one can say that such systems are

socially produced and reproduced means to effectively structure and regulate purposeful collective action, including social domination and the establishment of social order. Analytically, one can distinguish between instrumental and communicative motivations for the social production of social rule systems.

Instrumental, including exploitive purposes. Social rule systems are created and maintained in order to achieve 'collective goods' as well as to enable some agents to effectively dominate others.

Social rules, including descriptive, evaluative and prescriptive rules, are the cumulative knowledge and know-how in human groups and collectivities. They are established and developed in efforts to solve certain collective problems, to realize desirable states or goals, and to generate certain valued or effective activities. The knowledge is maintained, transmitted and reproduced in the form of social rule knowledge.

Included in collective knowledge are the norms and social institutions which enable actors to coordinate their activities for mutually desirable ends, and to participate in communication processes, problem-solving activities, and social decision-making. In other words, social activity is organized, on the basis of such rule systems, so as to achieve desirable patterns of behaviour and/or outcomes, or to avoid undesirable ones.

Social rule systems such as community norms and institutions are particularly important in two contexts. (1) They are strategically useful organizing and coordinating devices in contexts where the actions of different actors are interdependent and where, in the absence of social coordination, negative unintended consequences are likely to occur (such contexts include 'the Common's problem' or the unintended depletion of a scarce collective good such as water, forests, or other natural resource based on individual pursuit of self-interested resource exploitation. Moreover, these systems often emerge only after prolonged struggles to limit and regulate destructive social competition and conflict (Burns et al., 1985)). (2) Social rule systems, as means to organize and coordinate social action, are also important in contexts calling for resource mobilization sufficient to produce particular collective goods (temples, irrigation canals, dams, defensive forces, etc.).

Collective action problems (among others, 'free-rider' and 'prisoners' dilemma' type problems) are handled through the institutionalization of social norms prescribing certain behaviour (cooperation, honesty, collective discipline) and proscribing others (non-cooperation, cheating, dishonesty) in specified settings (Burns et al., 1985). Or an authority may be designated with the right to command obedience to assure coordination, sufficient resource mobilization, and collective discipline generally.

The purposeful structuring of social action and interaction through the establishment and maintenance of social rule systems is not only pursued for the collective or general good. Powerful agents may pursue it in order to advance their special interests. Thus, rule regimes may be designed and maintained, to a greater or lesser extent, to assure that some categories of actors are able to dominate, and to gain from or exploit, others *on a regular and systematic basis*. For instance, some property rights and systems of authority are established and maintained by interests in order to *institutionalize their power and status, resource control, and future strategic action capabilities*.

Relations of domination are further elaborated in the concrete interactions among the parties involved. Indeed, specific rules for such interactions are made, interpreted, and implemented in an *ongoing process of negotiation*. This entails anything from passive resistance to open confrontation on the part of subordinate groups. The latter, over time, may achieve substantial gains in the terms set for such interactions, in particular in specifying the limits of the superordinates' power or the disciplinary means at their disposal as well as guaranteeing areas of autonomy for subordinates. Changing external conditions which affect the balance of power among the groups often affect the possible outcomes of such negotiations.

Even rule regimes constituting domination relations may provide certain benefits and advantages to subordinate and periphery groups: such as protection of their property or their collective physical or social security. Elite groups try, of course, to legitimize (even with some justification) social organization that produces, among other things, general collective goods. Morever, even in areas of less obvious material or spiritual interest, subordinates often accept regimes, not only because sanctions are imposed, but because the regime provides a type of 'rule of law', specifying the limits of superordinates' power, guaranteeing areas of autonomy, freedom and self-organizing action of subordinate groups (Perrow, 1979:30).

Communicative and symbolic purposes. Human actors and groups establish and maintain social rules as a means to produce clear communications and to differentiate activities in precise and meaningful ways. This is, in part, a strategy to deal with social uncertainty, ambiguity and conflicts that might arise in their interactions. In different forms of social intercourse, including such activities as physically touching, hugging, and kissing, socially produced rule systems provide a basis of communication and contribute to making more or less clear distinctions between various types of
.

relations, for instance, sexual and non-sexual, family and non-family, play and serious (see Chapter 3). Actors participating in social relationships so defined can co-orient, anticipate and understand one another, and coordinate their activities. The shared social grammars also distinguish one type of social relationship — and corresponding patterns of transaction — from others in terms of who is included or excluded, what types of action are permitted, prescribed or proscribed, who has the right to do what, who has access to or control over resources used in the sphere, etc. They assure not only certain patterns of interaction and outcome. *They operate so as to communicate unambiguous meanings* to participants about what it is that they are doing, who is involved, how, when, and where. To be a 'knowledgeable participant' in the relationship means to have learnt the social rule systems, at least those essential to their role communications and interactions with one another.[17]

Human groups also create and develop social rule systems — conventions, customs and collective styles — to give symbolic identity to themselves and, thus, to differentiate themselves from other groups and communities. Such rules of symbolic differentiation may be found in the styles of dressing, eating, and conversing, which intentionally distinguish status groups and communities from each other.

Many statutory rules have significant symbolic/normative dimensions which may be just as important to the rule-makers and to those to whom the rules apply, as their intended instrumental effects (Twining and Miers, 1982:296). Legislation, penalizing the possession of certain drugs or making some types of racial or sexual discrimination unlawful, is sometimes of this character (Twining and Miers, 1982:196).

The uncertainty, and related risks, of social and physical existence are precisely the general problems which social rule systems, as social technologies, have been produced to deal with. Of course, as in any technology, the 'solution' itself often generates new problems and uncertainties, which it cannot handle itself. Regimes such as social stratification and international economic structures generate a variety of problems which cannot be effectively handled within those frames (Eisenstadt and Curelaru, 1977; Burns et al., 1986).

In general, rule systems should not be conceived simply as social constraints or limitations on action possibilities (Giddens, 1984). They are also templates and strategic guidelines. They reduce social uncertainty, which is important to most humans in many key action settings. In addition, they provide opportunities for social actors to behave in ways that would otherwise not be possible, and even to innovate and to pursue new alternatives. Some of them provide access to certain strategic resources, or enable agents to make claims or to shape collective action opportunities — and in this sense, they are socially determined capabilities or powers.

Factors underlying rule-following and compliant behaviour

Various regulative mechanisms and forms of social control underlie adherence to and implementation of social rule systems: legal sanctions, 'private' social network and organizational sanctions, public opinion, internalized moral codes, and ideology, among others. Those based on sanctions imposed by the state are familiar to legal theorists. In a general study of social rules, extending beyond legal systems, a spectrum of social control and socialization mechanisms can be identified and analysed:[18]

* laws are enforced by means of the coercive power of the state. In addition, in modern, democratic societies, the state makes substantial use of positive incentives and moral persuasion, and tries to enlist the support of intermediary organizations, in order to gain adherence to certain laws as well as government policies and regulations lacking full legal status. The enforcement of social rule systems through the overt use of state power occurs relatively infrequently in modern, Western nations. Rational–legal principles as well as property right notions are deeply ingrained norms and are a pervasive part of the social order
* norms and rule systems are enforced through organizational and network sanctions. Many of those found within business firms and government agencies have the ultimate backing of the state (judiciary, police) in that they are grounded on property rights or public law pertaining to government [19]
* mutual agreements and contracts, as between economic and/or political agents are enforced by the parties to the negotiations, their organizational apparatuses. These use persuasion and disciplinary means and, under some conditions, the backing of the state
* norms and rule systems are also supported by 'private social coercion', e.g. the Mafia or gang 'laws'. Some systems governing, e.g. certain aspects of market behaviour, are enforced through private, non-coercive sanctions, such as the threat of a consumer boycott, or the threat of a supplier, for instance the telephone company, cutting off the service
* public opinion is, in some areas of social life, a sanctioning force, particularly where, as in public life, actions are relatively visible.

This sanction is much more powerful in a relatively cohesive community with well-developed social network and organization in contrast to highly fragmented or anomic social systems

- many norms and rule systems such as moral codes are deeply internalized, as a result of socialization. Norms such as those relating to democratic practice, fairness, and justice are moral imperatives, or principles of life in many communities. These communities are accustomed to being organized in such terms. Their members would feel in many instances estranged or alienated if they behaved otherwise. Of course, such deep internalization also implies a potential network of social control, activated in response to deviant behaviour[20]

- not all rule systems to which human agents adhere — and adhere closely — are enforced through sanctions or even through internalization and ideological justification. Some systems are supported by the payoffs they provide (conversely, the losses they avoid). Thus, technical rules relating to the operation of a machine or complicated equipment may be closely adhered to, since this assures effective, safe operation of the machine. Such rule compliance has an instrumental basis. Of course, even technical rules are often reinforced through socially applied sanctions. Similarly, the top managers of enterprises may follow certain organizing principles and systems of rules in organizing production and making marketing decisions, because they have found or believe it profitable to do so [21]

- rule compliance occurs in part simply as a consequence of actors habitually implementing particular rules and rule systems in everyday activities. Enactment structures patterns of social experience. These are externalized/objectified manifestations of social rule systems (Berger and Luckman (1967) refer to 'recipe knowledge'). New members or participants are partially socialized in this way. Old members are continually re-socialized. Such 'covert socialization' is usually complemented with more overt processes, such as special supervision, training, and 'education'

- many rule systems, such as those connected with 'custom' and 'tradition' are followed because they are the established patterns for doing things and there are no obvious alternative patterns. Children learn many rules in these terms, that is simply imitating what adults and other children do and following these repeatedly over time. The rules and rule systems governing social behaviour are so many, diverse, and complex — particularly in the modern world — that to question or to try to replace each and every one would leave the human agent immobilized, unable to begin to act.

Typically, there is a combination of factors which motivate against all-too-frequent or intensive questioning of compliance with rules and the routines of simply complying with them. A basic stability in rule compliance obtains because actors adhere to a *meta-rule* usually acquired and strengthened during child socialization, that social rule systems are 'good', useful, and sooner or later rewarding. And moreover, the costs of opposing them and trying to adopt or create alternative systems are formidable, and most attempts fail.

The meta-rules which socialized members of communities accept are typically abstract and general, applying to social rules and rule systems which are provided by 'authoritative', 'good', or legitimate agents: norms, enactments, decrees, regulations, principles of knowledge and method, and so forth. Similarly, social rules and rule systems which have been arrived at through certain established and correct procedures, such as 'decisions of parliament', 'supreme court or presidential decisions', ' scientific tests and analyses', etc. can also fall under the *meta-rule which suspends serious reflection, questioning, and uncertainty. Once accepted and institutionalized, these enable the formulation and development of entire complexes of rules and the issuance of orders.* Lindblom (1977:18–20) points out concerning general rules of obedience:

> Every specific control can be used either as a method of direct control or as a method for establishing a rule of obedience which, once established, itself suffices for control as long as it stands ... One, several, or many people explicitly or tacitly permit someone else to make decisions for them for some category of acts (or sphere of activity).

Such a rule defines a domination relation, with a certain probability of obedience on the part of subordinate actors. Otherwise, each occasion for exercising influence would require mobilizing power resources.

In sum, participants in social relationships conform to the governing rule systems to varying degrees. Compliance depends on the status participants have within the group or community adhering to the systems as well as on the social sanctions enforcing them. Rule systems vary in significance as well as in the extent to which, and the means whereby, social sanctions are used to enforce them. The centrality of, for example, property rights in a modern Western society is underscored by the extensiveness of relevant legislation backed by the authority of government and, if necessary, by the use of means of violence. By contrast, various conventions and modes of behaviour are enforced largely through public opinion. Some rules, such as purely technical rules, may have intrinsic or self-realizing payoffs, and need not be enforced or sanctioned. Still others in the system are simply traditions or routines, without apparent competing alternatives.

Rules in practice: Conformity, deviance, and informal rules

One may study rules and rule systems much as students of law do, namely, by examining their particular formulations, the domains or processes to which they apply, their possible interpretations, the networks of various types of rules within a rule system, and the degree of consistency and precision of rules within a system. Such analyses are on the level of the study of knowledge and ideology (see Chapter 7).

Rule system theory, as an empirically oriented theory, is, in addition, interested in the extent to which, and the particular ways in which, social rules and rule systems are realized or implemented *in practice*. Furthermore, it is interested in the exercise of power and authority and in processes of sanctioning in connection with rule-making, interpreting and implementing. Related questions concern rule systems which require a minimum of sanctioning for their enforcement as opposed to those which can only be enforced through the massive and systematic use of force. In general, the theory presumes that social agents (individuals, groups, organizations and movements) struggle to varying degrees among themselves about the enforcement of rules, and about whether or not to maintain or to change them. These processes affect the degree and stability of social rule compliance.

In practice, rule systems are never precisely and systematically implemented in the settings to which they are supposed to apply. Nor are they implemented with strict adherence either to their 'letter' or to their spirit. Those involved in the setting to which a particular rule system applies may lack adequate knowledge of the system or necessary information about the specific action conditions in which the system is to be implemented. Mistakes are made. Situational constraints vary. Resistance is encountered from some actors; compromises or adaptations of rules are willingly or forcibly made. New rules are invented.

The actual or informal rule system worked out in practice through learning, negotiation, persuasion, conflict and the exercise of power among agents in the setting will differ to a greater or lesser extent from the formal system. The latter may be formulated in laws, sacred books, handbooks of rules and regulations, or in the design of systems which dominant groups or coalitions in the setting advocate and try to implement.

Mouzelis (1967:59–61) points out that participants in social organization are not simply automata or inert materials subject to formal rule systems:

> Organizational members do not comply automatically with formal rules. Their compliance is always problematic and unpredictable. It is this fundamental 'recalcitrance of human tools' which accounts for the unanticipated consequences of purposive action and control. The tension between the formal rules, which attempt to control organizational behaviour, and the 'recalcitrance' of such behaviour which defies full control and develops in an unpredicted manner, generates new situations and needs which in their turn bring forth a renewed attempt to control the situation by further rules. Thus, in a general schematic way the general pattern underlying most of the models of bureaucracy ... seems to be:
>
> Purposive control (rules) ▶ unanticipated consequences ▶ renewed control.

> Thus Alvin Gouldner in his *Patterns of Industrial Bureaucracy* stresses the dialectic nature of bureaucratic rules. Rule elaboration has the functional and often unintended consequence of decreasing the visibility of power relations between inferior and superior bureaucrats. In a culture with democratic egalitarian norms (like the American one), this simulation of power between the written law decreases impersonal tension and favours co-operation. But on the other hand, the imposition of rules has a dysfunctional aspect. Specifically, the detailed definition by rules of unacceptable behaviour increases the knowledge of employees about the minimum acceptable behaviour.

Any rule system in its practice — as distinct from the formal or ideal formulation — will contain reformulations (rewritten rules), 'unwritten rules', and ad hoc rules and procedures, which are known by those who practise the system. To those outside the system, uninitiated into the actual practices, the operative rule system may be largely unknown or invisible.

Rule system theory stresses three major factors which make rule systems in theory or ideal different from implemented or operative systems: (1) *The concrete action settings* to which a particular rule system is applied. The settings are defined by the particular social agents involved, physical and spatial aspects, the timing of activities and events. These aspects can be referred to as the specific social-physical-time complex in which social transactions governed by rule systems take place (see Giddens, 1984). The complex is a major factor affecting the degree to which, and the precise ways in which, a social rule system is implemented. (2) *The knowledgeability and capability of actors* involved in the implementation of rule systems. Social actors may know about a particular rule system and be willing generally to adhere to it, but *lack the practical or operative knowledge, including local knowledge of the setting in which implement-*

ation is to take place. Other types of capabilities or resources might also be essential to the enactment of social rules. One type of resource is, for instance, the means of action, such as tools and capital. (3) *The commitment of involved actors to the rule systems and their motivation to adhere to or to accept the rule systems* governing their particular activities in a given sphere. On pages 20–21 we discussed various social controls and incentives which underlie adherence to or acceptance of rule systems.

In general, these factors which affect the rule implementation process are important for explaining how a social institution or organization 'appears in practice'. In this sense various situationally specific or 'local orders', having a common regime as a base, may emerge.

Rule systems, as valuable social technologies, become resources and stakes in social interaction and the strategic structuring of social life. Thus, they cannot be viewed as simply 'neutral' or 'technical means' to realize certain purposes such as increased coordination or the solution to collective action problems. In part, this is because they are powerful tools of social structuration which have instrumental and communicative impacts on social action and interaction. They are also a power resource which social agents utilize in their struggles and negotiations over alternative structural forms and development of social systems, serving their interests (in the area of organizational analysis, see Salaman, 1980: 148). In part, this is because they are introduced and maintained by powerful agents to advance or protect their own interests, against the interests or will of others.

From the perspective of rule system theory, human agents (individuals, groups, organizations and communities) should be viewed not only as producers but implementers of social rule systems. In some instances, they adhere closely to such systems, showing a high degree of commitment and loyalty to them and even trying to impose them on others. In other instances, they only accept them, by virtue of sanctions or potential sanctions. These actors are likely to experience such systems — or specific rules — as impositions or constraints on their behaviour, as they try to pursue interests or rely on means which are incompatible with the rule systems. Indeed, they may oppose the rules, openly struggling to change or replace them. More typically, they simply try to escape or to deviate from established rule systems without major penalties (but this is only possible in some contexts and for some actors).

Overall consensus or the absence of opposition is not then a necessary condition for the establishment and implementation of rule systems. Indeed, stratification systems — in particular class, ethnic, or political domination, among others — typically elicit individual and/or collective opposition in one form or another.

However, the overt use of force may not be essential — at least not frequently — to the maintenance of a particular rule regime. Other conditions of domination and social control are usually available or developed. For instance, subordinate groups of actors may be collectively weak.

Such weakness in the face of a system of inequality can be the result of several factors, e.g. (1) groups of actors in subordinate positions are fragmented and lack awareness of their common situation, or lack sufficient material means and organizational competence, for instance women prior to women's liberation, Palestinians prior to the late 1950s, workers before the formation of unions and worker movements, and, in general, categories of actors which are a group-in-itself and not one-for-itself; (2) dominant groups encourage or perpetrate fragmentation among subordinate or exploited groups, through various 'divide and rule strategies' (Burns et al., 1985); (3) particular economic, organizational, institutional or cultural conditions bind subordinates to their superiors or to the system as such and, thus, inhibit collective opposition (examples here are paternalistic enterprises and rational–legal bureaucracies); (4) the institutional arrangements for initiating and bringing about restructuring of some features of the stratification system discourage or reduce incentives for solidarity and collective action among subordinate groups, instead permitting adaptation and development in non-radical directions only (e.g., civil, political and social rights) which permit piecemeal reforms, protect collective bargaining and assure a modicum of welfare.

Organized opposition to a regime of power and control consists of social agents — groups, organizations, and movements — made up of individuals who have developed a shared symbolic image of themselves and a shared rule system for organizing collective decisions and action. Such opposition is illustrated by a trade union, a political party, mobilized/organized communities and ethnic groups, religious, political, and social movements. These engage in struggles — in some instances in major social struggles such as class war, ethnic strife, and international conflict — which may lead, under certain conditions, to reform or transformation of established rule regimes, governing, for example, economic or political relationships.

The contextuality of rule-forming and reforming behaviour
Human agents continually form and reform social rule systems,

even if organizing principles and core rule structures are maintained over long stretches of time. The process of rule system formation and reformation — which implies the structuring and restructuring of social relations and institutional frameworks — occurs within *historically given conditions.* These entail the concrete social-physical-time settings in which social action takes place and decisions are made about rule-making, rule-interpretation, and rule implementation. Hence, the great stress in rule system theory on studying these processes *in specific contexts* with certain social agents predisposed to cooperate, conflict, or engage in power struggles with one another.

The strategic structuring of rule systems

Strategic action to form, reform, or transform social rule systems is a common, although not always highly visible socio-political process. (It can be analytically distinguished from the forming and reforming of rule systems in everyday activities with a minimum mobilization of power resources and group struggle.) Strategic processes typically involve political and other types of collective struggles among agents with conflicting visions of, or interest in, particular social rule systems. On the one hand, innovators and entrepreneurs seek to establish new rules or to transform a rule system. On the other hand, there may be others who adhere to an established complex and act to impede or to put down change attempts, including 'devious acts' initiated on the level of everyday activity. Deviance, either resulting from 'innovative efforts' or the acting out of sub-cultural rule complexes ('the Mafia'), need not, therefore, take the form of attempting to change or transform rules through political or collective processes. Rather, it may simply entail *everyday strategies to avoid the imposition or enforcement of rules by more powerful agents such as the state, an employer or parent.*

In formally organized systems, e.g. business firms and government agencies, but even local clubs and voluntary organizations, the process of adapting and transforming rule systems is typically given an explicit, formal status. Thus, one may have a legislative process with investigations, hearings, debates and the final decisions taken by parliamentary or other democratically elected bodies. The rule-making or rule-changing processes may also be organized with elite consultation and decision-making, e.g. tri-partite (business, labour and government) institutions as found in the Scandinavian as well as other European countries.

Social reproduction and transformation

A basic principle of the theory of actor-structure dynamics concerns the interplay between structure and action: major regimes in a society organize and regulate the transactions among social agents at the same time that transactions maintain, elaborate, or transform these systems. Along such lines, Hernes et al. (1976:515, 518) elegantly reformulates Marx:

> Both the ends men pursue and the means at their disposal are decided largely by their past and present locations in the social structure — by their biography and their social position. But in pursuing their goals men may modify the constraints under which they choose: actions may change the parameters of choice. Another way of saying this is to say that the plans individuals seek to carry out are determined by their expectations about the future and about the distribution of possibilities, by their interests, and by the means they control.
>
> Not only may a group change the conditions of its own existence in the pursuit of its interests, it may also change the conditions of existence for another group by opening new possibilities or imposing new constraints — by destroying or providing alternatives. It is important to note the asymmetries that usually exist in the capacities of groups to change the choice parameters for each other, and particularly their impact on the probability of social conflict.

Such notions can be formulated in rule system terms, providing a further specification. *In our terms, continuities and discontinuities of social structures correspond to the maintenance or transformation of systems of rules or rule complexes through human action and trans-action, including strategic action.* This conception provides a point of departure for actor-system descriptions and analyses of social reproduction, adaptation, and transformation in social life, as a function of human transactions.

The maintenance of social organization is explained in terms of such factors as social power and control networks, routine patterns of social transaction, strategic maintenance actions and sanctioning, and deep rule structures and organizing principles. Changes of the latter, in particular, are very costly or disruptive, even for those groups that might have much to gain from such changes. There is an inherent 'conservatism' in the deep structures of social systems.

Nonetheless, social rules and rule systems — norms, laws, role relationships, institutions and social orders — are not fixed, even at deep levels of core rules and principles. Although they may be relatively stable over long periods of time, they are subject periodically to serious challenge, resulting in some instances in transformation. In the transition from one social system — or type of society — to another, whole rule system complexes may be transformed. Thus, a social order consisting of a complex of rule systems is never in equilibrium, but rather is subject to tension and pressures for change. Latent as well as manifest processes of destabilization arise: power shifts occur among groups of actors adhering to opposing organizing principles and social rule systems; multiple rule systems converge on strategic economic or political action settings, thereby generating ambiguity, uncertainty and conflict; other practical problems of implementation arise, e.g. lack of essential resources or changes in constraints of the physical world or the social environment. Often rule systems no longer relate meaningfully or effectively to the specific historical context(s) in which they are applied. Adherence to conventions and established rules in such cases leads to ineffective action, performance failures, and, ultimately, delegitimation and transformation of the rule systems.

A universal theme in human societies is the struggle between the new and the old. This struggle can be readily formulated in rule system terms, with more or less identifiable agents adhering to and seeking to maintain established or conventional rule systems, while others — change agents, entrepreneurs, social movements — seek to reform and transform. Class struggle is one particular case of this pattern.

Human bonding in time and space
Through their roles consisting of rule sets within social institutions and organizations, actors are related in meaningful, and more or less predictable, ways to one another and other larger collectivities. Roles give direction and meaning to their decisions and actions. They feel themselves more or less meaningful parts of larger totalities — groups, organizations, communities, and societies — governed by identifiable rule system complexes. Of course, individual actors or groups may not be fully knowledgeable about or fully competent to make use of all of these systems. Typically, they are knowledgeable about strategic parts of the rule systems governing areas of activity on which their material existence, social identity or other major valuables depend. In general, such knowledge is practical, operative knowledge, not theoretical knowledge.

Shared rules and rule systems are essential links between human individuals and between them and the macro-social structures which they produce and reproduce in their social transactions. Social rule systems also link the present to the past and to the future. The systems which people follow currently have been produced and developed over long stretches of time. Through their transactions, social groups and communities maintain and extend rule systems into the future. In a certain sense, they 'reproduce' them. Of course, human agents modify these systems, and in this sense there is some degree of discontinuity. But in large part there is substantial continuity with the past, because major social rule systems are difficult to change radically. (In this sense they are part of an 'objective reality'.) They are complex, usually requiring a long period of time to develop and to learn. In modern societies, large numbers of individuals, groups, and organizations depend on them for guidelines in organizing, and making more or less predictable, their social actions and interactions in important action spheres such as work, community, and politics.

Social rule systems are human constructions. Through their implementation, however, they structure and restructure concrete material and socio-cultural conditions. Social rule systems which become crystallized and legitimated into major social institutions are experienced generally as objective structures or 'real'. They constrain social action and interaction as well as provide opportunities for new types of social activities. At the same time, these human produced systems structure the subjective experiences of, and provide meaning to, individual persons. They exist as concrete knowledge inside each active member of the community socialized into or sharing rule system knowledge. They guide individual social activity. Each is enabled to 'carry on' everyday practices as well as to understand how other actors in the community are likely to behave. Shared social rules are the basis for actors to have similar expectations. They also provide a frame of reference and categories, enabling actors to communicate about and to analyse social activities. In such ways, uncertainty is reduced, and social actors can more or less effectively transact with one another. Harre and Secord (1972:12) point out:

> The propositional nature of rules fits them to appear in accounts and commentaries on action. The question of the authority of a rule is a matter for empirical investigation. It is the self-monitoring following of rules and plans that we believe to be the social scientific analogue of the working of generative causal mechanisms in the processes which produce the non-random patterns studied by natural scientists.

Social rule system theory as a research programme
Social rule system theory provides a general language to describe and analyse social organization and its structuring.[22] In some cases the framework is used simply to single out particular types of rule systems and to examine the processes whereby these are socially maintained or changed. Later chapters describe and analyse, for instance, the shaping and reshaping of markets, collective bargaining institutions, and government administration and planning systems.

Rule system theory incorporates and extends a number of theoretical ideas and models developed within sociology and social science: (1) the conception of social definition of the situation and its influence on the organizing of social behaviour and meaning; (2) models of formal and informal organization; (3) models of institutional innovation and change; (4) concepts of roles and role relationships within organizational and institutional systems; (5) models of specific types of social organization and their performance patterns, such as markets, market structure and price formation, public administration and governance, socio-technical systems and technology.

Rule system theory stresses conflict and power struggles around the fundamental social processes of rule-making, rule-interpretation and rule-implementation. It directs our attention to meta-level transactions in society relating to institutional innovation and change, constitutional issues, the formulation of basic organizing principles for strategic areas of social activity, as well as the making and interpretation of law and other formal rule systems. Finally, it focuses attention on the practical implementation of laws, norms and regulations in concrete social settings.

The theory recognizes explicitly *multiple rule-makers and rule-interpreters*. They are often located in different parts of the social structure, in different class positions, in different institutional or organizational spheres, with varying roles, interests and resources at their disposal — not least in the strategic structuring and restructuring of rule systems (what we have referred to earlier as 'meta-power'). To varying degrees they cooperate (forming, for instance, temporary coalitions or more permanent networks and parties) as well as struggle with one another to maintain, adapt, or transform societal rule systems. Adaptation and transformation — at some level(s) of rule systems — go on in any case, because the world changes. Social actors are confronted with new problems, or old problems in new contexts.

Although social rule system theory is a general theory, its scope is limited. First, the theory is not concerned with individuals as such, in particular the psychological and social psychological processes whereby individuals learn, interpret and implement social rules. The theory does not provide a language and analytical tools to describe and analyse the formation and reformation of personal rule systems, that is 'personalities', and individual performances of social or personal rule systems.

Secondly, the theory, as developed thus far, is oriented more to social institutions and complex organizations, particularly economic and political formations, rather than to social rule system formation and implementation in communities and small groups and networks. It is likely that social rule processes are substantially different in large, complex organizations as opposed to tight-knit communities or small social units and networks. The latter may be essential to socialization processes whereby individuals are indoctrinated into major social rule systems. In general, the theory says very little about human socialization, although a number of useful questions can be immediately raised about such processes from the perspective of the theory.

Thirdly, as stressed earlier, not all patterning of social activity occurs through the implementation of rule systems. Ecological factors and natural conditions also play a role in the structuring of social life.[23] Of course, in response to such 'natural structuring', human groups may formulate social rules, in a certain sense capturing symbolically and meaningfully a given fact. Thus, social groups may have rules instructing their members to do certain things such as eating, drinking, nursing children, or engaging in sexual activity, which *they are inclined to do in any case.* Nonetheless, social rules articulating what human agents are inclined to do in any case often take on a life of their own and have unintended, aggregated consequences, possibly evoking efforts to formulate other rule systems. Of interest to the further development of the theory are specific rules, specifying how, when, and where biologically essential activities are to be carried out, and, in some instances, even proscribing against the satisfaction of basic biological needs, at least for certain groups of actors, times and places, as exemplified in fasting and chastity rules.

Fourthly, social rule system theory does not address forms of social activity which are ad hoc, temporary, or apparently random in character, even if much of the activity can also be examined in rule system theory. In some instances, such behaviour is important as a counterpoint to rule-governed behaviour or as a point of departure for institutionalizing new social rule systems.

In conclusion: there are substantial areas of interest for which social rule system theory does not provide analytical leverage and explanatory power. The theory, nonetheless, seems to offer a promising point of departure for systematic and cumulative social science research on social process and social organization — particularly from the perspective of agency-system dynamics.

3
The organization of social action and social forms

Introduction

A basic tenet of our approach to social organization is that *shared or partially shared rule systems* are key factors (1) in the organization of social activity and transactions among actors, (2) in the structuring of social experience and (3) in the formulation of social accounts (Harre, 1979a). While the analyses and illustrations in this chapter draw heavily on Goffman, particularly (1974) and Cicourel (1974), among others, who stress the organization and interpretation of social experience, *it shifts the focus more to the role that social rule systems play in the organization of social transactions.* Also of interest is the interplay between the stucturing and regulation of transactions and the structuring of perceptions and interpretations of social experience.

In *Frame Analysis* (1974) Goffman states openly that he does not address problems of social organization and structure. A careful reading shows, however, that Goffman has a great deal to say about the successful structuring of social activity and concrete transactions between actors. His many insights and contributions to the study of social organization are pointed up and developed, we would argue, by framing some of his work in social rule system theory.

We shall examine how people in everyday life construct social reality on the basis of shared rule systems, 'social grammars', and situational analyses (See Figure 3.1).

The construction process entails both the *organization of social activity* as well as *the structuring of social experience.* Goffman (1974:495) observes:

> It is known that on every occasion when two or more persons are in one another's immediate physical presence, *a complex set of norms* will regulate the commingling. These norms pertain to the management of units of participation, situated and egocentric territoriality, display of relationships and the like. And if talk occurs, then of course norms will apply regarding organization of turns at talking and initiation and termination of the encounter in which the exchange takes place.

More specifically, the participants in the situation define the situation and act out roles — that is, particular rule sets applying to certain categories of participants. The social reality which partici-

33

FIGURE 3.1
Model of social definition of the situation and nesting process

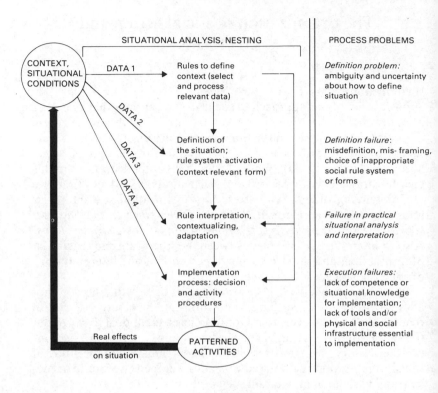

| SITUATIONAL ANALYSIS, NESTING | PROCESS PROBLEMS |

CONTEXT, SITUATIONAL CONDITIONS

DATA 1
DATA 2
DATA 3
DATA 4

Rules to define context (select and process relevant data)

Definition problem: ambiguity and uncertainty about how to define situation

Definition of the situation; rule system activation (context relevant form)

Definition failure: misdefinition, mis- framing, choice of inappropriate social rule system or forms

Rule interpretation, contextualizing, adaptation

Failure in practical situational analysis and interpretation

Implementation process: decision and activity procedures

Execution failures: lack of competence or situational knowledge for implementation; lack of tools and/or physical and social infrastructure essential to implementation

Real effects on situation

PATTERNED ACTIVITIES

pants in many everyday life situations construct is then, in a certain sense, a 'common' reality. The guiding social rule system, the socially grounded situational analyses, and the organization of experience play a central role here. Communication among participants also plays a key role, particularly in 'correcting' differences in interpretation and meaning. Such communication is organized and regulated by the general rules of language and discourse as well as by the particular sets of rules corresponding to participants' roles. The latter rules indicate, for instance, which actors in a relationship enjoy initiative and authority in dealing with matters of ambiguity and differences in interpretation and judgement.

Social rule systems and situational analyses are the bricks and mortar with which actors construct social reality. Referring to Alfred Schutz and H. Garfinkel, Goffman states (1974:5, 6):

Rules ... when followed, allow us to generate a 'world' of a given kind. A game such as chess generates a habitable universe for those who follow it, a plane of being, a caste of characters with a seemingly unlimited number of different situations to realize their natures and destinies. Yet much of this is reducible to a small set of interdependent rules and practices. If the meaningfulness of everyday activity is similarly dependent on a closed, finite set of rules, then application of them would give one a powerful means of analysing social life. For example, one could then see (following Garfinkel) that the significance of certain deviant acts is that *they undermine the intelligibility of everything else we had thought going on around us, including all next acts, thus generating diffuse disorder ...*

... nor has there been much success in describing constitutive rules of everyday activity. One is faced with the embarrassing methodological fact that announcement of constitutive rules seems an open-ended game that any number can play forever. Players usually come up with five or ten rules (as I will) but there are no grounds for thinking that a thousand additional assumptions might not be listed by others ... one is left, then with the *structural similarity between everyday life* — neglecting for a moment the possibility that no satisfactory catalogue might be possible of what to include therein — and the various 'worlds' of make-believe but no way of knowing how this relationship should modify our view of everyday life ...

Finally, [there is] the modern effort in linguistically oriented disciplines to employ the notion of a 'code' as a device which informs and patterns all events that fall within the boundaries of its application.

In this perspective, a certain inter-subjectivity is characteristic of social life. *But it is a relative inter-subjectivity.* It is rough, imprecise. Participants in a given social situation experience somewhat different social realities (as we shall see, sometimes very different), even when they participate together in the same or closely related transactions. This is because they have different levels of competence and knowledge, differentiated roles, and differences in resource control, action capabilities and interests. Accordingly, each participant's action conditions and situational analyses vary to a greater or lesser extent. Finally, their 'personalities' are interwoven in their role performances.

Differences among actors tend to be articulated or acted out, finding expression in conflicts and struggles around 'the social construction of reality'. The conflicts concern, for instance, which (or whose) rule system, rule interpretations and situational analyses shall prevail? Differences in perspective or structuring orientations are particularly likely among actors who belong to different cultures, religious traditions, classes and ideological groups, even where the same institutional arrangement is supposed to govern their activities.

A few or many of those engaged in particular interaction settings may conceal their 'deviant' perspectives, interpretations and analyses. Open expression would evoke opposition or sanctions, or, in general, alert others. They may engage in *'fabricating a reality' different than appearances* (Goffman, 1974). In this way divergent conceptions and experiences of reality are produced and sustained, although many or most participants may be ignorant of this fact. Of course, the 'fabricators' realize that a world of 'multiple experiences' of reality has been shaped since they contribute to its shaping. This is the place of lying, deceit, cheating and so forth in the construction processes. Goffman (1974:513) suggests:

> The human actor stores information in his skull and [that] these materials may be hidden from view by skin and bone; his facial features are the evidential boundary he employs during face-to-face interaction. Except, then, for leakage due to involuntary emotional expresssion, the actor is able (and often willing) to play an information game, selectively withholding from interrogators what they would like to know ...

In general, the construction of social reality is, in part, an open process and, therefore, vulnerable to ambiguity, ignorance and incompetence, and to misunderstandings and conflict. Goffman (1974:495) observes:

> Note these various forms (of social interaction) are constantly coming up for affirmation whenever individuals are in one another's presence. It follows, therefore, that any consistent breaching of these rules — whether unintentional or intentional, whether due to 'incompetence' or not — will have a generative effect, unseating all the interaction the rule breaker engages in. This is known from the tricks that have been played by experimenters (Stand 'too' close in talk and see what hapens), small boys (Keep pace with an old lady one sidewalk square away and see what she does), and interrogators (Take away his belt and shoe laces so he must present himself sloppily whenever he is brought to a session).

In the next section we examine the social definition of transaction situations and the process of socially organizing reality. The following section then deals with multiple definitions of the situation.

Definition of the situation, nesting and the organization of social action and experience

On entering or finding themselves in a social action situation, actors are faced with the basic contextual question:

> What sort of stuation is this;
> What is or should be going on here?

As Goffman (1974:8, 10–11) points out:

> Whether asked explicitly, as in times of confusion and doubt, or tacitly,

during occasions of usual certitude, the question is put and the answer to it is presumed by the way the individuals then proceed to get on with the affairs at hand. ...

I assume that definitions of a situation are built up in accordance with principles of organization which govern events — at least social ones — and our subjective involvement in them; frame is the word I use to refer to such of these basic elements as I am able to identify. That is my definition of frame. My phrase 'frame analysis' is a slogan to refer to the examination in these terms of the organization of experience.

In order 'to define a situation', the actors require data about the situation and rules to select, categorize and organize the data. A shared rule system for such purposes *enables a more or less socially coherent contextual analysis, communication among participants, and definition of 'what sort of situation is this'?* Moreover, it provides a collective point of departure for deciding ultimately 'what is it that we shall (or should) do in this situation?' and 'how shall we do it?'

As Goffman (1974:1–2) states, definitions of the situation are usually socially given:

Presumably, a 'definition of the situation' is almost always to be found, but those who are in the situation ordinarily do not create this definition, even though their society often can be said to do so; ordinarily, all they do is to assess correctly that the situation ought to be for them and then act accordingly. True, we personally negotiate aspects of all arrangements under which we live, but often once these are negotiated we continue on mechanically as though the matter had always been settled.

While this is largely true, Goffman overstates the generalization. Often enough, as we discuss later, actors struggle and negotiate over the appropriate definition of an action situation in which they participate. They can and may disagree at various stages or levels in the process of defining and 'nesting' the situation. Disagreement may be the result of ambiguities in the situation itself as well as of miscues and mistakes. But it often results also from the participants' adherence to differing organizing principles and rules.

Data from the interaction setting is selected, categorized and organized according to specific social rules or algorithms, which enable actors to define the situation: 'It is this sort of situation.' Successful definition of the situation with the help of shared rules typically activates, or leads to the social choice or selection of, a class of rule systems considered appropriate for structuring and regulating social action and interaction in the defined situation.

The choice will in turn lead to a focus on, and selection of, specific types of situational data. Some of the data will be that relevant for initially making a choice of sub-classes of rule systems and algorithms; it will be useful also in organizing the information required in the course of enacting rules and performing appropriate algorithms in the situation (see Figures 3.1 and 3.2).

The analytic descriptions above of the processes of defining situations and nesting are cumbersome. They veil the fact that the various decisions and selections are *typically routine,* arrived at quickly and without much reflection in situations which are well-defined and where actors have had a history of interaction and have developed relatively well-structured rule systems. Only in undefined or ambiguous situations, such as new or transformed situations, where conflicting rule systems are activated would hesitancy and delay be characteristic. The process of defining the situation would correspond to the elaborate 'working out' suggested in Figures 3.1 and 3.2.

If the interplay between a socially defined context, selection of rule systems, and implementation of specific algorithms is 'consistent', the process of interaction continues along a course which the actors recognize. This is another way of saying that the situational definition and action process are self-contained. Interaction will be more or less predictable.

On the other hand, miscues, misdefinitions, and disagreements — or a substantially new situation — all tend to disturb and even to abort the process. Participants are compelled to activate meta-rules and meta-processes, including meta-communication, in order to (re-)establish order, possibly by adapting or reformulating rules.

Consider the example of actors in a superior/subordinate (AB) relationship in a work setting (see Chapter 5). They meet one another in a concrete situation, let us say on the initiative of the superior. The latter in this case defines what type of situation they are in (although an explicit initiative will be unnecessary in most instances, since the subordinate will already have anticipated the type of situation). The participants will generally know which particular social relationship — that is, which rule regime — applies to their interactions in the situation. Hence, they know more or less how they are to act vis a vis one another. (Of course, there may be some ambiguity here, particularly in societies or organizations where actors have a variety of different types of possible relationships with one another. If the superior-subordinate relationship (AB) in the workplace applies in a spectrum of interaction situations, and assumes the same general form — a most extremely and unlikely case in modern, highly differentiated societies — then the likelihood of ambiguities and confusion will be minimized. The choice problem will be relatively simple.)

FIGURE 3.2
Process of determining the situation and activating a rule regime to structure and regulate social behaviour

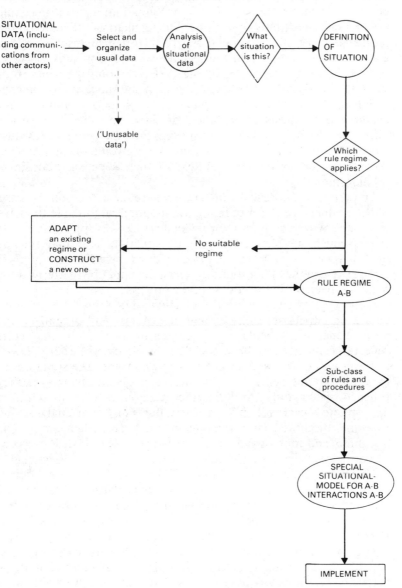

In their interactions represented, for example, by models such as those presented in Figures 3.1 and 3.2, the actors (A and B) are assumed to agree throughout the process concerning the critical decisions: namely, definition of the situation; appropriate rule regime and algorithms organizing and regulating interactions; the particular phase of the process where they find themselves in any given moment in time; and the specific decisions and activities (e.g. specific forms or sub-types of the A–B relationship) which they should be carrying out in each phase. If any uncertainty or confusion arises, they provide signals or cues to one another, for example B 'requests information or direction' and A 'provides directions'. Should a disagreement arise, the superordinate A would tend to insist on his interpretation and B would most probably accept this, at least in the context of their superior/subordinate relationship.

Of particular interest are instances where the actors, on the basis of the available rules for defining the situation, are unable to arrive at a satisfactory definition or to determine the appropriate rule regime which they should follow in the situation. They may even be in disagreement with one another without being aware of their differences, to the effect that they enact incompatible patterns, only discovering errors in the course of the process.

Definition of the situation, selection of a social rule system, choice of sub-classes of rules and algorithms, and organizing the performance of particular activities and interactions by the actors reflects *the nested structure* of social action discussed earlier. Viewed in this way, *action situation* is a dynamic concept. The situation, as experienced and defined by the actors involved, changes as they proceed in due course to define the situation, activate or select an appropriate social rule system, carry out situational analyses and rule interpretation, and implement rules and algorithms. The 'meaning' and tone of the situation change as the process goes on. Nevertheless, there is a definite structure or logic to the changing meaning and experience of 'context': the nesting of context definitions, specification of rule systems, and focus of attention and social regulation. The decisions in the nesting process are branch points determining entire families (as well as sub-families, sub-sub-families, and so forth) of potential action and interaction patterns.

Human actors not only construct and reconstruct the situation cognitively. They also structure it through acting in and upon it. Of course, powerful actors have more substantial impacts on the situation — on physical and social processes — than weaker actors. The exercise of this power may transform the situation beyond 'recognition'. The growth and accumulation of power enables agents to carry out such transformations, that is to make the world into something beyond the 'limits of their knowledge' or action frameworks and, therefore, something that they do not fully recognize or understand. This calls for re-cognizing the situation (changing descriptive rules and models). Ultimately, they tend to restructure the relevant action systems, for instance the rules for processing and organizing data from the situation as well as rules governing social decisions and activities in that context. This is often done in such a way as to take into account some of the objective changes in the context which have a bearing on their activities and outcomes. This dialectical interplay between action contexts and context-changing actions is one of the characteristic features of human development.

To sum up the discussion here: Our general model points up the interplay between 'action situation', social rule systems and situational analysis. The recursive nature of rule system processes is also pointed up:

(1) Some situational data is required to recognize or define the situation.

(2) Actors usually have socially shared rules to select and analyse data for the purpose of defining the situation. Rule systems can be more or less shared. Sharing is not the same as consensus. Some actors may adhere more or less to a social rule system because they fear sanctions or because they desire certain rewards which adherence is likely to bring. In general, the authority or power to socially define reality, in particular the processes of making and interpreting definitional rules as well as social rules generally, is unequally distributed.

(3) Once the situation has been defined, an appropriate rule regime can be activated or selected to structure and regulate transactions. The role-sets of rules applying to particular categories of actor not only guide their actions and interactions but provide a basis on which each can organize social experience (Goffman, 1974) and provide appropriate accounts for one another in communications about their activities (Harre, 1979a). Thus, the activation of a socially shared rule system, considered appropriate for the situation, is a function of context (providing certain data or information) and definitional rules and algorithms. This tends to exclude unintended meanings and interpretations as well as unintended behaviour. The likelihood of misunderstandings and spurious conflicts is reduced. Of course, such structuration depends on social rule or, in general, cultural knowledgeability on the part of the actors involved (Goffman, 1974:496).

(4) The transactions governed by the rule regime are not usually performed mechanically or completely routinely, but entail considerable adaptation in applying the rules to concrete circumstances. Hence, local or situational data as well as situational knowledge and analytic capability of the participants are essential ingredients in the implementation process. Participants carry out 'situational analyses' and engage in a continual mediation between local circumstances and the relevant rule regime. This is also observable in the organization and interpretation of social experience.

(5) Finally, the rule-regulated activities themselves have impacts on the situation, validating or possibly invalidating the definition of the situation as well as the feasibility of applying a particular regime.

In the remainder of this chapter, we shall develop these ideas, building on some of the work of Goffman, especially as formulated in his *Frame Analysis*. The next section analyses a few of the multiple, potential definitions and meanings of a situation and some of the transformations involved in socially organizing reality. Shared rule systems enable participants in an activity to generate complex patterns of social activity. At the same time, they enable the participants to systematically interpret and understand that complexity. Nevertheless, the construction of social reality is vulnerable and may be disrupted in several ways, as we discuss next.

Multiple definitions of the situation:
Levels of meaning and meta-processes
Typically, actors have available alternative perspectives on the 'same action setting', that is a social situation may be defined in several ways. A social activity such as 'kissing' may be a playful activity, a symbolic expression of family affection, or a sexual engagement, among several possibilities. Certain rules enable knowledgable actors to make these distinctions, to give tone or special character to more or less the same activity, and to do this in a consistent, relatively unambiguous fashion. (It also permits the intelligent, even strategic use of ambiguity in social transactions.)

Of course, participants in a social activity might have quite different views about what is going on. Nevertheless, they often manage to carry on effectively. 'Pretending' and 'fabrications' are common features of everyday social experience (see Goffman, 1974). Sometimes, the disagreements among participants may be openly expressed, but they carry on in any case. In some instances, those with an alternative framework and definition of the situation struggle to assure that their definition and rule system shall prevail. The final outcome is either a negotiated settlement, the imposition of one frame, or disengagement from participation of some or all of those involved. Since more than one definition of a situation and structuring of social activity is possible, participants may experience uncertainty about whether one or another of the possible definitions applies in a particular concrete situation. There are two forms of this ambiguity:

I. Two or more rule systems apply, where each system structures quite different patterns of activity, for example, 'work regime' as opposed to a 'leisure-time or fun-and-games regime'.
II. More or less the same general rule system is applied but the tone or quality of application takes substantially different forms.

Ambiguities of both types arise, for instance in relationships between persons of opposite sex in their work and leisure time activities. Expressions of 'understanding' and 'affection' between men and women need not necessarily imply 'sexual interest', nevertheless ambiguities and misunderstandings arise.

Resolving ambiguities about 'what should be going on here' is important to those involved in order that they know how to organize their activities and what to expect from one another. As Goffman (1974:304–5) points out:

> These ambiguities have to be resolved lest the individual be forced to remain in doubt about the entire nature of the happenings around him ... the frameworks (or rules)are fundamental to the organization of activity, because a whole tissue of organization derives from each ... Indeed, it seems a characteristic of human life that any activity we become involved in carries at least this much orderliness. On the other hand, it seems also the case that very brief ambiguities at the level of the primary perspective will be relatively common.

Both types of ambiguities referred to above are resolved by contextual information — time, place, the actors involved — and certain shared rules or algorithms with which to define (distinguish) situations. Type II ambiguities require, in addition, *knowledge of transformational rules. These enable participants to generate and to understand the different forms of the same or very similar social activity.*

Except in entirely new situations or situations where contradictory rule systems are advocated by different actors, knowledgeable members of a community or society have few difficulties handling Type I ambiguities. They recognize that a certain situation is the proper time and place for a religious ceremony, not a luncheon; or, conversely, they recognize a luncheon, even a formal luncheon, as something substantially different from a religious ceremony such as 'holy communion'.

But some activities appear similar (even if the fully initiated see clear differences) and serious confusion can result. For example, Goffman points out the problems that arise because psycho-therapeutic sessions appear initially to many patients as 'everyday conversations'. Yet, the rules of therapy treatment breach the frame of ordinary face-to-face dealings. Therapy patients are, therefore, compelled to learn these rules, indeed to learn quite another system for interpersonal interaction than those they are familiar with from everyday life. The discrepancies occur at just those points in inter-action at which an actor would otherwise be protected from excessive influence and from the formation of emotionally intense relation-ships. In this way, 'the patient is trapped into a special relationship' (1974:385). Goffman goes on to identify some of the peculiar rules of psycho-therapeutic interactions and contrasts them with rules of everyday interactions (1974:385–7):

(1) The client's information preserve can be penetrated by the therapist beyond the point at which the client might penetrate it himself. (The secrecy defense against a relationship is thus breached. This license, however, is not reciprocal.)

(2) Client behaviour which would ordinarily be treated as outside the main track, such as initiatory and terminal rituals, tone of voice, blushings, silences, slips, spurts of anger and the like (being person rights relative to role) are to be treated as proper subject matter for the therapist to address [in particular, to draw attention to and discuss, our comment].

(3) The reprisal principle of ordinary social intercourse is held in abeyance by the therapist, a wide range of 'acting-out' behaviour being tolerated by him in support of the doctrine that the client's behaviour is directed not at the therapist but at significant figures into which the therapist is project-ively transformed, in short, that the behaviour is not quite literal, although the client may be unaware of this.

(4) The client is encouraged to break the decency rule and the modesty rule prevailing in ordinary interaction. Not only taboo fantasies, but also petty, egocentric daily reactions are given the focus of attention as worthy of extended consideration. Also, the therapist recommends versions of the client's version of the therapist which would ordinarily be considered immodest and improper for a professional to support. But while the client's self is thus placed in the very centre of affairs, inflated sufficiently to fill the whole stage, it is the therapist's vocabulary drawn from doctrines of 'personal dynamics' (albeit in a respectively lay version) that the client is led to employ in these considerations.

(5) As part of the obligation to free-associate, the client must be ready to

consider his relationship to any and all his intimate others, divulging what would ordinarily be the preserve of these relationships, and in consequence, betraying them; so, too, with organizations, groups, and other structures.

(6) The client's negative response to the application of these rules and the reservation this creates regarding the session and the therapist is itself a legitimate matter for considering ('analysis of the negative trans-ference'), and so the protective distance this alienation ordinarily pro-vides is itself expropriated, becoming a matter for consideration, not a basis for an unstated stand.

Type II ambiguity concerns almost identical, or very similar pat-terns of activity, which are given substantially different meanings. Such ambiguity is handled through *meta-rules* which enable rela-tively sophisticated transformations and differentiation. The very same activity is carried out with quite different tones and 'meaning'. Unless participants know the meta-rules for transforming the rule system structuring the activity, they will mis-interpret and mis-behave, even though they appear — and believe themselves — to be doing more or less exactly as others, according to guiding rules.

The set of meta-rules handling ambiguity of this sort consist of two subsets: (1) meta-rules which distinguish appropriate contexts for the different qualities or meanings of the social activities in question; (2) the meta-rules to transform the activity rules from one quality or tone into another.

In the area of everyday life, one of the major distinctions in quality and tone, which actors must be capable of making in order to participate effectively as well as to understand what is going on is that between:

REAL OR SERIOUS ACTIVITY/PRETEND OR PLAY ACTIVITY

Many institutionalized transactions (courting, sexual play, arguing, fighting , and so forth) can be transformed into qualitatively similar activities which are understood by the participants to be something quite different (Goffman, 1974:44). The activities are already meaningful in terms of some primary rule framework, e.g. courting, arguing, or fighting. Participants have the competence to generate the activities as well as to analyse and understand their patterns. Knowledge of the meta-rules for such transformations enables participants to distinguish 'this is playful fighting' from 'this is serious fighting'. Goffman (1974:43, 45) introduces the concept of 'the key':

> I refer here to the set of conventions by which a given activity, one already meaningful in terms of some primary framework, is transformed

into something patterned on this activity but seen by the participants to be something quite else.

For participants, playing, say, at fighting and playing around at checkers feels to be much the same sort of thing — radically more so than when these two activities are performed in earnest, that is, seriously. Thus, the systematic transformation that a particular keying introduces may alter only slightly the activity thus transformed, but it utterly changes what it is a participant would say was going on. In this case, fighting and checker playing would appear to be going on, but really, all along, the participants might say, the only thing really going on is play. A keying, then, when there is one, performs a crucial role in determining what it is we think is really going on.

Goffman (1974:41–3) specifies some of the rules whereby serious, real action is transformed into something playful:

(i) The playful act is so performed that its ordinary function is not realized. The stronger and more competent participant restrains himself sufficiently to be a match for the weaker and less competent.
(ii) There is an exaggeration of the expansiveness of some acts.
(iii) The sequence of activity that serves as a pattern is neither followed faithfully nor completed fully, but is subject to starting and stopping, to redoing, to discontinuation for a brief period of time, and to mixing with sequences from other routines.
(iv) When more than one participant is to be involved, all must be freely willing to play, and anyone has the power to refuse an invitation to play or (if he is a participant) to terminate the play once it has begun.
(v) Frequent role switching occurs during play, resulting in a mixing up of the dominance order found among the players during occasions of literal activity.
(vi) The play seems to be independent of any external needs of the participants, often continuing longer than would the actual behaviour it is patterned after.
(vii) Although playfulness can certainly be sustained by a solitary individual toward a surrogate of some kind, solitary playfulness will give way to sociable playfulness when a usable other appears, which, in many cases, can be a member of another species.
(viii) Signs presumably are available to mark the beginning and termination of playfulness.

Knowledge of transformation rules such as the following is essential to effective discourse in everyday life and in behaving appropriately (properly) in the spectrum of settings in which humans carry on with one another.

TRANSFORM RULES

<rules/algorithms for producing a certain serious social activity>   ⟹   <rules/algorithms for producing more or less the same activity in non-serious/play forms>

.

This capability enables knowledgeable actors to distinguish between serious activity and the same or similar activity rendered playful or non-serious (which is an essential competence in many situations if one is to understand what is transpiring). The capability is also essential (necessary but not sufficient) to generating and regulating one's own behaviour in ways suitable for the particular context.

Of course, knowledge of the transformation rules and performance skills varies considerably among actors. Some may have serious difficulties with the subtleties of analysis. They end up behaving awkwardly or inappropriately, unable to grasp the subtleties of the different forms or to execute skilfully some forms, for instance of playful (alternatively, serious) social activity.

Social forms of action: The case of the kiss
Thusfar, we have argued that some activity enjoys (suffers from) multiple forms of expression and meaning: sacred, serious, playful, and so forth. In addition, there may be several forms of, for instance, seriousness. 'Kissing' provides familiar examples. The different forms of kissing are distinguished by particular rules of execution and of transformation. Most competent adults in Western countries can distinguish and execute competently the following:

● kissing affectionately one's closest relatives, e.g. one's mother
● kissing more distant relatives
● kissing as a form of greeting among friends and acquaintances
● kissing as a form of ritual greeting, even between persons who are not related, close, or acquainted
● kissing as a form of or prelude to sexual communion
● kissing as flirtation and play

Kissing is an activity, much like various touches and embraces, *which communicate a sentiment, meaning or idea*, at least within the group, society, or wider culture which shares the various rule systems relating to the activity. These acts have high and varied symbolic values and are appropriate, even required, in certain social settings or interactions. Many rituals are of this nature, e.g., the 'kiss of greeting or farewell' among some Europeans.

Social competence in kissing requires extensive rule knowledge. Competent actors in social discourse which involves kissing make successful distinctions among the different forms and meanings of kisses. The rules governing kissing specify, among other things, which categories of actor can be — or should be — kissed, in what ways particular forms and procedures of kissing should be carried out, when and where they may or should be carried out. (See

Chapter 7 concerning the structure of institutionalized transactions.) For example, we find relatively well-specified rules regulating kisses between intimate family members and friends, between distant family members, political comrades and between lovers. Also important is rule knowledge about kissing in settings which involve 'welcoming', 'saying goodbye', 'thanking' or 'showing gratitude', 'showing passion', and so forth.

In general then, one expects to find in any community or society widely shared, more or less specific rules indicating whom one is to kiss or not to kiss, which types of kisses are appropriate for which categories of persons, the settings or times which are appropriate (as well as inappropriate, such as during religious ceremonies, unless the ceremony, for example a wedding, specifically calls for the act of kissing. But at a wedding, a passionate, open-mouth kiss would probably cause some consternation, even in these permissive times).

Consider kissing among family members. There are a number of well-understood unwritten rules about the act. These relate in part to incest taboos as well as to role and status differences among members concerning the freedom to express affection or sentiment in general. Social rules in the USA (and also to a large extent in Scandinavia) indicate that a father should not kiss his son, or certainly not with strong feelings. A certain playfulness accompanied perhaps by backslapping is one acceptable pattern. Handclasps, light hugs, and a bit of 'sportsmanlike' encounters are appropriate forms for expressing intimacy and sentiment between male relatives and also acquaintances. A son's mother may kiss him up to a certain age, otherwise affectionate hugs are more appropriate. Kisses between mother and daughter, on the other hand, can be reasonably free. The father could never go so far with his daughter, particularly as she nears or enters puberty. Certainly, the 'kiss' should express affection or sentiment, not passion.

The 'greeting' or 'farewell' kiss is fairly common in Europe, among relatives, close friends, and even some acquaintances. Of course, 'lips should not meet' except for the closest of friends and relatives — and then only as a sort of tag. The greeting kiss is used in Eastern Europe on even the highest political levels. Leaders who are serious rivals engage in this ritual. To refuse to do so would be an insult and reveal publicly a serious tension or conflict.

While this practice is widely accepted — and practised — in Eastern Europe, Westerners would find it highly irregular and possibly shocking if their political leaders — or even worse political rivals — began to kiss and hug regularly at their meetings: for instance, if Reagan and Kohl (West Germany's prime minister) or

Reagan and Thatcher were to exchange kisses much as family members (see S. Brögger on the kiss as cultural symbol, 1976: 61–71).

The hierarchy of action

Human activity is hierarchically organized. Actions such as 'greeting another', 'shaking hands', and 'kissing' may be defined and described on different levels of resolution or detail. On the most abstract level are expressions such as 'greeting', 'showing respect', 'demonstrating affection'. On a more concrete level, the activities take specific verbal and non-verbal forms: shaking hands, bowing, kneeling, kissing, among others. Of course, these forms vary between different cultures and sub-cultures. Also, in any historically given society, actors usually have several alternative forms of, for instance, 'greeting one another', 'showing deference', 'giving orders', or 'sanctioning someone'. The selection of form depends, among other things, on the concrete action setting, its social definition, and the relative power, status and familiarity of the persons or groups involved.

An activity such as greeting another is executed by doing certain concrete things such as grasping another's hand, bowing, or kissing. These activities are in turn made up of a sequence of more detailed steps. Eventually, as we progress toward greater and greater detail, the 'steps' are expressed as control signals for arms, fingers, sensing contact with objects, rotating a joint, and motor control activities (see Powers (1973) for an earlier, highly original attempt to examine human activity as hierarchical in the sense we are discussing here).

Typically, the hierarchical character of activity is taken for granted in human communication. A task, sub-task, activity, or sub-activity will be mentioned or named in a directive or discussion of what is to be done. Those knowing the activity or task in a practical or action sense, share rules and algorithms for performing it. On the other hand, a child or an unsocialized person might ask, 'what do you mean?' or 'how?' This would require showing or communicating the lower order detail of each of the activities or tasks making up the sequence of an overall activity or task.

The degree of verbalization — the extent of elaborate description of social rule systems — will vary considerably from activity to activity. Some activities, even very social ones such as greeting others and showing deference or exercising authority, have a relatively low degree of verbalization, because there are few incentives to communicate about them. On the other hand, rule systems and algorithms governing activities which call forth discussion, for example in connection with collective decision-making, coordination, or large-scale organization, will be described more fully. Obviously, social rule systems (e.g., law, sciences, mathematics, languages and medicine) which are taught in schools and universities through lectures and books will be more elaborate and systematically verbalized than those taught through example and practice.

No instruction, rule, or rule system — whether communicated orally or in writing — is ever completely specified. At the same time, an instruction or rule is of no use to an actor if he or she does not know or understand what the words mean or how to carry out the directive, such as 'tell the assembly unit to set their gauges at 0.35mm for controlling the play in the drive axles'. To specify completely would be quite impractical and highly costly. A full specification or description would require communicating the complex rule systems and situational knowledge of actors sharing a common culture as well as the specific local culture in a given organizational or work setting. Most conditions and details are 'understood' by *knowledgeable* actors, and they communicate with one another, fully aware of this shared level of understanding.

Successful performance of lower level tasks and activities may depend to a great extent on local information. These may not be specified beforehand in detail in a rule system or plan, but must be 'worked out' on the spot. Also, even when rules and plans for activities can be specified in detail based on systematic knowledge, action settings change or are subject to variations which confront actors with special constraints or problems not anticipated in the original rule system.

Conclusion

Humans are knowledgeable agents (Giddens, 1984). Actors learn the shared knowledge of social rule systems in the communities, organizations, and societies to which they belong. They learn to apply this knowledge in a variety of settings. Such application entails considerable 'situational knowledge' about, and analysis of, these settings. Actors learn to adapt and transform rules both to be able to apply them in diverse and varying situations, but also to give special character or tone to what appears to be the same patterned activity, for instance to make the activity 'serious' or to render it 'playful' or 'make-believe' in character. In this chapter we have suggested that human actors learn various shared rule systems as well as transformations whereby they can generate new or qualitatively different social activities which are alike or very similar. These systems are *social forms,* utilized by actors to organize recognizable patterns of social activity. They enable actors to anticipate
.

and predict one another and to generate appropriate and effective activities vis a vis one another. In this way participants in a social process can coordinate conflict as well as cooperation. Social forms are not only distinguished (and distinguishable) in terms of such binary distinctions as 'serious' and 'non-serious'. There are usually multiple forms of, for instance, 'play' and 'contest'.

Distinctions are also found between instrumentally oriented activities which are organized mainly to achieve certain outcomes, on the one hand and, on the other, activities organized to realize through social action certain norms (or a normative climate) and to express certain sentiments.

Much of the remainder of the book, particularly the chapters in Part II, is concerned with institutionalized forms to structure and regulate social reality for the instrumental purposes (economic or political) of certain groups and classes of actors in modern society.

4
Actors, rules and social structure

Introduction: Human actors as rule-creating and rule-changing agents

Human actors produce, adapt, purge, and transform rule systems. Sometimes, this occurs as an aggregate effect of individual or subgroup innovation, entrepreneurship, or deviation. At other times, it occurs through concerted political action and the purposeful alteration or reform of rule systems, for instance, through legislation. Law-making is the most formalized and highly visible rule-making process in which actors engage, but we can observe rule-making at all levels and in all spheres of society. At times, it is institutionalized as in large organizations and international networks (such as those dealing with banking and financial institutions on the world level).

Typically, rule-making entails both formal and informal processes, where the informal may be most closely associated with rule-interpretation and rule-implementation, for instance, in a work place, within a labour union, in local and national politics, or in business dealings and contracts.

The institution of private property, for example, was not planned or developed by any government authority or legislative (Dam, 1982). Nevertheless, the efficiency and stability of this central rule regime depend upon complex, often arcane legal rules. Dam (1982:3) adds, 'Similarly, contracts were made and enforced before the full apparatus of contract law developed hand in hand with the evolution of more complex forms of commercial constraints, supporting the development of new kinds of contracts and providing the certainty necessary to their increased use.' He goes on:

> A similar process may be observed in the evolution from the gold standard to the gold exchange standard, as national statutes and regulations changed, not so much to create the new system as to cement it. After the Bretton Woods system collapsed in 1971, a number of changes in the rules adopted by the IMF [International Monetary Fund] were necessary simply to take account of the system of generalized floating that came into being in 1973. And in the 1980s one may safely assume that even if the system evolves into one based on multiple reserve currencies, many rule changes will be necessary to accommodate such a new system and to render it stable and workable.

Rule regimes vary in the extent to which they allow social agents the freedom of action or discretion to adopt or develop their own particular rule systems and algorithms. Freedom of action or discretion is, in part, a function of social power factors as well as situational factors. Although each and every rule regime is, in a certain sense, a 'negotiated order', some actors have more power than others to form and reform the system. In other words, they enjoy the privileges of being able to make the system — at least the formal system — conform more to their purposes and interests, rather than vice versa. Weaker actors, on the other hand, must either more or less accept the rule regime or deviate covertly from its regulations, in the latter case risking possible sanctions from those prepared to enforce it.

Some rule regimes, as noted above, may leave unspecified or ignore substantial areas of activity. They allow, or even expect, the actors to fill in and develop their own rules and procedures. Other regimes may specify social activity in considerable detail, yet allow participants the possibility of changing particular rules and principles within certain constraints. Such freedoms can be contrasted with social rule systems which govern behaviour in great detail and at the same time proscribe alterations of the system. For instance, some social rituals and administrative procedures are expected to be closely followed, deviance is subject to stringent sanction, and reforms are proscribed.

Legal codes, the codes governing programmes, decisions and procedures of a government agency, the instructions and rules governing task activities in a technically complex and demanding facility such as a nuclear power plant are more or less well-defined action settings and processes. They enable large numbers of actors to predict and to coordinate their activities, as a basis for the performance of complex collective sequences and hierarchies of different activities.

In a turbulent or poorly defined social setting, where at the same time the actors involved have a commitment to effective performance, they will tend to modify and replace rules or introduce entirely new rules. Often different participants will have somewhat different conceptions of appropriate or effective rule systems. In settings where there is some 'balance of power' (that is, a social system which is not purely hierarchical) the actors negotiate and renegotiate the rules prevailing at any given time. On the basis of such considerations, Strauss et al. (1963) developed their conception of an organization, in this case a mental hospital system, *as a negotiated order.*

The rules which were supposed to govern the social activity of the professionals such as psychiatrists, residents, nurses and nursing students, psychologists, occupational therapists and social workers were found to be far from extensive, clearly stated or binding (Strauss et al., 1963; Buckley, 1967). Hardly anyone knew all the extant rules or the applicable situations and sanctions. Some rules previously administered would fall into disuse, receive administrative reiteration, or be activated anew in a crisis situation. As in any organization, rules were selectively evoked, broken, and/or ignored to suit the defined needs of personnel in their concrete professional work, and the politics and struggles around this. Upper administrative levels especially avoided periodic attempts to have the rules codified and formalized, for fear of restricting the innovation and improvisation believed necessary in the treatment of patients. The settings and the problems which personnel had to deal with were ever-changing, the setting was turbulent. The multiplicity of professional ideologies, theories and purposes would never tolerate reification of a single, relatively fixed rule system.

In sum, the area of action covered by clearly defined rules was very small, constituting a few general 'house rules' based on long-standing shared understandings. The basis of organizational order was the generalized mandate — *a general rule or principle* — the single but ambiguous goal of returning patients to the outside world in better condition. Beyond this, the rules structuring actions to this end were the subject of continual negotiation and renegotiation — being argued, stretched, ignored or lowered as the occasion seemed to demand. Rules failed to act as universal prescriptions, but required judgement as to their applicability to, or effectiveness in, the specific case with its particular conditions.

On the other hand, agreements did not occur by chance but were patterned in terms of who contracted with whom, about what, as well as when. There was an important temporal aspect, also, such as the specification of a termination period often written into an agreement — as in instances where a physician bargained with a head nurse to leave his patient in her ward for 'two more days' to see if problems would work themselves out satisfactorily.

Strauss' model presents a picture of a hospital — and many other institutional spheres of social life — as a transactional milieu where numerous agreements are continually being established, renewed, reviewed, revoked and revised. The daily negotiations not only enable the day-to-day work to be accomplished, but feed back upon the more formalized, stable structure of rules and policies by way of a 'periodic appraisal process' to modify it — sometimes slowly and incrementally, sometimes rapidly and convulsively.

Rule systems and social action
An institutionalized rule system, a rule regime, is a system of rules

adhered to by actors in a particular group, organization, culture or society. The regime serves cognitive, communication, and action purposes. First, it is a source of expectations, a basis for actors to simulate and predict one another's behaviour in the sphere of activity to which the regime applies. It also may be used to communicate with one another in providing accounts, analyses, and explanations of behaviour. Finally, it guides and regulates social action and interaction of those agents subject to the regime in the social action sphere or spheres to which it applies. Among other things, it specifies who does what, when, how, and where (see Chapter 7).

A social rule system makes the course of social action and interaction more or less predictable to those knowing the system. This is important not only in institutionalizing particular forms of social coordination and cooperation, but in validating the system in practice. The rules give stability and continuity to social activity. In the absence of such shared rule systems, social life would be highly unpredictable and unstable. Shared rule systems enable individual actors to overcome uncertainty in their social environment, by making more or less predictable the behaviour of others. It also enables actors to overcome their own uncertainty about what they should do in a situation or how they should carry on.

Social rule system theory distinguishes several different types and levels of rules: rule systems which constitute social relationships, socially diffused rules of strategy and tactics, and actor unique or idiosyncratic rules. We discuss these briefly below.

1. Constitutive rules of social relations and transactions. We distinguish two subsets of constitutive rules, social process rules and role grammars, which essentially define or constitute types of social activities and relationships.

Social process or transaction rules, such as rules of social conduct, rules of the games, and general norms define permissible agents, acts, means, and settings. They contribute to organizing and regulating in socially identifiable ways the interactions among social actors. In this sense, they define what is supposed to be going on and, in particular, the permissible or legal moves (Rawles (1955), Searle (1965) and Garfinkel (1963) refer to constitutive-like rules).

Rule sets and grammars are role-specific systems of rules embedded within the social rule systems that constitute defined social relationships and organizational structures. Typically a regime differentiates categories of actors and assigns to each category specific rule sets or grammars, which constitute 'roles'.[24] Social grammars include two essential types of rules, classification and action rules. Classification rules distinguish different types of relevant objects, persons, activities, outcomes and events in the sphere to which the regime applies. Action rules sequentially structure or order acts as elements of transactions with others.

Actors occupying different social roles are then governed by different rule sets or grammars embedded in the rule systems constituting organizational structures and institutional frameworks. The actors collectively produce in their role relationships *transaction sequences, the structuring of which is based on the complementary grammars.* Such structuring of action and interaction sequences enable actors to understand their meanings, to anticipate one another's behaviour and to coordinate, even in cases where large numbers of agents in different roles are involved in complex transactions.

2. *Socially diffused strategic rules* (Searle (1965) refers to regulative rules.) These are rules or rule systems which are diffused socially and to some extent shared. However, adherence to them does not depend on collective sanctions. They are adhered to and followed because actors have learned, or been led to believe, that the rules are those capable of generating 'effective action'. They will pay off in some sense: rules of strategy and tactics, technical rules, and rules of optimal action. Examples are: suitable or effective openings in chess (which of course is a small subset of the entire set of legal openings); 'tit-for-tat' or 'live-and-let-live' as principles of response in certain situations (e.g., prisoners' dilemma settings (Axelrod, 1984)); rules for writing style ('elements of style'); and 'rules of thumb' for good business or successful politics.

In general, individual actors or agents (with their specific capabilities and levels of knowledge) adopt or develop particular rules or rule systems which elaborate or complement rules of social conduct and role grammars.

Typically, these socially diffused rules make sense only in the context of a defined rule regime and certain types of action situation (Wiley, 1983).

3. *Actor unique rules.* Although persons are often selected or socialized to fit into the framework of a rule regime, they also possess their own personalities (personal rule structures) and individually inspired or motivated rules.

These may fit into the organizational framework, complementing or elaborating it. For instance, personal styles and idiosyncratic rules enable persons in their roles to act more effectively within the framework. In some instances, however, individually inspired or motivated rules contradict organizing principles and major rules of a regime and predispose the individual to behave in a 'deviant' manner. Other actors may adopt and develop the deviant rules and styles, so that a socially diffused, deviant rule system competes with or threatens to replace the official or formal system (see Chapter 11). These actors tend to come into conflict with those committed to the established regime. Such conflict leads either to regime reinforcement and the suppression of deviance or to some degree of reform and restructuring of the regime.

Institutionalized rule systems exist outside of any particular individual. At the same time, the behaviour of individuals is not fully deducible from the rule regimes which govern social activities, in part because individuals have their own personalities and individually motivated rules as well as multiple roles. Moreover, individuals bring varying levels of knowledge and competence, and their own interpretations and strategies for following rule regimes to concrete interaction settings.

The different types of rule systems will be examined in more detail below, with a particular focus on the relationship between process rules and role specific rules. The interplay between these systems of rules — as actors pursue their interests and play their roles out in innovative and unique ways — is a major theme in social life and the locus of much social deviance and conflict between social agents and social structure.

Social conduct: Process and transaction rules

These govern the ways in which actors interact with one another: for example, rules of order for parliamentary bodies; rules and regulations governing wage negotiations; 'rules of the game' for contests, competitions, and politics; rules governing superior/subordinate interactions in enterprises or public agencies. Some process rules specify coordinated activity at *defined points or periods in an overall process*: exchanging information, linking sequentially or jointly activities carried out by different categories of actors, including joint decision-making such as negotiating agreements and voting.

Even in the case of conflict activity, appropriate process rules and procedures regulate the behaviour of participants: exchanging or sharing information to some extent as is done in labour/management negotiation processes, engaging in preliminary 'coordination' such as preparing an agenda for negotiation sessions, and so forth. Also, there are rules excluding certain types of action (or 'weapons'), as in the case of labour/management conflicts. In some countries, secondary boycotts and general strikes are proscribed.

Process rules can be characterized in a flow diagram by at least one *multi-actor nodal point for joint decision, coordination, or interaction*. Specific actors (or categories of actors) are linked to the rule-governed process. The process rules define where interaction

FIGURE 4.1
Social interaction process: negotiation

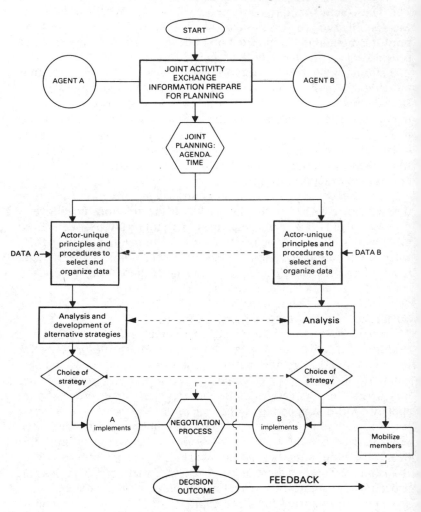

nodes are to occur: situations where the actors involved exchange information, make common or collective decisions (through negotiation, voting, or dictatorial rule), and carry out joint or organized tasks. Actors engaged in such a process are, to a greater or lesser extent, expected to link into, and to fit their own actor-specific rule systems and algorithms into the frame provided by the process rules.

The 'social nodes' in the process may be organized hierarchically or democratically. In the former case, one class of actors dominates another in their transactions (see Chapter 5). Process rules and procedures are the result of past innovations and formulations passed on through social control and diffusion processes. They are intended to structure and regulate decisions and activities, as in organizing work or political activity, or setting up an institutional framework for negotiation. In the latter case, for example, this would entail specifying rules for conducting negotiations, for deciding on agendas, and for dealing with the principal types of issues and conflicts expected to arise.

The task of preparing a system of social rules is greatly facilitated if already existing rule systems can be adopted, of course adjusting or amending the system to take into account special 'local' conditions and problems: for instance, one might adapt Roberts' or Chapman's rules of order to the governance of decision-making bodies at a university or the organization of a voluntary association's annual meetings.

Roles: Actor specific rule systems
Actor specific rule sets or grammars are *roles*, structuring and regulating social action and interaction of a category of actors. The grammars specify appropriate activities and interaction patterns with other defined categories of actors.

Everyday examples of social interactions governed by actor specific rule sets associated with role relationships are numerous and varied:

- superiors and subordinates in production organizations
- doctors and patients
- teachers and students
- customers and sales persons
- parents and children
- neighbours with one another

Schneider cited in Salaman (1980:128) points out the importance of the role concept in understanding and analysing the patterning of social action and interaction:

> Roles [such] as father, mother, factory worker, manager, friend and soldier. All these are separate and well-defined roles ... What makes role of such importance is the fact that it largely determines how human beings will act in certain areas ... the role of factory worker implies certain duties and certain rewards, certain relationships to management and its representatives, and other relationships to fellow workers.

Actors engaged in role relationships — and concrete interaction processes — will have greater or less freedom of discretion to complement, elaborate, and even to alter to some extent the rules and procedures governing their roles and role relationships. Indeed, role as a rule system embedded in an organizational or institutional framework, such as a modern factory, government agency, or army, never provides a full or adequate specification of social action and interaction patterns in the situations to which it applies. Actual performance calls for situational knowledge, knowledge about other agents (including their level of competence and typical strategies), situationally-specific problems with which they must deal, and useful strategies and styles for these purposes (see Chapter 11).

Personality and style: Actor unique rule systems
Although actors in a historically given culture or society share, in a certain sense, rule systems governing their social action and interaction in defined spheres of activity, they do not all have identical levels of knowledge about or the same interest in the rule systems. Nor do they all use, or adhere to, the rule systems in the same way or to the same degree.

Social agents (individuals, groups, organizations) have their own 'styles', exploit opportunities and deal with constraints differently. They may develop or adopt to varying degrees particular strategies, algorithms and rule systems of their own. By strategy we mean the approach an actor employs in using and developing relevant rule systems in a particular setting or class of settings. The strategy may encompass a complex array of principles and algorithms, entail considerable flexibility, and be more or less open to adjustment and reformulation. Or it may be relatively simple and easy to fathom, inflexible, and not open to reformulation. The point is that social agents work out their own singular systems and these regulate or govern, in unique ways, their social action and interaction.

Actor unique strategies and personality may complement the governing social rule system, in particular actors' roles in the system, or they may compete with or contradict the guidelines and directives of the system. By contradiction we mean that the actor unique rules, motivated and inspired by the person's own interests and goals or, possibly, associated with other important roles he or she has, lead to decisions and actions which are proscribed or judged undesirable within the social rule system.

In general, actor unique strategies and personalities of organizational members are to a large extent compatible with the frame of the organizing rule system. The roles actors play in social organizations are to a greater or lesser extent recognizable, even if there is considerable variation in personal styles. This is, in part, a result of recruitment principles and patterns as well as socialization and social controls; in part, it is an outcome of organizational design.

Social organization in modern society

Social relationships and organizational structures are conceptualized in rule system theory as supra-actor or structural phenomena (see Chapter 2). Figure 4.2 identifies *stable, institutional forms of social organization characteristic of modern society* (the distinctions are partly inspired by Weber (1968). We briefly discuss these types.

Institutionalized social relationships between individuals or groups. Institutionalized social relationships are constituted by relatively well-defined social rule systems. A population of actors share these systems orienting them to one another. The systems structure and regulate social action and interaction within the sphere or spheres to which the relationships apply, specifying how different categories of actors should interact, for what purpose, with what means and procedures, where, and when.

Community relations. These are social relations in a group whose members are oriented to the governing rule systems based on a sense that they 'belong together' or share a common destiny. Such systems specify a spectrum of rights and responsibilities of actors in multi-stranded relations and in a variety of social action spheres.

Association relations. Association relations are deliberately formed for a purpose. Stable, institutionalized forms of associative relations entail the application, adaptation, or possible reformation of established rule systems. These constitute the relationships and organize social action and interaction within the frame of these relations. The systems specify rights and obligations among participants within a circumscribed sphere or area of purposeful action to which they apply.

Network relations. These are social relations established deliberately as in mutual-help, professional and informal exchange systems. No organized authority or agency enforces the social rule systems governing social action and interaction, although internal elites may emerge and try to usurp the role of rule creators and enforcers.

Organization relations. These are deliberately formed relationships and structures with rule-creation and enforcement performed by a defined authority and administrative staff. The rule regime

FIGURE 4.2
Types of social organization

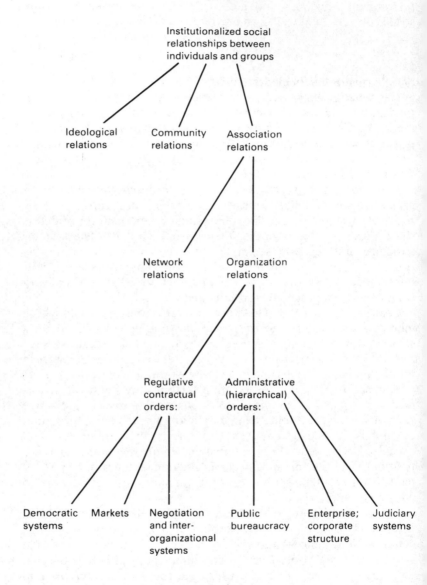

constituting such a relationship entails explicit role distinctions and
relations of domination. There is a person in authority — the
executive of an association, a managing director, a president, a

prince, the head of a church — whose action is concerned with implementing the regime governing the organization. A formal organization is usually legally specified for a given sphere with a defined authority and permanent staff. The latter operate according to rules and procedures specified in the regime. These systems may be voluntary or imposed. A regime is imposed to the extent that it does not originate from a voluntary or negotiated agreement among the the participants involved.

Regulative contractual orders: markets, negotiation systems, democratic political systems. Such regimes specify certain organizing principles for, and constraints on, participating actors, in constituting their relations and engagement in types of activity such as 'trade and barter', 'negotiation', and 'democratic decision-making'. The regimes are enforced by specified authorities and an administrative staff. In many cases participants themselves (buyer/seller; negotiator/negotiator; voter/leader) also contribute to enforcement.

Typically, such orders structure and regulate social action and interaction of participants to a much lesser degree than do administrative orders. Participants are not at the disposal of the administrative staff or regulative authorities. They enjoy considerable freedom or autonomy to organize transactions, form new rules and to enjoy benefits — or deal with losses — within the frame of the regime. The frame grants rights, relating to ongoing relationships and activities within the order, such as property rights, contractual rights, negotiation rights, civil and political rights, and protects them, although procedures for exercising these rights — and certain limitations on their use — may be specified by the regime.

Administrative orders: Bureaucracy, organized association, labour union or political party apparatus. In the purest case all specified social action and interaction within the defined sphere or scope of the order is structured and regulated by the regime, constituting the order. Compliance is enforced by a designated authority and administrative staff. The regime governs the actions of the administrative staff as well as those of members/participants in their direct relations to the organization. The administrative staff and the organized activities of the members are, in principle, at the disposal of the top authority, when it issues orders, including new rules. (However, as we shall see in Chapters 11, 12, and 13, effective resistance may emerge.) The regime structures and regulates coordination of action, decision-making and transactions including the distribution of responsibility and authority within the given sphere.

Two primary or fundamental types of social relation, domination and non-domination, can be distinguished within rule system theory. Domination relations, as organized in administrative systems, are characteristic of modern business enterprises and the state. Regulative organization — as institutionalized in markets, negotiation systems and formal democratic procedures — are special types of non-domination structures, in that the relationships among participants are, in principle, non-hierarchical. *However, the organizing principles and rules are enforced by authorities, and, therefore, entail a hierarchical component.* In this respect, such organization differs significantly from network relations, which, in principle, have no institutionalized relations of domination. These various types of modern social structure are described, illustrated, and analysed in some detail in later chapters, first theoretically in the remaining chapters of Part I and then empirically in Parts II, III, and IV.

Rule compliance
This section examines some of the reasons human actors follow rules and to a greater or lesser extent implement social rule systems. Several general types of factors are identified, which contribute to explaining rule-following behaviour and adherence to social rule systems. These give rules varying degrees of 'force' or compulsion, as reflected in verbal distinctions such as 'you must (not)...', 'you should (not) ...', it is (not) preferable that you ...', 'you may (not)...'.

We distinguish socially based inducements to rule-following from intrinsic and self-motivated inducements.

Social inducements to rule-following behaviour
The force of social rules in this case depends on more or less established social control processes, their type and effectiveness. Social inducements are as many and as varied as there are bases of social power and control (see Burns et al., 1985). For our purposes here, we distinguish two general types of social inducement, namely persuasion and sanctioning, with a variety of sub-types. Included here are processes of indoctrination and the structuring of 'definitions of the situation' and orientations toward social action and interaction. We also include here various means that social agents use in structuring 'rewards' and 'punishments' around social activity. That is, through remuneration and/or coercion, social rules are often imposed and enforced. As Perrow (1979:82) points out about bureaucracy:

> For Weber, authority in bureaucracies was rational–legal authority, a type of domination based upon legally enacted, rational rules that were held to be legitimate by all members. The rules were either agreed upon

or imposed. The fact that members accepted the legitimacy of the authority in no way altered the fact that rules could be imposed and coercion lay behind them.

Of course, in practice a network of social controls (in many instances with considerable redundancy) often operates to assure a high level of acceptance or adherence to social rules.

Table 4.1 points up not only the distinction between social inducements based on persuasion and the exercise of sanctioning power but the importance of the concrete social conditions under which social inducements are exercised. For our purposes here, we distinguish simply between situations of dominance/hierarchy where one agent or class of actors is in a position to impose a rule system on a weaker or subordinate class, on the one hand, and, on the other, those situations where no agent or class of actors is in a position to enforce compliance to a rule system on others. In the latter case, we do not wish to suggest that the actors are in any sense 'equal'. There may be considerable differences in their access to and control over resources, but these differences are not sufficient to permit unilateral inducement to rule-following. Weaker actors and groups are in a position to refuse to comply with rules or to negotiate changes in rules or in the conditions of their implementation.

In addition to obvious direct forms of social persuasion and control, there are *indirect forms, above all socially structured inter-*

TABLE 4.1
Socially induced conformity to rules

	Dominance/ Hierarchy	Non-dominance
I. Persuasion (social processes of communication, argument, appeals to ideology, norms, and beliefs)	Expert/Moral authority (including charismatic political and religious leaders)	Mutual persuasion, Dialogue, and Dialectics
II. Sanctioning power (social processes of social action and control, using control over or access to power resources: valuables including goods and people)	Unilateral exercise of monopoly power: coercion or remuneration	Mutual exchange and struggle (with actors mobilizing and using power vis a vis one another to enforce adherence to mutually agreed on rules as well as to negotiate new rules)
Legally based sanctioning power	Bureaucratic legal authority	Legally specified forms of negotiation and contracts

nalization: among others, persuasion which leads to commitment to a rule system principle or to certain conceptions of reality and rules to deal with it; the various forms of indoctrination which parents, highly integrated groups, and totalitarian elites employ in varying mixtures.

Intrinsically motivated and self-induced rule-following behaviour. The force of socially produced and diffused rules need not depend on obvious sanctioning or social control mechanisms. Rule-following patterns also derive from intrinsic and situational 'payoffs' associated with the activities and/or the cognitive–evaluative frame of the actors involved.

(a) The incentives to rule-learning and following behaviour may be intrinsic to the process of implementation or its outcomes. Thus, people may learn the language and procedures of bureacracies as well as strategies to deal with them not simply because overt sanctions are executed if they do not comply but because certain advantages are associated with acting 'effectively' vis a vis a bureaucratic agency. Similarly, actors accept and follow 'technical rules' in connection with the effective/efficient use of technology.

Actors adhere to social rule systems, even when they oppose some of their specific rules and rule sub-systems, because the systems (1) reduce uncertainty and (2) enable them to participate more or less efficaciously with others in socially established forms.

In general, compliance with some social rules provides its own rewards, partly by reducing uncertainty in social situations and partly by enabling persons to coordinate and interact more or less effectively with one another.

(b) Actors are attracted to and accept a social rule system because of the 'ease' with which it can be used and the high costs involved in adopting or developing an alternative system. This argument is particularly pertinent in the case of complex rule systems, the change of which would entail very substantial psychic costs as well as the costs of investing substantial amounts of time and energy.[25]

(c) Actors impose social rules or rule systems on themselves after convincing themselves of their rightness, correctness or appropriateness in structuring and regulating their behaviour (as well as that of others). A system 'fits' or appears compatible with personal experience as well as deeply felt values or norms. This implies that classes of actors who share a few very basic social principles along with common experiences are likely to develop or adopt rule systems compatible with this background.

(d) A social rule system may be appealing not only on normative or instrumental grounds, but on aesthetic grounds: the system has a certain elegance, a beauty of form which users find appealing. The

importance of this assessment rests ultimately, of course, on normative and value foundations.

(e) Typically, there is a combination of factors which motivates
against all-too-frequent or intensive questioning of compliance with
rules and the routines of simply complying with them. A basic
stability obtains because actors adhere to a *meta-rule* usually
acquired and strengthened during child socialization, that social rule
systems are 'good', useful, and sooner or later rewarding. And
moveover, the costs of opposing them and trying to adopt or create
alternative systems are formidable, and most attempts fail.

The child, in the course of its upbringing, like a wild horse, is
usually 'broken' through one or more strategies of parents and
adults. The meta-rule which it comes to accept is typically abstract
and general, applying to social rules and rule systems which are
provided by 'authoritative' and 'good' agents : norms, enactments,
decrees, regulations, principles of knowledge and method, and so
forth. Similarly, social rules and rule systems which have been
arrived at through certain established and correct procedures, such as
'decisions of parliament', 'supreme court or presidential decisions',
'scientific tests and analyses', etc. can also fall under *the meta-rule
which suspends serious reflection, questioning, and uncertainty.*

Much rule-following and compliant behaviour is undoubtedly
unreflective and routine (Giddens, 1984).[26] This proposition is not
inconsistent with earlier arguments: (1) Social rule systems are often
adapted and re-interpreted in the concrete situations in which they
are implemented. *Such innovations can be carried out in more or less
unreflective ways,* although not necessarily in routine ways. (2)
However, as a result of social conflict and/or experience of performance failure and crisis, social rule systems become the object of
reflection and non-routine alterations.

The 'civilization process' (Elias, 1978a) has entailed the establishment and acceptance of abstract *meta-rules of obedience* (based on
concepts and the ideology of rational-legal authority). *Once accepted
and institutionalized, these enable the formulation and development of
entire complexes of rules and the issuance of orders. One result is the
apparently almost endless elaboration and accumulation of rules and
rule systems so characteristic of modern society.* Lindblom (1977:18–
20) points out in this connection:

> Every specific control can be used either as a method of direct control or as
> a method for establishing a rule of obedience which, once established,
> itself suffices for control as long as it stands ...
> ... One, several, or many people explicitly or tacitly permit someone else
> to make decisions for them for some category of acts (or sphere of
> activity).

Such a rule defines an established relationship, with a certain probability of obedience. Otherwise, each occasion for exercising influence would require mobilizing resources.[27] As Lindblom (1977:21–3) observes about established rules of obedience and the capability of government to exercise authority:

> For any given population, a government exists for them to the degree that one of the groups exercising authority over them exercises authority over all the others or claims, without challenge from a rival claimant, a generalized authority for its orders over those of every other organization. It may not make effective its claimed priority in case of conflict and in some cases may not even wish to enforce a priority. But the generality and uniqueness of its claim to priority distinguish it.

The efficiency of authority explains its central role in government. Government control through ad hoc deployment of rewards and penalities — say, a bargain struck with each individual citizen on each of repeated occasions — is hopelessly expensive and time consuming for the vast tasks of government. Even if a government could employ a battery of ad hoc methods of enforcement, it could do so only because a large group of people stand willing to administer these enforcements.

Authority, the core phenomenon that makes government possible, explains how a congress or parliament can be more powerful than an army, how a Stalin can override the unanimous opinions of his colleagues in party leadership, and how a political boss can boss. Both the obvious features and the puzzles of politics are inexplicable except by reference to the authority relation and to the intricate network of relations that supports any specific authority relation. The great feats of political leadership and organization rest on the phenomenon of authority. So also do the crises that disturb political order. For authority can vanish with astonishing suddenness, as abruptly as people can change their minds about which *rules of obedience they are willing to follow,* as a long list of former rulers, including Haile Selassie and Isabel Peron, testifies.

'Communism,' a Soviet writer says, 'is the most organized society man has ever known.' He then goes on to say it is organized by rules, and that it achieves 'the habitual observation of these rules as a regular norm of conduct.' *The same can be said for any government.*

In government, authoritative rules of the game are controlling in the same way that they are in a game of poker or basketball. That again explains the volatility of politics in some circumstances. Abruptly — as abruptly as they can change their minds — *political leaders decide they no longer wish to follow an existing rule. It is then a new game.*

5

Rule systems, social power and the organization of modern society

The structure of societal rule systems and conditions of change

Social rules do not all have the same status in a group, organization or community. There are not only qualitative differences among them, but social agents use them in different ways and are committed to them to varying degrees: constitutional principles, laws, norms, moral codes, administrative rules and regulations, technical rules and guidelines. These often have different logical and socio-political priority and are typically created, reproduced and changed according to different mechanisms, although hard and fast distinctions cannot be made, except analytically. There are considerable overlap and shifts in the character of various social rules.

Social rule systems consist of multiple levels of rules (Burns et al., 1985). This is apparent in the case of formalized systems, but holds true for more informal systems as well. Concerning the multi-level character of rule systems, Hofstadter (1985:75) observes:

> Indeed, if appropriate qualifications are made for the informality of custom and etiquette, a strong argument could be made that normal social life is just such a system of indefinite tiers. Near the top of the 'difficult' end of the series of rules are actual laws, rising through case precedents, regulations, and statutes, all the way up to constitutional rules. At the bottom of the scale are rules of personal behaviour that individuals can amend unilaterally without incurring disapprobation or censure. Above these are rules for which amendment is increasingly costly, starting with costs on the order of furrowed brows and clucked tongues, and passing through indignant blows and vengeful homicide.
> U.S. Government is a multi-tier system, with its intermediate and substatutory levels such as parliamentary rules, administrative regulations, joint resolutions, treaties, executive agreements, higher and lower court decisions, state practice, judicial rules of procedure and evidence, executive orders, canons of professional responsibility, evidentiary presumptions, standards of reasonableness, rules establishing priority among rules, canons of interpretation, contractual rules, and so on.

The multi-level (and in some instances, recursive) character of social rule systems is well-exemplified in legal systems. Statutes are made by a rule-governed process, law-making, which is itself partly statutory (Hofstadter, 1985:75). Hence, the power to make and change statutes can reach some of the rules governing the process itself. Hofstadter (1985:75) adds:

> Most of the rules, however, that govern the making of statutes are constitutional and are therefore beyond the reach of the power they govern. For instance, Congress may change its parliamentary rules and its committee structure, and it may bind its future action by its past action, but it cannot, through mere statutes, alter the fact that a two-thirds 'supermajority' is needed to override an executive veto, nor can it abolish or circumvent one of its houses, start a tax bill in the Senate, or even delegate too much of its power to experts.

Such changes require quite other procedures, specified in the enacting rules to amend the US Constitution. Of course, the social organization of constitutional, legislative, and regulative rule-making, rule-interpretation, and rule-implementation varies substantially from country to country, and even within countries in different regions and at different levels of government.

The multi-level character of social rule systems entails the logical and institutional/political prioritization of some rules over other rules (Hofstadter, 1985:74). For our purposes here, these are the two major dimensions of priority in the multi-level structuring of rule systems:

(1) Higher level rules take logical and generative priority over lower level ones. Whenever there is a conflict between rules in a system, higher level rules take precedence over lower level rules, as in the case of conflict between a constitutional principle and a statute, where the former prevails (except in those specified cases in government systems where the constitution can be changed through legislation, see below).

Priority of rules is also manifested in rule formation, where a higher level rule sets the terms (defines inputs, the parameters, and scope) of lower level rules. In a word, the latter are generatively subordinate. Thus, specific government regulations concerning control of chemical or other emissions are formulated in line with the specific laws passed for this purpose. The regulations also reflect other legislation and regulations concerning government agencies, administrative principles and practices, and so forth; in this sense, the lower level rule does *not* follow deductively from its parental statute.

(2) Higher level rules tend to be more institutionalized, and immutable than lower level rules. Logically/generatively prior rules such as those in a constitution are more difficult to amend or replace than the logically/generatively posterior legislation.

In general, although social rule systems have a multi-level structure, many of our empirical studies illustrate how, in practice, rule system hierarchies are vulnerable, subject to erosion and periodic transformation. What may have been lower level rules are given priority over higher level rules — in concrete social action settings, often in connection with practical problems of implementation as well as with political struggle. In many instances, rule system changes do not evoke conflict and power struggle, but go on in ad hoc and piecemeal ways, through minimal adjustments and compromises, exception-making, and finding new interpretations. This is the case in connection with many technological innovations and developments (see Chapter 14).

The 'drift' of ad hoc and piecemeal adjustments is often patterned and cumulative, entailing emergent principles and rules. These may be given logical and institutional priority over previously higher order forms, at least by certain groups and organizations. In this sense, the new emerges from the old, although the relationship is a contradictory one.

In the study of social organization in modern society, one can make the following distinctions (inspired in part by Parsons; see Mouzelis, 1967:42).

Basic rules or organizing principles
of society or a social sphere
Basic rules, whether written or not, govern the relationships amongst social groups or categories of actors in a social organization or society. They also specify relationships to nature and natural resources, to supernatural powers and the unknown. Each social system has certain organizing principles or core rules governing external relations, the relationships to other social groups, organizations and societies.

Among familiar core rules are the following:

- property rights, that govern access to and control over wealth and income
- authority and regulative rights, specifying access to and control over powers of government, including the use of force
- religious rights, namely access to and influence over moral and spiritual powers

(Included here are the control relationships, whether hierarchical or egalitarian in character, between and among categories or classes of actors in society.)

The basic rules are not only utilized to formulate and elaborate specific decision rules, procedures, and programs of particular organizational forms but to legitimize these — or they make them meaningful in the sense that actors in a society adhering to the basic

FIGURE 5.1
Levels and processes of rule system structure

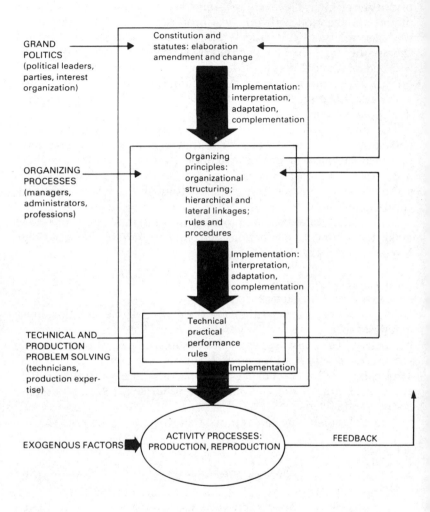

rules are capable of understanding the meaning or significance of a larger number of specific rules and procedures by virtue of their linkage to or origin in basic rules. Included among core rules are meta-rules governing the ways in which core rules may be altered — or indicating that they are absolutely not to be altered.

Organizational forms and institutions
These are the specific rule systems which organize people, resour-

ces, and activities in observable interaction patterns. For instance, they specify the ways in which government enterprises or private firms are to be organized and operated; how collective bargaining or democratic decision-making should be constituted. They provide the practical bases for social activity: the laws, contracts, regulations, programmes, and principles for social decision-making and action in defined spheres.

Operating and technical rules
These are the specific procedures and algorithms, including technical directives, which govern particular activities such as the processing of certain materials, the production of particular services or goods, negotiation activities, the regulation or administration of people, resources and information.

The processes whereby these different rules and sub-systems of rules at different levels are maintained and/or changed vary considerably. There are institutional, ideological, strategic as well as practical constraints. Obvious here is moral and political resistance to changing core principles and rules in a society, such as property rights, political rights, established ways to organize public services, since these are often well institutionalized, backed by powerful vested interests, and grounded in societal ideology and values.[28]

The establishment of new organizing principles or the transformation of conventional ones entails in most instances major political efforts including legislation. This is true even in the private economic sphere. Once a framework has been established however, actors may elaborate and innovate *within the frame* to a greater or lesser extent, in accordance with institutionalized rules and strategies. Such innovation takes place within certain constraints. Besides the limits imposed by the overall frame, there are those which arise from general societal norms and values. Also, some actors in the sphere — and possibly others outside — have vested interests in the structural development within the sphere, and mobilize to initiate change or to block it.

Changes in organizational forms and institutions are initiated in response to new problems or to demands which are consistent with the overall framework. Similarly, operative and technical rules also change in response to practical requirements of rule implementation and the realization of effective practices in concrete settings. Environmental contingencies, 'flesh and blood' actors, and efforts to improve or to elaborate rules are all factors which play a role in the adaptation and change of rule systems — in many instances, these improvements and changes are brought about without major managerial/administrative involvement or political/legislative enactments. That is, they are made more or less in accordance with the organizing principles and core rules governing a sphere of social activity.

Technical needs and developments — particularly in connection with technological change and innovation in practices — often give cause for the alteration of operating rules, and even some components of decision rules and organizational structures. Many of these consequences are not anticipated when the innovations are introduced. Rather, actors discover 'misfits' and other problems as they carry on, and find that they must deal with them by altering rules in order to achieve effective performances. Such rule changes are often limited initially, in large part, to technical and operational innovations.

Major restructuring or transformation of basic rules and organizational principles can result from 'bottom-up' processes where actors introduce new, apparently complementary rules or technical and operative rules. Cumulative changes in these rules eventually lead to ambiguities, uncertainty, and conflict with respect to the higher level rules and principles. These developments, in turn, evoke efforts to reform the latter in ways that make sense in light of the accumulated experience with practical changes in technical and operative rules.

'Top-down' restructuring or transformation typically has another social character. It often entails political mobilization and struggle among elite groups (with expertise, political power and capital). Changes limited to a single setting or sphere of social action require only that powerful agents or a coalition in that sphere get behind the idea and implement the change or changes. On the other hand, alterations or transformations cutting across spheres with social power distributed across spheres requires that change agents build up networks or coalitions of power cutting across the spheres (see Chapters 12 and 13).

In general, reformulations of higher level principles and meta-rules lead to lower level changes, but the reverse is less often the case, at least in the short run. Higher levels of rule systems are typically more difficult to change than lower level rules. Of course, powerful actors in a society are in a better position than most to exercise the meta-power to alter higher level principles and rules than most. However, even elite groups are bounded and restrained by much of the institutional framework of a society.

Rule systems and social power
There is a complex interplay between social power and social rule systems. On the one hand, established systems structure and regu-

late power relationships and the exercise of social control. At the same time, social power — and control over resources — enable agents to establish, maintain, or change rule systems for their purposes and to their own advantage. In general, three faces of power may be identified in connection with rule systems:

• social rule systems are biased, shaping to some extent the distribution of power in transactions among actors in defined social spheres
• actors' unique knowledge and strategies allow for greater or lesser action effectiveness and power within a given rule framework or institution
• social agents generally have unequal power to change or maintain rule systems

A particular rule regime entails an inherent distribution of social power. The rules of social conduct, for example applying to role relationships and institutional settings such as employer/employee, patron/client, traditional husband/wife relations, high status/low status relationships, typically provide one category of actor with more opportunities for initiative than another (as examined later in this chapter). At the same time, the rules reflect in large part the crystallization of power exercised in establishing or developing the particular rule systems. Inevitably, however, there are unanticipated and unintended power developments, and also negotiation about and adaptation of any given rule regime, no matter what the social power conditions obtaining at the time of its introduction or establishment.

The distribution of social power brought about through rule regimes may be recognized and exploited to varying degrees. Actors' awareness of, or ability to exploit, the possibilities may differ. This enables potentially weaker actors with considerable knowledge to improve their position, within certain limits, vis a vis stronger but less knowledgeable actors. Or what is more typical, the stronger with great knowledge are able to exploit more fully their opportunities in the situation at the expense of the weaker as well as other powerful actors with less knowledge.

Social agents also invent or adopt somewhat different strategies when acting within the framework provided by the rules of social conduct. That is, even with more or less equal knowledge of the rules of social conduct and institutional arrangements, actors differ in their ability to develop — or to know about and adopt — effective actor unique strategies and procedures. The ability to execute strategies also tends to be distributed unequally, thus enhancing or diminishing the ability of different actors to make use of their opportunities within a given social organization.

Finally, the actors governed by a particular regime of social rules have differing meta-power to maintain or change the system. In any given social system, the unequal powers embodied in a regime tend to be reflected or reproduced on higher meta-levels of structured social action and interaction. However, there is no one-to-one correspondence. The reasons are various: the unintended effects of rule regimes, the continual processes of learning, innovation, negotiation and struggle which alter meta-powers without social agents being initially aware of changes, and the uneven impact of exogenous developments on power and meta-power relationships.

The elites of society or of a social organization are predisposed to consider a rule regime as a system to be upheld or as an object amenable, at least partially, to manipulation and reform. On the other hand, the weak are more likely to experience the rule regime as something given, lying outside their domains of influence, regardless of whether or not they find the system attractive or acceptable. They are not likely to believe that they can change it in any substantial way. They must either make the best of their possibilities within the regime framework, or possibly avoid or escape its worst impositions.

Even elites and powerful coalitions may feel that the costs (resources, time, risks) involved in trying to change an established rule regime governing strategic spheres of social organization are formidable. They too may experience the system as more or less given — a social structure external to them, difficult to alter — at least in the short run. For instance, it can only be changed by struggle with other groups or through a major mobilization of society, an undertaking which may appear unfeasible or not worth the costs or risks likely to be involved. Such a change might entail altering a written constitution, where a complex, costly process of amendment is required.

Knowledge of specialized rule systems relating to particular institutional settings and social organizations is essential to effective participation in these settings. Examples of such social action spheres are: specific production settings and work places, administrative and public service settings, local or national politics, local community organizations and networks. Even among socialized members of a society, knowledge of the specialized rule systems which characterize modern society varies considerably. This variation is found among persons with different class and educational backgrounds, occupational and professional groups, rural and urban groups, and racial, ethnic and sub-cultural groupings within a society. Variation is also found among individuals and subgroups within a particular social category, as a result of individual learning capabilities, differential socialization and differences in experience and career. Variation in knowledge of specialized rule systems — some knowledge being more strategic in one society than others — translates into different performance capabilities and effectiveness in acting in the settings where the rule systems apply. These differential capabilities translate, of course, into differences among agents in their social power and interests, within an institutional sphere as well as across spheres of activity.

Social domination

Within the scope of our analyses of social organization, we shall focus particularly on social domination within organizations. Our point of departure is the Weberian concept of domination: namely an organized or institutionalized domination based on an administrative staff, e.g. the modern state or capitalist enterprise, with powers to enforce *the rules of domination* (corresponding to the compliance of subordinates to obedience rules).[29] This power may have coercive, remunerative, or normative bases (Etzioni, 1975; Burns et al., 1985; see also Chapter 4).

A system of domination presupposes that dominated groups depend on dominant ones for single or multiple aspects of their physical, material, and spiritual needs or wants. It emerges and develops socially as *a two-fold historical process through which sizeable population groups have been separated from the means of production, or violence, or salvation, or expertise, while other groups have monopolized and concentrated these means in their own hands.* The two-fold historical process of domination and concentration is the ultimate basis for the relations of domination, institutionalized in rule regimes. At its base then, any rule regime depends on precluded alternatives, which, as much as the available ones, lock in and bind the interests of subordinates to those of their superordinates. Typical examples are various factory and political regimes as well as religious, bureaucratic, or military orders.

Regimes of domination are further elaborated in practice. New rules and rule reformulations are made, interpreted and implemented in an ongoing process of negotiation between subordinates and superordinates. Changing external conditions, which affect the power balance between groups, may be crucial for the possible outcomes of such negotiations.

In sum, *organized domination is then a social relationship which distinguishes two or more groups and defines their rights, control over resources, rank and rewards, and rules of command and obedi-*

ence in relation to one another. One group or category of agents (subordinates) is structurally predisposed to obey a command or directive with a given content as well as accept other initiatives on the part of members of another group or category (superordinates or authority). Issuing directives, formulating governing rules, and taking other initiatives are then socially structured predispositions.

Like Weber, we stress command, but we also specify in domination relationships *the powers of superordinates to allocate resources and tasks, to establish and reform relevant rules, to evaluate, to sanction, and, in general, to take initiative vis a vis subordinates.* To varying degrees these are part and parcel of modern, institutionalized domination relations.[30]

Domination relations, as we shall see below, can be modelled as interlocking roles, which specify types of action, resource control, rights and obligations of each in relation to one another in defined spheres(s) of activity. The rule regime constituting a *system of social domination* specifies who dominates whom with respect to which sphere of social activity, types of relevant activity, and the where, when and how of interactions between superordinate and subordinate actors. Important here are controls over production activites as in work organizations, such as business firms and government agencies, allocation of production resources, products and gains, and prestige as well as control over control structures themselves (including the possible manipulation of non-formal structures and networks).

Domination relations within an organization or between groups and the organization may be defined widely or narrowly. In the latter case it is limited to a certain sphere, certain activities, certain tasks and procedures. Relatively narrow, and well-defined spheres of domination, are characteristic of modern (rational–legal) forms of organized domination (see Chapter 11).

The structuring of social interaction in domination systems

The following discussion presents a crude model of the type of rule regime governing domination relations between superordinates (A) and subordinates (B) in a work or production organization. The model points up the structuring of social interaction according to the regime.

Transactions in domination relationships entail by definition substantial differences in rights and capabilities (based on access to resources) to take initiatives, to sanction, and, in general, to exercise a degree of control over the social and other environments where the institutionalized relationship applies. In more egalitarian or non-hierarchical relationships, mutual initiative and 'negotiation' in a strict sense are characteristic features of social transactions. Our point is that there is a family of domination type grammars which can be substantially differentiated from non-domination grammars. (See related discussion in Chapter 7.)

A grammar of social domination consists of at least two types of roles for individuals or groups of actors, A and B. As indicated in Figure 5.1, it distinguishes two sets of rules for the categories of individuals or groups corresponding to the A and B roles. It specifies the types of action appropriate for each, what rights and obligations each have vis a vis one another, and their 'property rights' or control over resources in their sphere(s) of activity.

The different positions entail both power (commanding and sanctioning) and status (expertise, prestige) differences. Sanctioning capabilities entail A's right (legitimized or supported in the larger social context) to reward or punish B. Usually the conditions for such sanctioning are specified by a sub-set of process or procedural rules.

In addition to the organizing principles and rules structuring domination in work organizations, there will be specific rule systems having to do with the types of situations or settings in which As and Bs interact in their workplace: for instance, different task settings with only A and B involved, task settings with A and B in the presence of particular other actors such as top management, and settings for wage or labour/management negotiations. Special settings outside the workplace, for example sport clubs, churches, local community gatherings, may also be covered by the same general rule regime. Typically, however, the general system is adapted to take into account some of the particular norms and social codes appropriate for non-workplace settings.

As the model in Figures 5.2 and 5.3 indicates, the AB regime of domination provides role specific rule systems or social grammars (see Chapter 7) for each class of actors. These guide or specify for the occupants of each position their appropriate social activity and interactions with others. (As suggested earlier, role sets are typically complemented with personality or 'actor unique' rule systems.)

Actor A will have rights, among others, to initiate meetings, give orders, ask critical questions about and to evaluate B's work as well as to sanction B. The rules governing B's behaviour will specify the deference he should exhibit toward A, and such patterns as allowing A to initiate meetings, to give orders, to ask critical questions and to evaluate B's work; B is supposed to accept A's suggestions, evaluations and commands, including rule formulations, as inputs to organize and regulate his own activity and decisions.

FIGURE 5.2
The role structure of social domination

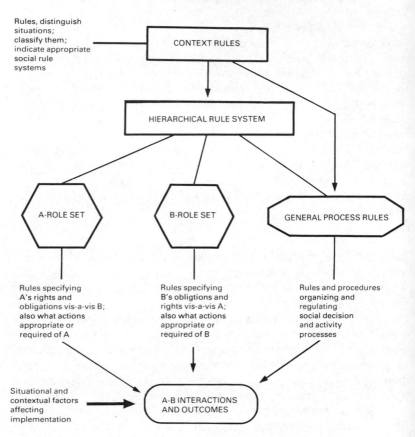

The rule regime will enable A and B to collectively generate certain understandable and abstractly predictable interaction sequences. These will not usually be rigid or mechanical, but stochastic, with actors having some degree of discretion to adjust and adapt their activity patterns and interactions according to particular circumstances and personalities. Therefore, they will exhibit variation over time as well as under differing interaction conditions. Many alterations in transaction patterns are carried out according to contextual rules, rules for interpretation and implementation, and those rules used in situational analyses (as discussed in Chapter 4).

FIGURE 5.3
Structure of social interaction:
the case of superior/subordinate in work settings

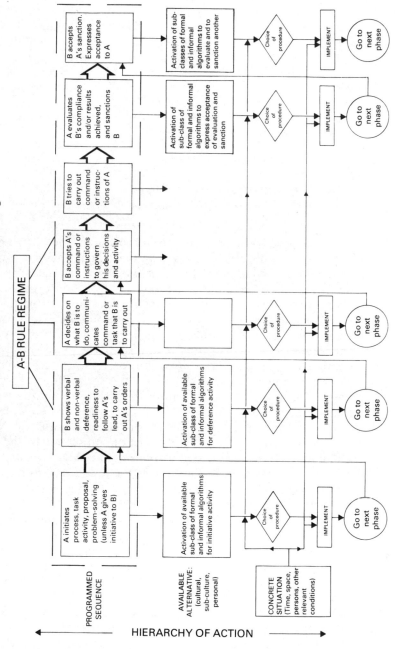

Figure 5.3 presents a very simple model to illustrate a rule-governed sequencing of social action and interaction under a domination type of regime. A initiates activity and commands B to do something (where the scope of A's directives are limited by law, by relevant labour contracts, and company policy); A's command activates specific algorithms structuring B's behaviour in the setting where the command is to be executed. The figure also represents the *hierarchy of social action,* in this case the fact that abstract categories such as the following may take a variety of specific, typically context-dependent forms:[31]

● initiate a proposal; allocate tasks
● show deference
● give instructions; indicate rules to be followed
● accept instructions and operative rules
● evaluate and sanction

There is usually a spectrum of procedures and algorithms — organized sets of rules — about how to carry out particular types of action, for instance to initiate a proposal, give commands, or to show deference. The participants in the process choose among these alternative possibilities in their interactions and, in particular, in performing concrete activities vis a vis one another. Their particular choices will depend on the specific context, local information and conditions, past history of the relationship, the presence or absence of other actors and so forth. Such differentiating factors — *within the global domination relationship* — contribute to the rich variety of observable patterns, even 'within the prison' of institutionalized relationships of domination.

The specific acts and sub-acts in social interaction are decomposed as in the structure of action presented in the figure. Ultimately, these will entail very concrete cognitive and motor activities, where nevertheless the latter *reflect the structuring and regulation of the AB rule regime* (thus, the linking of social structure and neurophysiological and muscular processes!).

The pattern of interaction between supervisors and subordinates (or employer/employee) in a work organization is a general one. Obviously, the specific forms of such interaction vary between cultures, industries and even between enterprises and plants (where 'local organizational cultures' may be observed). The subordinate agrees, in exchange for wages, to obey the supervisors assigned him or her and to carry out defined tasks. Such a contract differs from one which specifies concretely what is exchanged for what, as in contracts between enterprises, or a service contract. The *general principle* here is relatively simple: A is to initiate activity, give orders, allocate rewards, evaluate performances, and sanction; B is to accept A's initiatives, follow A's orders and accept A's assessments, judgements, and sanctions concerning work performance within a more or less well-defined task sphere or work setting. This principle provides a frame for the design and development of more specific rules and algorithms appropriate for particular work and task situations. The labour contract is largely open-ended, but this may vary considerably. Typically, it is applicable to new types of activities, tasks, and work situations, although subordinate groups may resist changes initiated by their superiors because they violate established 'understandings' and 'informal, unwritten rules'. Nevertheless, radical changes in specific tasks, techniques or settings to which the AB relationship applies take place over the long run, without substantially altering the basic principle of superior/ subordinate relations in work organizations.

Often, differing, even contradictory organizing principles may be activated or applied to social activity in particular settings. A rule regime of social domination, such as a superior/subordinate relationship in a workplace, may be contradicted by democratic norms and values in the larger society. Social agents, both superiors and subordinates, share to a greater or lesser extent these egalitarian norms and organizing principles. This sets the stage for change attempts, conflicts, and negotiated compromises as well as new syntheses.[32] Thus, the AB rule regime in practice tends to be somewhat different in the context of a larger egalitarian or democratic society than it is in non-democratic societies. The differences would typically be observable in culturally distinct forms of communication, supervision, and sanctioning. The extent of variation or divergence in forms would depend, of course, on the institutionalized force of democratic principles. Some adaptation of hierarchical relationships can be accomplished, without basically changing the hierarchical nature of the AB relationship. Thus, symbolic homage may be paid to egalitarian or democratic principles of social organization (through the use of 'first names', commands expressed as requests, and so forth) at the same time that the principle of supervisory domination prevails or takes precedence over realization of egalitarian principles, at least in production settings.

Rationally designed social action
Modern culture is to a large extent characterized by the systematic application of expert knowledge to rule formation and the organization of social action (Weber, 1968; see Chapters 11 and 17). This culture is particularly prominent in modern government, business firms, labour unions, and other practically oriented organizations

but also pervades political parties as well as voluntary organizations. *Expert knowledge — legal, scientific/technical, management 'science' (administration, accounting, marketing) — is used in the formulation and reformulation of rules to organize and regulate purposeful collective action.* Options or patterns of social action, which are believed on the basis of expert knowledge to be optimal or effective, are crystallized in the form of rule systems designed to generate the desirable patterns. Inappropriate actions, or highly risky patterns tend to be proscribed in rule formulation — guided by expertise which can assess or judge legality, costs and consequences.

FIGURE 5.4
Modern rule formation and rational social action

**Socio-political/
institutional frame**
for social production
and use of knowledge   **Expert knowledge:**
legal, technical,
management/economic
(organizational,
marketing, accounting)

|

Rule formation: rules
proposed, assessed,
selected, developed,
replaced, transformed

|

Rule implementation:
certain types of
'rational social action'
(lacking authentic
spontaneity, amateurism,
or devotion to tradition)

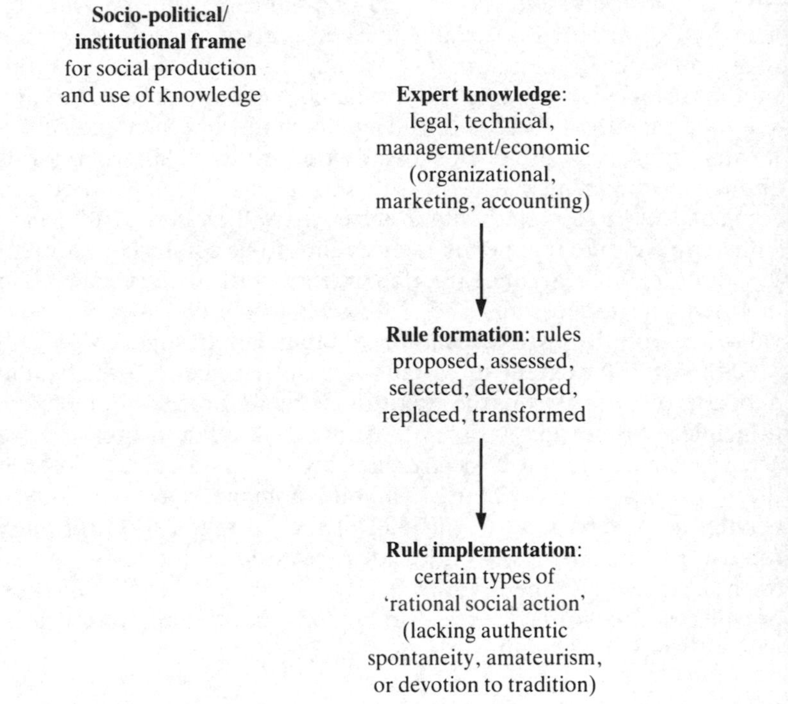

Important points here are:
(i) 'Rational' rule formation and reformation entail a social process of examining as well as formulating action possibilities which

are legal and which also serve the purposes or goals of those who dominate or exercise authority over the sphere or organization in question. Illegal actions tend to be excluded, but actors under modern legal conditions may take calculated risks in this respect. Within the realm of legal feasibility, certain activities are technically or economically indicated or preferable. Social rules and regulations generating or leading to these actions are then formulated. These become the directives for organized action, introduced and enforced by agents with authority and power capabilities within the sphere of organized activity.

(ii) The various types of expert knowledge — and the organized actions they deduce would be preferable or optimal — need not be consistent. Finding optimal types of actions, and optimal rule systems to generate these, may be very difficult and, in some cases proves unfeasible. As we illustrate later, these situations often provoke deviance and/or attempts to change laws, organizing principles and regulations as well as to develop new expert understanding and knowledge, so as to expand or transform action possibilities.

Different types of expert knowledge may be inconsistent in relation to particular questions of organized action, in that they indicate contradictory courses of action. The expert groups or communities often have rule systems with very different norms and regulations governing their modes of collecting, organizing, analysing and using information as well as formulating knowledge statements and rules for action. The purposes, norms and regulations, and methods relating to the structuration and regulation of social action differ so substantially that an integrated or coherent knowledge application and rule formation process becomes very difficult, if not apparently unfeasible. Later we explore such incompatibilities between, for instance, the logic of scientific social action and decision, and that of politics (Chapter 16). Similar analyses and conclusions can be developed concerning 'legal knowledge and procedures' and 'scientific knowledge and procedures'.

(iii) The organizing principles and rules which structure and regulate organized action are often compromises or syntheses which are believed to lead to optimal patterns. Thus, in the design of technologies, socio-technical systems, and social organizations, there are several objective or performance criteria: for instance, minimum cost, reliability, and quality of output. Typically, these objectives conflict with one another, and, therefore, compromises must be made. Optimal or well-established compromises are often crystallized in standard principles and rules, which become widely diffused. This is particularly observable in the systematic knowledge of professions such as engineering, architecture, management, etc.

In a certain sense, the rules and regulations of organizations are institutionalized means or strategies to organize and regulate social action for certain purposes within specified constraints, where the rules are based to a greater or lesser extent on the systematic application of expert knowledge (see Chapters 7, 11, 14 and 15).

(iv) General 'optimal' rule systems must be adapted to the concrete action settings in which they are to be implemented, that is particular local conditions. Situations where implementations have been relatively successful in the past may undergo substantial changes, again calling for adaptation in the rule systems. Thus, one distinguishes between a theoretically optimal rule system and the 'practical' system(s), which emerge and develop under action conditions not specified or taken into account in the formulation of the more theoretically or abstractly formulated system (see Chapter 11).

(v) In many instances, the outcome of a rule formation process is weakly or even inversely related to the expert knowledge inputs (see Chapter 15). To understand this in the context of a dominant 'technocratic culture', we must consider *the politics of rule formation.*

1. Class, ethnic, or other groups with competing or conflicting interests struggle over rule formation and reformation. In some instances, they mobilize different, contradictory 'expertise'. In other instances, some of the contending agents put stress on expressions of their interests or values, ignoring or minimizing considerations of expert knowledge and rationally organized social action.
2. Rule formation in which contending interests struggle results in compromises where expert considerations play only a secondary or partial role, because of priority given to compromise itself.
3. Situational knowledge is not incorporated into expert knowledge. The former may be local or particular in character. As a result, there tend to be substantial gaps or inconsistencies between the 'theoretical knowledge' of experts and the 'practical or operative knowledge' of those involved in concrete organizations and institutions. Rule formation based on practical knowledge and non-systematic considerations of effective action may replace or substantially reform 'expert inspired rules'. (See Chapter 11.)

Many of the case studies and analyses presented in Parts II, III, and IV of this book concern the interplay and contradictions between multiple rule systems and the ambiguity, uncertainty and conflict which such conditions evoke. Of particular interest is competition and conflict between rationally designed and pragmatically evolved rule systems (see particularly Chapter 11).

Conclusion: Power, strategic structuring and system development

Social actors transact with one another not only to communicate sentiments and to 'play', but to act out their roles and to pursue their interests within particular social structures. In the course of their transactions — in cooperation and in conflict — they produce (one or more) social organization(s) in practice. Their activities may in part be *strategic* in character, designed or pursued in order to maintain or change certain rule regimes which favour their interests or hurt the interests of others to whom they are opposed or antagonistic.

The power implications of social rule systems should by now be apparent. They structure and distribute opportunities for initiative, for access to and use of important resources, and for carrying out control activities in relation to other social agents. For example, in social settings where property or ownership regimes apply, unequal distribution of property resources shapes differential action capabilities and dominance relations. Certain opportunities, depending on access to and use of property resources, are available to 'owners or their representatives'. They will be in a position to exercise social power over others on the basis of their property control and to take initiatives, such as to try to maintain a rule regime or to change it in directions favouring them. On the other hand, those without substantial property would lack the same action opportunities, including the possibilities to shape future developments in a favourable direction, at least in settings where an ownership regime would apply.

Those lacking property resources may, nonetheless, be able to countervail or limit the full exploitation of property rights, by virtue of other rule regimes such as political democracy. The multiplicity of rule regimes, which to a greater or lesser extent, compete with and partially contradict one another, make for the ambiguity, uncertainty, and partial 'openness' in social transactions. In modern life the interplay between organized domination and principles of democracy, championed by different social agents, makes for tensions and the dynamism of modern Western society (see Chapter 17).

The social structures and patterns of activity which actors produce and reproduce in their transactions, including their strategic structuring and institutional design, need not be those they intended. This is particularly the case when they come into conflict with one another and 'negotiate', possibly in creative ways, resulting in out-comes none of the participants anticipated.

Unanticipated and unintended consequences of social action, including strategic action, often serve to erode and restructure established rule systems and their resource bases.

Social rule systems and rule system complexes of modern society are continually undergoing change: new rules, norms and laws are being made, old ones are re-interpreted and re-formulated. Some are made obsolete and are replaced or simply allowed to fade away from daily practice. This suggests the social praxis of rule formation and reformation.

These notions correspond to Giddens' view that social institutions should be conceptualized and analysed as emerging out of concrete social transactions rather than operating teleologically per se or according to abstract, necessary 'societal purposes' (Giddens, 1979; 1984; also see Maynard, 1985). However, the production/reproduction of local social orders — while certainly affecting macro-structures — is often not the main or dominant factor in macro-structuration. In the framework developed here, powerful elites and agents are seen to act strategically and to struggle — mobilizing power resources at their disposal — to establish and maintain institutional arrangements which seem to them to satisfy their interests. These arrangements are typically *designed* — as, for instance, the many economic and political institutions examined in Parts II, III, and IV of the book have been to a large extent designed — by elite actors in order to produce certain desirable patterns of transactions and outcomes. In other words, they are intended to operate 'teleologically'. Such strategic structuring and institutional design and development, core processes in the shaping and reshaping of modern social organization, are major consider-ations in following chapters.

6
Consensus and conflict in social life

Introduction: Opposition in social life
Consensus and conflict, stability and change, are combined in any social process (Giddens, 1979). The challenge analytically is to show — through investigating the structuring of social action and the role of social rule systems in this structuration — the concrete ways in which social integration and differentiation, cooperation and conflict, combine at different levels and in the different phases of social activity.

Social rule system theory distinguishes three types of opposition in human affairs:

(1) *Social contradictions* are inconsistencies or incompatibilities *between,* and also possibly *within,* rule systems.
(2) *Disagreements or disputes* are expressions of opposition among social agents concerning: beliefs about the world, decisions, actions, or the rule systems which organize these.
(3) *Social conflicts* are said to occur whenever agents struggle with one another, mobilizing power resources and sanctions, in order to give precedence to one, interest, belief, decision or action over another; or to give priority to one rule system over another.

In the following paragraphs, we discuss briefly these types of opposition and their interrelationships. Of particular interest are the conditions under which social contradiction become manifest in disagreements and conflicts among social agents.

Contradiction and disagreement
By contradiction we mean:

- multiple rules systems or rules apply to the same action setting and indicate opposing courses of action in one or more situations
- a rule system cannot be implemented because of interests opposing it, if not for other reasons, such as insufficient resources, time, energy, or physical capacity. This leads to the emergence of a new rule system that subverts the old one (as in new formal or informal rules)

Contradiction between rule systems manifests itself in disagreements among actors about what decision, action, or rule system

89

FIGURE 6.1
The structure of contradiction and conflict

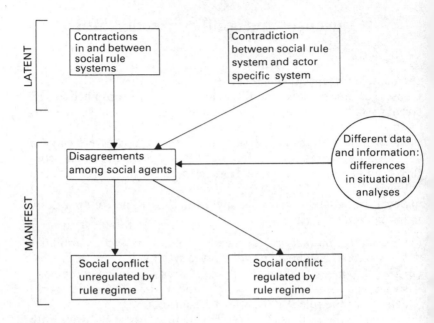

should apply or take precedence in governing social activity in the setting.[33]

Contradictions, in terms of rule system theory, arise whenever agents adhering to different rule systems or sub-sets of rules try to apply the systems to a given social activity or action sphere at the same time and place. Such inter-system contradiction may be distinguished from contradictions occurring as a result of disagreement among social agents, who share a rule system complex, about which of their rule systems, subsystems, or procedures apply. Their disagreements, in this case within a frame of general consensus, occur as a result of ambiguities in the rules, divergence in their situational information and analyses, or confusing or highly uncertain action settings (see note 33).

Clearly, contradictions may remain entirely latent unless attempts are made to apply the incompatible rule systems in the same social process or activity. Or the actors involved anticipate or perceive the likelihood of manifest contradictions in concrete action settings, which have yet to arise.

The greater the incompatibility between social rule systems, which different agents or groups try to apply or impose in social action settings, the greater the uncertainty, confusion, and likelihood of dispute. Given their very different frames of reference and logic of social action, the agents usually select different data for their decisions and activities. If they were to use the same data, they would do so in disparate or inconsistent ways. Exchange of data and 'information' will usually be inefficient, even counterproductive, in terms of providing a basis on which to understand one another's behaviour or to guide their actions in relation to one another. The organization and regulation of social action and interaction, in general social integration, becomes highly problematic under these conditions.[34]

The diversity of and contradictions between rule systems — which underlie many manifest disagreements and conflicts in society — can be traced to *differential organization of, and socialization in, modern complex societies.*

In a complex, differentiated society, individuals and groups (class, occupational, professional, ethnic, religious, and cultural) acquire unequal knowledge of, and commitment to, the dominant rule regimes. They are by and large recruited (and self-recruited) into different institutional spheres — work, community, politics. In these spheres, different rule regimes apply, specifying disparate organizational forms, social relations, and roles. Moreover, individuals have different power positions, functions, and interests in the spheres. They attempt to realize their different interests. Thus, the various social categories of people — and to some extent, their children — identify with, and develop commitment to, dominant rule regimes to varying degrees. In addition, they may also be socialized at the outset into alternative, marginal, or deviant rule regimes associated with various sub- or counter-cultures. Ideological doctrines and consciousness-raising processes make actors or groups of actors more or less sensitive or predisposed to anticipate and oppose contradictory rule systems. This is especially so in the case where agents involved have had a history of conflict.

In sum, socialization with respect to dominant regimes, corresponding to major economic and political institutions, is never complete or fully consistent, because of the complex differentiation of modern society. Moreover, groups (as well as individuals) accumulate to some degree unique experiences and have differential predispositions to deviate or to innovate with respect to established rule systems.

The utilization of — and differential socialization with respect to — diverse organizing principles in modern society are major factors underlying many inherent contradictions and patterns of conflict in society (see Chapter 17).

Not all contradictions and disparities, as we shall see, manifest themselves in disagreements and conflicts among agents. There are various buffers which veil the divisive forces lurking behind apparent social order. At the same time, human groups create and develop rule regimes to regulate and control disagreement and conflict. Without such buffers and controls, collective life in a modern society would be much more problematic than it is.

Social conflict
Disagreement among agents becomes social conflict in the proper sense when they act intentionally to harm or sanction one another. Major social conflicts are likely to arise in interaction settings where the social agents involved try to apply contradictory rule systems, in pursuit of ideal or material interests. Group, organization, or institutional settings which bring together such social agents are particularly prone to social disagreements and conflicts. Obvious examples are racial and ethnic conflicts within settings such as labour unions, community organizations, political parties, and larger collectivities such as nations. Similarly, conflicting interests between labour and capital are manifested within major economic, governmental, and political organizations and institutional settings in capitalist societies.

In all human societies, there are conflicts and struggles over rule formation and implementation: those with vested interests in a system of domination, e.g. based on property and/or political rights, try to maintain the system, making minimal adjustments and concessions, while those who are subordinated and/or marginalized will, at least on occasion, struggle to reform or transform the system, establishing new rules and regime complexes. The concern of the latter may be principally oriented to the order itself and/or some of the specific outcomes which put them at a disadvantage.

In modern societies, at least three types of organized groups are mobilized and attempt to influence rule formation and reformation: class organizations, status groups, and moral or ideological communities. These groups are organized in relation to major opposing interests or cleavages.[35]

Classes. Class agents and organizations consist of specific groups or collectivities with a common relationship to the means of production or more or less common 'market location'. In Western nations, these agents struggle around issues relating to private property relations, production relations and conditions, and distribution mechanisms. For instance, they struggle to exclude or include groups from a market, to alter ownership or production relations, or for control or redistribution of the resources allocated via markets (Kitschelt, 1985:275).

Status groups. These are collectivities (ethnic, religious, occupational) that mobilize around issues concerning their rank in the distribution of social, economic and political power relative to others. They advocate the maintenance, defence, restoration, or introduction of exclusive communal identities, moral codes, legal privileges, and rules for organizing social interactions among status groups. Their demands are derived from group specific — particularistic — norms, or a conception of justice in which one's status in social hierarchy should determine one's position and fair share in the social order. Status groups mobilize around issues concerning their rank in the distribution of social, economic and political power relative to others.

Both class organizations and status groups mobilize and struggle around the distribution of resources and power and the organizing principles that such distributions imply.[36]

Moral communities and social movements. These consist of mobilized collectivities with a vision of social organization opposed to existing arrangements. Such collectivities may consist of peripheral communities and nations, which aim simply to maintain and develop their own community life (e.g. Lapps in Scandinavia, Utopian communities).

Typically, they are excluded from the socio-political institutions that function as a core sphere. Thus, 'their struggle' concerns entering and exercising influence over the structuration of society, more than over 'distributional issues' and 'relational issues' which concern class and status groups. In some cases, such collectivities consist of movements which seek to substantially alter the existing arrangements. As in the case of many early Communist and Socialist movements, they may also be excluded from the core sphere, either by legislation, electoral rules, or by their own programme. Some communities and movements follow an 'isolationist' strategy, attempting to remain outside established society.

Kitschelt refers to the 'Green' and 'anti-industrial–military-bureaucratic-complex' movements. The Greens in West Germany have arisen in opposition to the increasing control of social relations by formal organizations and bureaucratic politics. On the one hand, they seek to undermine, or at least restrict, this type of organizational control; and to combine it with more self-management by *all affected members of society*. On the other hand, they refuse to embrace, and often reject, the dominance of the axial principles of class and status, embodied in the institutions of social regulation.

One may analytically distinguish pervasive structural relations among major groups in society, such as those based on class and status, from particular organizational relations and spheres of society where the representatives of these groups interact. Domination systems entail specific groups controlling resources and having certain economic and political prerogatives (based on private property, organizational power, public authority). Such systems, as suggested earlier, engender contradictions of interests and predispositions to tension and social conflict. Sustained conflicts between, for instance, classes and/or status groups may be organized and regulated by specific institutional and organizational arrangements established for such purposes. Such conflict regulation and social integration is discussed in the following section.

Conflict regulation
One may distinguish analytically between two general types of social opposition based on whether or not it is contained within particular institutional arrangements:

(1) Intra-systemic opposition. Such dispute/conflict arises *within* a larger institutionalized rule system which serves to structure and regulate disagreements and conflicts and their outcomes.

(2) Inter-systemic opposition. This type of opposition arises in connection with encounters between social agents, adhering to very different regimes or regime concepts, without or outside of any common overriding regime. Frequently, in such cases social contradictions are not distinguished or differentiated from the actual conflict.

In the case of intra-systemic opposition, actors share to a greater or lesser extent at least one overarching rule system, which is a coherent basis for structuring their social relationships and patterns of social interaction. Within this integrating regime, disputes, and conflicts between major actors, for example capital and labour, are organized and regulated. This is accomplished by means of legislative rules, collective bargaining systems, electoral procedures, etc. These institutional devices enable social agents to pursue their interests and values, at the same time they serve to reinforce and develop the overarching rule regime, and the collective sense of a shared culture and underlying political consensus.

Concepts introduced earlier may be applied here to enrich the description and analysis of conflict-containing, overarching rule regimes:

(i) Process and transaction rules govern conflict interactions, specifying acceptable (or proscribing unacceptable) actions and 'weapons'. These rules may also indicate the phases of the conflict, its timing, and rules about ending it. The role of third parties and other institutions may also be specified. Thus, disagreements are not only anticipated but are regulated to a greater or lesser extent within the regime, as in the case of collective bargaining or parliamentary institutions.

(ii) Role systems define rule sets which govern the behaviour of particular categories of actors, e.g. an employer association or enterprise, and its appropriate orientation to labour unions. They specify legitimate or appropriate strategies and 'weapons', such as a 'lockout', and some of the conditions about their use.

(iii) Actor unique rules or rule systems are the particular strategies and tactics which agents adopt and develop on their own, in some instances at variance with the institutionalized rule system governing their conflict relationships. These may be quite predictable and even incorporated in the system, as where the actual (as opposed to centrally agreed) wages are measured and injected, according to certain rules, into the next negotiating round under the label of 'wage-drift' (see Chapter 10).

The conditions for the establishment and maintenance of an overarching rule regime complex in society are both structural and cultural. Several of the structural factors are (see Tumin (1982); Moore (1966)): (1) groups and classes obey/respect a central authority; (2) the central authority is relatively strong; (3) the state, that is the centrally controlled bureaucracy, is strong enough to provide coherence, and effective administration, but not so strong as to wield absolute power; other societal groups and classes in society are independent and powerful enough to exercise a number of important rights, regardless of the desires of the central authority; (4) coalitions are formed between and among groups, classes and the central authority in such ways as to maintain a certain power balance. Conflicts occur without eliminating groups and with alternating victories and defeats.

A key cultural factor in the successful establishment and maintenance of an overriding rule regime is the sense of shared, for instance, national identity and the identification of major groups with collective welfare and well-being. Such identification arises in many instances in the context of military, political, or economic competition in regional or international arenas. At the same time, as Tumin (1982) suggests, such identification, and the commitment it engenders, depends, at least in part on institutionalized principles of solidarity and fair play within collectivities. Such principles allow groups, classes and other collectivities in the society to pursue their interests and to express their views within certain limits, without fear of repression or elimination. No group is strongly inclined to bring down or radically destabilize the society on behalf of its own special interests.

Tumin (1982:146–7), in developing such ideas, points out, following Moore (1966), significant differences in the degree to which aristocracies in various countries opposed democratic developments:

> The theme of diehard opposition to the march of democracy is a rare and minor current among the landed aristocracy of England in the 19th century. One cannot find in English history the counterpart to those German conservatives whose parliamentary representatives rose in demonstrative applause to the ringing challenge of Herr von Oldenburg auf Januschau: 'The King of Prussia and the German Emperor must always be in a position to say to any lieutenant: "Take ten men and shoot the Reichstag!"'

Tumin (1982:147) goes on to argue that, in contrast to Prussia and Germany:

> The aristocracies of England, Sweden and Denmark had become firmly committed to national unity and survival by the end of the sixteenth century in each case. The same can be said about the other major groups in these countries. This does not mean that these groups ceased struggling for power and privilege. But they did so within the 'rules of the game'. In none did they seek to bring down the nation–state to advance their own class interests. Indeed, in England, the Conservatives in the 1800s led the fight to extend the franchise to the working class. They suspected that the workers were just as loyal to 'England' as they were themselves.

Tumin emphasizes the importance of the commitment to national unity above narrow self-interest as well as to democratic norms in the stabilization of a nascent democratic system (1982:147). In doing so, he argues that in England, Sweden and Denmark, aristocrats played by the 'rules of the game', an institutionalized strategy which capitalists later inherited, at least in Sweden and Denmark.

In the absence of an overarching regime, disagreements and intense conflicts are likely to arise between groups, organizations, and communities with opposing rule regimes or principles of social organization. They will disagree about and struggle over such questions as, for example, the principles for organizing people in work, politics, or community, the rules governing the distribution of valuable resources and income, and questions relating to equality, liberty and freedom.

Intense social conflict, tending to escalate into violence, is likely whenever contradictory rule regimes advocated by different groups, classes, or communities are not subject to any *higher order or overarching regime*. The latter is essential to constraining contradictions, and organizing and regulating concrete disagreements and conflicts between human collectivities.

Of course, such conflict may be controlled by the dominance of one of the social groups or by a third party or central authority. The dominant group or central authority provides a global regime. However, the system would typically fail to command general loyalty or legitimacy among those groups and classes adhering to opposing rule systems. Any erosion of the bases of the dominant power would unleash tension, a deep sense of insecurity and powerful predispositions to intense conflict and conflict escalation. At the same time, conditions of serious conflict and insecurity, combined with repression, block the possibilities of establishing and developing an overarching, legitimate regime. A vicious circle obtains.

Even in societies with an overarching rule regime, the latter is rarely fully shared or adhered to among major groups, because of the differential organization of, and socialization in, the society. One might expect, consequently, that rule regimes and particular rules would be endlessly contested. What is surprising in the light of the complex array of conditions organizing and regulating social life, is that social life is not more confused, more conflict-ridden, or more chaotic.

The explanations are several. First, there are various mechanisms serving to buffer social groups and society from forces of division and chaos, for example:

- actors internalize contradictions, evoking 'personal' or 'local' resolution rather than social or more global resolution processes
- lack of information as well as intentional deception about disagreements
- deception, hypocrisy, 'game playing' as buffering mechanisms
- pragmatism and the sense of a need to keep the business of life going
- ideology and interpretation which lead actors to overlook or to treat disagreements as mistakes or misunderstandings, thereby maintaining an image of consensus and homogeneity
- contradictions remain latent

As pointed out earlier, in addition to various everyday mechanisms which serve as buffers, specific social institutions are established to systematically regulate disputes and conflicts, e.g. political institutions, collective decision procedures such as voting, formal bargaining systems, arbitration boards, courts (see Chapters 10–13).

In general, there are various buffers and social controls, *a complex web of regulatory systems, sanctions and incentives,* which induce people to adhere to established rule systems and to produce 'social order', as discussed in the preceding chapter. The ubiquity, variety, and complexity of controls in modern society often go unnoticed, since most social actors take a substantial part of them for granted, even if this 'taking-for-grantedness' is greater in some spheres of society than others and also varies considerably from nation to nation.

Rule regimes tend to shape, as a consequence of their very implementation and functioning, their own penalties and rewards. When adhered to by a collectivity, a rule system becomes externalized: a reality which must be taken into account in making decisions and taking action in settings where the rule system applies. Opposing or deviating from the rule system, *in contexts where others adhere to it,* may be costly. Complying with it is likely to be rewarding, particularly if an actor's aim is to interact and coordinate with others, or to avoid the costs of miscues and misunderstandings.

In Parts II, III, and IV, we explore several types of contradiction and conflict, which social organization engenders and also regulates.

7
Grammars of social institutions and the structuring of spheres of social action

Introduction: Institutional spheres of social action

Since Weber, there has been a sustained interest in the social scientific analysis of institutions. Institutions are characterized by certain social relationships and patterns of social interaction, self-contained 'integrity' and autonomy, and tendencies toward structural stability (Streeck and Schmitter, 1984:5). Weber pointed us to stable forms in modern society such as bureacracy, markets, and political parties. These or similar institutions are examined in Dahl and Lindblom (1963), Lindblom (1977), Hernes (1982), Streeck and Schmitter (1984), among others.

Following this research tradition, we shall focus in this chapter on major, formally organized economic and government institutions. Our purpose here is to suggest ways, using social rule system theory, to systematically investigate the structure and dynamics of social institutions and their corresponding rule regimes.

(a) Social institutions may be studied and analysed in terms of social rule regimes, finite sets of constitutive rules specifying, for example, who may or may not participate, which transactions are valid or legitimate and which are excluded, and in what ways valid transactions are to be organized.

(b) The same analytical method can be used to compare on a finite set of dimensions characteristic properties of rule regimes corresponding to very different types of institutions — such as markets, political systems, and administration — which are found in any given modern society.

(c) Finally, the framework provides an analytic basis to study entire subsystems of modern society, such as 'the economy' or 'the political subsystem', which consist of *sets of institutionalized relations and transaction spheres*, each core relation governed by a different rule regime, which may be incompatible to varying degrees, together making up a *regime complex*. Thus, the 'economic system' with its processes of production, distribution and market transactions, and policy-making and regulation is seen as governed by a rule regime complex encompassing the market, collective bargaining, enterprise organization, and the other social forms making up the modern capitalist economy. This angle of attack leads to the examination in later chapters of the interfaces between different rule regimes, the extent to which they are or are not compatible, the meta-rules and strategies which actors use in dealing with contradictions, and the central problems of institutional dynamics and development.

Universal rule categories of social institutions

Any institutionalized relationship is structured and regulated by one or more social rule systems. This is axiomatic to rule system theory. Such relations correspond to certain forms or modes of transaction, power and authority relationships, exchange and conflict. Transaction modes also define or constitute a particular sphere of social action.

A rule regime is a social rule system enforced and sustained by legal as well as non-legal sanctions (see Chapter 2). It governs specific types of social transaction or spheres of action. At the core of each rule regime are the rules specifying legitimate or acceptable social agents, their roles and role relationships, rights and obligations in these relations, legitimate or acceptable activities (and conversely, illegitimate and unacceptable activities), legitimate or appropriate times and places for the rule-governed activity, and prescribed or acceptable techniques and technologies.

Each transaction sphere governed by a rule regime has then identifiable activities and processes, particular types of actors (roles, positions, status) and agents (groups, organizations, other collective actors), 'defined interests and purposes for transacting', types of transaction which are appropriate or acceptable, and types of acceptable and unacceptable resources and means of action. The 'social logic' of an action sphere is a manifestation of the rule regime which structures and regulates the sphere, and of the sanctions that typically are associated with these regimes. All social institutions which structure and regulate concrete transactions among human agents consist of a *finite set of rule types*. The rule types correspond to *basic categories of social transaction*. These categories are specified abstractly in the general model of social action (see Figure 7.1).

The correspondence between categories of action and types of rules in social institutions occurs precisely because institutions are designed to structure and regulate action. The language of action becomes the basis for conceptualizing and developing social rule systems that we call institutions. At the same time, the social rules structuring and regulating social transactions provide the language among participating agents for describing and accounting for action in their communications. (The basic categories of social transactions represent essential distinctions relating to acting in or upon the world and 'making a difference'.)

FIGURE 7.1
General model of social action

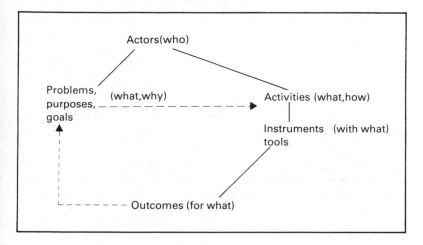

The rules and rule structure of a social institution contain directions for the choices that are to be made in connection with structuring and regulating interactions among human agents. *A social institution — consisting of a finite set of rules — answers to a greater or lesser extent the questions:* who, what, why, how, when and where (see Table 7.1). In some instances, 'the answer' allows a certain discretion or partial freedom: actors are free to provide their own answers, at least within very broad frames.

In sum, a social institution provides specific content to the universals of social transactions, by determining the values of social action dimensions. As we shall show later, this feature of social institutions allows them to be systematically compared, *since all share the finite set of rule types characteristic of social institutions governing human transactions* (Eisenstadt and Curelaru (1977:66–9) and more recently Marin (1985) also suggest types of ground rules for structuring and regulating social interactions). At the same time, one type of transaction sphere, e.g. markets, can be clearly distinguished from another type, e.g. administrative systems.

The rules of any social institution governing transactions may be grouped and analysed according to these basic categories or types of 'questions'. Thus, in our investigations and analyses of institutions

TABLE 7.1

Universal rule categories of institution grammars

Who?

Principles or rules defining who may participate (or conversely who may not) in a given social relationship or sphere of action where the relationship governs action and interaction. Also types of participants and their roles may be defined in terms of their purposes, types of activities, and resources (see later).

Why, for what aims?

Principles or rules specifying appropriate or legitimate values, purposes or problems which are to motivate actors to act in the relationship. Again, these may be specified differently for different types of actors.

Rules also specify what outcomes or results are appropriate or valid in connection with actions and interactions, for instance pecuniary payments (which are distributed according to a certain principle).

What action?

Principles or rules specifying acceptable activities/ transactions. (The rules may be of an excluding nature, indicating activities, types of social decision-making and transactions which are inappropriate or illegitimate.) The transactions specified (or excluded) will relate to particular types of activity such as communication, exchange, conflict, power processes. They specify the rights and obligations of different categories of actors (i.e. defining their positions and roles) in relation to resource access or control and to one another (relations of domination).

How?

Principles or rules specifying how social decision-making and transactions are to be carried out, what procedures are to be followed in specified activities. Included here are various procedures and techniques, social algorithms and rituals.

With what means?

As a further specification of appropriate or legitimate activities and procedures, there are often rules defining acceptable resources, technologies and instruments generally that may be employed (or alternatively, may not) in transactions in the sphere.

When, where?

Principles or rules specifying appropriate or legitimate contexts for the institutionalized activities, actors and resources, in particular the time and place of the activities. These rules in a very concrete sense specify differential settings, thereby locating the sphere of activity.

we look for the answers to these questions — or values on the corresponding dimensions of social action — specified in the rule regimes that constitute the institutions.

'Institution grammars' are never complete. The degree of incompleteness is a variable. Some institutions and their grammars

.

are highly elaborate, structuring and regulating in great detail. Others provide wide latitude to the actors to 'fill in' as they see fit or find necessary in the concrete, often varying situations in which they find themselves.

The incompleteness of institutions and their grammars arises in part because no real situation or process can be fully specified: there are an infinite number of possible specifications. Even when one makes a finite selection, there are limitations on the specifications which can be implemented (except for entirely artificial situations such as theatre). Human actors are part of the biological and physical worlds and transact ultimately in physical time and space and as biological and psychological beings. These conditions impose constraints on the specification and implementation of the rules which are to govern social action and interaction in the concrete world. Also, external social agents and systems impact on the sphere and make for contradictions and developments which could never have been fully anticipated or specified in advance.

Those unspecified or open areas of institutionalized activity, which participants themselves fill in with their own rules, strategies, and ad hoc decisions, make for *social uncertainty*. The uncertainty may take several forms. In some instances, a set or range of options may be specified. Those involved know more or less what possible activities and processes may occur. In instances where they know the predispositions and strategies of different actors, they can reduce uncertainty. In other instances, a more open-ended situation prevails and social uncertainty would be greater.

Apart from filling in 'options', the actors may reformulate system rules with rules of their own which derive from sub-cultures, local experience, or individual and ad hoc innovations. These 'innovations' reflect, in part, historical background and the cultural (or sub-cultural) realms to which particular actors or groups of actors belong. However, in addition, there are also purely practical and ad hoc rules which agents learn and develop through concrete experience and problem-solving. Thus, they acquire knowledge about different action settings or contexts, and interpret and apply an institution grammar in accordance with the types of contexts in which they find themselves. Moreover, certain sub-sets of rules and procedures may be formally defined as appropriate but are known to lead to undesirable consequences, at least from the perspective of some of the participants. Chess players learn from personal experience, from experienced chess players or from 'theories of chess', that legitimate chess moves, for example opening moves, entail different risks. Some moves leave the player so vulnerable that one is advised never to make them. These 'traps', which inexperienced players may readily fall into, can be exploited by experienced players.

What is from an institutional perspective a *prevailing rule regime* is from the perspective of participating actors *social grammars and role sets* (along with procedural norms). The grammars structure and regulate social actions and interactions of agents in the sphere to which the regime applies. They provide a set of classification rules (distinguishing types of objects, persons, activities, and events) as well as action and evaluative rules to structure or order actions as sequential elements of transactions. Actors occupying different roles are governed by diverse role- or position-specific grammars (see Chapter 4). Role grammars are at the same time embedded in the social rule systems making up institutions. Actors in established social relationships collectively produce transaction sequences. The structuring of the action sequences is based on the distinct but inter-oriented role grammars, along with procedural norms and rules of the game.

Knowledge of social grammars enables participants not only to guide their actions vis a vis one another, but to anticipate, interpret and understand what others are doing, and to 'simulate' transaction scenarios among participants and their outcomes. They also provide a basis for communicating with others about their on-going activities and for formulating accounts of what is happening and why (Harre, 1979a).

The grammars constituting institutions distinguish one type of social relation — and corresponding set of transactions — from others in terms of who is included and who is excluded, what types of action are permitted, prescribed as well as proscribed, who has the right to do what, who has access to or control over resources used in the sphere, etc. Thus, social rule systems, when implemented, give an 'identity' to and pattern the transactions in which actors are engaged, for instance 'market behaviour' as distinct from 'political activity' or 'governance'. Such rule systems are established — and are maintained — in order to realize the purposes of particular groups or even the majority of a society. They generate not only certain interaction and performance patterns, including distributional effects; *they operate so as to communicate unambiguous meanings to participants about what it is that is going on, what it is that they are doing, who is involved, how, when, and where.* To be a 'knowledge-able participant' in action governed by an institutional grammar means to have learnt the grammar, at least those parts of it essential to their communications and interactions with others.

Thusfar we have stressed abstract qualities of social relations more than the specific context in which the relations are implemented. A social relationship between actors A and B should be seen in relation to an activity or problem X *where this complex is embedded in a context or class of settings C, that is, specific social and physical localities or situations.* Institutionalized social relationships are always enacted in particular places and times, situational conditions and activities, and in general the fabric of social life. Thus, hierarchical relationships, defined in settings where instrumental performance or results are stressed, have a substantially different social grammar — or rationality — from those hierarchical relationships which are more geared to symbolic expressions and the articulation of status differences.

Social institutions and transaction analysis
The rule systems governing social relations in a specified social action sphere consist of four sub-systems of rules (see Figure 7.2):

- Constitutive rules are those core rules that serve to give identity to a social institution, defining who, what, how, where and when in ways, distinct from other systems.

FIGURE 7.2
Structure of institution grammars

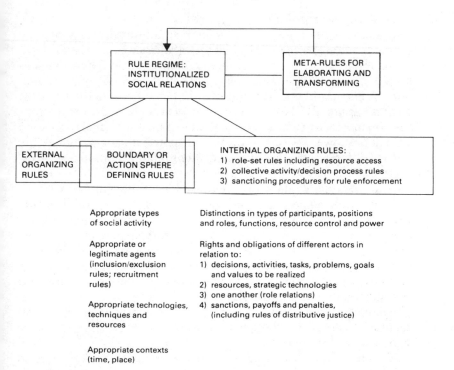

- Organizing rules, which structure and regulate relationships among participating actors and between actors and resources and activities within the defined institutional sphere.
- Boundary differentiating and regulating rules that structure and govern information, materials, transactions and persons which move across the boundary of an institutional sphere.
- Meta-rules dealing with ambiguities and conflicts between rules and sub-rule systems; they include institutionalized strategies to adapt and reform rule systems.

Constitutive rules and the universals of human transactions
These rules distinguish 'sphere transactions' from non-sphere transactions. The distinctions concern participants/non-participants, acceptable or legitimate resources and procedures, types of acceptable or legitimate transactions, and so forth. In other words, the 'inside' is distinguished from the 'outside'.

The constitutive rules of an institutional grammar specify what may (should) be included *and what is excluded from* the sphere governed by the grammar. The set of binary relations covered in complete grammar is indicated in Table 7.2.

Organizing rules: internal relations
The rules of an institution grammar structure and regulate the relations among participants, their social roles and role relationships, for example, those organizing and regulating social spheres such as markets, bureaucracy and politics. They define not only what is appropriate, valid, or even required in the sphere (and conversely what is excluded). They also structure and regulate some or many of the possible relationships among participating actors, their rights and obligations toward one another, their responsibility or accountability toward different activities and tasks, their relationships to resources, and specific time and place aspects of the transactions. Therefore, we look for the rules defining the relationships specified in Table 7.3.

Thus, while some organizing rules are constitutive rules in that they serve to distinguish the institutional sphere from other spheres, many of these rules do not serve to distinguish unambiguously social action in this sphere from that in other spheres. They are non-unique, organizing and regulative rules as well as technical and ad hoc rules (introduced to fill in gaps and to make the larger design actually work in concrete, practical settings).

Among the organizing principles and rules which structure and regulate internal relations in a institutional sphere, the following types can be distinguished:

Role set rules. Social roles or positions in an institutional sphere

TABLE 7.2

Transaction analysis I: universal binary relations on which institution grammars distinguish spheres of social activity

(i)	Actor/non-actor: who is included or excluded. Criteria specified determining conditions for participation.
(ii)	Action/excluded action: what activities are considered appropriate, valid or legitimate in the sphere. Some may be prescribed (types of activity which should be engaged in); others proscribed (types of activity which should not be engaged in).
(iii)	Instruments/excluded instruments: what resources, tools, or technologies are considered appropriate, valid or legitimate in the sphere.
(iv)	Purpose/excluded purpose: what are appropriate motives or purposes for actors to have; or what problems and tasks are actors supposed to deal with in the sphere.
(v)	Outcome/excluded outcome: what outcomes and developments are considered appropriate, valid or legitimate and those that are excluded.
(vi)	Context/non-context: in which specific settings are the rule-governed activities to take place (When ('time'), where ('place')).

are constituted by rule sets (a sub-set of the regime) structuring and regulating a particular category of actors in their relations to other categories of actors, to socially defined purposes and goals, to tasks and to problems (see Figure 3.1). Rule sets enable occupants of roles to guide their decisions and activities, to anticipate how others will respond to their acts and also what to expect of others, what demands can be placed on them, what strategies can be pursued in relation to them. These specify characteristics of the relationships among participants: their rights and obligations toward one another, their responsibilities toward certain activities and tasks, their rights of access to or control over key resources and technologies in the sphere (see below). (Of course, not all rules utilized by actors in roles are those specified by the institution grammar. Some will reflect local culture and innovation or, indeed, may be entirely actor unique. In some instances, these will contradict the formal role set. In fact, restructuring of social rule systems often comes about as a result of the inability or refusal of actors to follow the formal rules.)

Participants in an institutional sphere need not be differentiated to any substantial degree by the governing social rule system: for instance, they may be treated more or less as 'equivalent agents'. This is observable to some extent in collegial and other types of social

TABLE 7.3

Transaction analysis II: set of possible relations which internal organizing rules of an institution grammar specify

(vii)	Actor/actor: actors may be distinguished according to position, status or role, and their relations, rights and obligations vis-a-vis one another specified.
(viii)	Actor/action, outcome/actor: rules also — at times consistent with (vii), at other times not — specify what types of activity are linked to particular actors or classes of actors and what outcomes should accrue to them: in the first case generating an actor/activity matrix; in the second an outcome/actor matrix.
(ix)	Actor/instrument/technique: rules may also specify which resources, tools or technologies different groups of actors have access to and on which criteria these linkages are determined (e.g. property rights or political rights).
(x)	Actor/purpose: what are appropriate motives or purposes for different categories of actors to have or what problems and tasks should different types of actors engage in.
(xi)	Context/actor/action: in which specific settings or contexts are particular participating actors or actor/activity combinations to be involved, i.e., who acts when, does what, where.
(xii)	Context/activity: what is done when and where.

networks. On the other hand, some rule regimes make fundamental distinctions in social roles within the sphere, as between employers and employees and between political representatives and citizen–voters in democratic systems.

Social rule systems, in distinguishing different roles in a transaction sphere, give expression to strategic dimensions of human interaction as well as spell out major principles for role relationships and permissible strategic manoeuvres, for instance:

HIERARCHY/NON-HIERARCHY (or DOMINATION/EQUALITY)
NEARNESS/DISTANCE (or INTIMACY/IMPERSONALITY)

The articulation of such binary distinctions is examined later in this chapter.

Resource access and control rules. Such rules were suggested above (p.106). They concern property rights or control over property or resources such as water, minerals, and land which may belong to the public or communal domain (often there are issues and struggles relating to the definition of 'property'; and 'rights' associated with it change historically and also vary from nation to nation). Some of these rules are *not* linked to particular roles but apply generally, for instance, specifying procedures for the transfer of property, rules for resolving conflicts over property ownership and control, and so forth. *Activity/Decision rules.* These are usually linked closely to particular roles. However, some may have a more general status, specifying how collective decisions in general should be made, that is multi-laterally or uni-laterally, publicly or privately, or as an outcome of public debate or of closed negotiations. Also, techniques or procedures may be specified for carrying out certain activities that are not role related.

Outcome rules. Such rules specify how resource gains or income are to be distributed among participants, how rewards and punishments for activities are to be applied. The organizing principle may be one of 'collective responsibility' or one of 'individual responsibility'. Distributional rules may be, for instance, egalitarian, non-egalitarian, or performance based.

Organizing rules: External relations

These rules arise since an institutional sphere by definition entails a boundary distinguishing the 'inside' from the 'outside'. The boundary is socially defined and maintained. Since information, materials, transactions and persons can move across that boundary, social agents establish rules structuring and regulating these linkages and flows, or preventing such flows altogether.

The types of organizing rules specified above apply here as well. There are differences, however.

(i) The more interactions and flows across the boundary of the sphere, the more complete and elaborate the regulating rule system is likely to be. In such cases, the external organizing rules often become an 'institutional sphere' themselves, for instance, an 'associational sphere' (Schmitter, 1979) which structures and regulates the interactions between peak organizations of state and business and labour. (The opposing strategy, one of maximum 'avoidance', is also a way of organizing social relations.)

(ii) Rules designed to govern linkages to a given sphere may or may not be backed by sanctions sufficiently powerful to gain the compliance of internal and external agents. A social sphere can be said to dominate other spheres when its agents are able to impose external organizing rules — or gain stable adherence to these rules — from actors in other spheres. In many instances, such rules are subject to negotiation and struggle, with a high degree of uncertainty regarding ultimate outcomes.

Implementation and maintenance of a rule regime become problematic if the boundary of the relevant sphere of activity cannot be regulated. Outside information, resource inflows, and influence attempts will tend to destabilize and erode the practice of the institution grammar.

If the internal rule regime cannot be sustained, *an institutional sphere no longer obtains — or certainly not the same type of sphere.* Effective challenge to and erosion of rules within a sphere not only may change its character but may shift the boundary of the sphere. Thus, what was a 'market rule system' governing the supply and demand of labour becomes subject to a system of collective negotiation and administration. The institution grammars governing these latter systems differ substantially from market systems (see Chapter 10).

Meta-rules
These are the rules for dealing with ambiguity and contradiction among rules or rule systems and for changing constitutive and organizational rules. (See Chapters 5, 12 and 16.)

Elaborated social grammars are, generally speaking, not legislated, although politics may initially determine basic organizing principles which form the core of an institutionalized sphere. Typically, much of the grammar is worked out in practice in 'everyday activities', and adapted and developed in the course of acting in concrete social settings. The basic practical grammar at any one time is the resultant of multiple and conflicting rule systems which are brought to bear on the concrete activities and processes in the transaction sphere. Old rules are continuously adapted and reformulated in the face of situational variation and changes; new rules are tried. In some instances, there may emerge or enter agents who try to reform the regime in major ways. *Meta-rules and meta-processes generally play a strategic role in these practical activities of rule system elaboration and development.*

Key binary distinctions in social grammars
The model of universal features of social grammars, even in those cases where there remain undefined or unspecified features, provides us with a guide to examine and analyse any institutionalized social relationship or sphere of social action. Knowledge of such grammars enables scientific observers — as well as participating actors — to distinguish one social sphere from another, in terms of specified agents, types of transactions, and contextual factors such as time and place. Grammars also indicate what are appropriate motives or reasons for social actions and interactions, their purposes or meaning.

A social grammar contains principles or key rules which constitute characteristic forms and features of the social relationship, e.g. a certain type of domination. In this way, *the universal dimensions of social transactions, in this case domination, are given a particular content.* The content consists of institutionalized choices with respect to binary oppositions or dualities such as the following:[37]

> HIERARCHICAL/NON-HIERARCHICAL
> INTIMATE/DISTANT
> FORMAL/INFORMAL
> COOPERATIVE/COMPETITIVE
> PEACEFUL/CONFLICTUAL
> INSTRUMENTAL/EXPRESSIVE
> OBLIGATORY/VOLUNTARY
> SEXUAL/NON-SEXUAL
> PROFANE/SACRED

(As shown later, several such dimensions may be combined in the structuring of social relations.)

The binary distinctions and contrasts underlying different institutionalized grammars reduce ambiguity and social uncertainty.[38] They indicate to actors what types of social grammars are appropriate. The grammars articulate basic institutionalized choices about the character of relationships, giving each a particular identity and providing an appropriate set of rules to express or realize in social transactions the underlying value choices. Unambiguous meanings are communicated to participants about what it is that is going on and what it is that they are or should be doing.

Consider the hierarchical/non-hierarchical dimension in social relationships. The family of 'hierarchical type grammars' can be substantially differentiated from non-hierarchical grammars.

Transactions in hierarchical relationships entail by definition substantial differences in ability to take initiatives, to manipulate or to dominate and, in general, to exercise autonomous control over the social and other environments where the institutionalized relationship applies. In more egalitarian or non-hierarchical relationships, mutual initiative and 'negotiation' in a strict sense are characteristic features of transactions.

Using the set of finite questions which social grammars answer to a greater or lesser extent, we may distinguish hierarchical and non-hierarchical types of grammars in the terms shown in Table 7.4 (this is far from complete, but illustrates the direction in which a more comprehensive analysis can be taken).

Obviously in employer/employee relationships, an employee interacts differently with his fellow employees from with his employer or representatives of the employer (management). Such patterns are structured and regulated by the rule systems which the

TABLE 7.4

Hierarchical and non-hierarchical grammars

Who, What, How, When, Where?	Hierarchical		Non-hierarchical	
	A Employer (parent)	B Employee (child)	A Colleague (peer)	B Colleague (peer)
Who has initiative?	(+)	(−)	(+)	(+)
Who has authority?	(+)	(−)	(+)	(+)
Who communicates evaluations?	(+)	(−)	(+)	(+)
Who sanctions?	(+)	(−)	(+)	(+)

participants know and more or less follow in both guiding their own actions and interactions and anticipating and interpreting those of others (again, see earlier remarks on actor-specific innovations and styles).

Hierarchical grammars may be distinguished further in terms of, among other things, their scope, intensity, and elaborateness:

(i) *Their extensiveness, the range of social settings or spheres of social action to which they apply.* A single-stranded relationship applies to a single, strictly limited sphere of activity, whereas a multi-stranded relation applies to a number of spheres and is in a certain sense more general.

(ii) *The extent that the relationship is interpersonal as opposed to collective* (class, status group based on dimensions such as age, sex, ethnicity, occupation, etc.). This distinction may concern political rights which may be highly individualized, as in most modern democracies. In some cases minority *groups* are given special 'collective rights', for instance to veto certain types of public decisions or policy. Collective forms refers also to transactions between representatives of collectives.

(iii) *The type(s) of social setting or situation* where the relationship applies or is activated. Instrumentally oriented dominance relations, such as an employer/employee relationship, tend to have a different type of social grammar and action logic than dominance relations oriented to the articulation of status differentials and privileges.

(iv) *The types of sanctions and controls* involved/permitted. Also important may be special conditions internal and external to the relationship which serve to secure compliance and maintenance of the regime and which are taken into account in domination grammars and distinguish them accordingly.

(v) *The extent to which the hierarchical relations are simply bilateral or well-defined parts of larger multi-lateral systems.* Social grammars in a community or society are rarely based on a single binary distinction. Typically, they combine or incorporate several binary distinctions. Hence, hierarchy may be combined with a certain intimacy as in some master–slave or master–servant relations. Or, on the other hand, equality is combined with 'social distance' or 'impersonalness' as in abstract citizen–citizen relations by a legal order. Table 7.5 suggests how hierarchical and non-hierarchical relationships are distinguished further in terms of (1) the extensiveness of the relations and (2) the individual/collective character of the relations.

Social grammars in these cases provide markers enabling partici

TABLE 7.5
Relational dichotomies in social grammars

		DOMINATION	NON-DOMINATION
INDIVIDUAL[2]	Single-stranded[1]	Superordinate/ subordinates Employer/employees Experts/clients	Buyer/seller (competitive market) Colleague/colleague (professional networks) Peer/peer
	Multi-stranded	Master/slaves Lord/serfs Patron/clients Parent/children	Friend/friend
COLLECTIVE	Single-stranded	Employer (association)/ labour union Regulator/organizations Class/class	Nation/nation (in international representative bodies) Federative organizations Inter-organizational networks
	Multi-stranded	Caste/caste Ethnic domination Other collective domination	Community/community Ethnic equality

1. A single-stranded relationship applies to a single or limited sphere of activity. A multi-stranded relation is more general, applying to a number of spheres.
2. Individual refers to relationships where in large part individuals interact, whether in hierarchical or non-hierarchical forms. Collective forms refer to transactions which in large part are between collectives, or representatives of collectives, for instance, interorganizational or intergroup interactions.

pants to 'express' in their interactions such dimensions as domination combined with intimacy or 'equality' combined with a certain social distance. Typically, any established relationship is defined by a set of binary distinctions. Moreover, some dimensions dominate others, that is a *hierarchy of binary distinctions provides the underlying consistent logic to the relationship, as manifested in patterns of transactions.* In this way, a relationship, for instance of domination, is articulated properly in rules specifying B's obedience or acquiescence to A's commands and unilateral decision-making. But, in addition, the domination may be interwoven with other (secondary) distinctions such as 'informality' or 'sexuality', which either reinforce, dilute or contradict the primary one. Moreover, the hierarchy of binary distinctions may, under certain conditions, be transformed. In individual relationships the primary stress might shift, for example, from domination to openness and intimacy. Or a relation of friendship/non-sexual is transformed to friendship/sexual. Such transformations occur frequently enough that most adult actors are knowledgeable about them and possess various strategies to try to prevent or to achieve such transformations (strategies which are recognized as part of the 'game between the sexes'). Besides these 'interpersonal transformations', social transformations may occur on the macro or collective levels where, for instance, a relationship such as sexual domination in marriage (based on property rights, defined duties, tax laws, naming laws, etc.) is transformed through legislation and social movement into a more egalitarian relationship.

In general, institutional relationships governed by rule regimes with defined binary distinctions are not fixed, but are subject to stresses and transformations. For instance:

(i) Egalitarian relations may develop into hierarchical structures in practice, or vice versa as the result of differential accumulation or loss, respectively, of power resources and action capabilities. Or countervailing forces operate structuring more egalitarian relations. These developments may be entirely 'local' or ad hoc in character. Or they may reflect an emerging pattern or even a movement bringing about this restructuring, in part through political and legislative efforts.

(ii) A relationship defined in a specific context such as between employer and employee may develop into a more encompassing relationship covering several different spheres of social life.

Institutionalized social grammars deal with potential tensions and uncertainties within social relationships. For instance, 'friendship relations' between persons of the opposite sex (and also in some cases between persons of the same sex) generate sexual tensions. Binary distinctions as part and parcel of social grammars enable those involved in such relationships to define and to maintain a relationship of a certain type: that is by avoiding certain gestures, activities and interactions, on the one hand, or by not avoiding them, on the other. Of course, these are culturally and historically specific. Thus, the class of 'friendship grammars' can be distinguished further in terms of those which provide rules for sexual intimacy, principles and algorithms for expressing such intimacy, and those which carefully and delicately enable 'friends' to avoid sexual interactions. Table 7.6 suggests these distinctions.

TABLE 7.6
Role defining rules in complex social relations

Social action setting	Sexual	Non-sexual
Friendship rules apply	Rules concerning expressions of sexual desire, sexual intimacy and receptivity	Rules concerning avoidance of expressions of sexual desire, intimacy, etc. (e.g. avoiding touching certain parts of the body, certain types of kisses, hugs etc. which are 'sexual in character'
Commercial rules apply	Rules for clients and prostitutes to interact, including client expression of sexual needs or demands	Usual business rules

In each institutionalized social relation, the role-sets which are embedded in the rule regimes tend to be compatible or 'to fit' one another. They constitute social grammars of conduct for individual actors. Without them, the actors would continually 'bump into one another', each mis-guiding his or her own actions and mis-judging or mis-simulating the actions of the others. (Consider automobile drivers, some of whom would operate with certain traffic rules and others with quite different rules; or the case of political relations where those adhering to highly formal, ritualistic grammars interact with others who adapt or restructure the grammars, adhering, they believe to the spirit of the basic rules.)

In general, actors who follow incompatible rule systems in their interactions with one another not only will have substantial problems coordinating, but will experience increased confusion and uncertainty. Interactions will be unstable, resulting either in withdrawal or attempts to rewrite or reform one or the other or both rule systems. Thus, friendship interactions are not stable and manageable if 'the nature of the friendship', e.g. non-sexual or sexual, is not understood and distinguishable through adherence to rules such as those indicated in the table above. A classic case for comedy as well as serious fiction/film/theatre is the interaction between persons of the opposite sex (or, in some instances, of the same sex) where one person wishes 'simply to be friends' while the other seeks romantic/sexual engagement. Social grammars assist to a greater or lesser extent in sorting such matters out. They enable the actors to communicate in non-verbal forms with one another about the nature of the relationship. Of course, they may each believe the relationship is something other than it is, misreading signals, or engaging in 'wishful thinking' and ignoring signals (see Chapter 3).

Furthermore, one or the other of those involved in a relationship may try *to signal a shift to a different type of relation*. This leads to a phase of 'negotiation', with the other either accepting or rejecting the shift. Nevertheless, the *actors have non-verbal forms of communicating based on following or not-following certain social grammars which distinguish types of relationship*. When those involved disagree about the nature of the relationship — or the type of relationship each wants — the *social grammars do not, of course, help resolve this*.

This situation may be distinguished analytically from one where the available social grammars for friendship relations fail because those rules pertaining to relationships between the sexes are unclear (or fail to make clear distinctions between 'sexual' and 'non-sexual' interactions). Such a situation may arise in societies where the relationships between persons of the opposite sex are undergoing radical changes, including growth in complexity (e.g., attempts are made to combine more and more variables distinguishing relationships). The situation also arises when those involved have not adequately learned the social grammars (that is, they are not fully competent actors), and therefore have difficulty making clear to one another what type of relationship they have or want. (For instance, boys and girls in puberty often find it difficult sorting these matters out.) One would expect that the problems are much more formidable in cultures where the rules for non-verbal as well as verbal communication about these questions result in a great deal of distortion, confusion, or simply blockage.

Major types of institution grammars
in modern society: Sphere analysis

Any society is characterized by a set of institutionalized social relations which structure and regulate transactions among actors, both individual and collective. The grammars of social institutions may be grouped into families in terms of their regulating *primary modes of social interaction. These are: domination, group or collective decision-making, and negotiation and exchange.* Social relations can be distinguished, for instance, on the basic dimension of hierarchy/ non-hierarchy, where domination is distinguished from modes of social interaction such as collective decision-making and mutual negotiation and exchange.

A social relation of domination entails certain rules concerning initiative, the communication of evaluations, and the performance of sanctioning acts, as analysed in Chapter 5. To be subordinate means to follow the initiatives, guidelines, evaluations and decisions of a superior who communicates these in the context(s) or settings where the relation of domination applies. According to the rules of some grammars, subordinates have opportunities in concrete situations to break some rules or to negotiate ad hoc changes in the grammar. One may compare the organizing principles governing social domination based on *property rights and civil law and* those based on *public law.* In the case of non-domination relations, one may compare, as we do here, market, network, associational and democratic political systems.

The organization of data about, and the comparative analysis of, social institutions can be made on the basis of the *finite set of rule categories and structure of rule regimes.* The universal features of social transactions relate to such questions as: who, what, why, how, when, and where. These dimensions are the basis for describing and analysing the dimensions of social institutions or, more precisely, families of institutions (see below).

In this way, families of institutions are seen to share certain relational properties, and to differ from other families on some or all of these dimensions. Those cases sharing a given cell or set of cells are distinguishable from one another in terms of well-defined differences in their rules or in the context-dependent application of the rules in specific social settings (see Table 7.7).

In our discussions in this section we limit our attention largely to general types of institutional spheres (each with a variety of sub-types): markets, democratic political systems, private and public administrative systems, judiciary systems, the associative sphere, and social networks and communities.

Even in the short run, the spheres of social action are never neatly separable. In any given case they are linked and inter-penetrating. For instance, a group such as a labour union exercises its political rights as an interest organization. Through its ties to a political party, it compels the political leadership of a country to intervene and to regulate labour markets. On the other hand, political leaders might use their ties to labour unions to end or to regulate strikes and other

TABLE 7.7a
Institutionalized forms of modern social organization

	Regulative orders			Administrative orders		
	Democratic systems	Markets	Negotiation systems; inter-organizational relations	Private enterprise	Public bureaucracy	Judiciary
Who	Citizens/members; representatives; parties	Buyers, sellers	Negotiator/ negotiator; Representative/ representative representative	Owners/managers; employees	Administrative chiefs; civil servants; citizens/ residents, regulatees	Judges; prosecutor/ claimants; defendants; lawyers; (juries)
Major participation/ exclusion principles	Citizenship/ membership, principles concerning rights to vote and/or represent	In some cases only certified or authorized sellers and/or buyers	Legitimate or authorized representatives or 'negotiators'	Exclusion based in first instance on owner/non-owner distinction. Owner may authorize agents and/or employ persons in the firm	Authorization of agency; civil servant employment regulations; legal criteria for 'clients' receiving services (health care, pension, etc.) and/or for subjection to regulation	Appointment (or election) of judges; certification of other experts; persons with actionable claims
For what purposes	Make collective or public decisions, e.g. elect leaders, decide on laws, policies, actions	Exchange of goods, services, money in self-interest	Reach agreement on contracts, and specific rules in contract, including rules for implementing contract	Pursue economic interests: 'value-added' for owners and investors; income for others	Provide certain public goods and services; implement policy or ensure compliance with laws/regulations	Determine judicial truth; punish offenders of law
What action, transaction	Vote; mobilize and organize voters and other forms of support; decide on representation, new rules, policies	Buying, selling; 'negotiating'	Exchange information, negotiate, decide contracts, rules in contract	Produce and sell goods and services; employ and organize people and resources	Produce and distribute certain legally specified goods and services; monitor, evaluate and sanction compliance with law; employ and organize people and resources	Present evidence, counter-evidence, cross-examine; deliberate and make judgements

TABLE 7.7b
Institutionalized forms of modern social organization

	Regulative orders			Administrative orders		
	Democratic systems	Markets	Negotiation systems; inter-organizational relations	Private enterprises	Public bureaucracy	Judiciary
How	Voting rules and procedures for selecting representatives, making collective decisions (various types of rules for calculating votes and determining choice)	Transaction procedures to be followed in buying/selling	Negotiation rules and procedures to be followed	Organizing principles; management principles; strategies for making production, investment decisions	Agency organizing principles; public administration rules and regulation	Court procedures for presentation of evidence, expertise; legal reasoning procedures; procedures for making decisions
With what means	Means of communication, resources, machines, and other tools which may be used to mobilize and organize voting	Permissible 'legal tender', specification of restriction of types, amounts of borrowed money	Legitimate means 'partners' may use to try to induce agreement: 'weapons' and inducements (exclusion of certain 'weapons' and inducements)	Production technologies and techniques; raw materials; labour power which may be used in producing goods and services	Production technologies and techniques; raw materials; labour power which may be used in production of goods and services and/or in regulative acts	Expertise, techniques and technologies which are permitted in producing and presenting evidence
When, where	Specified settings, times and places for mobilizing votes, voting in making collective decisions (extra-ordinary times may also be defined)	Specified settings, times and places where buying and selling of goods/services should (may) take place (may be unspecified)	Periods, places where negotiations are to take place	Legitimate places and times to organize production of certain goods and services	Specified times and places for agency activity	'Court' meets and deliberates at certain times and in particular places

industrial conflicts. Thus, a 'labour market' becomes in part an administered sphere, where 'labour market organizations' (often with some state involvement) adhere to certain inter-organizational and negotiating rules and also negotiate new rules to structure the market (see Chapter 10). Rule systems should enable us to shed light on such questions, by indicating useful analytical distinctions and by providing a framework whereby the similarity of apparently dissimilar phenomena can be recognized and the differences among similar phenomena specified.

Thus, while we categorize business enterprises, government agencies and judicial systems as hierarchical in character, they differ substantially, among other things, in their legitimizing principles, prescribed or permissible modes of social action, ways of making changes in rule systems. Moreover, as pointed up in the tables, a sphere of activity such as 'public administration' includes *diverse organizations and types of activity*. These range from welfare service agencies through various types of regulatory agencies to police and military organizations. Although these different organizations share a number of common elements (such as their hierarchical character), they also differ substantially in specific organizing principles, modes of operation, and capability of change. In a word, they are constituted on the basis of substantially different rule regimes.

Even in the case of markets such as commodity markets, there is considerable variation in the extent of regulation. Some sectors have elaborate administrative structures, whereas others approach the economic ideal of a competitive market. Consider the following cases: (i) public utilities and public transport companies, even when they are private, are administered. Administration pertains to: prices, service standards, the mix of products offered. Moreover, restrictions on 'sellers' are found. Usually only a few enterprises are permitted to enter the market and to sell the commodity or service such as air, road, rail or sea transport. (ii) the pharmacy industry is highly regulated, a regulation going back many hundreds of years. (iii) agro-chemicals and pesticides are increasingly subject to government regulation. Even buyers of such commodities are usually subject to substantial regulation. Certain toxic chemicals cannot be purchased without certification of competence or a licence. (iv) automobiles are regulated in terms of safety features as well as pollution-control requirements. (v) food products are regulated as to addictives, level of bacteria permitted, colouring, etc.

The concepts and principles introduced in this chapter are developed further and applied in the following chapters.

Studies and analyses of modern social organization

In this chapter we have sketched a framework for the analysis of social institutions and, ultimately, of social order. The general model is as follows, where the social rule system not only structures and regulates but gives the transactions recognizable identity and, for the participants, 'meaning' (See Figure 7.3).

FIGURE 7.3
Rule systems, social transactions and meaing

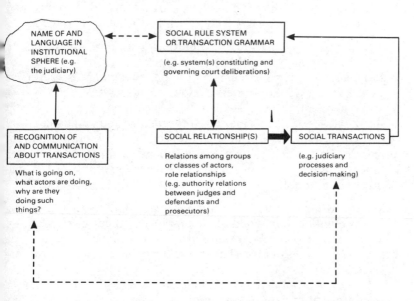

In this context, the distinction between 'social rule systems', as cultural forms, and their context-dependent manifestations in operating social organizations, should be stressed again. Historically specific organizations, enterprises, government agencies, and negotiation systems are the result of implementing social rule systems in concrete social action settings. People and resources are mobilized in the processes of implementation. Attempts to implement two or more social rule systems in a given sphere of activity result in ambiguities, confusion and conflict among those involved. Informal rules, bridging institutions, but most importantly, meta-rules, are created by human agents to deal with such problems. Social rule systems as such *do not act or interact*. Human agents do.

In the following parts of the book we apply and develop social rule system theory in analyses of the structure and dynamics of a few major types of social organization in modern society:

- markets
- formal organizations including government
- wage negotiation systems
- socio-technical and expert systems
- planning and policy-making systems

While the studies reported are only fragments, they apply and develop several key concepts and principles of rule system theory:

- multiple rule systems and their interplay with respect to concrete spheres of social transactions
- social actors, groups, organizations and movements as bearers as well as makers and reformers of rule systems
- social cooperation, conflict, and struggle among social agents in the processes of rule formation, reformation, and implementation
- the historical phases of rule system formation and transformation, and the factors, including value shifts, power shifts, performance failures and de-legitimatization, which generate observable historical patterns

Even more importantly, the studies presented in the following chapters point up that two fundamental social processes consist of:

(1) *the formation and reformation of social rule regimes,* entailing the social processes of formulating, excluding, selecting and ordering rules in relation to one another.

(2) *the implementation of social rules,* involving situational analysis and interpretation, the use of tools and resources, and, in many instances, the mobilization of power and authority to enforce social rules.

II

MARKETS AND COLLECTIVE BARGAINING SYSTEMS

8

The structuring of markets and other distributive systems

*Tom R. Burns and Helena Flam**

Introduction: Markets as regulative social organizations

In this and the following two chapters we use social rule system theory as a framework to develop models of market structure and dynamics.

Economists generally view a market as a system where buyers and sellers, all engaged in the purchase and sale of identical or similar commodities, are in 'close contact' with one another and 'buy and sell freely' among themselves. A competitive market is one with a 'large number' of buyers and sellers, with minimal or no social or legal restrictions on entry (Boulding, 1955:45; Samuelson, 1958:368–85; Mansfield, 1975; Sven-Erik Sjöstrand, 1985; among others).

From a social organizational perspective such definitions are peculiarly imprecise:[39] What is meant by 'contact', 'close contact', and 'freely buying and selling'? Many of the major questions — not only analytical questions but those arising in connection with practical problems — of market formation and development are taken as given: How is contact arranged or organized? According to what rules and procedures do 'barter and trade' take place? What rules govern market entry and exit? Which social agents — and in the context of which social relationships — establish, maintain, enforce or challenge these various rules, including rules of access or openness? And what means do they utilize in these efforts, and at what cost? Granovetter (1985:483) observes:

> Classical and neoclassical economics operates ... with an atomized, undersocialized conception of human action, continuing in the utilitarian

---

*In collaboration with Philippe DeVille and Bernard Gauci.

tradition. The theoretical arguments disallow by hypothesis any impact of social structure and social relations on production, distribution, or consumption. In competitive markets, no producer or consumer noticeably influences aggregate supply or demand or, therefore prices or other terms of trade. Albert Hirschman has noted, such idealized markets, involving as they do 'large numbers of price-taking anonymous buyers and sellers supplied with perfect information ... function without any prolonged human or social contact between the parties. Under perfect competition there is no room for bargaining, negotiation, remonstration or mutual adjustment and the various operators that contract together need not enter into recurrent or continuing relationships as a result of which they would get to know each other well (Hirschman, 1982:1473).

From the perspective of our theory, modern markets are *regulative social organizations*, where in many instances market entry opportunities and the definitions of and procedures for 'buying' and 'selling' are socially specified and regulated (see Chapter 4). Market behaviour is in part governed by legal and other normative rules and principles; in part by actors' orientation to relative scarcity and their beliefs about the probable actions of others, insofar as the latter affect the same resources (Weber, 1968:32).

The rule systems structuring and regulating market organization are established by one or more agents, including, but not limited to, the state. Non-government structuring agents are, for example, associations of sellers, professions, status groups, and communities which have an interest in patterning economic exchange activity and its outcomes.

Socially enforced market rules define freedom of access and transaction possibilities and procedures. Sellers, buyers, the state or other agents engage in formulating and implementing the rules which structure and regulate market behaviour. At the same time, those participating in economic exchange are formally free within the socially produced and maintained rule frame to negotiate, reach collective agreements, sign contracts, exchange and enjoy or suffer the gains and losses respectively of their transactions.

From a sociological perspective, market regulation, 'collusion', and 'intereference with market forces and outcomes' are universal processes.[40] They are part and parcel of the human production and strategic structuring of their conditions. The structuration of markets is largely, but not solely, a function of power, exchange, and conflict processes where social agents try:

(i) to formulate and reformulate market rules so as to advance or to protect interests, their own or those of others.

(ii) to prevent 'instability' and disorder, thus decreasing uncertainty and increasing predictability and calculability.

(iii) to make market rules which satisfy certain norms, values, and relationships in a community or society.

Market rule formation, including rules determining freedom of entry, may occur in various ways, for instance:

- *legal and administrative rules* are formulated and implemented through political and government processes. Laws and regulations such as the following result: 'persons under 18 years of age may not purchase alcoholic beverages'; 'persons may not be denied access to goods and services on religious, racial, or sexual grounds'
- a group of sellers and/or buyers establish *rules of market entry* or access and *rules and procedures for transactions*. The rule system may or may not be sanctioned by the state
- a status group, voluntary organization, or community *support norms, including informal rules*. For instance, certain 'outsiders' are excluded from a market on the seller and/or buyer side. Such community norms and informal rules may contradict legal rules.
- sellers, the government, or other agents — each with its own principles and *rules of application* — provide credit to potential buyers, and in the case of the state transfers to potential buyers, thus expanding or, in times of restrictive policies, contracting credit

In general, laws, group and community norms operate to structure and regulate market entry, transaction possibilities and procedures (and, therefore, costs). Market rules, for example those regulating freedom of access of potential sellers and buyers as well as those rules and procedures affecting transaction costs, imply price changes and quantity changes (see Chapter 9). In this way, they influence supply and demand relationships and prices. These relationships are suggested in Figure 8.1.

In this chapter we focus on certain aspects of market structuring and characteristics of market organization. The following chapters examine the conseqences of social structuration for economic performance, such as transaction costs, prices and wages, and market stability.

A general model of market structuration
Markets are social organizations, structured and regulated by more or less well-defined social rule systems. These regulate entry to the market as well as market activities such as buying and selling, negotiating and implementing contracts. Below we outline our general model of market structuration.

FIGURE 8.1
General model of market structuration

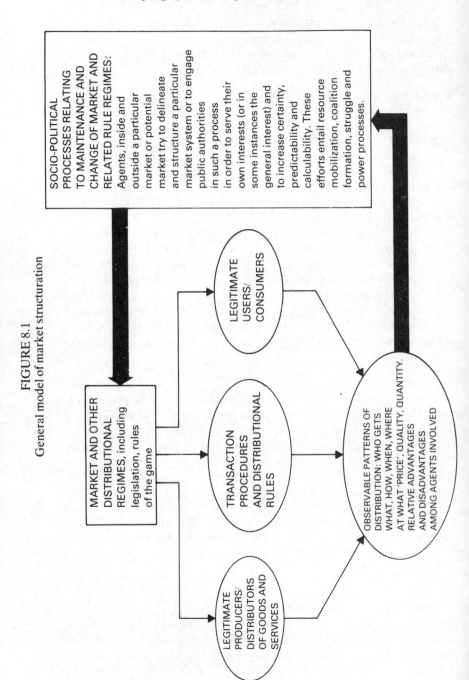

Multiple structuring mechanisms
There are two basic ways market organization is brought about:
from the top down or from the bottom up. Some combination of the
two is the usual case. (See Figure 8.2.)

I. Strategic structuring, informal or formal, whereby social agents,
   including the state, establish a rule regime regulating market access
   and transactions. Some rules reflect special interests or a dominant
   coalition of interests trying to ˙limit or expand participation and/or
   levels of transaction. In some instances, rules are designed to protect
   the interests of buyers and/or sellers and even third parties. Hence,
   the social as well private benefits of many of the rules and procedures
   which organize and regulate markets (see Model I, Figure 8.2).

II. Emergent structuring, whereby participants discover or adopt certain
    similar strategies within bounded rationality and situations with cer-
    tain opportunity structures and incentive structures. Social network
    and ecological properties result in relatively well-defined aggregate
    performance characteristics (see Model III, Figure 8.2).[41]

Some of the market rules structuring and regulating transactions are
backed by sanctions. This proposition — along with the distinctions
in types of rules and rule structures — provides a point of departure
to develop a general, comparative theory of markets.

Market rule systems have a history and a political economy
The systematic study of markets as social organizations calls for an
investigation of the ways in which agents establish(ed) and maintain
the rules governing a market or set of markets. (See Chapter 10 on
labour markets.) What interests do these agents have? What power
resources do they mobilize and use in structuring and restructuring
market systems? What struggles and conflicts occur around attempts
to maintain or change market rule regimes?

A market rule regime will often reflect the interests of particular
social agent(s) or a dominant coalition in expanding or limiting
participation and/or transactions.[42] Typically, multiple agents —
public and semi-public authorities and branch or professional associations — are involved in the structuration of markets. Their
interests and models of socio-economic reality often differ, setting
the stage for conflict and negotiation over market regimes.

The modern state is obviously deeply involved in the formation
and enforcement of many of the rule systems governing market
entry and market transaction procedures. The state (or, more precisely, branch-specific agencies of the state) formulates and tries to
enforce market rules governing market entry, excluding certain
transactions, requiring particular procedures be followed in transactions, specifying qualities and conditions of goods and services,

FIGURE 8.2 (a)
Market structuration processes

I. General political economic model

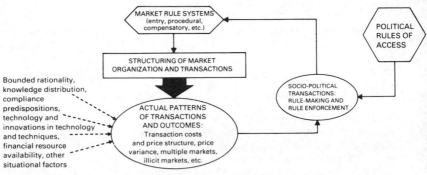

II. Neo-classical model (Baker, 1984)

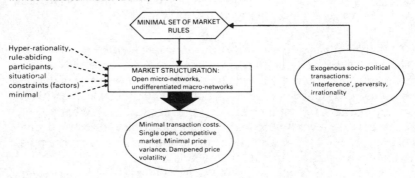

standardizing weights and measures, and regulating participation of buyers and sellers in the market(s). Of course, in many instances the regulations are not extensive, particularly in the case of regulations governing buyers of simpler consumer products.

State involvement may result from its responsibility for the health and welfare of citizens in modern societies. Or it may derive from political pressures, either important lobbies, political groups, or Nader-like groups acting on behalf of unorganized and weak consumers. There may also be professional groups within state agencies who feel it their responsibility to assure that markets operate in ways consistent with basic laws, values and norms in the society.

Other social agents — for example, professional associations such

FIGURE 8.2(b)

III. Emergent structuration (Baker, 1984)

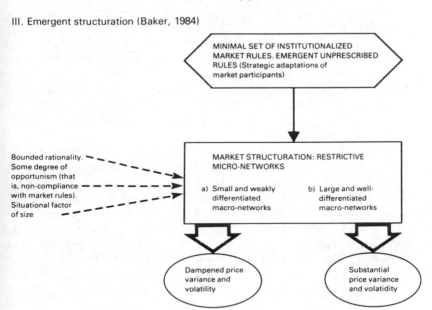

as those of physicians and lawyers, labour unions, industry or trade organizations, and informal cliques — are also often involved, in establishing and maintaining market rule regimes.

Market rule regimes are usually only partially guaranteed by the state, ultimately through recourse to force. Indeed, in a few instances, market structuration is carried out and maintained illegally, for example in violation of laws requiring that certain procedures be followed in making transactions, or proscribing barriers to entry.

In modern capitalism, government agencies, political leaders and parties, social movements (e.g. consumer and environmental movements), lobbies of varying sorts, as well as effective critics and public opinion leaders (such as Ralph Nader) are involved in the formation and reformation of market rule systems. While our emphasis may be in large part on legal and formal means of establishing and enforcing market rule systems, informal and illegal means are also important — and even decisive in some areas. Sellers may form illegal or quasi-legal 'cartels' or private regulatory associations which establish and enforce rules, employing a variety of strategies and sanctions to exclude non-members from their markets and to require that certain transaction procedures be followed. Professional groups, such as pharmacists, use *both* legal backing as well as the authority and other resources of their profession to prevent 'non-professionals' from selling competing products (or even selling the same products; see Chapter 14).[43]

Market rule systems include certain actors, types of transactions, and commodities while excluding others
Four of the types of variables specified implicitly or expicitly and regulated by the rules are: legitimate or acceptable sellers, legitimate buyers, legitimate market procedures and transactions, and legitimate commodities.

Social constraints on the the freedom of entry ('openness') — that is a market organized according to rules which exclude certain participants and/or types of transactions — is central to our theory. Exclusion of certain types of agents may occur through laws, informal norms and selection rules. These are activated, developed and applied by governments, trade and professional associations and credit institutions. Some of these rules determine 'rights to participate'. Others (such as property rights and rules governing credit availability and access to credit) operate more indirectly, limiting participation by denying actors resources essential to participation, in a word: their *capacity to pay*.

The exclusiveness (or 'openness') of markets varies and will depend on institutionalized rule systems. It depends also on knowledge, resource distribution, and technology. Thus, relatively open markets may exhibit a low degree of participation (or a narrow range of transactions) because effective participation may require: (1) considerable technical knowledge (either of the commodities bought and sold and/or procedures to be followed in preparing and carrying out transactions), (2) available capital and other strategic resources, (3) political and normative support, or other enabling factors.[44]

Market social organization — a specific rule complex — has performance consequences
Some of the consequences such as price formation are systemic in character. Others relate to the distribution of gains (and costs) among participants and between participants and non-participants. Such distributional effects may evoke political processes which serve to stabilize or destabilize the system (see Chapters 9 & 10).

Systemic consequences. The rules structuring and regulating a market system increase, decrease, or leave unchanged transaction costs. They also partially structure supply and demand and influence in this way price structure and variance. *Moreover, rules excluding buyers or limiting certain commodities tend to generate illegal markets.* That is, the social organization of a market and the resulting patterns of transaction shape incentives and pressures for deviant behaviour. For instance, rules which are highly exclusive of buyers and/or limit transactions provide 'potentials for gain' through the exploitation of opportunities on illicit markets. Some actors may be tempted to exploit these potentials. The greater the potential gains, the stronger the temptations.

Distributional consequences. Market rules (above all, when combined with property rights) result in monetary and non-monetary gains and losses for different types of participants (as well as non-participants). For instance, sellers excluded from a market thereby 'lose' opportunities to sell certain commodities and to realize gains by doing so. Similarly, excluded buyers are denied the freedom to enter the market or to choose desirable commodities.

Other distributional effects of market rules pertain to consumption patterns, particularly those which are socially important in group status relationships and relativities. Competing social groups may be led, through a bandwagon effect or through invidious comparisons and envy, to purchase more than they would otherwise do, market distribution rules permitting. Through observation and social communication, they observe what others are doing and react in ways which shift the demand curve outwards.

On the other hand, the widespread diffusion of a commodity through 'mass markets' may also lead to its 'devaluation' (Hirsch, 1977; Douglas and Isherwood, 1980). As more and more come to possess (and use) the commodity, its 'status value' may decrease, reducing demand for it. This effect will be stronger the more the commodity is one that defines status, or a special life-style (entailing ownership of particular types of residences or cars, sorts of travel and vacation, the use of diamonds, etc.).

Market exchanges and their outcomes often impact on non-market participants. The impacts may be positive or negative. A 'negative impact' may arise from consumption patterns or other effects associated with a market offending the sensibilities (values, norms) of non-participants. For instance, the widespread sale of alcohol, the quasi-legal sale of drugs and guns, or legalized prostitution may be highly disturbing for some. Negative impacts also rise through 'third parties' (the state, taxpayers) having assumed the costs of enforcing market rules.[45]

In sum, we analyse a market as a *social organization which not only generates certain price characteristics but distributional properties*, in a word *who gains and who loses from the specific social rules constituting the structure.* This conception of markets as social organization stresses that price reduction and efficiency may be severely constrained by market regimes, *which have support on moral grounds of communities or the state.* This points up, as in several of our other analyses, the contradictory interplay between market rationality and social (or normative) rationality in modern society.

Distributional properties of markets are particularly important factors in their stabilization

Markets which result in outcomes that are unsatisfactory or unacceptable to important power groups within or outside a market tend to evoke counter-action and efforts to change market rules. Those who may be gaining from existing rules are likely to resist change attempts, at least attempts to change the rules serving their interests. Such a situation often leads to conflict and struggle over particular market rules or over the entire system. The outcomes of the struggle determine the specific structure — and structural stability and future development — of the market system.

Thus, for each and every market there is a partially unique political economy. This meta-level structure may not be apparent or visible. Indeed, it is often taken for granted by those involved. Such a structure becomes transparent only when emergent groups or new coalitions — for instance, in the form of a social movement, oligopoly, labour union or lobby — attempt to bring about restructuring. As a result, conflicting interests and the mobilization and exercise of power are likely to be manifested. This is fairly obvious in the case of labour markets, but it also holds for markets where special interests, the state or the public want to limit (or conversely, to expand) entry.

Consider the case of inalienable land 'rights'. Some actors, such as industrialists, real estate agents, developers and speculators have had an interest in making a commodity out of land so that it could be freely bought and sold. In the past, status groups, such as a landed aristocracy, whose position of prestige and authority rested on control of land, resisted commodification of land. In a similar vein today, albeit for entirely different reasons, recreational and environmental protection interests oppose the commodification of land and water, which they wish to preserve for public use (as opposed to developing for commercial or industrial purposes). *A struggle ensues between groups advocating two different controlling principles.* Ultimately, different state agencies, political parties, special interests and social movements may be deeply involved in the issues and struggles around what boils down to the access and distributional rules governing land and water use (see later discussion and also Chapter 13).

Our model of markets directs us to a systematic consideration of the interests including representatives of the 'public interest', the relative power which these various interests can mobilize, and the institutional framework within which interest groups and organizations can formulate or change market rule systems as well as assure their implementation. This provides a useful point of departure for the analysis of market structure, stability and instability, and development tendencies.

The structural stability of a market
This depends to a large extent on the configuration of support and opposition among major agents with an interest in the organization and functioning of the market in question.

Stability of a market rule system — and its implementation structure — will obtain whenever: (1) no major interest finds the current regime disadvantageous (although agents may employ different criteria in making their assessments); (2) those actors, either participating in the market or outside it, who oppose the present market rule system and might have an interest in change are unable to mobilize and exercise power to bring about change in market rules. (Their weakness may reflect an inability to establish and maintain a stable coalition and/or to formulate a viable or effective alternative to the existing rule system.)

Market actors who have an interest in change may simply *perceive* that there are no possibilities to alter the market rule regime, or that the costs of doing so would be prohibitive. In this case, interest in change is not translated into objective demands. They lack, for instance, power to overcome the resistance of those committed to the existing system.

Market actors, as well as those outside agents concerned with market performance and outcomes, are unequal in their capability to influence the market rule system. Not only is such 'meta-power' unequally distributed, but actors vary in their motivation to exercise such power in maintaining or changing particular market rules. Consumers in mass markets are notoriously weak in mobilizing and organizing to realize their interests, for instance concerning the organization and functioning of such markets.

Meta-power to influence a rule system is always a function of the power resources which may be mobilized in relation to a *particular channel of influence*. Some channels, such as open political arenas, often require considerably more mobilization of power resources and entail overcoming more resistance or procedural inertia than others, for example technical/administrative settings where policies are formulated and implemented.

Some market interest groups, by virtue of their economic resources or importance to the economy, have substantial possibilities to influence legislation through lobbying, through their network linkages with political elites, or through their direct engagement in political parties. For instance, in the USA, the AMA (American Medical Association), the 'oil lobby', the 'legal lobby', or the 'farm lobby' have the capacity to strongly influence legislation affecting their interests — either completely or by partially blocking the interests of others in reform, or in desirable alteration or innovations in existing legislation.

Other powerful groups, such as organized crime, Mafia, or local merchants (not that these should be viewed as a single type of market actor) will usually have very limited or no possibilities to affect national *legislation*. On the other hand, they are often in a position to influence the implementation of national legislation or local legislation — through personal contacts, bribery, extortion, and so forth.

Even powerful, legitimate groups at the national level have only very limited possibilities to influence areas where there are strong moral sentiments opposed to the changes which they would like to bring about. Also, in legislative areas where their 'interest' is not considered 'appropriate', their influence possibilities are likely to be strictly limited or at least ad hoc in character.

Social rules specifying who, what, how, where, and when of markets

Groups and organizations based on class or status interests, operating on their own or in coalitions, attempt to structure and regulate markets in which they have an interest or at least to engage public authorities in such social control processes. These groups and authorities direct their efforts at determining:

• the rules specifying who can participate in the market as a seller or a buyer [46]
• the rules defining what commodities with what particular qualities are included and considered legitimate
• the principles, and possibly the procedures, for determining prices
• the rules regulating transactions and disputes concerning transactions and contracts
• the rules specifying which agents, in particular organizations of sellers and/or buyers, can legitimately act collectively in and upon markets (structuring their members' (and opponents') interests and strategies)

- the regulatory and enforcing agencies (private, semi-private, or public) which formulate the rules organizing markets and supervise and regulate a market, seeing to it that rules are followed and enforced

Generally speaking, there is considerable variation in the organization and functioning as well as development tendencies of empirically observable markets. This is traceable in part to the rule systems structuring and regulating market transactions. Rule regimes contribute to shaping supply and demand curves, thereby affecting price and market performance (examined in the following chapter). For example, rules such as zoning laws regulating land use affect supply and demand for land in the form of differentiated commodities: farmland, commercial zone, industrial zone, residential zone. Specific conversions from one zone type to another significantly change the price per acre. Often key property owners are in a position to influence zoning laws and regulation, thus substantially affecting 'development possibilities' and their own incomes and profits.

(1) Markets may be categorized, described and contrasted in terms of such features as:

- their particular rules and degree of exclusivity (or conversely, their 'openness')
- the degree that market procedures and transactions are specified (and standardized) and regulated by social rules, legal as well as non-legal. We include here unwritten rules and informal norms
- time and space constraints limiting times of year, month, week and day for transactions as well as places where transactions can (or should) be carried out. Again, these are specified and enforced as formal and informal social rules

(2) Market rules, such as participant exclusion rules, consist of various rules having different sources and levels of legitimacy. Legally sanctioned rules are, of course, enforced by the state. Some formal rules may be established by a trade or professional association, such as the AMA. The sanctions used to enforce these rules are in some instances backed ultimately by the state. In addition, there are often a variety of more informally determined rules as well as unwritten rules, which market participants learn in order to act effectively in the market.

(3) Many markets are characterized by rules which allow only certain agents to sell. Formally the state may exclude sellers who do not satisfy certain requirements in terms of their capital base, insurance, legal status of the company, as well as considerations of com-

petence and certification (to handle the commodities in question, such as toxic chemicals, drugs, etc.) Such requirements are obvious in the case of sellers who sell transport services, such as air or bus travel, or those who produce and/or run nuclear power plants.

(4) Similarly, there may be legal and administrative restrictions on buyers, in terms of their technical competence and financial resources (who can buy and use powerful pesticides, poisons, uranium, nuclear power plants, etc.). Typically, a certification process is required in such instances. The certification process is also observable in the purchase of drugs requiring a physician's prescription.

In sum, approval or certification by a regulatory agency, professional association, or their representatives may be required in order to participate in certain markets, either as seller and/or buyer. But there may be 'informal exclusionary principles' as well: unwritten rules whereby established market actors keep out newcomers. Of course, potential market actors may exclude themselves, because they feel that they lack the competence, the necessary resources or support required for effective participation (including capital, access to capital markets, or political and other support). Finally, there may be 'purely economic constraints' on market entry: insufficient resources to buy, to produce, or to engage in selling. Even these circumstances have their grounding in the social rules of property rights, resource accumulation, and access to economic resources.

(5) Not just any exchange completes a market transaction. The legitimacy or appropriateness of transactions and procedures followed in arranging a transaction are specified by rule sets. There is an entire language, including in many instances a formal, legal language of agreements and contracts. There is also a complex interplay between buyers and sellers, entailing sets of sequential procedures designed to safeguard interests. The procedures concern, for instance, quality controls, guarantees about delivery, product failure, guarantees against default, and so forth.[47] *For each market or commodity type, the set of elaborate procedures will vary, reflecting the legislative and institutional history governing that market, the configuration of powerful interests which have shaped and which maintain the rules governing that market, as well as purely technical and professional considerations.*[48]

Social actors, rules and market structuration

In this section we want to suggest more concretely ways to investigate market rule systems, the formation of new rules, changes in rules structuring and regulating markets, and the social agents (the state, other authorities such as a trade association, key groups of buyers and/or sellers, etc.) engaged in bringing about market structuration. The discussion begins with general observations on labour, commodity and credit markets. Later we discuss specific cases of market structure and dynamics (see Chapter 10).

The labour market as well as commodity and credit markets are subject to restrictions placed on sellers and buyers. Historically speaking, legislation excluding children and limiting the work-day came first. In Great Britain, an alliance formed between the worker movement and the Tories in pushing through such legislation. In Sweden, male trade unions, the Social Democratic Party, and employers supported legislation against women's nightwork in 1911. Various women's organizations and female members of the Social Democratic Party opposed such legislation and had seen its defeat earlier in Parliament (1909). As a consequence of this new legislation, women printers, for example, were forced to accept worse-paid jobs and no new female apprentices were accepted. Swedish laws of 1901 and 1916, similarly, banned women from work in mines and as stevedores. Examples of such restrictive legislation regulating the labour market are many: minimum wage, seniority rights, open or closed shops, safety and environmental conditions, employment and retirement age, part-time employment, rank among the most important.

As these examples from Great Britain and Sweden suggest, there may be no obvious basis for deriving what specific interests a given class or status organization will pursue, nor is there an a priori way of unequivocally determining what interest coalition(s) will form in the market. *These entail matters of strategy in response to contingencies,* of course with certain general predispositions, deriving from class or status relationships. The two examples also point up that in each case of market structuration it is possible to identify the differing interests pursued by class and status groups as well as political parties, so that one may descend from the world of abstractions such as 'the clash between economic and communal types of rationality' (Smelser, 1963) to empirically observable and analysable processes.

In a similar way, one may approach the 'clashes' between the sacred and the profane, or a moral community and the market (see also Chapter 9). The case of American life insurance illustrates another instance of market delineation and development associated with a coalition of interests. In this case restrictions imposed on buyers and sellers were not at stake, but instead the legitimacy of a new type of commodity and the emergence and expansion of a new type of market. The case for this market was pushed by occupational specialists (insurance men), welcomed by many state legislatures, impoverished parishes, and religious and non-religious liberals, at the same time that it was opposed by religious fundamentalists (Zelizer, 1978; 1981). The history of regulation of medicines provides another illustration of the politics of organizing and delineating commodity markets. But, in this case, as in the case of many new markets promoted by professionals or occupational specialists, the issue has been the restriction of 'open markets' and the establishment of a distinction between illegitimate and legitimate sellers and commodities. Over the past two centuries, professional, but also university, state and public interests, on their own or in combination with others, opposed 'illegitimate sellers' outside pharmacies, at the same time establishing an increasing number of regulations and control agencies to monitor, register, and ban 'illegitimate medicines' sold outside and within pharmacies. The rapid growth in industrially manufactured preparations increased the influence and regulatory powers of governments at the expense of professional groups, particularly as a result of public discontent and reactions to failures in professional regulation (see Chapter 14).

The modern state — in many instances, pressured by producers or sellers, lobbying groups, citizen groups, or socio-political movements — establishes rules and regulates markets or potential markets to varying degrees: (i) It considers certain products, transactions or sales should be banned altogether because they are believed to be harmful to life or property or because they violate strongly held norms and values. (ii) It prevents forms of transaction which entail fraud, deceit, or extortion; or which are likely to lead to costly miscalculations, misunderstandings, conflicts, or damage to important third parties, etc. These motivate regulations and procedures to be followed in certain transactions such as the buying and selling of property or of major energy facilities such as coal-fired plants or nuclear power plants. (iii) It allows only certain sellers believed to be competent and reliable or able to satisfy certain social status or membership criteria. Such exclusion rules may be felt to assure product quality or reliability or to maintain an important monopoly within a group (the argument that product quality or reliability must be assured often veils interests in protecting a monopoly). Or the rules may be motivated by a desire to prevent violation of community norms and values, and, therefore, only sellers satisfying certain social status or membership criteria (age, sex, religion, ethnicity) are acceptable. Again, powerful economic or nation–state interests may underlie to a greater or lesser extent such claims. (iv) The government considers only certain buyers as suitable on the basis of their satisfying competence or resource criteria or purely social status or membership criteria such as age, sex, religion, ethnicity. These rules may be motivated in part by a genuine desire to prevent accidents or harm to person or property. Or, as in the case of restriction of sellers, they may be instituted to prevent violation of important community norms and values. (v) The government involves itself in formulating or at least legitimizing the price determining principles or rules which prevail in a market (and, in general, as we discuss more fully later, this can entail the determination of the distribution rules which govern various goods and services).

Variations in price determination mechanisms in commodity markets illustrate the range of organizing principles and rules which govern diverse markets. Let us briefly compare three different sectors which we have investigated in Sweden (Flam, 1985): paper and pulp, housing, and agriculture. The first approaches a proper market. Its prices are not regulated, even if, as other markets, it is subject to periodic price stops and, on occasion, is blackmailed to slow down price increases by the government threat of price stops. In this market, enterprises set prices as a function of international price developments, exchange rates, and production costs. In contrast to the pulp and paper market, the housing sector entails an intricate combination of public regulation, market forces, and bargaining between associations of landlords and tenants. Local associations use as a frame of reference central guidelines within the public housing sector. (Guidelines have been established by the national representatives of public housing authorities and the national tenants association.) Moreover, in the case of both apartment houses and homes, the pricing of housing is affected by government-provided mortages and rent-subsidies, government loans to construction firms, and government regulations affecting construction costs. Finally, in the agricultural sector, prices are largely administered. They are set centrally in a series of successive legislative recommendations, agreements, and negotiations, the rules for which are carefully formulated, and the participants in which are carefully specified. The latter include representatives of farmer unions, employer and employee union representatives, and specified government departments. Consumers are not directly represented.

Clearly, the three sectors of the economy have different agencies engaged in price determination and are governed by very different principles.

In general, prices in many economic sectors are determined by well-defined, organized parties which engage in bargaining according to established rules and procedures (Chapter 10 examines labour markets). These parties and procedures may change over

TABLE 8.1
Price-setting agencies

Economic sector	Firm	Voluntary organization of buyers and/or sellers	Government
Paper	●		
Agriculture		●	●
Housing	●	●	●

time — each economic sector has its own organizational history. Typically, the participants involved in price determination in each sector differ, although exceptions may be found. For example, in Austria, the wage frame, interest rates, and one-third of all prices, are set by the same group of decision-makers, among whom the representatives of organized labour and capital are central.

Both differential access to, and inequalities in, markets are a frequent source of conflict and political action. One typical course of action is to call for public intervention. Public involvement in markets has historically assumed several forms:

● legislating rights for all citizens
● affirmative legislation (minority rights)
● subsidies to either providers or consumers of goods and services, even if the means of production and provision remain in private or semi-private hands
● government take-over of the means of production/administration of goods and services

Obviously, these forms of public intervention in markets have very different impacts on market behaviour and outcomes. Even legislation concerning rights may be formulated in diverse ways with substantially different consequences for market access and development; for instance, the establishment of equal (citizen) rights of access, under conditions of great economic inequality, will result in very stratified patterns of participation, for example in housing markets, whereas a system providing for actual use rights or ownership will not only operate differently but have radically different distributional consequences.

Public interventions in markets are typically related to issues and struggles around political and civic rights. Where civic, political and social rights have emerged, often after prolonged struggles, they interact with and assert themselves over and against property rights.

In nations where such rights have failed to be fully established, sizeable population groups remain outside or have only minimum access to important commodity markets.

The legal structuration of markets can, therefore, function either affirmatively or negatively: in the first case granting to specific groups or all citizens access to certain goods and services, thus improving their market capacity; or in the latter case, prohibiting specific groups of citizens and non-citizens access to or the right to ownership of particular goods and services, thus reducing their potential and actual market capacity.

Affirmative or prohibitive legislation is a strategic means for organizing markets. Such legislation may differentiate or equalize access rights and capacities. Laws and regulations increasing or limiting access to goods and services interact in various ways with the market buying capacity and social (ascribed) status of consumers, structuring their market opportunities and choices. Moreover, such legal regulation also influences what goods are produced, distributed and consumed, the ways this is done, and the actors or groups who benefit and lose from this arrangement.

Civic rights, in contrast to social rights or affirmative or prohibitive legislation concerning access to markets, may enable not only sellers but also groups of potential consumers to engage in self-organizing production in order to improve their consumption possibilities. Through such self-organizing, they can gain access to goods and services, which could not be obtained on the basis of individual buying capacity or social (ascribed) status. The self-organization, usually in the form of cooperatives or mutual assistance societies, within which collective resources are pooled, has also led, at times, to the take-over of the means of production and the self-provision of these goods and services. Self-organizing has presupposed, and is accompanied by, struggles for civic rights. Such laws constitute a basis for a particular positioning in the markets, that is a particular status by virtue of organizational affiliation, or 'affiliational status', in short. At places of employment, self-organizing in the form of employee unions has contributed, as to some extent has employer paternalism itself, to the emergence of employee benefits, provided, financed or co-financed by employers.

To sum up our discussion of social rules determining potential buyers' access to, and opportunities in, markets: these can be distinguished according to four dimensions which limit or facilitate their access to commodities:

• market capacity (property, income, credit)
• ascribed social status (ethnicity, nationality, gender, age)

- status by virtue of organizational membership or affiliation
- status by virtue of legislation (citizen/minority rights, including those underpinning claims for government transfers)

In general, access to commodities in terms of market capacity is often in conflict with or counterbalanced by access rules formulated in terms of the three kinds of status suggested (social, organizational, legal). Thus, for instance:

(i) It is known that ethnics and blacks in the USA, even if they have adequate market capacity, cannot realize it in mortgage and home markets, because of discriminating rules (informal) concerning, for example, their credit worthiness.

(ii) In some countries foreigners cannot own businesses or land.

(iii) In many instances, only the members of trade unions have the right to job training, that is, non-members are excluded.

(iv) In some countries citizens have the right to social security in old age, in many instances irrespective of previous market capacity.

(v) Specified minorities are in some instances given access to certain goods and services (such as education and housing), disregarding their market capacity. Affirmative action legislation in the USA is an example of this.

(vi) On the other hand, specified groups (non-white) may be barred, as in South Africa, from access to certain commodities, types of education, types of ownership, and so forth on the basis of legislation distinguishing the groups as white, black, or coloured (e.g. including Indian or Asiatic).

Ethnic or class organizations, religious groups and ecclesiastical orders, professions, political parties, and governments are among the types of agents who have organized, in pursuit of diverse goals, market and non-market distribution systems. When successful, they monopolized, or came to share with other agents, the role of provider of certain goods and services, buttressed often by legislation granting them statutory rights.

In general, one can describe and analyse economic sectors in terms of the types of agents providing goods and services, the types of access and distribution rules, and consumer status distinction rules which prevail. In this way, one not only distinguishes different types and degrees of market openness, but also non-market or quasi-market distribution systems.

If the types of agents selling and providing goods and services are juxtaposed with the criteria according to which consumers gain access to the goods and services, Table 8.2 can be constructed, which suggests different distribution regimes for goods and services. Some sectors may be largely or wholly characterized by market

TABLE 8.2
Distribution regimes

	Market capacity	Social or Legislated status	Government enabling/ retarding measures	Organizational status
Firm	Market proper with commodities	Status restricted market goods	Subsidies to firms and/or buyers or fines imposed on buyers	Private employee benefits
Voluntary organization	Commodified collective goods	Status-restricted collective goods	Subsidized collective goods	Collective goods for members only
Government	Commodified public goods	Affirmative goods such as housing, food for underprivileged groups	Public goods proper, provided by the state	Public employee benefits

regimes. Distribution of goods and services occurs on the basis of market rules governing transactions between private sellers (firms) and consumers, relying entirely on their market buying capacity. In other words, *the exchanges take place without considerations of the ascribed, organized, or legislated status of potential buyers. Other goods are distributed more according to the social status of consumers or potential consumers.*

Rules of access are formulated in terms of group affiliation, based on ascribed or acquired status. Such goods are typically not available on open markets, unless special laws require it (in which case organizations often establish informal rules to circumvent legal requirements). *It is organizational affiliation which determines access to goods and services.* Typically, when affiliation ends, so does access.

While we have the concept of public good — produced and distributed by the government for all citizens or certain status groups — we lack a term for goods and services provided through voluntary associations. We refer to them here as collective (or 'community') goods.

Table 8.3 presents agents and types of goods and services produced and distributed outside markets, such as those provided within private firms, government, and voluntary organizations. Market capacity does not play a role in access to the goods and

TABLE 8.3
Non-market provision of goods and services:
Private and public

Type of goods or service	Firm	Type of agent Voluntary organization	Government
Education/job training	Enterprise school, on-the-job training	Professional, trade union, ecclesiastical	State school and public job training
Health care	Enterprise medical care and hospitals	Health coop, trade union, ecclesiastical orders	Public health and public hospitals
Housing	Enterprise provides housing	Housing coop	Public housing
Pensions	Enterprise-organized insurance or pension schemes	Union-arranged pension plans	Social security

services produced and distributed through these systems (unless, of course, a 'black market' with these goods and services is established, as is the case in many Eastern European countries). Such systems obviously operate according to a different action logic or rationality than market systems (see Chapter 10 as well as Chapter 13). This is typical of many 'services' such as education, health care, housing and pensions, particularly in Western European countries. These goods and services may at the same time, especially in the USA, be distributed as commodities through markets.

Among different nations, various combinations of provider/distribution systems may be observed in different sectors of the economy. Accordingly, some sectors have more the character of markets, while others operate according to *non-market or quasi-market regimes of distribution*. In other words, the goods and services in question will vary in the degree they are 'commodities', 'private goods', 'collective goods', or 'public goods'. In each case, certain types of conflicts about control over the provision of, and access to, goods and services have historically determined the observable combinations (consequently, the configuration and orientation of loyalties and interests of recipients and potential recipients of the goods and services). As we have pointed out earlier, statutory rights have played an important role in such structuration, as they reinforce or help to replace established market organization, price mechanisms, and commodity exchange. Frequently, interests emerge, which come into conflict with the prevailing market organization and its consequences, making statutory rights and regulations themselves targets in ensuing struggles.

In the following pages (and Chapter 10) we discuss several different cases of markets and quasi-markets with varying rule regimes, and patterns of functioning, also their development as a function of interest configuration, distribution of power, and market stability.

Case studies of market formation, regulation and organization

Commodity markets and the Chicago Board of Trade

In an excellent study of the 'social organization of commodity markets', Leblebici and Salancik (1982) develop a model and carry out an analysis which is highly compatible with the theoretical framework developed here. Drawing on Commons (1959) and Crozier and Thoenig (1975), they consider markets to be structured systems regulated by collective or working rules (1982:230):

> The system of working rules defines and structures the interorganizational network, defining not only the conditions of exchange but the parties who exchange.

The authors conducted a study of the Chicago Board of Trade (CBT), a quasi-public regulatory agency. The Board was established in 1859 on the basis of a corporate charter granted by the Illinois legislature. The charter enables CBT to establish and enforce rules which maintain a limited open and competitive market. It authorizes the CBT also to arbitrate the resolution of transaction conflicts. Membership of the CBT is around 1,400.[49] Membership rights can be sold by members, but eligible applicants must be sponsored by a reputable member and elected to membership in a secret ballot by the board of directors. While median membership fee (price) was $2,450 in 1950, it reached $232,000 in 1979.

The CBT was developed to guarantee the continuity of transactions between buyers and sellers of commodities (1982:30–1). This development can be traced through legislation, adjudication, arbitration, prosecution and informal action. Leblebici and Salancik (1982:231) write:

> Today a well-run organized futures market has certain features that make it a reliable institutional mechanism for trading. First, it has a

FIGURE 8.3
Chicago Trade Board and commodity markets:
grain, silver, soyabean oil

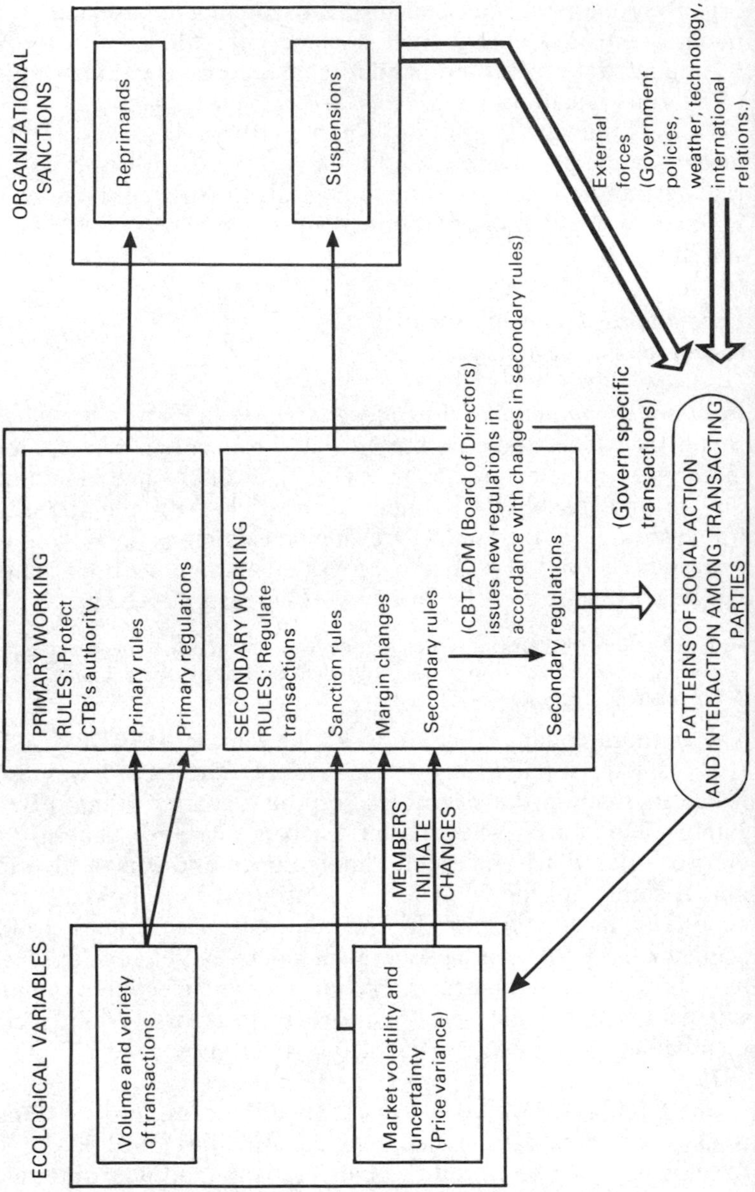

contract that enables principals to instruct their agents to trade on their behalf in terms of price and quantity alone, even though buying and selling an actual commodity requires more information; the commodity must be inspected, its quality determined and its location specified... A standardized future contract makes familiarity with the properties of the commodity and the preferences of the principals unnecessary. Secondly, an organized futures market limits actual trading to its members. This limitation generates each member's interest in the survival of the exchange because of the value of his membership and further forces demands that the other members be reliable. Third, an organized futures market has a clearing house that 'enables the transition from trading on forward contracts, where the identity of the parties involved is necessary information to judge the safety and reliability of the contract, to trading in future contracts, whose validity depends on the faith and the credit of the organized exchange itself and not on the individual parties to a transaction' (citation from Tilser, 1981).

Leblebici and Salancik (1982) distinguish the structure of the CBT rule system regulating inter-organizational relations on the Chicago commodity markets. It consists of two general types of rules: (i) *process rules* regulating transactions among agents and (ii) *organizational rules* establishing and maintaining the authority and powers of the regulatory agency.

Rules and regulations of the first type deal with such matters as: (1) the trading conditions and delivery procedures for specific commodities; (2) procedures for the resolution of internal disputes; (3) the clearing of contracts signed in exchange; and (4) setting margin requirements, that is the sum of money deposited by both buyers and sellers to assure performance of the terms of the future contract. (A margin is a performance bond or security, not a payment of equity or a down payment on the commodity.) The CBT determines the rules specifying minimum initial margin requirements and the maintenance of margin levels (subsequent deposits to cover fluctuations in the market price of a commodity). Leblebici and Salancik (1982:233) point out that this class of rules is an important tool used by the Board of Directors to influence market fluctuations directly.

The organizational rules for CBT deal with (1) issues of governance, (2) where and when market transactions may take place, (3) other conditions under which a member enters into transactions, and (4) the types of transactions permissible (or more specifically, the procedures to be followed in carrying out an acceptable transaction).

The structure of the CBT rule regime is indicated in Figure 8.3 (Leblebici and Salancik (1982)). The figure also points up several of the important relationships which find expression in the propositions and analyses of the article. In particular, these concern processes and conditions which bring about changes in the rules.

The authors argue that rules are transformed in connection with increased levels of uncertainty in the exchange environment (e.g. price volatility, but other factors might be international supply and demand developments, credit developments, and inflation which could impact on commodity trading).

The focus of their analyses is on grain (which includes wheat, corn, oats, and soybeans), plywood, silver, ice broilers and soybean oil transactions. These were selected because of the availability of continuous time series data and their importance in CBT transactions.

The authors find that market volatility was a major determinant of changes in process rules, but only those enacted by the membership (rule changes carried out by CBT administrators could result from factors other than market forces, such as changes in the rules themselves, which might call for codification, elaboration or clarification). They found that margin rules (see earlier discussion) were the process rules most sensitive to changes in market volatility.

On the other hand, organizational rules are changed in response to overall changes in market activity (such as the volume and variety of transactions).

*Constraints on market formation and
emergence of new commodities*
Zelizer (1978; 1981) shows that certain strong norms about human beings, such as the sacredness of children and of life and death matters, led initially to substantial resistance in the USA to insurance on children's health and life and to life insurance. The impediments were not so much political–legal in character (although in the case of child-life insurance, there were serious attempts to block this type of insurance), they were moral.

The general thesis motivating Zelizer's research is that there is cultural resistance to introducing certain items into markets, that is 'commodifying such items'. Above all, these are items relating to sacred aspects of human life, death, and emotion. Attempts at such innovations will result in structural strains, ambivalence, and even conflict in the marketing process (1978:593). In the case of life insurance, man and money, the sacred and the profane, were brought together. 'The value of man become measurable by money' (Zelizer, 1978:605). Zelizer points out (1978: 590, 598):

Life insurance became the first large-scale enterprise in America to base its entire organization on the accurate estimate of the price of death.

It was necessary to know the cost of death in order to establish adequate policy benefits and determine premiums. The economic evaluation of human life was a delicate matter which met with stubborn resistance. Particularly, although not exclusively, during the first half of the 19th century, life insurance was felt to be sacrilegious because its ultimate function was to compensate the loss of a father and a husband with a check to his widow and orphans. Critics objected that this turned man's sacred life into an 'article of merchandise'.

Zelizer found that the solution which marketing found was to 'sacralize life insurance'. The monetary evaluation of death was transformed into a ritual. She concludes (1978:605):

> Death yielded to the capitalist ethos — but not without compelling the latter to disguise its materialist mission in spiritual garb. For instance, life insurance assumed the role of a secular ritual and introduced new notions of immortality that emphasized remembrance through money. A 'good death' was no longer defined only on moral grounds; the inclusion of a life policy made financial foresight another prerequisite. One finds, in addition to religious legitimation, attempts at moral and social legitimation of the industry. The public was assured that marketing death [benefits] served the lofty social purpose of combating poverty...

Further studies

Medicine markets have been structured and regulated by professional groups and the state, determining who can produce and sell, who can buy and under what conditions. Technological developments in medicines and in the production of preparations have destabilized organized medicine markets historically (all highly organized and regulated markets are vulnerable to such destabilization).

Some 'medicines' and medical techniques have been removed from markets ('decommodified') and distributed through non-market systems, and a few have been removed altogether from legal public access (such as LSD). In Chapter 14 in connection with our analysis of the dynamics of regulating new technologies, we consider the case where human sperm and artificial insemination have been decommodified in Sweden.

Major attention is given in Chapter 10 to one of the most highly structured and regulated quasi-markets in modern economies, namely labour markets. Not only is there a great deal of legal regulation but major rule systems and means of enforcement are negotiated periodically between employer and employee representatives.

Conclusion

In this chapter we have introduced a set of concepts with which to describe and analyse the social organization of market as well as non-market distribution systems.

In analysing market organization and functioning, we have stressed that one should examine: (1) legislation and other social rules applying to a given market, and (2) relevant social agents, conflicts, and power struggles pertaining to rules determining legitimate sellers and buyers, commodities, pricing mechanisms, and regulatory agencies.

Legislation plays an important role insofar as it reinforces or changes the organization of a market or an entire sector. Civic rights along with statutes, licences, regulations and general social norms directly affect the organization and development potentials of a market, because they constrain or enable actors to actively shape or reshape it. Such rights affect the market on its production or supply side. On the other hand, civic rights as well as affirmative–prohibitive legislation constrain or facilitate the access of potential recipients or buyers to goods and services, thus affecting consumption patterns. In this way, markets are affected on the demand side. At the same time, organizations operating in markets use constitutional rights and legislation in order to define and challenge the legitimacy of buyers and sellers, of commodities, pricing mechanisms, and regulatory agents. Outside organizations may cooperate or engage in conflict with those internal to a market.

In a word, constitutional rights and legal systems — and group interests and strategies in utilizing these — play a major role in the social organizing and functioning of market (as well as non-market) distribution systems.

Obviously, market social organization is embedded within a larger social structure, where social agents act in ways which, intentionally or unintentionally, affect market structuration and performance (Polanyi et al., 1957; Etzioni, 1985; Granovetter, 1985). Thus, the organization and performance of any given market will depend on the larger social context: the ideological/normative and institutional framework within which any given market is nested. This framework impinges on the market, contributing to its structuration and performance characteristics. At the same time, market behaviour and developments impact to a greater or lesser extent on the larger structure.

The analyses of this chapter have ignored, among other things, innovations in production, products and marketing which may facilitate the break-down or erosion of market exclusion rules; in particular:

.

- types of products and transactions emerge which are not defined or adequately conceptualized by established rules
- the innovations are covered by the rules but visibility of transactions is reduced, and, therefore, monitoring and social control effectiveness are impaired
- the amounts of economic gain to be realized become so great that the established penalities are trivial or meaningless

In such ways, market developments may burst asunder rule regimes governing the market. According to our theory, however, social agents, as they learn about the new types of products, product transactions, and related conditions try to establish and enforce new rules. This is particularly the case of communities with relatively strong moral or ideological commitments. Often, there are political struggles around these initiatives, as those who wish to maintain 'the freedom of the marketplace' or 'the established regime' resist those who attempt to institutionalize new ones (see Chapter 14).

9
Market organization and performance properties

Tom R. Burns and Helena Flam*

In this chapter we examine more closely the types of rules organizing markets and the impact such rules have in influencing transaction costs, supply and demand curves, and price structures. Here we can only outline our models and arguments (for more comprehensive formulations and analyses, see Burns et al. (1986)).

Types of market rules and their economic impact
The rule regime(s) governing market transactions not only govern the types of transactions allowed (or accepted) but the agents permitted to engage in these transactions. Other conditions of economic exchange are specified as well, such as the specific procedures to be followed and time-and-place conditions (situational requirements and/or defined 'areas of freedom'). Below we examine market rules which are typically instituted by public and semi-public authorities, or branch and professional associations.

We consider the market rules defining and regulating legitimate sellers, buyers, and transactions and the impact these have on supply and demand and on price formation.

Seller access rules
Market rules may bar entry to suppliers, unless, for instance, they meet certain professional criteria (such as competence, expertise), financial conditions, or purely socially defined criteria (sex, age, religion, ethnicity, network membership, etc.). Given a more or less homogeneous product, such restrictions will tend to reduce supply.[50] As a result, prices will tend to be above the level likely if participation were more open (in other words, less exclusive).[51]

Proposition I. Rules reducing the number of potential suppliers limit supply. If the interaction among buyers and the restricted set of sellers remains competitive, the supply/demand relationship with price P_2, represented in Figure 9.2, would obtain.

*In collaboration with Philippe DeVille and Bernard Gauci.

FIGURE 9.1
Market social organization

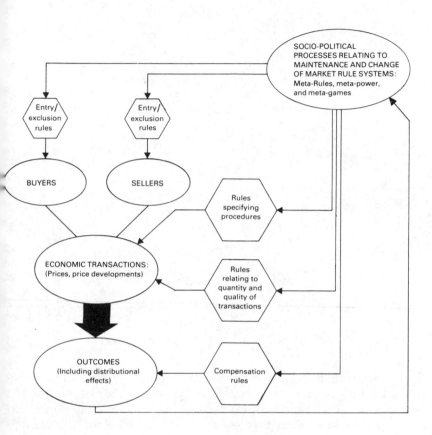

Buyer access rules
Many market regimes contain rules *which exclude buyers*. There are usually several bases for exclusion, these differing from market to market. The underlying criteria will also vary from society to society, although, for instance, among OECD countries, there will be considerable overlap.

● safety and order considerations. Buyers may be excluded because they lack certification attesting to their competence to handle or use the products in question (toxic chemicals, guns, other dangerous equipment). Entire groups may be excluded from a large number of markets, e.g. children and those who have a history of mental illness or criminal records

FIGURE 9.2
Supply/price adjustment under seller exclusion

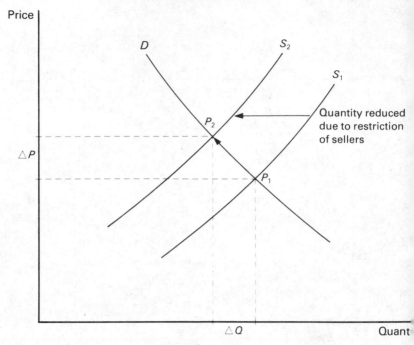

- social status or membership considerations. Such status characteristics as age, sex, ethnicity, religion, and so forth may be the
basis of exclusionary rules. The making of modern 'mass markets'
entails the erosion or removal of rules maintaining elite or community markets (Weber, 1968)
- financial considerations. Buyers may be excluded because they
fail to satisfy financial or similar criteria. Without suitable
resource bases — or access to credit — many markets would
remain relatively exclusive, open only to small populations, e.g.
housing markets, automobile, and other 'household property'
which requires considerable capital investments. Indeed, mortgage and consumer credit institutions have played a major historical role in the expansion of such markets and the sustained
growth in demand. At the same time, these institutions have rules
for providing credit (satisfying 'credit worthiness' criteria), which
not only enable a new class of buyers to enter the house, automobile and similar markets, but also directly or indirectly exclude

groups or classes. These rule system complexes contribute of course to 'life-style' formation and differentiation

To the extent that rules excluding 'unacceptable or questionable buyers' are effectively enforced, *the restrictions reduce demand and, therefore, for a given supply curve, induce lower prices than would otherwise be the case.* In other words, if freedom of entry were more open to a population of potential buyers, the price sellers could ask would tend to be higher for a given supply curve.

Again, as we have suggested earlier, the barriers to entry may not arise only from such exclusion rules.

- Potential buyers judge themselves (whether accurately or not is beside the point for they act according to their beliefs) to lack the expertise to handle/use the product and therefore never try to enter the market. They may lack sufficient economic resources to engage themselves
- Potential buyers lack market knowledge or information essential to participation. Therefore, even if they have the resources and the expertise to use the product, they do not know the market exists or is open to them
- And, of course, capable buyers may not enter because they have no interest in or need for the products, or they have attractive alternatives

Proposition II. When, through market exclusion rules, the number of potential buyers is reduced, demand will be less, and the supply/demand relationship with price P_2 in Figure 9.3 will obtain. provided the interaction among sellers and the restricted set of buyers remains competitive.

Decommodification and banning rules

The rule regime governing a particular market will exclude *certain types of potential commodities* as illegal (weaker forms of such a rule are expressed in terms of 'unacceptable' or 'inappropriate'). For instance, prostitution and the sale of sexual services are banned in some societies (and many states of the USA). Certain chemicals and drugs, such as DDT and LSD, are banned in many countries. The sale of nuclear weapons is universally banned (although there is evidently a potential market for such weapons). Total or partial restrictions may also be imposed on imports and exports. Thus, the US Congress has in some instances banned weapon exports to countries violating human rights and the Swedish parliament excludes weapon exports to countries engaged in hostilities. Import stoppages, quotas or tariffs are well-known means to exclude

FIGURE 9.3
Demand/price adjustment under buyer exclusion

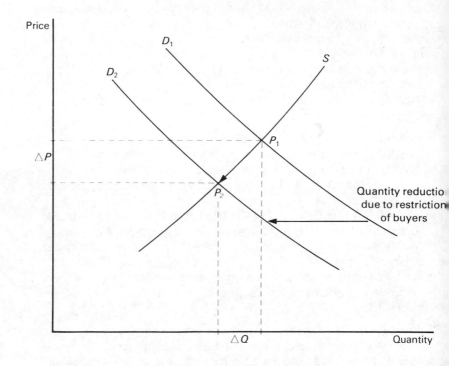

foreign products in order to protect domestic producers. Subtler forms of such protection may entail the requirement that foreign products have failed to satisfy certain quality requirements, which effectively excludes them, at least in the short run.

As we discuss later, economic agents may breach such exclusion rules because they can realize major gains with low risks by buying and selling banned products. A major consideration in this analysis is the enforcement — and the cost of enforcement — of exclusion rules by the state, by a relevant business community, or by a trade association.

Proposition III. Supply and demand do not arise in the case of commodities or transactions which are banned altogether, *and* where potential buyers and sellers comply with the rule regime (that is, any potential market is socially excluded).

Some economic agents may be prepared to breach norms in order to exploit opportunities for gain by establishing and/or participating in an illegal market. Whenever at least one illicit seller and at least one illicit buyer manage to link up, we have the limiting (and of course non-competitive) case of the preceding two propositions. (Transaction costs in this case would include those usually connected with obtaining information and organizing transactions plus the costs incurred in trying to avoid detection and countervailing or suffering the punishments for being caught in illicit activities.)

Transaction rules and procedures
A market rule regime will exclude some transactions which are not carried out according to correct procedures. Such procedures include recording the transaction, making sure that agreements are witnessed, and obtaining certification of a buyer's competence to handle or use certain products such as dangerous pesticides. Many of these rules and procedures are designed to protect the interests of buyers and/or sellers or, in some instances, even third parties. In this sense, some of the rules and procedures organizing and regulating markets have social as well as private benefits. At the same time, the transaction requirements increase transaction costs to a greater or lesser extent. As we discuss later, the debiting of such costs may be distributed in a number of ways, in some cases to minimize the costs to the participants, for instance, when third parties (e.g. taxpayers) carry out and/or pay for the various procedures (see note 57).

In general, increased transaction costs in connection with rule specified procedures for conducting exchanges tend to increase prices.[52] Such 'price increases' may not be visible if the buyer is the one who invests time, energy, and money in the procedures (we do not presume a perfectly competitive model here; see later discussion). The procedures are often organized and managed by a third party who charges a fee, for example a 'settlement fee' which according to legislation or established norms the buyer is supposed to bear. Such costs would not show up in the 'official market price', but certainly would be a part of the 'price paid'.

Proposition IV. Rules specifying procedures to be followed in executing economic exchange will increase transaction costs to the extent that the procedures entail the investment of time, energy and resources (possibly including payments to agents to organize and manage the procedures). Rule-induced price increases would lead to a lower level of demand, other things being equal.

As we have stressed earlier, legitimate public interests may motivate the imposition of transaction procedures (and increased costs). In some cases, there may be a net gain in terms of reduced prices and expanded markets. This would occur, for instance, when the increase in transaction costs connected with the imposition of market norms and procedures is more than compensated for by the avoidance of costs associated with conflict, litigation, and high uncertainty. Sellers on a regulated competitive market where uncertainty and expensive conflicts have been reduced would be predisposed to reduce margins on their costs. Prices might be pressed down even further because additional sellers are willing to enter the market in the face of 'greater security'. Lowered prices, along with product and transaction guarantees, serve to expand the population of potential buyers, other things being equal.

To sum up our discussion: market organizing principles and rules, applied to the access of suppliers or buyers to the market, and to defining acceptable transactions and trade procedures, affect supply and demand and, ultimately, prices. Although our analyses are only preliminary, they suggest the general form and direction which more comprehensive studies could take (Burns et al., 1986).

The enforcement of market rule systems
In this section we shall try to develop our arguments further, exploring the types of social controls used to enforce market rule systems. Ultimately, we are interested in the consequences such controls have for market prices and structures as well as for community norms and relationships. A basic premise of our framework is that the enforcement of market rules — and the reliability of participants in complying with them and non-participants in accepting them — will depend on the social structure in which markets are embedded (Granovetter, 1985; Polanyi et al., 1957; these treatments of embeddedness represent substantially different theoretical perspectives from the one presented here).

Two general types of social control system are distinguished below (see Burns et al. (1985) for further distinctions and analyses of social controls).

Communities with strong moral or ideological commitments
Strong ideological or moral sentiments in a community will increase the likelihood that market participants will adhere to market rules, e.g. exclusion rules, that are based on these sentiments. Rules derived from major social norms in the community would be experienced as legitimate. For example, social rules arrived at through democratic, religious, and legal institutions to which members of the community are committed would also be experienced as legitimate and felt to be binding. Concretely, this would mean that market participants — sellers as well as buyers — would probably resist the temptation to exploit possible economic gains by breaching, for instance, exclusion rules. *Formal, that is administrative,*

enforcement costs (policing, sanctions, etc.) would be relatively low. (This is one of the important economic consequences of ideology and moral sentiments (North, 1981).)[53] But actual market behaviour tends to correspond closely to that specified by the governing rule system. Other things being equal, the supply and demand curves arising under the market exclusion rules would be more or less predictable, corresponding to those presented in the previous section. *Illicit 'supply/demand curves' would not be found or would be highly transitory. There would be little or no market outside the legal or official one.* Members of the community are predisposed to react with universal condemnation of those who breach the rules, particularly rules representing core community norms and values. The treatment of such deviants would serve as an example to any others with weak moral fibre..

Communities with weak moral or ideological commitments and administrative regulation of market behaviour

In this case ideological or moral commitments to market rule systems, in particular exclusion rules, are weak or non-existent. Such a situation may have a variety of historical roots. (i) The sense of community or nation is undeveloped, and the territorial unit is held together by administrative or military means. Market expansion is largely promoted by the state, which through taxation and other policies induces previously isolated or economically sufficient population groups to become involved with the market economy. This is the case in many developing nations where market entrepreneurship is low or resistance to market penetration is high. (ii) The community is a cohesive one, but the rule regime lacks legitimacy, possibly because it is imposed from the outside or is viewed as incompatible with community norms and values. Under such conditions, adherence to the rules would be uncertain even in a strongly moral and cohesive community. (iii) The community has undergone rapid changes, in terms of social mobility, changes in technology and everyday practices, so that many are uncertain about what rules are legitimate and about the extent to which other members of the community continue to adhere to norms and moral commitments. Such a moral climate combined with high market uncertainty, or opportunities to make substantial gains, sets the stage for opportunistic behaviour (see Baker (1984) for a discussion of 'opportunism' in markets, and also the possible linkages between market uncertainty and opportunistic behaviour). (iv) Important interest groups, speaking with authority, attack the rule regime, arguing on behalf of 'free markets'. Not only do such attacks, when successful, open up certain markets, *but they erode the normative structures of society*

which contribute to the enforcement of market rule systems.
Generally, such structures are public goods — and a cultural infrastructure — whose value is incalculable not only for the society as a
whole but for effective economic performance. (v) Market mechanisms are inefficient because of resource scarcity and cannot sustain
their own legitimacy in the eyes of participants. That is, the demand
for goods and services cannot be met, which provokes deviance that
is often tolerated or even encouraged by the authorities, for instance
in the case of the widespread black markets in developing countries.

In the absence of moral or administrative controls enforcing
market rule systems, market participants or potential participants
are likely to break the rules. (Even in communities with relatively
high moral standards and discipline, substantial *resource scarcity
tends to erode practical adherence to norms and acceptance of market
regulation.)* Illicit or black markets would be common (possibly
becoming the norm in practice). For example, sellers sell to unlicen-
sed or illegal buyers (children, criminals, the mentally disturbed,
persons or enterprises lacking certification to handle, for instance,
dangerous equipment or chemicals); buyers are willing to purchase
goods and services from illegal sellers; banned commodities (such as
weapons, dangerous drugs, child prostitutes, murderers-for-hire,
and so forth) would be available; finally, there is a general propensity to ignore or to breach the transaction procedures which are
supposed to be followed in carrying out market exchanges.

In general, cheating, deceit, and the buying and selling of stolen
or banned goods, as well as incompetence and confusion would
prevail. Supply and demand curves as socially generated relations
would be unstable and subject to unpredictable shifts as actors
would conceal information from one another and find ways to take
advantage of one another. *Many markets would disappear
altogether, because the validity and reliability of transactions could
not be guaranteed.* Not only would uncertainty and opportunism be
maximized, but the risks of escalating conflict and a struggle of all
against all, including the widespread use of non-market weapons,
would be increased.

Of course, few societies — or markets within them — are so
'normless'. But the 'thought experiment' points up the economic
risks that are involved once the social regulation of transactions and
market participation has broken down. The social costs would also
be high, and some of these would not be ascertainable until long
after damage to health, life, and property — not to speak of the
moral foundations of society — had set in. For these reasons,
among others, community leaders with moral authority, and some
economic interests, demand the establishment and enforcement of

market exclusion rules. Granovetter (1985:489) refers to Kenneth Arrow's suggestion that societies 'in their evolution have developed implicit agreements to certain kinds of regard for others, agreements which are essential to the survival of the society or at least contribute greatly to the efficiency of its working' (Arrow, 1974:26).

Granovetter adds:

Now one can hardly doubt the existence of some such generalized morality; without it, you would be afraid to give the gas station attendant a 20-dollar bill when you had bought only five dollars worth of gas. But this conception has the oversocialized characteristic of calling on a generalized and automatic response, even though moral action in economic life is hardly automatic or universal (as is well known at gas stations that demand exact change after dark). [Granovetter, 1985:489]

In market areas where it is unfeasible or highly risky to rely on the moral or ideological commitments of market participants, groups of market actors, a trade association, or the state may establish an administration to try to uphold market organizing principles and rules. Such an initiative is, in some instances, motivated by genuine moral considerations, such as outrage at increasing dishonesty and breach of societal norms. Sellers, on the other hand, are frequently motivated by a desire to exclude competing sellers who could not qualify according to the entry criteria which they would institutionalize. But the sellers might be interested not only in increasing their own profits and security, but in establishing among buyers confidence in respectable and reliable sellers.

Groups of buyers may also support certain exclusion rules, both to increase product reliability and possibly to keep 'riff-raff' out of some markets. Often the motive here is to maintain social status structures and distinct life styles. Housing markets in the contemporary world provide excellent illustrations of this phenomenon.

State involvement in establishing and maintaining administrative controls tends to reflect a variety of interests and demands. The role of business lobbies, for instance, in advocating protection of their trade and the credibility of their associations in the eyes of consumers, is well known. But consumer as well as 'anti-consumption' movements (for instance, the temperance movement and the anti-drug movement) can play an important role in government intervention and regulation. The pressures for government enforcement of market rules occur also through more normal political channels — political parties make such issues a part of their programmes. Professional groups in state agencies in some instances feel it is a professional responsibility or challenge to deal with market conditions that are eroding normative structures and the public order within their areas of concern —- weapons sales, for instance, or the marketing of dangerous chemicals and equipment.

The effectiveness of administrative controls depends on: (i) the availability and reliability of the data on transactions; (ii) the strength of sanctions which can be imposed for transgressions; (iii) the competence and efficiency of those responsible for enforcing market rule systems, in particular exclusion rules; (iv) the gains and risks associated with agents breaching market rules and regulations; (v) the support of the community, where the compatibility between the legal rules of the state and community norms is one significant factor influencing the level of support.

Of course, potential deviants are often capable of mobilizing resources and developing stratagems to avoid or to minimize control over their actions. The interplay between regulators and those regulated should be seen as a *dynamic social game,* where the actors may alter their strategies and the rules of the game may be changed.

One of the most common ways in which administrative controls are extended or made more effective is through *market participants themselves helping with monitoring and policing.* Their readiness to do this will vary with the seriousness with which the illegal activity is viewed and the personal or social costs of engagement. Participants may engage themselves in social control activities for other than ideological and moral reasons, as pointed out earlier. This happens in three ways.

(i) Legal sellers try to limit the entry of new competitors. They argue that only they can assure the proper levels of required quality, professional competence and reliability. Their interests need not only be material, however. They may wish to protect their reputations, or that of their profession or business association, against criticism or political intervention arising from reactions to 'uncertified sellers' or the sale of low quality or unreliable products. The long-term economic and political consequences of such reactions cannot be foreseen. For instance, the state might intervene with stringent controls which could greatly harm their interests professionally and economically.

For reasons similar to those just mentioned, sellers in many instances try to prevent 'illegal' sales, e.g. the sale of banned products or the sale of products to illegal buyers. Failure to control such transactions within their own ranks could lead, among other things, to the loss of professional autonomy and prestige. Granovetter (1985:492) points out that traders such as diamond merchants who are embedded in a close-knit community monitor one another's behaviour closely:

Like other densely knit networks of actors, they generate *clearly defined standards of behaviour* easily policed by the quick spread of information about instances of malfeasance.

(ii) Buyers themselves may also be prepared to help enforce exclusion rules. Again, they need not be motivated by moral principles, although this type of action, among sellers as well, plays a certain role in many modern societies (for instance, the Scandinavian countries). Rather, they react forcefully to defend their social status and the general social order which in part is associated with exclusive markets. Not more than two decades ago in the USA a hotel or restaurant in the southern states that was prepared to serve blacks elicited outrage from some whites who experienced this as a threat to their own status, not to speak of the threat to their conception of social reality.

In the case of exclusive clubs, restaurants, and hotels, sellers try to maintain exclusion rules which are considered essential to their clientele's social status and life-style distinctions. In doing this, they employ a variety of stratagems, legal as well as illegal, to limit entry (other than simply very high prices). For instance, they require places to be booked ahead of time with reservations made available only to known or referenced clients, they insist on membership, refer clients elsewhere, use insulting treatment, and so forth.

In general, the rules excluding lower status or outsider groups (distinguished on the basis of class, ethnicity, religious or other social dimensions) from certain markets are often enforced with the assistance of buyers who are legitimate participants. They have a social interest in maintaining their position of distinction and privilege. (At the same time, considerable economic advantages in the form of cheaper prices and greater variety might be lost as a result of the failure to establish large mass markets.)[54]

(iii) Excluded buyers or sellers also contribute to rule enforcement out of envy, greed, a sense of injustice, moral outrage, or concern with the welfare of the larger community. They do this by monitoring and reporting on those who engage in illicit transactions.

The point is that a regulatory agency may receive considerable 'external assistance' in enforcing exclusion rules, for instance, through one or another group of community 'watch-dogs'. This will increase the likelihood of more or less successful control, even in the absence of a resource-rich and competent regulatory agency.

Nevertheless, like sin, some illicit markets are extremely difficult to wipe out (indeed, many of these trade in the 'commodities of sin': drugs, sex, gambling, stolen goods, etc.). Even with a more or less effective regulatory agency and support from many quarters of society, illicit markets continue to operate, rising and falling not only with supply and demand cycles but with political and administrative cycles of enforcement.

Paradoxically, effective enforcement of market exclusion rules leads in some cases to greater incentives to breach the rules. This is particularly characteristic of commodities which are highly attractive or necessary. But it occurs also in markets where regulations and procedures for transactions are complicated, transaction costs are high, and many market actors are predisposed to opportunism.

For instance, the supply of an illegal drug will be reduced if the police control drug traffic effectively. One effect of this is that habitual users or addicts will be prepared to pay higher and higher premiums to obtain the drug.[55] Consequently, the incentives increase for illegal dealers as well as legitimate dealers (such as pharmacists and, indirectly, doctors) to engage in illicit drug traffic. Even if the likelihood of being caught is significant the temptation would be compelling for those agents who are motivated largely by a desire for high economic gain because the gains increase as supply is reduced under conditions of sustained demand.[56]

Given the inability of the police and other regulatory agents to eliminate 'the need' for such commodities when there are powerful incentives to engage in illicit transactions for economic gain, such markets can scarcely be eliminated altogether, and certainly not in a modern, complex society. (Of course, if those apprehended are executed or given life sentences, both supply and demand would be reduced, but such sanctions are inconsistent with the other principles of modern societies which aspire to present a humane image.) Vigorous efforts to eliminate sinful markets under such conditions will have the unintended effect of increasing the price of the illegal commodity, thus enhancing the incentive for some to engage in its commerce. The interplay between social regulation, supply and demand, and market patterns is complex and, in some instances, as suggested here, counter-intuitive.

As pointed out in note 57 the principle for allocating enforcement costs will affect the interplay between legal and illicit markets, and in particular the closure and stability of legal markets. Enforcement costs that are imposed on legitimate sellers and/or buyers will generate incentives to breach the rules in order to reduce costs and prices. If legitimate sellers bear most of the enforcement costs and increase their prices accordingly, the incentives for sellers or potential sellers to engage in illicit transactions will increase, since they may well sell under the legal price with comfortable profit margins. The greater the discrepancy between the 'legal price' and the 'illegal price', the more likely buyers will be tempted to shift from the white to the grey markets, particularly if the social stigma attached to participating in such illicit markets is weak, the likelihood of being detected is small, or the legal punishments relatively minor.

One strategy for dealing with difficult-to-control illicit markets is to partially legalize them. This is a well-established strategy in regulating certain markets because moral and ideological sentiments or political will are weak and social controls are largely ineffective. The strategy is observable in many countries in dealing with 'victimless crimes' (which may only have been considered 'crimes' during certain periods or in certain countries) as in cases of prostitution and gambling.

Thus, prostitution and gambling are legalized and regulated in some countries within a rule framework that includes specific exclusion rules. Those selling their services may be required to register and to undergo regular medical check-ups, and to follow certain norms about soliciting and about the times and places where they operate. Even clients may be regulated (through medical controls, as was done in the houses of prostitution established for German soldiers during the First World War).

To sum up this section: the two ideal types of market regulative systems — the diffuse rule enforcement of intense moral and ideological communities and the well-defined, organized enforcement of administrative agencies — entail different modes of social organization and functioning. Administered market regulation entails the explicit economic costs of employing people and mobilizing resources to police and sanction illegal market behaviour. Two of its characteristic activities are formal: legal monitoring and sanctioning. Typically, these are carried out by specially recruited and trained agents according to explicit, well-defined policies and rules. Moral/ ideological control processes are often more informal, even implicit. The sanctions may be both self-imposed and community-imposed, without the quality or quantity of sanction being systematically explicit. Consequently, market participants are likely to find the 'calculation of costs and net-gains' very difficult to carry out and, in principle, inappropriate. Moral/ideological and administrative control systems will, in general, affect transaction patterns, pricing behaviour and market stability/instability in different ways and having quite different impacts.[57] As the discussion above points out, regulative modes are often combined in various ways. Also, considerations of community norms and ideology may converge with the economic or professional interests of market groups to maintain or reform a particular market organization.

Market structuration as a function of social factors

Our framework suggests a variety of illicit or black markets, distinguished by participants violating one or more rules of a market regime, for instance:

- commodities which are altogether banned are bought and sold, for example, hire-killing, political bribery (the selling of favours)
- commodities are sold to persons in amounts exceeding that allotted or prescribed for these persons (from zero upwards). (In the case of 'zero allotment' the buyer is of course an illegal buyer)
- certain commodities are sold by 'illegal sellers' and/or purchased by 'illegal buyers'
- buying and selling are organized and carried out in ways which breach prescribed procedures and norms
- commodities are bought and sold at prices above a legal ceiling or below a legal floor. Or they are sold in amounts or according to measures contrary to prescription

In some instances, there is an asymmetry: sellers are legitimate sellers but transacting with illegal buyers, or vice versa. In other cases, both sets of actors are transacting in banned commodities or organizing transactions in totally illegal ways. Finally, illicit sellers and illicit buyers may together establish a market, for example, moonshiners produce and sell illegal alcohol to minors. This market in the purest case would not overlap at all with legal markets. It would have its own rules, communication networks, supply and demand curves and price structure.[58] The possible exchange patterns are as follows:

I.   *Banned commodities*: Both the seller's participations and that of the buyer are illegal (e.g. selling and buying/consuming heroin).

II. *Illegal selling*: A seller engages in deceptive or fraudulent behaviour (e.g. overcharging credit or using inaccurate scales).

III. *Illegal buying*: Deceptive or fraudulent purchases, (e.g. buying weapons or dangerous equipment with false certification; writing false cheques, etc.).

IV. *Legal exchanges*: Neither the buyer's nor the seller's participation is illegal.

The social control of deviant market behaviour in large, complex societies, and even in relatively small societies undergoing rapid change, is rarely complete or secure. Illicit markets emerge and develop. Crimes are committed and in many instances pay off well.[59] Also incentives for 'deviant behaviour', besides those arising under potential 'supply and demand conditions', may be generated and sustained through social pressures and controls applied by deviant groups. For instance, the Mafia's 'code of silence' — and the often stringent sanctions supporting it — stabilize illicit markets, even if considerable police and community pressure is mobilized to eliminate the markets. (The Mafia's strategies are not limited to sanctioning marginal participants, but to buying off as well as threatening those persons and agencies with the responsibility of preventing illicit markets.)

In the preceding section we argued that the enforcement of — and predisposition of market agents to adhere to — market regulating rules will depend on the social structure in which markets are embedded. Even in highly ethical communities, the readiness to enforce and to comply with these rules will be a function of the degree to which particular market activities defined as illegal or immoral are considered appropriate for social control. In part, some types of deviance are considered much more serious than others, as we now discuss.

Rossi et al. (1974) conducted a study in the US in which 200 respondents were asked to rank 140 criminal acts on a nine-point scale of seriousness (a score of 1 reflected low seriousness while a score of 9 reflected high seriousness). Most of the activities in Rossi's study which entailed market transactions are included in Table 9.1 (adapted from Zaltman and Wallendorf (1979)). It shows the mean ranking of the action on the nine-point scale and the amount of variance, and it indicates whether buyers or sellers are considered the responsible agents in the illegal transaction. (Since many of the criminal acts have very close means, the rankings can only be used as rough approximations of the perceived seriousness of the crimes.)

TABLE 9.1
Seriousness of illegal exchange activities

Rank	Crime	Mean	Variance	Illegal behaviour of Buyer and/or Seller
1	Planned killing of a policeman	8.474	2.002	
2	Planned killing of a person for a fee	8.406	2.749	Seller/buyer
3	Selling heroin	8.293	2.658	Seller
10	Selling LSD	7.949	3.048	Seller
25	Manufacturing and selling drugs known to be harmful to users	7.653	3.280	Seller
26	Knowingly selling contaminated food which results in death	7.596	5.202	Seller
28	Using heroin	7.520	4.871	

Table 9.1 (*continued*)

Rank	Crime	Mean	Variance	Illegal behaviour of Buyer and/or Seller
34	Selling secret documents to foreign governments	7.423	5.772	Seller
49	Selling marijuana	6.969	7.216	Seller
54	Selling pep pills	6.867	5.683	Seller
63	Manufacturing and selling autos known to be dangerously defective	6.604	5.968	Seller
71	Performing illegal abortions	6.330	5.723	Seller
73	A public official accepting bribes in return for favours	6.240	6.467	Seller
75	Knowingly selling stolen stocks and bonds	6.138	4.960	Seller
78	Theft of a car for purpose of resale	6.093	5.085	Seller
79	Knowingly selling defective used cars as completely safe	6.093	5.023	Seller
82	Knowingly selling stolen goods	6.021	4.463	Seller
90	Knowingly selling worthless stocks as valuable investments	5.821	5.021	Seller
92	Selling liquor to minor	5.789	7.572	Seller/buyer
94	Using stolen credit cards	5.570	5.832	Buyer
97	Lending money at illegal interest rates	5.653	5.775	Seller
98	Knowingly buying stolen goods	5.596	5.794	Buyer
102	Using false identification to obtain goods from a store	5.438	6.628	Buyer
103	Bribing a public official to obtain favours	5.394	6.198	Buyer
108	Soliciting for prostitution	5.144	7.687	Seller
110	Overcharging on repairs to automobiles	5.135	6.455	Seller
116	Overcharging for credit in selling goods	4.970	6.213	Seller
118	Smuggling goods to avoid paying import duties	4.918	5.618	

Table 9.1 (*continued*)

Rank	Crime	Mean	Variance	Illegal behaviour of Buyer and/or Seller
121	Knowingly using inaccurate scales in weighing meat for sale	4.786	5.902	Seller
126	Fixing prices on a consumer product like gasoline	4.629	6.069	Seller
127	Fixing prices on machines sold to businesses	4.619	6.218	Seller
128	Selling pornographic magazines	4.526	7.826	Seller
129	Shoplifting a book in a bookstore	4.424	6.551	
132	False advertising of a headache remedy	4.083	7.972	

Adapted from Rossi (1974).

If one compares the seriousness with which a seller's illegal activities are regarded with the seriousness of a buyer's participation in the same activities, typically the seller's participation is ranked as more serious than the buyer's. This is shown in the following comparisons (Zaltman and Wallendorf, 1979:129).

- selling heroin (No 3) with consuming heroin (No 28)
- offering bribes for favours (No 103) with accepting bribes for favours (No 73)
- knowingly selling stolen stocks and bonds (No 75), selling stolen automobiles (No 78), and selling stolen goods (No 82) with knowingly buying stolen goods (No 98)

The degree to which market behaviour defined as illegal is considered appropriate for social control varies not only from market sector to sector but from community (or sub-culture) to community (sub-culture). Patterns of averages conceal variation in attitudes and norm-enforcement among groups within a community and also with respect to socially differentiated 'others'.

Indeed, the market participants of a community may adhere rather strictly to exclusion rules when dealing with each other, but may relax the rules considerably in contacts with outsiders. Thus, we find sellers among Arabs, Jews, and other ethnic communities making *clear distinctions between different categories of buyers*, above all in terms of whether buyers belong to the sellers' ethnic community or not. What may be sold to one may not be sold to another. And, of course, the well-known pattern of price differentiation for different categories of buyers on the 'same market' is also widespread.

For Weber, however, the emergence of modern, rational capitalism was based, in part, on the systematic 'lifting of the barrier between internal and external ethics' (Weber, 1961:232). Collins (1986:88) points out:

> In virtually all premodern societies there are two sharply divergent sets of ethical beliefs and practices. Within a social group, economic transactions are strictly controlled by rules of fairness, status, and tradition; in tribal societies, by ritualized exchanges with prescribed kin; in India, by rules of caste; in medieval Europe, by required contributions on the manor or to the great church properties. The prohibition on usury reflected this internal ethic, requiring an ethic of charity and the avoidance of calculation of gain from loans within the community. In regard to outsiders, however, economic ethics were at the opposite extreme: Cheating, price gouging, and loans at exorbitant interest were the rule. Both forms of ethic were obstacles to rational, large-scale capitalism: the internal ethic because it prevented the commercialization of economic life, the external ethic because it made trading relations too episodic and distrustful. The lifting of this barrier and the overcoming of this ethical dualism were crucial for the development of any extensive capitalism. Only this could make loans available regularly and promote the buying and selling of all services and commodities for moderate gain. Through innumerable daily repetitions, such small (but regular) profits could add up to much more massive economic transactions than could either the custom-bound or the predatory economic ethics of traditional societies.

Market organizing principles and institutionalized rules of market behaviour are historically and socio-culturally specific. Among modern, industrialized nations, there is considerable but certainly not complete agreement. Obvious cases of disagreement concern the sale of alcoholic beverages, guns and drugs. Alcohol for consumption is banned altogether in many communities. In others it is heavily restricted and in some it is available to all but a few groups (the young are excluded under a certain age). And in a few countries, of course, there is no formal exclusion. Similarly, the organization and regulation of labour and credit markets varies considerably from country to country and even within a given country, from one sector to another and from one time to another.

To understand the background to such differences in market regimes, *one must explore the historical, institutional, and cultural specifics of nations* which relate to market structuration and regulation. Religion and ethnicity, political and social movements (such as temperance movements in the USA and Scandinavia), and the development of the state and of professional groups ('health advocates' and scientifically educated moralists) will play a role in differentiating the market structures of one country from those in others.

Since market systems are embedded in larger social structures, and these structures vary across communities and nations, they become segmented, both nationally and internationally. Buyers and sellers in different communities and nations, with varying moral and administrative practices, will be subject to somewhat different exclusion rules. *Even very similar rules will tend to be interpreted and enforced in different ways.* Markets dealing with more or less the same commodity will make up a patchwork, a more or less heterogeneous ecology of markets.

National and regional variation in market organizing principles and rules — and in their interpretation and enforcement — will have a segmenting affect on price formation, including differences between white, grey and black markets for the same or similar commodities. Complex price structures will emerge for the same or similar products. Such market segmentation and price differentiation do not arise only from variation in exclusion rules and their enforcement. Other social structural factors may have similar effects and should be systematically studied if any well-grounded theory of markets is to be developed. For example, consideration should be given to the social barriers to information, to communication, and to the formation and development of social networks in communities and nations. Class, ethnic, and religious cleavages in society are well-known sources of such barriers. Other barriers to communication and social organization arise from differential control over and access to wealth and credit in the society; and from differences among the major social groups in political power — that is, their ability to translate political power into economic power (in part through establishing and maintaining particular market rule systems).

Summing up and concluding remarks
Our general framework indicates the following:
(1) Markets are social organizations and, therefore, structured and regulated by social rule systems.
(2) The shape and stability of supply and demand curves — and price and market performance characteris´ics — are a function of the rule regimes articulating and governing a market or a set of interrelated markets.
Obviously, more purely economic factors — natural scarcity,

TABLE 9.2
Comparison of market regimes

Types of market rules	Type of market rule regime	
	Minimally regulated market	Substantially regulated market
I. SELLER ENTRY RULES	Relative openness of market for both sellers and buyers. Prices will approach marginal costs of additional units of production. Political ideology and distribution of socio-political power support minimum regulation.	Restricted seller entry. Prices higher than on the minimally regulated market. Opportunities for enhanced and/or more secure economic gains for included sellers. On the other hand, excluded sellers motivated to change rules and/or sell illicitly.
II. BUYER ENTRY RULES	Also, technological solutions found to communication and information processing problems. Failure to solve these problems, even in absence of much formal regulation, would induce actors to follow (according to Baker's model (1982)) unprescribed rules which segment market and result in price variance and volatility	Restricted buyer entry. Demand and prices lower than on the minimally regulated market. Excluded buyers miss opportunity to satisfy desires or needs. They may be willing to pay premium prices for satisfaction. Opportunities for sellers to enhance income by selling to illegal buyers.
III. TRANSACTION PROCEDURE RULES	Minimum of required procedures. This contributes to cost minimization, other things being equal. There are limited opportunities to develop markets for procedural services. Also, incentives are relatively weak to establish illicit markets based on circumventing required procedures.	Substantial required procedures. Prices will tend to be higher than on the minimally regulated market (under conditions where prices include costs of procedures). Opportunities generated for 'suppliers' of procedural services (lawyers, brokers, deed-searchers and other experts). Also, incentives to form illicit markets which do not follow the prescribed procedures.

Table 9.2 (*continued*)

Types of market rules	Type of market rule regime	
	Minimally regulated market	Substantially regulated market
IV. TRANSACTION QUANTITY AND QUALITY RULES	'Buyers beware'. 'Sellers be wary'. Sellers add to price risk considerations or discount expected losses. Buyers also 'add to the price' their assessment of expected losses from product or service failure etc. High uncertainty, confusion, deceit, conflict. However, see below about the importance of 'personal relationships', particularly for large transactions.	Market rules assure certain standards of quality, standard measures and weights, etc. Reduction of risks for buyers and also for sellers, and in general reduction of uncertainty. Contributes to the development of 'mass markets' – and economies of scale etc. – which depend on general or universal standardization and the establishment of impersonal, generalized trust.
V. COMPENSATION RULES	Minimal. 'Guarantees' and 'compensatory rules' are formulated and enforced in small communities and networks, where economic agents know and trust one another (within certain limits). Personal relationships reduce uncertainty and risks for opportunism in systems where few ideological or administrative controls regulate market transactions	Guarantees required to protect both buyer and seller interests. Protection of interests on a 'universal' as opposed to a personal level. Rules requiring seller to compensate buyers (and even possibly third parties) for losses. Raises prices, however, in predictable ways.

changes in factor costs, reduction in costs through economies of scale, rationalization and innovation — play substantial roles in market performance and price developments. But even in these cases, one can expect corresponding or related changes in market rules. Major changes in scarcity and technology in a sphere of social action typically lead to innovation in and restructuring of the rule systems governing social transactions in that sphere (see Chapters 14 and 17).

(3) Market rule systems operate on the components of social transactions, giving identity to and shaping patterns of social activity. They determine, for instance, (i) which specific types of buyers and sellers may participate (alternatively, which actors or groups are excluded); (ii) which commodities (with certain qualities, measures, etc.) may be exchanged; (iii) what procedures should be followed in carrying out market transactions and what constitutes a legitimate transaction (or type of transaction); (iv) where and when transactions may be performed.

We have suggested a few of the ways in which a market rule system — and changes in such a system — operates to limit or to expand participation of sellers and/or buyers. Similarly, it can limit or expand goods and services acceptable for trading (where both overall volume and/or variety are likely to be affected). Finally, the rule system may contract or expand required procedures, thus lowering or raising transaction costs.

Rule systems influence the price structure and other performance characteristics of markets by affecting the levels of market participation, the volume and variety of transactions, and transaction costs. Furthermore, our model implies the following:

(i) Rules limiting sellers enhance the opportunities for 'the select' to make economic gains (and impose 'opportunity losses' on those excluded). Since prices tend to be 'artificially high' under such social constraints, there are incentives for excluded sellers to collude with price-sensitive buyers to change the rules, either legally through political or similar action or through illicit market activity.

The costs of bringing about legislative or policy changes will often be high, if not prohibitive, at least in the case of many small or primarily local agents. On the other hand, the opportunities to operate successfully as an illicit seller will be greater for small or less visible agents. Of course, this can be offset in part through administrative measures and effectiveness. In systems with relatively effective administration, the problems and risks of apprehension and punishment increase as the illicit sellers enjoy success and expand.

(ii) The exclusion of some groups of buyers also creates incentives for illicit participation, since sellers may, other things being equal, enhance potential profits by selling illegally to excluded buyers. Again, the effectiveness of administrative or moral controls plays a decisive role.

(iii) Markets with stringent rules about commodity quality and other properties generate incentives for illicit markets under conditions where there is a potential demand for products below standard. Again, the likelihood of such a development will depend not only on the potential demand for such products but on administrative effectiveness and moral commitment in the community.

(iv) Market systems requiring extensive procedures in connection with exchange activity increase transaction costs as well as generate opportunities for service providers (unless these services are provided gratis by third parties such as the state). However, high transaction costs increase the incentives for buyers (and also for some sellers or potential sellers) to circumscribe market procedures, particularly when the costs are considered unnecessary or unproductive (as pointed out earlier, transaction procedures and related costs may be viewed as useful means to reduce high uncertainty and the risks of substantial losses, conflicts and litigation, etc.). Market rule systems do more than impact on legal market prices and market behaviour. They increase or decrease the incentives for the formation of illicit markets. These incentives are also affected by the ways in which enforcement costs are distributed, as argued earlier.

(v) A major new line of analysis offered by our approach is the consideration of the distribution of gains and losses arising from market rule systems. This question has only been briefly explored here, but the direction such analysis would take is fairly straightforward. Each rule system generates an array of benefits and losses (or lost opportunities). These concern not only different categories of market participants, such as buyers and sellers, but third parties. Here we include those 'third parties' who are denied access because of their lack of market capacity (income, property, credit), yet who experience their exclusion as an 'externality' which requires regime changes. Gains and losses are not only monetary in character. There are gains and losses in other value terms, such as those concerning core societal principles (honesty, lawfulness, solidarity, etc.).

(vi) Such societal consequences and distributional effects become the issues or dimensions of conflict around which groups of actors struggle to maintain or to change market regimes.

10

Collective bargaining regimes and their transformation:
The rise and decline of the Swedish Model

Anders Olsson and Tom R. Burns

Introduction

Conflict and struggle, to varying degrees, are endemic to capitalist societies. In modern, Western nations special institutions have been established and developed in order to structure and regulate conflicts between capital and labour. This institutionalization of conflict — and the establishment of conflict resolution mechanisms — takes the form of particular rule regimes: labour legislation, collective bargaining, mediation and arbitration boards and procedures, collective agreements, grievance procedures and so forth.

Collective bargaining, in particular, is governed in modern Western nations by certain regimes. The organizing principles and rules specify, among other things: the ways in which wage negotiations are to be organized and conducted; whether centrally, branch-wise, or locally; the factors considered in determining a frame for wage increases; the issues other than wages which may be legitimately negotiated in bargaining processes (or those strictly forbidden); and the possible linkages between issues, for example between wages, work rules, and productivity measures.

One characteristic feature of capitalism is its periodic destabilization and restructuring (DeVille and Burns, 1977). This chapter focuses on collective bargaining as one institutional area in which to examine certain destabilizing forces and the agents and social games involved in system restructuring. The study points up:

(i) the interplay between established rule regimes and concrete socio-economic developments: the transformation of the economy, shifts in strategic functions, the relative decline of industry and the emergence of the service economy, the growth in power of private and public white-collar groups associated with the transformation of the economy, and the societal struggle over income distribution in an economy which is stagnating as well as undergoing transformation.

(ii) social conflict and the exercise of (meta-)power in connection with efforts to structure and restructure social rule systems organizing and regulating particular economic processes and transactions, in this case collective bargaining and wage determination. Collective bargaining is something more than a rule-governed exchange between two parties, be it in economic or other terms. Flanders (1969:14) has stressed that even though a collective agreement may be called a collective bargain and it may have the legal status of a collective contract, it does not commit anyone to sell or buy labour. The collective agreement is meant to ensure that whenever a transaction does take place in the labour market, it will take place according to the provisions of the agreement. *These provisions are a set of rules intended to regulate the terms of employment contracts. Collective bargaining is thus in its essence a rule-making process. The effect of the negotiation of collective agreements is to impose certain limits on the freedom of actors in the labour market, without extinguishing their freedom.* (See Flanders 1969, especially pp. 14–16.)

Based on the power resources at their disposal, the actors join in negotiations to shape and invent new rules. The rules are then jointly determined by representatives of employers and employees who share responsibility for their contents and observance, often with legal underpinnings. Collective bargaining is thus analysable not only in terms of its economic consequences, but also as a process of 'private politics', a rule-making process which resides outside parliament. It follows that a union may be as interested in establishing its rights and action capabilities vis a vis employers as in achieving immediate material gains.

This chapter considers the organization of collective bargaining in the US auto industry, drawing on the important work of Katz (1982). The structure and some of the properties of the collective bargaining rule regime are specified. Recent restructuring of the regime as a function of the crisis in the US auto industry from the late 1970s is discussed briefly.

We examine the structural formation and reformation of the Swedish wage bargaining system, particularly 'The Swedish Model' of centralized wage negotiation and administration. The theoretical–methodological focus is on identifying several key organizing principles which give the system its identifying properties and stability, at the same time that institutional failures of, and emerging struggles around, established principles destabilize the system and set the stage for transition to other systems. We periodize the time frame since the Second World War on the basis of characteristic organizing principles prevailing in each period. This provides a point of departure for the systematic comparative analysis of the different systems in the various periods in terms of key performance variables. The concluding section discusses the future prospects for organized, stable collective bargaining in Sweden and some of the implications of the study for institutional innovation.

Collective barg.;ning in the US auto industry

The collective bargaining system in the US auto branch is a relatively well-defined social organization, developed and maintained by certain interests. The regime is derived, in part, from the general institutional framework for management/labour negotiations in industrial sectors of the US.[60]

Of course, specific interests have adapted and developed the system — by means of industry-wide as well as local innovations in a historical process.

The rule regime governing collective bargaining in the auto industry contains the following specific rule systems: (a) the social organization of collective bargaining, (b) rules governing negotiable issues (that is legitimate issues for bargaining) and linkages among issues in bargaining, and (c) the principles governing wage formation (arrived at through collective bargaining and holding for long periods of time). We present and discuss briefly these systems, as they operated until approximately 1980.

Organization of collective bargaining

(i) Wage negotiations were conducted nationally at the same time that they were company specific. Separate agreements were reached and, since 1955, contracts for three years were signed between the United Auto Workers (UAW) and General Motors, Ford, Chrysler, and American Motors. Of course, there was considerable overlap in the forms and content of these different agreements.

(ii) Although plant level wage negotiations took place and contracts were signed on this level, these were monitored closely by the national union to prevent wide divergence in the wage terms of local agreements. Many features of the local agreements, particularly those concerning wages as well as local strikes, required approval of the national union.

(iii) Work rule/work condition negotiations were the main issues of local negotiations: seniority ladder forms, job characteristics, rules concerning job bidding and transfer rights, health and safety standards, production standards and other rules affecting shop floor production. These issues could reflect — and allow for — local preferences and norms as well as adjustments to special local work conditions.

(iv) Disagreements and conflicts arising in connection with con-

FIGURE 10.1
Collective bargaining systems: the auto industry in the USA

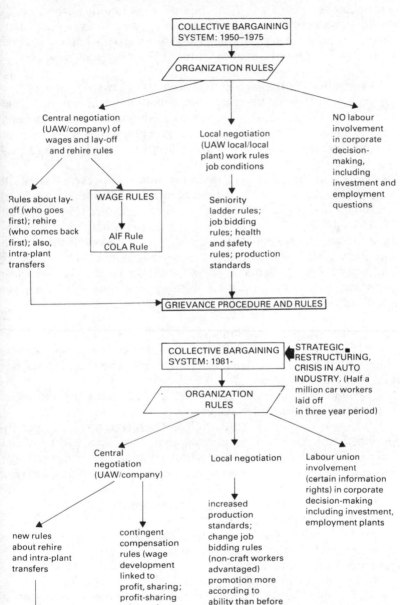

tracts — their interpretation and enforcement — were handled through a grievance system with binding third party arbitration. This was the end point of contract administration. Disputes concerning production standards, new job rates and health and safety issues were not resolved through recourse to arbitration but handled through other procedures and institutional arrangements.

Rules governing issues and linkages among issues in bargaining
(i) A key rule here separated wage bargaining from work rule bargaining. In part, this reflected the division between national and local bargaining. Nevertheless, even bargaining over work rules at the national level was kept in large part separate from wage bargaining.[61]
(ii) Collective bargaining in the auto industry focused largely on wages and contractually based job control (work rules). Corporate decisions — and labour participation in such decisions — were largely outside the scope of management/labour bargaining, in contrast to some developments in Europe, particularly Scandinavia and Germany where 'co-determination' became a major new ideology and institutional principle. (As we shall see later, union absence from corporate decision-making in this period contrasts with some recent developments in the US auto industry.)

Rules governing wage development
Katz (1982) refers to 'formula-like' rules governing the determination of wage and fringe benefit development. The two most important of these rules were:
    (i) Annual improvement factor (AIF) which, since the mid-1960s had amounted to three percent per year.
    (ii) Cost-of-living adjustment (COLA) escalator which originally provided full cost-of-living protection in the 1970s had provided approximately 80 percent protection (that is, 0.8 percent wage increase for 1 percent increase in the consumer price index (CPI)).

Stabilization of the rule regime: Actor commitments, effective adaptations, and the favourable economic context
The collective bargaining regime served to stabilize industrial relations in the US auto industry during the period 1950–1980. The prolonged strikes and tensions that characterized the industry in the immediate post-war period were avoided (Katz, 1983:6).
    The formula-like wage determination rules provided continuity in wage determination over time and across industry at any given point in time. Wages were more or less rigidly set from 1948–1979 among the Big Three producers (GM, Ford, and Chrysler) with few minor

exceptions. The level and structure of wages covered the entire industry. It was not modified to any great extent through local bargaining, according to Katz (1982) (it would be very useful to determine the extent of 'wage-drift' and variations in this over time). What were the factors underlying major actors' commitment to and support of the rule regime sketched above, particularly the wage rules at the national level and the work rules at the plant level?

COLA and AIF formulas, the core rules concerning wage determination, enjoyed support among all the key actors. Of course, the motivation for support varied among these actors:

● for the national union leadership, the steady adherence to the rules provided for standards of good performance in bargaining. Rank-and-file members could not fault the union leadership for securing wage increases that satisfied the rules during contract re-negotiations
● for rank-and-file members, the rules provided steadily and certainly real wage improvements. Also, the rules and resulting wage patterns satisfied workers' concerns about equity
● for management, adherence to the rules minimized conflict with labour. The uncertainty of wage developments and risks of major confrontations were thus reduced. This was particularly attractive in the context of stable growth in sales and high profitability

Also, management/labour adherence facilitated long-range planning (of labour costs). The continuity in labour costs provided by the wage determination rules was especially attractive to auto management, because of the long lead-times associated with new product development and investment planning[62]

The collective bargaining regime in the auto industry was relatively stable in large part because of the commitments of key groups of actors. The context of economic growth and generally favourable conditions for the industry played a key role, as pointed up by the impact of the crisis of the late 1970s discussed below.

In sum, the system with relatively rigid wage determination rules was attractive to major actors because it reduced the contentiousness of bargaining and the likelihood of strikes at the same time that it offered substantial gains to all. For management it provided wage cost predictability by limiting the uncertainty surrounding labour costs. It provided auto workers with more or less guaranteed real wage increases and at the same time satisfied equity norms. For the national labour leadership, the system reduced or eliminated the risk of major confrontations with unpredictable outcomes, at the same time that the satisfaction of rank-and-file members with their gains was maintained.

Given the above assessments, none of the major actors was inclined to change the regime, unless entirely new problems arose or the context of old problems changed markedly, which the regime could not deal with effectively. Attempts to change the regime in any substantial way would be conflict evoking — and with highly uncertain outcomes — at least in the context of the period, 1950–1975. Even in the absence of crisis or serious challenge, a rule regime is never fixed. Amendments, supplements and other elaborations as well as revisions are made periodically. Such piecemeal and limited changes — to be contrasted with the more radical changes that took place after 1980 — tended to preserve the basic structure of the regime.

One major factor underlying the limited adaptations in the rule regime prior to 1980 was market pressure. For instance, when national agreements were renegotiated in the midst of the post-war recessions, a few cents of the scheduled COLA increases were diverted to cover the increasing costs of the expanding fringe benefits won by the union in the national negotiations (Katz, 1982).

In the late 1960s and early 1970s when labour markets in the construction market tightened, the auto industry's national agreements provided an additional few cents for skilled tradesmen on top of the rule determined wage increases. In other words, the rule was adapted somewhat to take into account the shortage of skilled labour.

Also, local or regional conditions provided a point of departure for some deviation. Indirect changes in wage determination occurred at the local level through local agreements providing special definitions of job classifications. The concrete operation of piece-rate systems also modified wage levels, but by the late 1950s piece rates, with very few exceptions had been eliminated from the industry.

Economic crisis, struggle, and rule regime transformation
From the late 1970s until rather recently the US auto industry has been in a deep crisis. At the end of 1979 industry employment was approximately 1,000,000. By August, 1982, this had been cut in half (Katz, 1982). Three factors played a role in the crisis: (a) the rise in auto imports, particularly from Japan; (b) the deep recession during this period; and (c) structural shifts in demand, the overall decline in auto sales in the USA.

The major loss of sales of US auto companies resulted in very substantial layoffs which the UAW could not prevent (indeed, such decisions are within management's prerogatives, according to the prevailing rule regime, whereas in Sweden this is a matter for negotiation with labour unions). In this context, management took the initiative to try to radically alter rules concerning wage formation and work rules. They achieved striking successes in these efforts, as described below. The changes may not prove irreversible.[63] Nevertheless, they stand for the time being in sharp contrast to the rule regime which governed wage developments and collective bargaining in the period 1950–1980.

Although the bargaining around proposed changes in the rule regime was tough, the UAW was in no postion to effectively resist the changes, given generally unsympathetic governments, particularly the Reagan administration. Essentially, the AIF and COLA rules have been eliminated, replaced by 'contingent compensation schemes'. The latter connected wage increases to company performance, above all profitability. In some cases, profit sharing plans have been introduced.[64]

The drastic changes in wage-determination rules have been parallelled by reformulation of work rules and practices. These rules, as pointed out earlier, had a local job control focus. The threat of even more layoffs as well as of outsourcing of component supply (in some instances to Mexico) weakened the bargaining power of the unions. They were forced to accept extensive modification of work rules with a view to lowering production costs (and increasing productivity). Several of the major features of these changes were:

(a) production standards have been raised.
(b) job bidding rights have been modified to reduce the frequency of intra-plant transfers.
(c) production classifications have been broadened so as to include 'incidental machine maintenance' for non-craft workers.
(d) promotion rights (and the rules governing them) were reformulated to emphasize ability as much as seniority (previously only seniority had counted).
(e) the flexibility with which labour was to be deployed was increased (Katz, 1983).

In conceding substantial changes in wage determination and work rules, the UAW obtained in return the right to be kept informed and consulted about management strategic decision-making. In general, it was recognized as having a legitimate interest in such questions. That is, union representatives gained greater access to corporate decisions, in part in order that they could monitor corporate earnings and decisions on the plant level in connection with the contingent compensation schemes, in part to be informed and consulted about major business decisions planned or under discussion that would affect future employment. The unions insisted on these principles if they were to accept peacefully the new regime with company-based contingent compensation and major work rule concessions at local levels.

The rise and decline of the Swedish Model

Introduction

In this section, we describe and analyse the development of the Swedish wage negotiation system. First, we examine briefly the historical process, particularly after the Second World War, in which major actors struggled and negotiated in the formation and reformation of wage negotiation systems.

The discussion points out that a dominant coalition of employers and blue-collar union representatives, backed by Social Democratic governments, were instrumental in establishing the regime of centralized negotiations which ultimately became known as 'The Swedish Model'. The discussion also considers some of the challenges to it from within and from outside the system. During much of the post-World War Two period, the coalition of representatives of industrialists and industrial blue-collar unions dominated other interests, such as white-collar unions in the private sector, public sector employer and employee representatives, and local unions.

Since the mid-1960s, however, the power of the dominant coalition was eroded — and the Swedish Model which it had established and maintained was destabilized — by changes in the organization of the Swedish economy, the formation of a comprehensive welfare state, the growth of large white-collar labour collectivities (highly unionized) and intensified competition between employee collectivities, particularly between white-collar and blue-collar groups. Formal and informal organizing principles and rules were changed. Struggles are currently going on about the future organization of the system.

As we have seen in the previous section, each negotiation regime entails identifiable organizing principles and rules. For instance, there are explicit or implicit rules concerning which actors are included in bargaining (and those excluded). In the Swedish context, unions and companies outside the main employers' association and blue-collar association are excluded from negotiation activities, not to speak of 'syndicalist' and other radical groups). A regime also defines certain issues as 'legitimate'. In Sweden, wages and employment conditions, including fringe benefits, are legitimate issues. Management prerogatives were, until the 1970s, non-negotiable. Finally, certain principles govern the institutionalized strategies to ensure internal discipline in the ranks of the employers' association and the central blue-collar union (LO). Moreover, each party supports the other to a greater or lesser extent in maintaining internal discipline. This has been done, in part, by refusing to negotiate with, or to generally deal with, 'deviant' members. In the post-war period four major negotiation regimes can be identified. In the following subsections, we shall examine and provide a brief historical description and analysis of the formation and reformation of a few major features of these regimes, and the social agents and struggles involved in their development. Later, we shall briefly examine the performance characteristics of the four major negotiation regimes, as observable in patterns of wage formation and industrial conflict.

The decentralized system: An historical sketch
In Sweden the first associations of workers were founded in the mid-nineteenth century by skilled workers employed in small manufacturing enterprises (Ullenhag, 1971). Later during the 1880s, more militant unions were formed which were aimed more at countervailing the power of employers. During this time the social democratic movement developed and came to be closely associated with the rising unions.

In 1898 the 'Lands Organization' (LO) was constituted. It was from the start a *defensive institution* with a mandate to support unions which were facing lockout by employers. It had no mandate to support union strike initiatives (Ullenhag, 1971). This principle guided the strategic behaviour of LO until World War II. The major strike and lockout of 1909 reinforced the principle (see later discussion). An offensive LO would have been too vulnerable to the large lockouts — a major strategy pursued by the employers' organization at this time to destroy unions. Instead, the national industrial (sector based) unions held the initiative. These unions aimed in general at controlling the numerous, spontaneous strikes which occurred. Such strikes were often ineffective. At the same time, there were various good grounds — and numerous occasions — for industrial disputes. Until 1905 the employers made every effort to undermine unions and collective agreements. The high level of conflict in this formative period of the Swedish wage negotiation system was the result of union organization, the establishment of strike funds, development of militant strategies, the growth of union solidarity, and other social power developments in connection with the emergence of the labour movement.

Already in 1906 SAF, the Swedish Employers' Association, and LO concluded the 'December Compromise'.[65] SAF's policy at this time, as opposed to some employers who tried, without success, to break unions, was to recognize to a certain extent the rights to organize and negotiate but to insist on management's rights to manage. In exchange for recognizing the unions, SAF required its own affiliates to include a clause in all collective agreements affirming the principle of management prerogatives (Martin, 1984:196).

The rising power of the unions seriously challenged the dominance of the employers (Korpi, 1983:45). On two occasions in the first quarter of the twentieth century, major industrial conflicts took place. The 'great strike of 1909' resulted in a serious setback for the unions, LO losing half of its members. In the years following there was a marked decline in the number and scope of industrial disputes. Sixteen years later, on the other hand, the 'great lockout of 1925' was a failure for the employers, demonstrating that the lockout weapon was no longer a decisive weapon. Over 117,000 workers were locked out, compared to 71,000 in 1909. The employers drew the conclusion that it was no longer feasible to crush or seriously weaken the labour movement as they had almost succeeded in doing in 1909 (Westerståhl, 1945:146,154).

During the 1930s, key actors, the Social Democratic government, the central employers association (SAF) and the LO found the time opportune to establish and formalize a rule regime for industrial relations and collective bargaining. On the one hand, employers had failed, as mentioned above, to counter the growth and power of the union movement with the militant strategy of threatening and utilizing the lockout weapon. On the other hand, the LO had up to this time played an entirely defensive role. It had little interest in centralized negotiations due to the threat of SAF lockouts. Nevertheless, by now the Swedish labour movement was relatively well-established. Its political party, SDP, was the major force in a coalition government (with the Farmers' Party). The time was ripe for a shift in principles for organizing industrial relations, particularly LO's and SAF's roles. Also, the Social Democratic government was particularly interested in a new rule regime for industrial unions since its economic crisis policy was threatened by industrial instability in several sectors. And, of course, international uncertainties and threats during the 1930s reinforced the sense that 'a new order' should be established.

The result was the 'Main Agreement of 1938' (The Saltsjöbaden Agreement). This agreement between LO and SAF established an entire complex of rules and procedures for negotiations: rules to regulate strikes and lock-outs, rules governing the annulment of agreements, and rules for dealing with conflicts at companies of particular 'societal importance'. The agreement also established a labour market committee consisting of LO, SAF and neutral representatives. This committee had the responsibility of interpreting and enforcing the Agreement (see Westerståhl,1945).

The Main Agreement not only institutionalized conflict and conflict regulation, but institutionalized the division of power between employers and unions. Owners and managers were to continue to dominate management and production decisions, while workers could associate in labour unions and negotiate about wages and work conditions. The Main Agreement did not change the role of the LO in wage negotiations. The latter continued to be handled by the national unions and their locals. Nevertheless, even in the absence of central administration, *normative principles* were established which had a global organizing and coordinating effect, in particular the stress placed on 'cooperation' and 'negotiation' rather than on confrontation. (The shift in normative climate was reflected in the substantial decline in the incidence of industrial conflict and in working days lost due to industrial conflict.) In addition, there were a number of 'informal rules' which for decades played a strategic role in the organization of collective bargaining processes. For instance, from 1931 a 'priority rule' was established which made the Swedish metal workers' union, the largest and most powerful union in the LO, the front-runner and wage norm setter in negotiations.

- During the Second World War the labour unions and employers' associations were bound, as in many other countries, by a frame agreement. After the war, these agreements were terminated and the labour market agents returned to the pre-war arrangements of independent negotiations.

In 1946 LO recommended to its unions that they try to raise their wages substantially. The result was a relatively large increase of 15 percent and a threat of accelerating inflation. Therefore in 1947 (in agreement with the Social Democratic government), LO advised its member unions to show restraint. However, the average wage increase was 10 percent, viewed by the government as excessive. The government then urged LO to accept a wage-freeze. LO and its membership complied, simply extending the old wage agreement for another year. The following year the Social Democratic government wished to repeat the procedure. LO agreed but wanted to show special consideration for groups which had lagged behind. It turned out that so many special exemptions had to be made that the agreement would have been impossible to manage. Therefore, LO agreed to extend the 1947 agreement for yet another year. After two extensions of the agreement, LO was compelled in

1950 to release the accumulated demands for wage increases. The negotiations resulted in wage increases of 23 percent!

The decentralized system proved unable to effectively regulate wage negotiations and developments. This was, in part, because it allowed only two extreme responses: 'stop' and 'go'. The obvious weaknesses of such an arrangement in a small, open economy were a major motivation behind the formation of what became known as the Swedish Model.

The Swedish Model of centralized negotiations

In preparations for the 1952 negotiations, LO aimed to coordinate the various branch negotiations, allowing some exceptions from a general agreement for those unions with claims for disadvantaged groups of workers. The powerful metal workers' union and the building workers' union were sceptical. They and a number of other unions wanted to advance and negotiate their own claims. In the end, LO was only trusted with the task of negotiating an index agreement with SAF. SAF, however, demanded centralized negotiations in exchange for an index agreement. Only five LO unions (out of 44) were opposed to such centralized negotiations. Ultimately, SAF's proposal prevailed, imposing a new structure on wage negotiations at least temporarily.

The economy was sluggish in 1953 and 1954 so the Social Democratic government felt no need to press LO on wage restraint. In 1955 the economy picked up and prospects for wage increases in 1956 suggested that the government's stabilization policy would be in serious trouble. Already in 1955 LO had felt that centralized wage negotiations would be desirable for 1956 and, indeed, a central contract was signed with SAF.

In 1957 LO informed SAF that they could not participate in centralized negotiations. Instead, independent union negotiations were initiated. These gave meagre results, only fractions of a percent. LO was compelled to try to negotiate with SAF and , eventually, signed a two-year agreement. According to the newly promoted chairman of LO, Arne Geijer, SAF was responsible for the initiative to establish central negotiations. SAF managed to close the ranks of its members and hold a united front against the unions, particularly those unions such as Metal and Building workers which were somewhat opposed to central negotiations. SAF tactics succeeded in making clear to LO and its member unions that their best alternative was to support central negotiations. This was the backdrop for the 25 years of centralized negotiations between LO and SAF for the private sector.

The central white-collar union, TCO (White-collar Union Central

Organization corresponding to the all blue-collar LO), was included initially in the attempts to organize central negotiations. This cooperation fell through because of LO's adherence to a principle of combined absolute/percentage increases in contract formulation, whereas the white-collar unions would only accept percentage forms (since the latter maintain wage and income relativities, an important goal for white-collar unions in regard to white-collar/blue-collar income relations). The Swedish industrial white-collar union (SIF) signed central agreements with SAF in 1952 and in 1956, under the auspices of TCO. Since 1957, SIF and SAF negotiated centrally. Later (from 1969) a central cartel of private white-collar workers (ISAM – eventually, PTK, the Private White-collar Union Cartel) negotiated with SAF. Parallel centralization occurred on the public side.

From 1956 until 1966, the negotiations entailed a *priority rule.* SAF and LO negotiated before all other groups. After they reached an agreement in March or April, the other negotiations commenced. The SAF–LO agreement was a starting point and a norm. This contributed to a uniform wage development for both LO and white-collar groups (TCO). There were, however, large differences among unions in gains from local, *unauthorized* wage increases in the private sector. Similar differences arose between the private sector and the public sector where the latter did not have opportunities to sign, and to draw benefit from, such local, unauthorized contracts. Eventually rules were negotiated and established assuring compensation to blue-collar and salaried groups for the wage drift of LO groups enjoying unauthorized wage increases.

In sum, the centralized system of collective bargaining consisted during the period 1956–1966 of the following structural features (see Burns and Olsson, 1986; Lash, 1984):

(i) The private labour market peak organizations, LO and SAF, negotiated contracts within an established framework of rules and understandings. These agreements to a greater or lesser extent governed wage levels and structures in the LO/SAF area.

(ii) The LO enjoyed considerable but not complete control over its member unions and over shop floor negotiations and wage developments. While unofficial strikes were few, unauthorized wage increases ('wage-drift') were a persistent 'problem' during the entire period, often equalling the wage increases of the central agreements (see Table 10.1, pp. 204ff). (Such increases, not authorized by the central LO–SAF agreement, are referred to as wage-drift and are 'negotiated' at branch, enterprise or plant levels.) Branch unions and locals negotiate unauthorized increases, in part due to pressures from their members to maintain traditional relativities, not taken into account in the central agreements. Also, local labour shortages offer opportunities for ambitious blue-collar employees to effectively demand increases above the authorized levels, thereby improving their income levels. Employers often went along with these demands, either to avoid trouble with their union locals or to express genuine support for a more differentiated or what was felt to be, locally, a more suitable wage structure.

(iii) SAF was relatively successful in coordinating the employers' associations and in exercising control over individual employers. Nevertheless, SAF's sanctions — warnings, chastisement, and fines — against members' agreements to unauthorized wage increases never succeeded in eliminating the problem. As indicated above, individual employers, in the interest of good management–labour relations, would go along with special 'corrective' or 'compensatory' demands. In many instances, managers would take the initiative themselves in order to ensure adequate recruitment of qualified workers or to reinforce management discipline and to provide incentives for increased productivity (Burns and Olsson, 1986).

(iv) Up until the mid-1960s, LO/SAF exercised successful hegemony over the collective bargaining system. Private white-collar negotiations and negotiations in the public sector followed and were guided by the norms and developments in the LO/SAF area.

(v) Informally, a neo-corporatist institutional framework — with labour, capital, and state representatives in consultation and negotiation — prevailed. This provided the structural basis in Sweden for systematic regulation of labour markets and wage formation and, in general, the formulation and implementation of economic policy. However, *in the case of Sweden the state operated largely as a silent partner, having functioned largely on the meta-level in facilitating the formation of organizing principles and norms to govern collective bargaining.* The interests of the state, as indicated earlier, were in reducing industrial strife and controlling wage development and inflationary pressures.

The Swedish model was sustained over a long period (until the early 1980s), because two powerful and important agents, SAF and LO as well as key political actors had an interest in maintaining it. LO gained the opportunity to implement its solidaristic wage policy. SAF could moderate wage-increases and settlements and ensure a low level of industrial strife. The Social Democratic government succeeded in its economic policy and stabilization goals.

Elite efforts to maintain the system in the face of countervailing forces are pointed up by the informal rule of not allowing contracts other than the LO-SAF contract to be introduced into negotiations between SAF and splinter groups. SAF signed only 'contingent agreements' with independent unions; similarly, LO forced independent companies (outside of SAF) to sign such contingent agreements. This exemplifies how a participation (or exclusion) rule may be enforced. LO and SAF conspired successfully to restrict entry to the wage-bargaining arena.

While Swedish wage levels were among the highest in the OECD countries, sustained improvements in productivity and high rates of rationalization resulted in competitive relative unit labour costs, at least up until the early 1970s. Sweden's growth in industrial production and gross domestic product (GDP), although not spectacular during the period 1955 to 1970, was considerably better than those of the UK and USA, comparable to those of Germany, Austria, Belgium and Switzerland, and only surpassed by up-and-coming countries such as France, Italy, and of course, Japan. The inflation rate, while not in the low class of Germany and Switzerland, nevertheless was respectable up until 1970. As is generally known, Sweden's unemployment rate has been very low, an achievement which it has sustained until today. This accomplishment, which reflects a serious policy commitment, appears even more noteworthy in view of the poor performance on this score of most other OECD countries.

The Swedish collective bargaining system became a source of pride — and in some other countries with unstable industrial relations, an object of envy. The rate of industrial strife, in contrast to the turbulent 1920s and early 1930s when it was among the highest in Europe, has been one of the lowest in the Western world. This performance was blemished somewhat by the rise in unofficial strikes and the several major strikes which took place in the 1970s and early 1980s, a subject to which we return later (see Table 10.1).

The overall excellent economic performance of Sweden up until the late 1960s cannot be attributed only, or even mainly, to its centralized system of bargaining. Nevertheless, in a society with a powerful labour movement and the highest level of union density, the performance is noteworthy. Certainly, the collective bargaining system contributed to labour market discipline and stability, an essential ingredient in the economic performance of any industrialized country.

The Swedish Model in transition

1966 was a momentous year, with several noteworthy developments. A major industrial conflict threatened, but LO and SAF managed to reach an agreement. The agreement gave LO workers a 12 percent increase over three years. Included here was 4 percent compensation for reduced working hours. At the same time, the salaried employees managed to negotiate an increase of 18–20 percent in a three year agreement. This was a challenge to LO, to be followed by further challenges. The LO was particularly critical of the compensation of salaried workers for the wage-drift of industrial workers. Wage-drift reflected tough rationalization in industry, LO argued, and white-collar groups should not draw benefits from it, through for instance automatic compensation. Such tensions between blue-collar and white-collar collectives and between the private and public sectors became an increasing threat to the stability of the Swedish wage negotiation system and its effectiveness in regulating conflict.

1966 was the first year when salaried employees employed by the state and local authorities enjoyed the full right to negotiate and to strike. *This changed the power base for the publicly employed. It also increased the number of full-fledged negotiating agents and complicated negotiations considerably in what had been a highly centralized system.*

Several innovations in contracts were introduced around this time. A persistent issue in the central negotiations concerned the problem of dealing with industrial branches where workers who did not enjoy opportunities for wage-drift gains expressed discontent. Until 1966, the principal solution had been to try to settle such matters ahead of — and therefore separate from — the main negotiations. Rising discontent and the number of requests for exemptions from the main agreement reached the point where it became very cumbersome negotiation-wise and administratively to continue with such an arrangement.

Ultimately, SAF and LO agreed to introduce a wage development guarantee for its members along with a new clause in the main agreement allowing for higher increases in branches with low wage levels. This arrangement reflected a fundamental understanding between LO and SAF on the princple that a long-term stable wage development was desirable and that this depended in part on a *'fair wage structure'*. The new arrangements were to have substantial and unforeseeable impacts later.

The discussion following the negotiations led to a proposal from SAF for a coordination of all negotiations which entailed absolute increases (as opposed to percentage increases). Economic experts were to decide on the total level of such raises. Deductions for wage-drift and other labour costs were to be made to ensure the maintenance of internationally competitive labour costs and investment propensities. The remainder after deductions was to be divided between blue-collar and white-collar collectives.

Both the blue-collar and white-collar central organizations, LO and TCO respectively, rejected the proposal. Instead, SAF, LO, and TCO agreed to establish an expert group of leading economists from their organizations to investigate the role of wages and salaries in the economy. The 'EFO group' (Gösta Edgren, Karl Olof Faxen, and Claes-Erik Odner) formulated the *Scandinavian or EFO model* for the Swedish labour market (Edgren et al.,1970). The rules of the model determined an available economic latitude for wage increases in the private sector based on growth in productivity. The rules for distribution of available income were to be negotiated in collective bargaining. It was understood that the distribution would be carried out, in part. according to the 'solidary wage policy', which was pushed by low income unions in LO, in order to improve the income levels and wage relativities of low wage workers. According to the model, public sector collectives would receive increases matching those in the private sector. These matching increases were expected to be inflationary, since they would not be based on corrresponding increases in productivity.

Clearly, the model combined the major concerns of the two dominant actors at that time: SAF's interest in limiting wage formation in the private sector to a level consistent with productivity increases and in assuring the leading role of the private sector in wage formation; LO's interest in assuring sustained, and reasonably predictable, real increases for blue-collar workers and at the same time in maintaining its leadership role and the integration of the blue-collar labour movement. This was particularly important vis a vis the low-income unions (such as textile, transport, and retailing), who would be reluctant to accept the wage-restraint discipline imposed by the rules of the EFO model.

After 1967 LO and TCO initiated discussions on the possibilities of coordinating their negotiations. These were aborted when SIF, a major union in TCO, publicly criticized the idea. LO continued to press for greater coordination. Indeed, LO seems to have been the only major agent on the labour market which has had a sustained interest in coordinating negotiations on the labour market as a whole. In 1969 the industrial white-collar union (SIF) along with the foremen's union (SALF) moved to counteract the LO position by signing an early agreement with SAF, that is prior to LO (and the Metal Workers' Union).

Upon obtaining the right to strike, salaried workers in the public sector became an increasingly important factor in the wage determination process. The total number of employees in the public sector substantially increased during this period in connection with the very rapid growth in public expenditures and of the 'welfare state' generally (see Table 10.1, pp. 205ff).

LO's share of total union memberships dropped from 81 percent in 1950 to 64 percent in 1980. This is one of several indicators of LO's loss of dominance in the collective bargaining system. Actors which emerged and increased in importance were public worker unions, public employers' representatives (state and municipalities), and white collar unions in the private as well as public sectors. The latter established large cartels and formulated militant policies. For instance, the white collar unions in the private sector formed a cartel (PTK), which negotiated with SAF. In this complicated setting, LO and SAF were no longer hegemonic. The wage negotiation process became an equation which a sizeable group of actors attempted to solve, *in the absence of institutions which would enable them to directly negotiate and to settle with one another.* Instead, labour collectives tended to negotiate with one another indirectly through their employer counterparts.

Several of the new types of negotiation problems and conflicts which emerged in conjunction with these developments were: (a) Salaried employees became more insistent in their demands for compensation for industrial workers' wage-drift, on the one hand, whereas LO insisted on compensation for salary merit increases among salaried employees. A major source of conflict between LO and the private white-collar cartel of unions (PTK) has been the issue of the *formula for wage-drift compensation.* In 1977 an 80 percent compensation rule (instead of 100 percent) was forced on the white-collar cartel, PTK by SAF through threatening a major lock-out. However, the struggle has continued and was a major factor in the breakdown of cooperation between LO and PTK. Along similar lines, Metall, the Metal Workers Union, tried (1980) to introduce a policy that salaried employees be laid-off just as blue-collar workers are subject to layoffs under current operating principles. (b) There emerged and deepened tensions and disagreements between private and public sides of the white-collar workers' movement. (c) There were also increased tensions and conflicts between communal worker unions and private sector unions within LO over questions of wage-drift. (d) TCO unions and the 'academic white-collar unions' competed and struggled in the private as well as the public spheres.

At the end of the 1960s and during the 1970s unofficial strikes became an increasing problem (see Table 10.1). By international standards, the strike-wave was minor. However, it was seen as undermining LO's position. The continuation of wage-drift, reaching particlarly high levels in some years during this same period, also pointed up the inability of LO and SAF to control their members. Employers reached agreements with local labour unions which violated the spirit, and often enough the letter, of central contracts.

As a result of growing unrest on the labour market, the formal agreement for 1970–1971 provided for very high wage increases. Then in 1971, in reaction to the downward business cycle, LO signed an agreement involving moderate wage increases. As this agreement expired, the business cycle started to turn upward. At the same time the oil-crisis struck. A downturn was expected in Sweden. In this context LO signed a low increase contract for one year. Since business continued to boom, company profits soared. Wage-drift jumped markedly.

The exercise of wage restraint became increasingly problematic. The Social Democratic government hoped to establish a new principle for wage negotiations. The basic problem was that the government could only influence the central actors to a very limited degree. These in turn enjoyed only modest influence over their members and wage determination. Local actors continued to generate wage-drift and to contribute to the wage explosion in the mid-1970s. At the same time, the various 'wage development' indexes or guarantees spread wage-drift developments throughout the economy, private as well as public sectors.

Increasingly, the 'question of taxes' became a labour market question. A few white-collar unions, had made this an issue already in the 1960s. But high marginal tax rates in Sweden — which became particularly pronounced in the period around 1970 — made it increasingly difficult for these unions to raise the disposable income of their members (rising inflation was also to play a role in limiting gains in real disposable income). The LO under Arne Geijer opposed linking the tax question to wage and income questions. This agenda rule held until the new LO head, Gunnar Nilsson, came into power in 1971.

It had become obvious to most that taxes had to be brought into the discussion of wages and income, at least in a country with tax rates as high as Sweden's. The Social Democratic government also realized that it was no longer possible to raise additional tax revenues through income tax. A 'package solution' was attempted during the so-called 'Haga Meetings', 1974–1976, with the participation of the employers, the major central unions and the state. Proposals, initiated by the government, became 'informal agreements' coupling wages and salaries, taxes and unit costs of employees with each other. The new deal entailed reductions in income taxation in exchange for labour unions showing wage restraint. At the same time, the loss of revenue to the state was to be counter-balanced by increases in 'employer fees' (a percent tax on employee income which the employer is obliged to pay the state). These fees increased by 4 percent annually between 1973 and

1977, driving up the unit labour costs of Swedish workers and salaried employees.

Thus, not only did centrally negotiated wages increase substantially in the mid-1970s, but wage-drift and employer fees as well. The result was a dramatic increase in total employee costs (more than 22 percent increase from just 1974 to 1975).

The Swedish model depended on growing income available for wage increases, that is, an expanding economy.[66] Economic growth could be divided between profits, wages and the demands of a growing public sector. This model faced formidable problems when economic stagnation set in and persisted at the same time that the public sector and transfer payments continued to expand. The slowdown in growth transformed what had been a more or less 'positive-sum game' into a zero-sum game. At the same time, the increase in the number of powerful actors — without an institutional framework to coordinate and regulate the new, destabilizing interactions — contributed to the relative decline of the powers of each actor to influence the wage and salary systems in favourable directions.

In these changed circumstances, the SAF–LO coalition could no longer dominate incomes policy, wage negotiations and wage developments as they had done earlier. New actors with diverse interests and aims were included in the collective bargaining system. The wage formation process developed into a wage-carousel where the demands of one labour union pushed up the demands of others. None of the actors enjoyed sufficient control over the situation to be able either to fulfill its goals or to establish a new system. This situation led to high uncertainty and increasing conflict potential.

In 1980 the unthinkable in Sweden happened. Labour market tensions resulted in a major conflict with more than 20 percent of the labour force on strike or locked-out. The Swedish economy was at a near stand-still for almost two weeks.[67]

A new and uncertain mood set in after 'The Great Conflict'. On the one hand, the general attitude was 'never again'. On the other, some key actors concluded that a new collective bargaining system was needed. The large companies in the engineering branch — Volvo, Electrolux, LM Eriksson, Saab-Scandia, Asea, among others — were the most open and assertive about this. They increased their earlier pressures to return more to branch level agreements (and perhaps ultimately to a system where enterprise level negotiations would prevail).

Although negotiations in 1981 followed the normal, centralized pattern, SAF had already decided to act upon the initiative of the Engineering Federation (VF). A change in SAF's statutes was necessary in order to shift to branch level negotiations. This shift was made in 1982, allowing VF to carry through its plan for more decentralized negotiations.

Later, in the course of the 1982–83 negotiation round, VF signed an agreement with the Metal Workers' Union (Metall). It also signed an agreement with the salaried employees union (SIF) in the private sector. The strategy pursued by the federation was similar to that used by SAF in the 1957 negotiations. In this case, however, SAF stalled the central negotiations while VF was allowed to deal directly with Metall. Metall felt that to oppose VF, possibly by striking, in order to maintain centralized negotiations would have been a move very uncertain of success and would have denied them opportunities to settle old claims with VF (which was the carrot that VF offered). Any other response would have been difficult for Metall to justify to its members.

Branch negotiations between employer federations and labour unions became the dominant pattern in 1984, although LO tried to coordinate the negotiations on its own (that is without support from SAF). The negotiations resulted in high nominal wage increases.

Inflation in Sweden reached one of the highest levels among OECD countries. The Social Democratic government took several initiatives, in particular calling 'national meetings' in 1984 with the participation of the government, unions and employer organizations to discuss questions of wages, income, and economic policy. Vague agreements to adhere to a five percent wage increase ceiling were made. LO, supporting the Social Democratic government's policy, managed with considerable effort — and not without some assistance from the government — to keep its memberships within the five percent frame. On the other hand, there was considerable uncertainty during Spring, 1985, whether the white-collar unions would adhere to the five percent ceiling or not (with LO threatening to tear up its contract if adherence was not achieved). A major strike of public sector employees was unleashed in May, stopping all air traffic and a number of other important services. The strike continued for three weeks and resulted in an agreement above the five percent ceiling (although the public unions viewed the 'excess' as promised compensation for losses the previous year).

New internal and external problems and conflicts
Swedish industrial relations, and in particular labour–management negotiations, face problems and challenges today which did not exist earlier or were of an altogether different character at the time the Swedish Model was established and functioned more or less effectively.

Some of the major problems and conflicts which have emerged

and become more serious over the past 10 to 20 years are:

(i) The set of economic and political constraints and opportunities within which collective bargaining takes place have been transformed. Above all, major changes have occurred in the macroeconomic and political context: (a) The Swedish economy has become increasingly internationalized, with growth in the size and importance of the export sector; at the same time, the international economy has been, since the early 1970s, turbulent and unstable; (b) there has been economic stagnation since the late 1960s (see 'change in GNP' and 'change in industrial production' in Table 10.1), which has evoked struggles among groups trying to maintain or increase real income levels at one another's expenses; (c) an immense welfare state and public sector has been established, with its heavy demands, through taxation, on private income; (d) The problems of achieving economic stabilization in a complex, externally dependent economy have become formidable. Policies and institutional measures which worked relatively well earlier no longer assure stabilization, in part because the problems are to a certain extent international in character and the nation–state, particularly a small one, has great difficulty dealing effectively with them on its own. Also, various government policies, including taxation, and labour market legislation have had a complex, inconsistent impact on wage negotiation processes and on labour markets generally.

(ii) Labour market actors and their relations have been transformed. The major developments here have been (a) the emergence of powerful salaried employee unions and the substantial growth of the public segment, where the latter has quite different 'game rules' and development logic than the private sector (particularly the open, internationalized ﹒ ﹔ctors) and (b) the erosion of LO–SAF dominance over collective bargaining and wage development in Sweden.

The salaried employees have established themselves as important actors. This has made the labour movement more heterogeneous. Moreover, there is no intimate linkage between the Social Democratic Party and the salaried employees' unions corresponding to that between the SPD and the LO.

Important and powerful enterprises, such as Volvo, Electrolux, LM Eriksson, Saab–Skandia, as well as the export sector generally, explored new systems of production organization and payment, geared to the demands of their production and markets, particularly export markets, as well as to rapid changes in technology. As a result, these actors became less and less disposed to accept the SAF's authority and attempts to impose discipline.

(iii) New types of tensions, negotiation problems, and conflicts have emerged in connection with the appearance of new actors and relationships. Thus, a collective bargaining system which had been relatively simple, dominated by SAF and LO and their central members, has been restructured by the appearance of new and powerful actors, in particular the salaried employee unions, both on the public and private sides. In general, there has been an intensification of inter-group competition and distributional conflicts. This concerns, above all, struggle among labour union cartels such as LO and the private white-collar cartel (PTK), and public sector unions and private sector unions (these tensions and conflicts are found also within the LO).

(iv) The struggle between the public and private parts of the economy has become more open and systematic. Employers and unions on the private side act in consort to improve wages and salaries in the private sphere relative to the public sphere. And, in turn, public sector unions and/or employers try to counteract or nullify the private sector moves. The public sector unions insist that they want no more but also no less than groups in the private sector. On the other hand, SAF, LO, and PTK are in general agreement that manufacturing employees should get more. The public/private struggle concerns not only income distribution and wage relativities, but also questions of initiative, status and power in collective bargaining processes.

(v) Central–local tensions and conflicts. This is not only a question of wage drift, unofficial strikes, and local tendencies to oppose and to deviate from central agreements and 'income policies'. It also relates to the demands which local organizations and interests make on the central organizations. In some cases these demands relate openly to freedom to take initiative and to 'negotiate on their own', as exemplified in the move of the employers of the engineering branch (VF) to decentralize wage negotiations, at least to the branch level. The problem of central–local tensions — not a new phenomenon in the Swedish context — has become more acute over the past 15 years, in part because of the very success of the central incomes policy (that of solidarity) bringing about substantial income compression; and, in part, because of turbulence, uncertainty and failures of economic policy, in the face of global shocks, recession, and inflation.

Periodization and empirical performance of the Swedish WNS[68]

Introduction: Four epochs of social organization
In this section we periodize the post-war history of the Swedish

wage negotiation system (WNS) into four periods or epochs. These are defined according to system organizing principles and functioning. This should be stressed: *The epochs are divided according to regime principles and not according to economic criteria.* The economic circumstances are of course of great importance, *but they provide the setting in which the actors play, they do not determine the logic of the situation.*[69]

Each epoch can then be characterized by a rule regime with certain organizing principles and core rules. The regime associated with an epoch structures fields of action and games relating to wage negotiation: participating actors, rules of the game, legitimate issues and strategies, structures of action opportunities and payoffs. This results in certain observable patterns of performance but also efforts to maintain or reform the particular wage negotiating system. Thus, our analysis of the social organization of the Swedish WNS is combined with quantitative analyses of wage agreements, wage-drift, and industrial conflict rates, among other variables.

In a certain sense, we associate different analytical models with the four epochs, where each epoch is expected to exhibit differing patterns of negotiation and conflict, negotiated outcomes, and wage performance. We should stress that we are not trying to explain the performance of the Swedish economy during the years encompassed by the four epochs. Our aim is a more modest one, concerned with explaining some of the performance characteristics of the wage negotiation system.

In the first epoch (I), the organizing principle of the WNS was decentralized, that is branch specific, union-level negotiations for blue-collar workers. This system was transformed into a system with centralized LO–SAF negotiations, which characterized the second epoch (II). In the transition from epoch II to III, the centralized system with LO–SAF hegemony was transformed into a bi-polar system with centralized private and public negotiations. A dominant game in this period entailed competition between public and private employee collectivities, played out through their negotiations with representatives of public and private employers, respectively. At the end of epoch III, the wage negotiation system was transformed further into a multi-polar system, involving complicated income distribution struggles between public and private, blue- and white-collar collectivities. While in epoch II LO and SAF could disregard — or settle more on their own terms with — other groups of employees, in the later epochs other collectivities had the power to insist on their terms.

The social organizational features of the four epochs are summarized below:

I: 1946–1955. The epoch of decentralized, separate branch-level wage negotiations. The period, starting after the Second World War, ended with the establishment of central wage negotiations. During this period LO and SAF had little to say about the conduct of wage negotiations. There was an informal rule prevailing that the Metal-Workers' Union negotiated first and the others followed. The latter had the opportunity to base their demands on the agreement achieved by Metall, the largest and most powerful union. Also, the LO-economists, Rehn and Meidner, argued that the unions should try to get as much as they could when business went well and there was a high demand for labour.

LO was in no position to enforce wage restraint. Systematic restraint could be achieved temporarily only through exhortations of LO and the Social Democratic Government and/or through deflationary policies.

II: 1955–1965. The 'Golden Age' of the Swedish Model, with central negotiations and SAF–LO hegemony. SAF and LO in large part dominated the wage negotiation process and outcomes. Their negotiation results served as the norm for the rest of the labour market. Central negotiations between SAF and LO were conducted according to a formula of rules which took into account productivity increases, international and national economic developments (see p. 193 concerning the EFO model). Wage agreements were reached which were in large part consistent with stable economic development.

However, during this period, wage negotiations became more and more difficult, in part because of the great number of exemptions which had to be made in order to assure the cohesiveness of LO (and individual union acceptance of central negotiations).[70] Public and private white-collar unions played no major roles in the wage bargaining processes. Public employees did not have the right to strike and, therefore, were in no position to launch a major challenge to the system. Moreover, both the public and private white-collar employees were organized into several unions and served more as networks and opinion forums than bargaining agents.

Public sector employment grew substantially during the period as a result of the rapid expansion of the welfare state. There was a parallel increase in the number of white-collar employees in the private sector. White-collar workers in both the public and private sectors increasingly joined unions. Nonetheless, only 57 percent of the white-collar workers were organized compared to 90 percent of the blue-collar workers; LO had 3.3 times as many members as the white-collar workers' peak organization (TCO). The latter, in contrast to LO, has never been a bargaining agent or a major

political force. Without a doubt LO, with its close informal ties to the Social Democratic Party, was the dominant peak organization on the employee side and a formidable counterpart to SAF, particularly in the context of Social Democratic governments.
III: 1966–1973. The decline of SAF–LO hegemony and the establishment of bi-polar centralism. There emerged a new central arena, public sector wage bargaining, with powerful new actors, the public sector unions, challenging the dominance of LO and SAF. These unions refused to be governed by several of the principles and formulas governing the earlier epoch.

In 1966 public employees obtained the legal right to strike and quickly became full-fledged negotiation agents. Their unions were eager to settle old scores. For instance, public employees neither benefited directly from wage-drift which many production workers enjoyed, nor did they have guarantees or compensation for wage-drift. Certain categories of employees had fallen substantially behind in their wage development. (Although 'civil servants' were presumed not only to have higher status but to enjoy higher incomes than industrial workers.)

Through a major strike against the school system, teachers achieved major increases in their salaries in 1966.

In 1969 the white-collar unions in the private sector (SIF, SALF and CF) managed to get together for the first time and signed a five year joint agreement with SAF. This signalled the entrance of yet another powerful actor into the Swedish WNS, although a formal cartel was not established until 1973. The long contract period of the agreement proved to be a major liability in the turbulent early 1970s and effectively excluded them until 1973. The private white-collar workers fared worse during this period than they had earlier, relative to blue-collar workers. While the latter received increases on the average of 9.1 percent, the former got only 7.4 percent under their contract terms. They were to make up for this initial failure by organizing into a powerful cartel, PTK, and negotiating much more militantly, particularly with an eye on blue-collar developments. This contributed to the formation of an additional central arena.
IV: 1974–1985. Multi-polar centralism with a set of powerful peak collectivities. This period was characterized by multiple arenas at the central level and new forms of coalition formation. LO and SAF no longer dominated wage developments. A new set of actors fully exercised their rights to battle over their share of income. A sustained competition between the public and private sectors of the economy had begun. Relativities between public and private employee collectivities became increasingly difficult questions.

More than 70 percent of the white-collar employees in Sweden were by now organized. The private white-collar cartel, PTK, negotiated with SAF for the first time in 1974. Wage competition between blue- and white-collar unions and between private and public sector collectivities became fully established. These struggled with one another at the national level over income distribution.

A characteristic feature of the epoch was the preoccupation with complex calculations of relativities and the formulation of complex guarantees (indexation) of relative developments among different collectivities. Furthermore, a new type of game emerged where new coalition partners in negotiations were sought. Sometimes LO and PTK negotiated together vis a vis SAF, sometimes not. A constellation of public sector unions, known as the 'gang of four' — an on-and-off-again coalition of blue-collar and white-collar collectivities in the public sector — was established to try to enhance their bargaining power and to improve their position relative to the private sector collectivities.

These struggles and games gave rise to high uncertainty and serious tensions and threats, leading to strikes in some cases and setting the stage for the 'Great Conflict' of 1980. This also became a period where there were manifest struggles over maintaining, reforming, or transforming the wage negotiation system.

System performance variables
We have examined a number of quantitative variables which could be expected to be affected by the particular organizing principles, rules of the game, and negotiation procedures of the WNS systems in the different epochs which have been identified. Among the variables examined are wage formation for blue- and white-collar workers, including wage-drift for the former, industrial conflicts including 'wildcat strikes', and the relationship between formal agreements and wage-drift. In addition, organizational data on unionization, employment and other economic indicators are presented.[71] *Means and standard deviations (SD) are given for each epoch.*

Analysis and conclusions
Epoch I, as period IV, was a turbulent period with high variance in wage developments, in inflation, in changes in industrial production, and in changes in industrial profits. The international inflation in 1949–1950, in part in connection with the Korean war, spurred this development. Also, central control over performance outcomes and developments was very limited.

TABLE 10.1a
System performance variables

Variables	Epoch			
	I 1946–55	II 1956–65	III 1966–73	IV 1974–
Blue-collar workers				
Total wage including wage-drift	9.26%	7.18%	9.06%	9.8%
SD	6.3	1.5	1.8	3.7
Real total wages	5.0%	3.2%	3.9%	− 0.1%
Formal contract	5.0%	3.2%	4.9%	5.8%
SD	5.1	1.2	1.8	2.6
Wage-drift	4.2%	4.0%	4.2%	4.0%
	1.4	0.9	1.2	1.8
Formal contract/ wage drift	1.0	0.8	1.3	1.7
SD	0.8	0.3	0.5	0.9
Correlation agreement × wage-drift	0.86	0.01	−0.30	0.38
White-collar workers				
Total wage increase	—	7.3%	7.4%	9.5%
SD	—	1.2	1.1	3.8
Real total wages	—	3.04%	2.12%	− 0.15%
Formal contract	—	4.9%	6.0%	7.3%
SD	—	1.6	1.2	4.25
Wage-drift	—	2.6%	1.3%	1.8%
SD	—	0.8	0.3	0.8

TABLE 10.1b

Variables	Epoch			
	I	II	III	IV
Conflict variables*				
Conflicts	174	49	162	536
Wildcat strikes	—	(0.45)	38	50
Unionization variables				
Relative size of LO to white-collar collectivities	4.4	3.3	2.2	1.8
White-collar degree of organization	—	57%	63%	>70%

*Working days lost in 1000s per year.

TABLE 10.1c

Economic background variables	I	II	III	IV
Change in GNP	3.8%	4.1%	3.6%	1.4%
SD	2.0	2.0	1.8	2.1
Inflation	4.4%	3.9%	5.2%	10.3%
SD	4.8	1.6	2.2	2.0
Unemployment	2.7%	1.7%	2.2%	2.0%
SD	0.4	0.4	0.4	0.3
Change in productivity	—	4.5%	4.6%	1.4%
SD	—	1.5	1.0	1.8
Change in industrial production	5.6%	5.5%	4.5%	−0.2%
SD	6.2	2.5	2.4	3.9
Industry profits	—	5.4%	4.2%	3.2%
SD	—	0.9	0.9	2.2
Public sector employment (1000's)	—	—	1057	1391
Increases in employment tax, including social security (white collar)	—	0.7%	1.1%	2.1%
SD	—	0.2	0.6	2.2

Sources: See note 71.

The data indicate that during the first period the average blue-collar wage increase was 9.3 percent per year. The variation was enormous, with a minimum of 0 percent (wage freeze) and a maximum of 21.6 percent. The standard deviation was 6.3. This was a period of stop–go cycles, where the government tried to stabilize the economy with macro-economic policy measures. Wage increases were higher only in the fourth epoch, and the variation in the first period has never been matched since. The largest part of the increases occurred in the union branch negotiations which averaged 5 percent. The largest variation was also to be found in these agreements. Still, a large part of the wage increases stems from wage-drift. This was on the average 4.2 percent during this epoch, with a standard deviation of 1.4. The average of the ratio of agreement wages to wage-drift was 1.0 with a standard deviation of 0.8.

The performance pattern in Epoch II differs substantially from that of the first Epoch, including the variance in wage-drift (although average wage-drift itself did not differ significantly. This pattern holds for the entire post-war period). Worker wages grew on the average with 7.2 percent per year, white-collar workers wages with 7.3 percent. Compared to the earlier as well as later periods, variance in key performance variables was low. Industrial conflicts, including 'wildcat strikes' were rare.

The economic circumstances during this period were very favourable. GNP growth was on the average 4.7 percent during the period, inflation on the average 4.1 percent. Productivity grew on the average with 4.5 percent, industrial production with 6.6 percent.

Compared to the preceding period, wages grew considerably faster in Epoch III, but variance remained relatively low. Particularly noteworthy was the emergence of a negative correlation between increases in wages through formal central contracts and wage drift. (In the preceding period the correlation had been close to 0.0.) There was a three-fold increase in the rate of industrial conflict (measured by working-days lost in industrial conflicts), putting it on a level comparable to that found in Epoch I (still very low by international standards).

The economy performed fairly well. GNP grew on the average with 3.6 percent, industry production with 4.5 percent, productivity with 4.6 percent, while inflation was on the average 5.2 percent. The state's finances were sound, public sector employment was growing, so were also taxes and payroll taxes (which grew on the average with 1.1 percent a year).

In Epoch IV, the average nominal wage increase is the highest of the four periods. The variation in wage increases was only greater in the first period, which resulted also from a pluralist negotiation system. Although wage drift varies the most compared to the other epochs, the variation in contract wages is even larger. The correlation between wage-drift and agreement wages became positive in this epoch. During this period the average working-days lost in industrial conflicts rose to 536 000/year from 162 000/year in the preceding epoch. A substantial part of this is due, of course, to the 'Great Conflict' of 1980. Nonetheless, other indications were the substantial increase in 'wildcat strikes' and in the number of negotiations which required mediation.

The fourth epoch is not only characterized by substantial changes in the WNS, but by a growing sense of crisis. The 1973 oil price shock and the subsequent adjustments show up strongly in the economic variables. GNP only grew with 1.4 percent on the average, productivity with 1.4 percent. Industrial production actually decreased with on the average 0.2 percent while inflation was on the average 10.3 percent. Further aggravating the picture is a deficit in government finances and sustained increases in payroll taxes (on the average 2.1 percent a year).

Our data analysis stresses the changes in the variance of key performance variables associated with restructuring of the WNS in the periods we have identified. Variance was relatively low in period

II, but even period III can be characterized as a period of effectively 'organized social discipline'.

One of the most striking findings is the transformation of the correlation between changes in contract wages and changes in wage-drift. Wage-drift, as suggested earlier, is mainly the result of *local* negotiations and labour market conditions, while contract wage formation is the result of central (or in Epoch I branch) negotiations and the strategic efforts of peak organizations to steer wage developments. The correlation between wage-drift and contract wage formation was positive in the first and last periods, but zero and negative in the second and third periods, respectively.

The observed relationship in the second and third periods was the result of effectively organized control. The negative relationship in period III probably reflected the widespread use of wage development guarantees. According to these, wages and salaries were adjusted for wage drift in the preceding year.

The postive correlation between contract wage formation and wage-drift in Epoch IV indicates the inability or unwillingness of central actors to control or limit the struggle over income distribution. White-collar peak organizations as well as non-industrial blue-collar workers tried to make up in favourable central agreements for relative losses arising from wage-drift which benefitted industrial blue-collar workers. On the other hand, the latter attempted, through wage-drift, to regain part of what private white-collar unions and public sector unions had won through formal central negotiations.

The present crisis and the uncertain future

Institutional innovation, meta-games, and legitimacy
The Swedish Model, once a source of great pride and self-assurance, is today a system in crisis. Its legitimacy and sanctioning powers have been eroded. Its capability of resolving conflicts and regulating the labour market is increasingly wanting. It no longer appears able effectively to restrain wage demands and wage developments consistent with those of Sweden's major trading partners.

Institutions, even the most successful ones must change, because the world around them changes. They also change because the social actors engaged in them, and their power relationships, change. The actors learn and develop new goals and strategies and, as a result, place new demands on the institutions. In this context, it is essential to see institutions as human devices, social rule systems, which enable diverse actors — even agents with somewhat different perspectives and interests — to coordinate their decisions and actions, to solve common problems and to resolve social conflicts in relatively effective ways.

The Swedish collective bargaining system was designed to reduce and to regulate conflicts between employers' and employees' organizations. It was never designed to deal — and the experience of the past 20 years has shown it incapable of dealing — with serious conflicts between labour groups and organizations, in particular between white collar and blue collar unions, as well as between collectives in the private sector as opposed to those in the public sector. As a whole, the system is segmented, with disorganized or uncoordinated but interlinked, indirect negotiations. This has contributed to the 'wage carousel', with leapfrogging and instability as various labour unions and collectives struggle to stay ahead or to catch up with one another.

The current complex of problems are institutional in character. One may speak of a mismatch between the institutional set-up and the typical problems and conflicts to be handled. Such mismatches give rise to innovations and attempts to restructure the set-up. Often, such restructuring leads to serious group conflicts, in part about the types of innovation required to shape a genuinely new and effective system. At the present time in Sweden there is a stalemate around the maintenance/transformation of the system. On the one hand, the established Swedish model is unable to deal effectively with a set of new and difficult problems. On the other, key actors such as the state, the Engineering Federation (VF), LO, SAF, etc. are unable either to impose their respective proposals for solution or to agree to common organizing principles which could serve as a legitimizing point of departure for the establishment of a new system. In part, this is because of the absence of a dominant actor or coalition to establish and develop a new system, with new understandings and new principles and rules. Key actors and groups on the scene (e.g. the Engineering Federation, major export companies, the Metal Workers' Union, LO, white collar unions on the private side, those on the public side, and the state) have very different ideas or confused ideas about how a new system should be organized, for instance, to what extent it should be centralized (and, in a certain sense, a continuation of the present system); or what relationships should obtain between the private and public segments; and what principles — or more precisely, what ranking of principles — of distributive justice should prevail in income determination (see Table 10.2).[72]

In our view, then, one of the major shortcomings, if not the major one, of the Swedish Model is its incapability of regulating — or

TABLE 10.2
Swedish viewpoints on correct principles of additional wage increase

Respondents' type of occupation and sector of employment; blue collar (LO) or white collar (TCO) union membership	Differentiating payment principles most correct (or right)(%)	Egalitarian payment principles most correct (or right) (%)	Other answers including don't know and uncertain replies (%)	Total percentage	N
Blue-collar workers					
Private sector	52	38	10	100	176
Public sector	34	45	21	100	157
LO members	40	44	16	100	286
White-collar workers Private sector	71	21	8	100	156
Public sector	56	28	16	100	158
TCO (and academic union) members	59	27	14	100	248
Entire sample of Swedish population (age: 18–70+)	53	32	15	100	1027

	Differentiating principles least correct (or right) (%)	Egalitarian principles least correct (or right) (%)	Other answers including don't know and un-certain replies (%)	Total percentage	N
Blue-collar workers Private sector	20	35	45	100	176
Public sector	21	25	54	100	157
LO members	21	33	45	100	286
White-collar workers Private sector	9	58	33	100	156
Public sector	21	48	31	100	158
TCO (and academic union) members	18	52	30	100	248
Entire sample of Swedish population Age: 18–70+	19	42	39	100	1027

Notes

The table is based on answers to a survey question concerning the most correct or right principle with which an employer should distribute additional income available to employees. Among the principles were those of 'performance achievements', 'degree of responsibility', 'level of education', 'equal percentage increases', and 'equalization' (to minimize differences in wages).

The table is based on grouping together differentiating principles, on the one hand, and more equalitarian principles, on the other.

The survey was conducted by the Swedish Institute of Opinion Research (SIFO) on a random sample of the Swedish population (1,017 persons aged 18–70+) and was part of a larger study investigating attitudes towards distributive justice, wage relativities and occupational status.

resolving — destabilizing conflicts among labour unions and struggles between public and private segments over income distribution.

The segmented collective bargaining system with powerful independent unions making relative comparisons and struggling with one another — often indirectly through negotiations with employers — generates a difficult and in a certain sense unpredictable, wage negotiation process. From the perspective of many employers and employees in the export and open sectors of the economy, the system is ineffective and, indeed, entails considerable risks. If the outcomes of wage negotiation games are not predictable, a realistic planning of labour cost developments and investment decisions becomes unfeasible. Thus, one important motivation in sustaining the system weakens or disappears, thereby eroding commitment or loyalty to the system among some major actors. Moreover, there are powerful tendencies in the system to generate wage agreements which ignore some of the pressing demands and constraints of international markets and export branches.

Major export companies such as Volvo, Electrolux, LM Eriksson, among others, as well as the export sector as a whole are interested in establishing a wage negotiation system — and rules of the game – which stress increased productivity, flexibility in dealing with market and competitive demands, and reliability (as a basis for long-term planning).

In this context, VF's moves to decentralize collective bargaining, to branch and possibly enterprise level, at least in VF's area, are understandable. Some labour groups and unions have supported this initiative tacitly or found it sufficiently attractive — in terms of favourable wage structure and employment conditions — to go along with the effort (e.g., the Metal Workers' Union and SIF, the private white-collar union). Nonetheless, VF's meta-power to restructure the collective bargaining system — or to 'pull out' to a certain extent — is very circumscribed, particularly since they will sooner or later be forced to deal with the government and public sector unions who have a rather different vision of what should be done. (Of course, a strong, conservative government with a mandate would be in a position to facilitate VF's efforts, but this does not appear politically likely in the foreseeable future.) While there is general dissatisfaction with the collective bargaining system, no clear, potentially stable alternative has been formulated or found general support, yet.

The questions facing Sweden today concern: the ways in which wage negotiations should be organized over the entire labour market, what basic principles or policies are to govern 'wage demands' and 'relative income developments' in the system, and* what are appropriate levels of wage demand and development under various economic contingencies. Different agents or groups push and shove for substantially different systems: more or less decentralization, more initiative in the private sector as opposed to more in the public, greater versus less income differentials, and so forth.

Challenge of the future

What are some of the requirements of a new collective bargaining regime in Sweden? An effective and stable system, at a minimum, must be more or less compatible with external requirements, such as the demand to sustain competitivity of the Swedish export sector. It should continue to regulate employer–employee conflicts as well as contribute to reducing or effectively controlling inter-union struggles over income distribution and relativities, which we have found to be so destabilizing since the late 1960s. This implies effective regulation of the tensions between private and public segments and their destabilizing effects. An effective collective bargaining system would also regulate wage expectations and demands, both in the private and public sectors. These norms should indicate, how 'gains', for example in productivity, are to be shared, both with the employees involved directly in achieving the gains and with external groups in other sectors and in the larger society.

Any new system, if it is to function effectively, will have to enjoy wide support — that is legitimacy — among key groups and actors involved in wage negotiations. This includes labour market agents, key Swedish companies particularly in the export sector, and last but not least, the Swedish state (which, as the largest employer, is an active agent within the negotiation context and not simply a source of laws and regulations).

Legitimacy of a rule system reduces the costs of enforcement (North, 1981). At the same time, core principles and rules are typically backed by powerful sanctions to assure general adherence to system norms and procedures. Those who breach the rules are effectively sanctioned. Others who show constraint and adhere to the system are visibly and significantly rewarded. Legitimacy of core principles combined with formal and informal sanctions to enforce operating rules and procedures assure a reasonably effective system of social controls in modern society. Typically, such levels of sanctioning are no longer available to private actors, at least not in Sweden. Thus, SAF's fines against wage-drift had only symbolic value — and not much at that in the case of contemporary Swedish multi-nationals such as Volvo, Electrolux and LM Eriksson. Earlier, of course, fines would hardly have been necessary except against a very few recalcitrants, since there was widespread adherence to an ideology which gave SAF status and authority.

Gaining the necessary social support and legitimacy, particularly under the ambiguous and fragmented conditions prevailing today in the Swedish labour market setting, will be very difficult. Neither the state, VF (and its major export firms), LO nor other key agents can shape the new system on their own. In part, this is because most actors are unlikely to accept unilateral initatives, without making strategic responses of their own. *A new regime will have to be negotiated and legitimated on the basis of principles, and with enforceable sanctions*, which most find compelling or reasonable *in the present material and socio-cultural circumstances in which Sweden finds itself.*

No socio-economic institution — with flesh and blood actors — can be 'rational' in any strict sense. Human agents have conflicting goals and interests and develop new, sometimes destabilizing strategies. These processes invariably generate uncertainty and confusion in the system. An institutional frame may at best make certain desirable patterns of behaviour and developments more likely than undesirable ones. This should be the level of ambition for a new Swedish Model (Burns and Olsson, 1986).

III
BUREAUCRACY AND FORMAL
ORGANIZATIONS

11
Multiple rule systems:
Formal and informal social organization

In this and the following two chapters, we examine the intersection of multiple social rule systems in social organizing. In part, we shall examine the distinction between 'formal' and 'informal' social organization. While we draw upon and develop some of the important findings in the relevant literature, our analyses suggest new perspectives on the problem and new research questions.[73]

Among other things, we formulate the principles of bounded rationality and insufficient exclusivity to explain why multiple, intersecting social rule systems arise, even in action settings where a single formal system with legal or other legitimizing status is intended to exclude or dominate other systems.

Introduction: Monolithic and polylithic action settings

Simple and complex rule system settings can be analytically distinguished. The former are organized, in the ideal case, by a single, coherent social rule system. Complex settings are those where multiple systems, to some extent contradictory, are espoused by different groups of actors.[74]

Weber (1968:32) observed:

> The fact that, in the same social group, a plurality of contradictory systems of order may all be recognized as valid, is not a source of difficulty for the sociological approach. Indeed, it is even possible for the same individual to orient his action to *contradictory systems of order.* This can take place not only at different times, as is an everyday occurrence, but even in the case of the same concrete act. A person who fights a duel follows the code of honor; but at the same time, insofar as he either keeps it secret or conversely gives himself up to the police *he takes account of the criminal law.* To be sure, when evasion or contravention of the generally understood meaning of an order has become the rule, the order can be said to be 'valid' only in a limited degree and, in the extreme case, not at all.

Single coherent rule systems are predominantly found in traditional societies, but also in certain areas of modern societies, such as, for example, the closed systems of some religious orders. *Modern social organization is characterized, in large part by multiple, partially inconsistent social rule systems* which intersect with one another. This applies even in the case of a legally constituted, formal organization which, due to its legal or official status, prevails, although not totally, over other competing systems. *In practice, no formal organization, even one based on legal rights to take priority over other systems, achieves total exclusion.* The degree of exclusion and prevalence is an empirical question. In part, this is because of the well-known fact that no formal rule system is completely sufficient unto itself. Its major organizing principles, sources of legitimacy, sanctioning powers or other resources lie to some degree outside it. The formal system can never be effectively implemented without consideration of the concrete conditions of implementation which always require adjustments and adaptations in the rules. Finally, participants in the organization bring into it external statuses, relationships, network and organizational ties, each with their own social rule system, which may interfere with or contradict the formal system.

In general, those involved in a given action setting bring more than one social rule system to bear on the activity. This situation arises also in cases where, as we mentioned above, one particular system has an exclusive legal or official status. Even when actors pursue designated goals, trying to use legally or officially indicated means in their efforts to solve concrete practical problems that arise in the setting, they may end up modifying either or both.

A major question concerning the activation and application of multiple rule systems in a social action sphere is: what are the relationships among these different systems and between the groups which espouse them? In this way, we are led to distinguish situations where, on the one hand, the multiple, intersecting systems are more or less compatible with one another — in the purest case motivated by the same purpose or interest and subject to a coherent design — and where, on the other, they are motivated by opposing interests or cultural values and contradict one another. Furthermore, the power relations among the actors or groups advocating different systems becomes critical, since these will in part decide which of several competing or contradictory social rule systems will prevail.

Several distinctions can be made which will prove useful later in organizing our discussion of multiple rule system settings. First, monolithic and polylithic social action settings are distinguished.

I. Monolithic situations. A single social rule system, applies.

Either the actors involved consider no other system applicable or these other systems are effectively excluded by the group or organization as non-legitimate.

A weaker case would entail multiple systems which in large part are coherent and, for all intents and purposes, can be treated as a single, coherent system. As we suggested earlier, a formal system may be complemented with additions and extensions which are in large part compatible with it, for instance, enabling effective performance in a concrete situation with new types of machines or technologies.

II. Polylithic situations. Here we assume that the multiple rule systems are to varying degrees contradictory. They may be contradictory in at least two senses: (1) they indicate contradictory courses of action; (2) both systems require the use of resources, action in time and space which exceed the physical, social or psychological capabilities of the agents to whom the systems apply.

Contradictory systems may be differentiated from one another and made to apply at different times and places. This becomes then a special case of I. Of interest for us are cases where this is not or cannot be accomplished. Two patterns are observable:

1. In the case of *system dominance* one system is the legitimate or official one and dominates. *However, as suggested earlier, domination is rarely total, since* its rule system is never complete and one or more participating agents are able to introduce 'illegitimate' or 'unofficial' rule systems. In general, the illegitimate or unofficial system appears in areas where official control is weak or ineffective and can be circumvented, and even openly opposed.

2. In the case of *system pluralism* two or more contradictory systems are advocated openly by agents acting within the sphere to which an official or formal system applies. In some cases, one and the same agent may introduce and try to follow the multiple systems. Often, participating groups have varying commitments to diverse systems.

The result of such pluralism is that the social action situation is characterized by ambiguity, confusion and open conflict. In this case, one observes the 'erosion' of a given formal system. The result may be a 'garbage-can process' of decision-making and administration, with a high degree of unpredictability and confusion (March and Olsen, 1976). In some cases, the actors may achieve 'a negotiated order' (see Chapter 4, pp. 53–4). However, this is, in a certain sense, at the expense of the official or formal order.

A basic premise of our investigation of social organization is that, in modern societies, more than a single social rule system is likely to be activated in any concrete social action setting. In some settings this implies that various social agents struggle to realize or, indeed, to impose on others diverse systems or substantial variants of a given system. Thus, within a defined social setting many 'organizational forms', groups and relationships are likely to be found, in part co-existing, in part in competition and conflict with one another.

As we discuss in more detail later, one social rule system may have an official or legal status, such as a business enterprise or a government agency, which other systems such as friendship networks, political groups and 'external' formal organizations lack. (Multiple systems may also apply legitimately to the same area, as Chapters 12, 15, and 16 point up.)

In this sense, social organization in a given action setting should be viewed as a *partially bounded arena* — to varying degrees open — within which social groups, coalitions and interests try to assure the force and implementation of different social rule systems, and engage in conflict and negotiations. Their success depends to a greater or lesser extent on their power within the organization and their location — and access to power resources — within a societal stratification system (Salaman, 1982:134).[75]

We are interested, above all, in instances where at least one rule regime introduced or established in an action sphere has an exclusive legal or official status — a legitimacy with powerful backing to exclude or to prevail over other systems. At the same time, other social rule systems[76] are introduced and established through concrete *socio-political processes* of complementing, reinterpreting, and adapting, or avoiding, replacing and transforming the official or formal system. This conceptualization is our point of departure for examining the 'formal–informal' dichotomy from the perspective of social rule system theory.

Rational–legal organization

The organizing principles
A formal organization is a rule regime with legal or official status. It has a continually operating staff and has been deliberately established by particular social agents or groups in order to organize collective action for certain purposes (Weber, 1968:52; Blau and Scott, 1962:5).[77]

The rule regime specifies and distinguishes what superiors and subordinates are to do (and also what they may not do). The specialization found in these organizations entails rules and regulations specifying task areas and spheres of jurisdiction, lest members overstep their proper jurisdiction and spheres of activity and threaten the stable functioning of the organization (Dahl and Lindblom, 1963:248).

Many of the organizing principles and rules making up such administrative or bureaucratic systems are familiar to students of organization (Weber, 1968; Blau and Scott, 1962; Albrow, 1970; Scott, 1981:68–71):[78]

(i) Separation of the membership from roles, relationships, resources outside the organization. Roles and duties are to be performed impersonally and exclusively and are, therefore, not to be subject to the personal or emotional feelings or to the norms and values of family, political or other relations.

(ii) A system of limited, well-defined domination relations, the designation of which is provided by formal laws as well as rules and regulations of the organization itself.[79]

(iii) The divisions of authority (domination) and responsibility, as well as specialization generally, are fixed and specified clearly in the organization's rules and regulations.

(iv) Legal, economic, and technical knowledge are used in formulating the organizational rules and regulations governing social action within the organization. At the heart of Weber's idea of formal rationality, Albrow (1970:65) points out, 'was the idea of correct calculation, in either numerical terms, as with the accountant, or in logical terms, as with the lawyer.' Therefore, special expertise is required in formulating the rules and, in many instances, in implementing them.

Rational domination is accomplished in part through the sustained application of systematic knowledge (legal, technical and economic) and in part through the principles of recruitment, removal, promotion, and remuneration of staff. These latter principles are designed to assure not only sufficient competence but also *discipline — prompt execution of rules based on expert knowledge.*

(v) The rules and regulations governing the organization arc more or less stable and exhaustivc, are written and can be learned.[80]

(vi) The principle of recruitment is meritocratic, matching applications to positions in terms of their knowledge, skills, expertise and motivation rather than in terms of their social status, connections, political sympathies, etc.

(vii) The principle of involvement states that officials are hired or appointed on the basis of a contract, not elected.[81] They receive fixed remunerative payment and should enjoy career opportunities, where the latter contribute to the enforcement of internal discipline.[82] Promotion, which is typically governed by relatively well-specified rules, is conducted either on the basis of merit or seniority. It is restricted to the organization itself. The promotion decisions themselves are made according to the judgement of superiors.

The readiness of members to accept or adhere to the organizational regime, including rules of obedience as well as those of a technical character, depends on separating members of the organization from 'external' contacts and involvements — at least during the time of their daily engagement. In other words, external roles, relationships, network and organizational memberships, as well as resource control are in principle excluded.[83]

In the purest case of bureaucratic organization, members are separated from the means of administration or production. These are concentrated in the hands of those who dominate the organization.[84]

Thus, stable and systematic rational–legal domination is achieved not only through the legal (and legitimate) sanctioning of the relationship, but also through systematic organization of resource distribution which structure the dependence of members on the organization, and through principles of recruitment and occupational involvement which increase the likelihood of compliance. Such compliance has an *impersonal character*. Weber (1946:215–16) states:

> The 'objective' discharge of business primarily means a discharge of business according to *calculable rules* and 'without regard for persons'.
> 'Calculable rules,' is of paramount importance for modern bureaucracy. The peculiarity of modern culture, and specifically of its technical and economic basis, demands this very 'calculability' of results. When fully developed, bureaucracy also stands, in a specific sense, under the principle of *sine ira ac studio*. Its specific nature, which is welcomed by capitalism, develops the more perfectly the more the bureaucracy is 'dehumanized,' the more completely it succeeds in eliminating from official business love, hatred, and all purely personal, irrational, and emotional elements which escape calculation. This is the specific nature of bureaucracy and it is appraised as its special virtue.

Elaborating the framework developed in Chapter 7 (see Table 7.7), we specify and organize the structuring principles and rules of rational–bureaucratic organizations in summary form in Table 11.1. Such a regime type is readily distinguishable from those of democratic organizations, patrimonial and patron–client relations, markets and judicial systems.

The triumph of rationality

As Weber anticipated, bureaucratic forms of domination have spread to most areas of social life and characterize to a great extent the modern world. Viewing this development as an 'organizational revolution', Lindblom (1977:28) writes:

TABLE 11.1
Principles and rules of rational – legal organizations

Who participates?
Members are hired or appointed on the basis of a contract. They are not elected nor do they own or inherit the position. They are free to leave. Moreover, their recruitment is based on their possessing certain skills or knowledge which they have received elsewhere or they are capable of receiving in on-the-job training. Some are hired for positions requiring professional qualifications, 'ideally substantiated by a diploma or gained through examination.'

Why, for what goals?
Members participate (it is implicitly understood) for material as well as possibly for 'spiritual' reasons. They receive a salary and possibly a pension right. Also, it is understood that the members have opportunities to exercise their technical, legal or other competence. There is typically a career structure, with promotion possible either on the basis of merit or seniority, and according to the judgement of superiors.

The goals or purposes of the organization are defined by law or by the top leadership of the organization. It is not necessary that there should be consensus about these goals, but it is necessary that members adhere to them and the rules designed to achieve them (within the limits specified by law or contract).

What do they do?
The roles, role relationships, and task and transaction structures are also specified by the rule regime (see Chapter 5). In particular:

(i) duties of position or office are clearly specified and organized on a continuous, regulated basis.

(ii) extra-organizational roles, role relations, tasks and duties are excluded from the sphere or area of organization.

(iii) organizational tasks are divided into functionally distinct spheres or jurisdictional areas, each furnished with the requisite technologies and other resources, authority and sanctions.

(iv) positions are clearly arranged hierarchically, the rights of control and duties of obedience between them being specified. (Obedience is not to the person who holds authority (i.e. person-specific domination) but to the regime itself, the impersonal order in which the member works.)

How?
Organizational rules and procedures specify how tasks are to be performed. These are, in part, technical and/or legal in character. Rationally organized formal procedures involve correct calculation, either in technical terms as with finance and statistics, or in logical terms, as with law. (In such cases, a certain training is necessary both in formulating such rules as well as in implementing them.) Administration is conducted with (and based on) written records and documents.

Other means of production and administration are also explicitly or tacitly specified: tools and equipment, monetary resources, and sanctions. (Again, these belong to the organization, not to the members.)

When, where?
The activity sphere of the organization is specified legally or in the rules and procedures governing the legitimate functions and spheres of action of the organization.

Millions of people are ... members of bureaucratically organized labour unions, employer groups, fraternal orders, veterans associations and farm organizations; and their children are encouraged to sample bureaucracy in the Scouts and Little Leagues. Some of these bureaucracies are enormous. By numbers employed, the largest in the USA is the Defense Department with over a million civilian employees (and another 2 million in the armed forces), followed by the American Telephone and Telegraph and General Motors, each with roughly 800,000.

An unplanned revolution has been brought about by men who, without making a political issue of their dimly perceived intentions, drew most of the work force out of small farming and small enterprise into the authority relations of the modern bureaucratic enterprise. It is a revolution that in industrialized systems has fundamentally changed the work patterns and other forms of human interdependence for most of the gainfully employed. Not a revolution pursued for egalitarian, democratic, or other humane motives, its motives are profit and power; and it succeeds for no more lofty reason than efficiency. But it is no less a revolution for that. It has altered politico-economic organization more than the French, Bolshevik, or Mao's revolution. And it has established a new order in the USSR and China no less than in the West.

The reasons for the successful diffusion of bureaucratic forms are many (Dahl and Lindblom, 1963:247). Of particular importance is the fact that bureaucracy organizes social action and imposes controls which are highly advantageous to elite groups and even to large numbers of people, while being costly largely to relatively peripheral groups:

- leaders in business, government, trade unions, churches, hospitals, universities and elsewhere utilize the organizing principles of bureaucracy
- citizens, customers, workers, church members, patients, teachers and others not only tolerate such forms of organization, but even on occasion demand it

Weber viewed such bureaucratic organizations as a special form of administration, that became fully developed only in the most advanced institutions of capitalism and in the modern state (Scott, 1981:68). Weber (1964:337–8) observed:

> The development of the modern form of the organization of corporate groups in all fields is nothing less than identical with the development and continued spread of bureaucratic administration. This is true of church and state, of armies, political parties, economic enterprises, organizations to promote all kinds of causes, private associations, clubs, and many others... Its development, largely under capitalistic auspices, has created an urgent need for stable, strict, intensive, and calculable administration. It is this need which gives bureaucracy a crucial role in our society as the central element in any kind of large-scale administration.

In Weber's view, the spread of the bureaucratic form was part of a general process of rationalization in modern society. Its *spread was inevitable* because its characteristics of *precision, continuity, discipline, strictness, and reliability* made it technically the most satisfactory form of organization for those who sought to exercise organizational control. Thompson (1980:10–11) argues:

> He (Weber) was describing the form of administration that went along with rational legal authority — in contrast to the kinds of administration that accompanied two other quite different types of authority, the traditional and the charismatic.[85] The reason for its triumph is *not* adequately summarized in the single word 'efficiency'. Weber's explanation for its success includes a wider list of operational virtues: precision, speed, unambiguity, knowledge of the files, continuity, discretion, unity, strict subordination, reduction of friction and of material and personal costs. Certain other developments in industrial society also favour the spread of bureaucracy, such as the speed up in communication and transport, the adoption of modern accounting methods, the demand for equal treatment by citizens in a democracy and the growth of mass production and mass administration. Weber was thus offering a general theory of *modern culture*, centered on the process of progressive rationalization in all spheres.

The type of rule regimes corresponding to bureaucratic organization provides systematic, stable forms to exercise social domination and to organize collective action. (1) On the one hand, it does not require consensus among the participants about the goals or the rules and procedures of organized action. It only requires their acceptance of, or adherence to, the rule regime. (2) On the other, the system enables one group, those who set up or who manage the organization, to dominate on the basis of legal rights and enables an administrative staff to ensure the compliance of other actors or groups (the members or employees who are subject to the rule regime, including the rules of obedience) (Albrow, 1970:38).

Bureaucratization is then an institutionalized strategy of social control. It entails a legal authority or power-holder organizing and regulating collective activity and excluding 'unofficial' power, norms and resistance (Crozier, 1964).

Vast human, financial, and other resources can be mobilized and controlled. In particular, the activities of many persons can be specified and coordinated on a more or less continuous basis[86] and incentives are furnished for persons to join and participate according to the organization's regime.

The cunning of unreason: Informal rule systems
In the following sections of this chapter, we examine social organ-

ization as a function of multiple, intersecting social rule systems and, in this context, deal systematically with the formal–informal dichotomy. Our strategy is to consider any social action setting as subject to more than one social rule system. At least one of these systems may have an official or legal status in the situation, to the exclusion of other systems. Nevertheless, the latter may be activated and followed to varying degrees in the situation, thereby complementing, interfering with, or even replacing the formal system.

The formal–informal dichotomy
It has become conventional knowledge in organizational studies that public, official or formal rule systems are often not those *found to be operating in practice.* In many instances, informal, unofficial or even illegal rules govern the day-to-day operations and structure of an organization or institution. Of course, these systems may incorporate to a greater or lesser extent some of the formal rules.

Informal rules, particularly those contradictory to formal rules, are usually explained by referring to 'local sub-cultures', 'problems of implementation', 'discrepancies between goals and means', etc. In our view, *the phenomena are so pervasive in modern institutions that no single factor will explain them. Rather it is a syndrome, reflecting deep-seated structural properties of modern social organization.*

In public administration and the political sphere, one refers to 'formal rules' as those of a public, legal nature. In the private sphere, particularly in relations of production and ownership, the formal system is that designed and institutionalized by top management and owners. Ultimately, this power is based on the legal rights of owners vis a vis employees, enabling them to hire and fire, to promote and demote. Such powers are tempered in most modern capitalist societies by legal and negotiated constraints on the exercise of employer power.

Formal rules are, then, those formulated by authorities and power-holders and institutionalized in law as well as administrative codes and handbooks. In a certain sense, they are official, at least within a particular social organization or community. In many or most instances they are legal in character, supported ultimately by the state. Legal backing gives such rules both a public character and ultimately a powerful sanction (or threat of such).

The legal or formal establishment of an organization does not mean that all activities and interactions of its members conform strictly to the official organizing principles. Along such lines Blau and Scott (1962:5–6) observe:

Regardless of the time and effort devoted by management to designating a rational organization chart and elaborate procedure manuals, this official plan can never completely determine the conduct and social relations of the organization's members.

In every formal organization there arise informal organizations. The constituent groups of the organization, like all groups, develop their own practices, values, norms, and social relations as their members live and work together. The roots of these informal systems are embedded in the formal organization itself and nurtured by the very formality of its arrangements. *Official rules* must be general to have sufficient scope to cover the multitude of situations that may arise. But the application of these general rules to particular cases often poses problems of judgement, and informal practices tend to emerge that provide solutions for these problems. Decisions not anticipated by official regulations must frequently be made, particularly in times of change, and here again unofficial practices are likely to furnish guides for decisions long before the formal rules have been adapted to the changing circumstances ...
Finally, complex networks of social relations and informal status structures emerge, within groups and between them, which are influenced by many factors besides the organizational chart, for example by the background characteristics of various persons, their abilities, their willingness to help others, and their conformity to group norms. But to say that these informal structures are not completely determined by the formal institution is not to say that they are entirely independent of it. For informal organizations develop in response to the opportunities created and the problems posed by their environment, and the formal organization constitutes the immediate environment of the groups within it ... It is impossible to understand the nature of a formal organization without investigating the networks of informal relations and the unofficial norms as well as the formal hierarchy of authority and the official body of rules, since the formally instituted and the informally emerging patterns are inextricably intertwined.

'Informal organization' is often understood as that which operates in practice. Participants in the concrete action setting(s), particularly subordinates, are typically the main sources of these rules. Those responsible for the formal, public rules may know about and support, and in some instances take the first initiative in, informal rule formation.

Operating rules in many instances reflect the formal ones, but not always consistently:

(i) some formal rules are implemented with a high probability but they are subject to minor adjustments and adaptations to concrete circumstances.

(ii) other formal rules are substantially reformulated in implementation but traces of the original can be found in observable practices.

(iii) certain informal ryles will reflect 'opposition', based on class, ethnic, or other group interests, and to a greater or lesser extent are the negation of the formal ones.

(iv) many informal rules have little or no direct connection to the formal system. Actors introduce and develop them in areas not covered or only partially covered by the formal rules. Such areas are particularly associated with: (a) activities extraneous to the purposes of the formal that nevertheless impinge socially on it, for example as a result of friendship, kinship, or political networks and the interests and demands mediated through these networks; and (b) 'new developments', new spheres of responsibility and new technologies that call for new organizing principles, new types of roles and social relationships, which the formal rule system fails to provide (it may even impose fetters on adjusting effectively to these developments).

(v) Some informal (meta-)rules are developed to deal with rule inconsistencies and ambiguities.

In general, participants bring into or develop within formal organizations informal rule systems and action patterns: including power and status relations, communication networks, sociometric structures and working arrangements (Scott, 1981:83). These systems have relatively well-defined structures, although, typically, they are not articulated as explicitly or systematically as formal systems.

In the following sub-sections, we examine and illustrate types of formal and informal social organization.

Multiple social roles and role hierarchy
Disjunctions arise between rules and roles required by formal organization and those stemming from other regimes to which an actor is also subjected. This problem is particularly acute in settings where one or more competing regimes pertain to a sphere of activity to which the formal organization applies. For instance: ethnic, class, religious, or other collective identities — and the rule systems these imply — permeate a person's life, often without his or her will or awareness, whereas some organizations require the neutralization or suppression of these identities. A formal system obligates or rewards achievement-oriented behaviour and competition and the other proscribes them, at least within the relevant action contexts; 'rules of conduct' within a corporation or political organization entail certain types of lying, cheating and general dishonesty in the affairs of business and state, respectively, while a participating actor has high moral standards and may be deeply religious, thus, in effect, adhering to systems proscribing such conduct. Examples are numerous of contradictions between the organizing principles,

global norms, roles and role relationships of diverse, but converging systems of social organization.

Persons in a modern society enjoy (suffer) a plurality of roles. As a result 'person' becomes the meeting place or arena for multiple and sometimes conflicting role designs and demands. Role conflicts and tensions are endemic to modern society but arise to varying degrees, and are handled with different institutionalized strategies, in various social organizations.

To begin with, role sets in organizations vary in the extent to which they exclude certain types of activities (sexual engagements, political activity, etc.) or, indeed, other role encumbencies. For instance, persons in 'moral leadership roles' are often not allowed to engage in activities which would taint or erode their leadership position. Combinations of priest and 'gambler' or priest and 'Don Juan' are not acceptable in the definition of the priest role, whether formally or informally. Of course, such combinations are the stuff of good stories and movies — or at least provide illustrations of the personal temptations with which a priest must deal. The same applies to politicians in democratic societies, concerning their adherence to principles of personal morality and avoidance of conflicts of interest (between political responsibility and economic ambitions).

The greater the exclusivity of organizational roles, the greater the limitations of personal, social, and political rights of encumbents. In a certain sense, the exclusive role *dominates* other roles or potential roles in that its rule-set defines the opportunities and boundaries of other roles. Nuns, monks, and priests in the Catholic Church may not assume the marital or parental roles. Indeed, a variety of other potential roles are excluded by formal rules or policy. Goffman (1974:270) writes:

> In the sixties, the Vatican ruled that Sister Marie Bernadette of the University of Detroit could not take a part — any part — in a college production but granted permission for Sister Michael Therese to become a pilot to further the work of the Church in Kenya; in both cases, the sisters made news, and the news pertained to the person–role formula. Note that a double perspective ought to be applied here. Just as role may call for a player who has certain 'incidental' social qualifications, so a player may feel obligated to restrict his choice of role because of public expectations regarding someone with his profile of social attributes.

Not all role 'contradictions' are moral in character. A role may be seen as so demanding in terms of time, energy, and responsibility, that certain other roles are simply excluded — *on practical grounds, not ideological ones*.

Much of the above is fairly obvious in the case of most modern, formal organizations (companies, government agencies, the army, police, hospitals, and so forth) which limit the demands other institutions and roles can make on their members in their capacities within an organization — at least during those times and in those places where they are subject to the organization's rule regimes. Engagements in other roles are sometimes permitted but under well-defined conditions and controls. In some cases, the regulations are stringent. Thus, the claims that other roles and their activities can impose are restricted, for instance with respect to time and place.

The design of roles or role relationships may be imposed by large-scale organizations through recruitment policies and career requirements which assure either exclusion or effective domination of other roles. Often, such structuring of role complexes begins already at the recruitment stage, with selection of persons who have demonstrated the desirable characteristics. Further on, the rules set for personnel or member remuneration, removal and promotion — and the pressure of compliant peers — help to establish the centrality of the organizational role with respect to other roles.

In sum, particular organizational roles vary in their degree of exclusivity and claims on encumbents' time, energy and loyalty. Individuals as well as classes of individuals have to develop more or less stable hierarchies of roles. The hierarchies are determined by the predominance or priority usurped by a certain institutional sphere or organizational system in society. For instance the sphere of employment and career usurps such a central position today in the West, while other institutional spheres, such as 'family', 'local community', 'political sphere', etc., have difficulties in asserting themselves with equal force. Only relatively few individuals are fortunate enough to imprint their preferences and predispositions on the multiple positions they occupy. Even fewer can grant centrality to spheres of life which have a peripheral position in the societal hierarchy.

Administrative systems

In study after study, organizational members are observed to follow or to develop rules which are extraneous to, and even contradictory with, the official or formal rules (Zimmerman, 1973:251). Perrow (1979:40–1), among others, has discussed the wide discrepancy between, on the one hand, the official hierarchy and organizational rules and, on the other, the unofficial ones:

> It is a remarkable phenomenon in many cases, and well-known to most people who have to spend their working lives as managers in organizations. Departmental secretaries in many universities have power far

beyond their status. David Mechanic's well-known essay, 'Sources of Power of Lower Participants in Complex Organizations,' touches on this and other examples. Melville Dalton, in his excruciatingly unsettling study of a manufacturing plant, reveals top people with no power and those three or four levels below with extensive power. Sociologists have been particularly fond of the contrast between the official and the unofficial because it indicates that organizations are natural systems rather than artificial or mechanistic ones — living things that the men within them create out of their own needs, rather than rational tools in the hands of a master. They are right, of course: between the conception and the reality...falls the shadow. The first thing the new employee should learn is who is really in charge, who has the goods on whom, what are the major debts and dependencies — all things that are not reflected by the neat boxes in the table of organization. Once he has this knowledge he can navigate with more skill and ease.

Perrow (1979:41) suggests that we should not expect the official map to be completely accurate because:

(1) It is never up-to-date — it does not reflect power shifts or trends toward future distribution of power, for instance in the case of a subordinate who accumulates power and influence and will be promoted over his boss in a year or two;

(2) It does not pretend to make all the many and finely graded distinctions that operating personnel in their concrete problem situations have to live by — e.g., three departments may be on the same official level, but one of them is three times the size of the other two and may carry a commensurate increment in power;

(3) It does not reflect all transactions in the organization, but primarily those disputes that can be settled formally;

(4) Most important, the hierarchy functions primarily for routine situations; new situations with legal, technological, economic or political changes, if they persist, can make for shifts in power and authority;

(5) Finally, hierarchical principles are sometimes violated intentionally; when, for example, the head office cannot get enough information about a division's operation, it sends in a spy.

For organizational theorists, an additional set of questions is required, for instance: What are the systematic bases for the deviations? What forms do they take? What conflicts and struggles arise in connection with them?

Political systems
Similar gaps between the formal and the informal are reported in political systems (see Mathews, 1960; Matthews, 1968:571–6). For instance, actual practices often diverge substantially from official

democratic forms. Concerning legislative behaviour Matthews (1968:573) points out:

> Contemporary students have not only found that unwritten rules of behavior exist in a variety of legislative settings, but they have also been able to describe the content of these normative expectations, estimate how widely they are accepted, describe how they are enforced, and suggest their consequences for the operation of legislative bodies.

Matthews goes on to point out some of the specific informal rules governing behaviour of members of the US Senate (1968:573–4):

> The first unwritten rule of Senate behaviour, according to Matthews, is that new members are expected to serve a proper apprenticeship. The freshman senator receives the committee assignments the other senators do not want; the same is true of his office suite and his seat in the chamber. In committee rooms he is assigned to the end of the table. He is expected to do more than his share of the thankless and boring tasks of the Senate, to keep his mouth shut, to listen and learn. According to the unwritten rules of the chamber, the freshman is to accept such treatment as a matter of course. Those who do not, encounter thinly veiled hostility and loss of esteem.
>
> The great bulk of the Senate's work is highly detailed, dull and politically unrewarding. According to the rules of the game in the Senate, it is to these tasks that a senator ought to devote a major share of his time, energy, and thought. Moreover, a senator ought to specialize, to focus his time and attention on the relatively few matters which come before his committees or that directly and immediately affect his state. Still another rule of Senate behavior is that political disagreement should not influence personal feelings, that senators should avoid personal attacks on colleagues and strive for impersonality in debate. Moreover, senators must be willing to bargain — to operate on the basis of the reciprocal trading of favors. This requires self-restraint, tolerance, and an essentially non-ideological approach to political life.
>
> These norms perform important functions. They provide motivation for the performance of legislative duties that would not otherwise be performed. They encourage the development of expertise and division of labor and discourage those who would challenge it. They soften the inevitable personal conflict of a legislative body so that adversaries and competitors can cooperate. They encourage senators to become 'compromisers' and 'bargainers' and to use their substantial powers with caution and restraint (Matthews, 1960:102–3). Without these rules of the game, the Senate could hardly operate in anything like its present form.
>
> Yet while the consensus about these norms is impressive, they are not universally accepted or lived up to. Men who come to the Senate after distinguished careers in public or private life find serving an apprenticeship a trying experience. Members of the chamber with active presidential ambitions are unlikely to build a national reputation through faithful adherence to the rules of the game. Men with highly insecure seats, or those representing unusually diverse and complex constituencies, often find the injunctions about legislative specialization and self-

restraint in floor debate difficult *to reconcile with the exigencies of political survival* [our italics]. Finally, while senators are necessarily tolerant of differences of political viewpoint, the ease with which senators can conform to these informal expectations depends upon their ideological position. A man elected to the Senate as a 'liberal' or 'progressive' or 'reformer' is under pressure to produce legislative results. The people who voted for him want national legislative policy changed. Yet if the liberal senator gives in to the pressure for conformity to the rules of the game (prevailing in the Senate), he must postpone the achievement of these objectives. If he presses for these objectives regardless of his junior position, he will become tabbed a nonconformist and will lose popularity with his colleagues. This might not be so serious a sanction if respect by one's colleagues were not extremely helpful in getting legislation passed. 'In the Senate,' one member is quoted as saying,'if you don't conform, you don't get many favors for your state. You are never told that, but you soon learn' (Matthews, 1960:114).

A study of the legislatures of California, New Jersey, Ohio, and Tennessee conducted by John Wahlke, Heinz Eulau, William Buchanan, and Roy Ferguson (see Wahlke et al., 1962) is based upon interviews with virtually every member of the bicameral legislatures of these four states. The rules of the game mentioned by these legislators are presented in Table 11.2.

This study along with that of Matthews allows us to make some general statements about the functioning and enforcement of rule regimes in American legislative bodies. These informal, yet dominating rules are generally understood and accepted by virtually all members of the legislative systems. They comprise on the whole, 'a body of mutually compatible rules'. They are systematically enforced by such informal but highly effective sanctions as obstruction of the nonconforming members' interests and legislative bills, social ostracism, mistrust, and loss of political perquisites and rewards. The rules create group cohesion and morale, promote predictability of legislator behaviour, restrain and channel conflict, and expedite the conduct of the legislative business.

Beyond the formal–informal dichotomy

Mouzelis (1967:70–1) argues that the formal–informal notion 'is a very convenient tool, as it draws the attention of the student of bureaucracy to the inherent and continuous tension between rational co-ordination of activities and the spontaneous pattern formation of interpersonal relationships and unofficial values and beliefs'. The latter are not controlled by the formal, official organization in many instances and, indeed, often they stand in oppsition to it. Mouzelis (1967:70–1) adds:

TABLE 11.2
Rules of the game most frequently perceived by legislators in four
American state (percentages)[1]

Rules[2]	California (N = 104)	New Jersey (N = 78)	Ohio (N = 160)	Tennessee (N = 119
1. Performance of obligations: keep your word; abide by commitments	64	47	28	24
2. Respect for other members' legislative rights: support other members' local bills if they don't affect you or your district; don't railroad bills through; etc.	32	26	24	47
3. Impersonality: don't deal in personalities; don't engage in personal attacks on other members; etc.	30	27	32	31
4. Self-restraint in debate: don't talk too much; don't speak about subjects on which you're uninformed	17	9	18	59
5. Courtesy: observe common courtesies; be friendly and courteous even if you disagree	19	19	24	26
6. Openness of aims: be frank and honest in explaining bills; don't conceal real purpose of bills or amendments	24	8	22	12
7. Modesty: don't be a prima donna or publicity seeker	9	19	23	21
8. Integrity: be honest, a man of integrity	13	19	18	11
9. Independence of judgment: don't be subservient to groups or individuals outside the legislature	16	19	11	14
10. Personal virtue: exhibit high moral conduct, no drunkenness or immorality	13	0	24	8
11. Decisiveness: take a stand, don't vacillate	10	8	11	15

Rules[2]	California (N = 104)	New Jersey (N = 78)	Ohio (N = 160)	Tennessee (N = 119
12. Unselfish service: don't be an opportunist; don't use your legislative position for your personal advantage	5	19	14	4

1. Percentages do not equal 100, because most respondents named more than one rule.
2 Fewer than half the rules mentioned are summarized above.
Source: Mathews (1968; 575)

Such a concept gives a dynamic and dialectic aspect to organizational analysis and provides a useful starting point for the study of organizational change. ... When one enters a concrete organization in order to observe closely the behaviour of its members, it becomes extremely difficult to distinguish what is formal and what is informal in their actions. These two aspects, in concrete cases, are so inextricably mixed together, that any systematic attempt at their differentiation is bound to fail ... Moreover, a great insistence on the formal–informal dichotomy might distract our attention from the systematic study of the organization as a whole system (in which the formal structure is one of its many aspects).

Mouzelis concludes by stating that the formal–informal dichotomy does not do justice to the study of social organization, pointing out the numerous and sometimes inconsistent ways in which it has been used. He distinguishes four categories of meanings of 'informal' (1967:147):

(i) Informal is deviation from expectations of those hierarchically superior. But there are multiple rule systems (and behavioural demands and expectations), not always congruent, 'which the individual takes into consideration before acting: for instance, the expectations of the top hierarchy, of his immediate superior, of his colleagues, his family and of many other reference groups. Thus, in such cases, where conflicting expectations claim the attention of the actor, most often there is not a clear-cut decision to follow one set of expectations at the expense of others; rather, the ensuing behaviour is the result of a compromise or fusion of the various expectancies in the mind of the actor.' He concludes that the informal–formal dichotomy does not do justice to the situation.
(ii) Informal as irrelevant to organizational goals. Thus, some activities of bureaucrats (e.g. gossiping) whether legitimate or illegitimate are called informal insofar as they are not directly relevant to the work process.
(iii) Informal as unanticipated. Here Mouzelis refers to the

unanticipated consequences of social action (irrespective of the legitimacy or goal relevancy of this action). There are inevitably discrepancies between administrators' intentions and concrete results.

(iv) Informal as real or concrete. Here the concept is used to distinguish between defunct or inapplicable rules, on the one hand, and, on the other, concrete behaviour or what really goes on in the organization (bureaucratic cookbook versus informal structure).

The importance to organizational research of the formal–informal distinction is apparent in view of the pervasiveness of the occurrence of multiple, intersecting social rule systems in organizations. Nevertheless, we lack a broad theoretical statement about this distinction. Organizational theorists have in large part failed to make systematic distinctions between different types and origins of informal rules and to explain satisfactorily their pervasiveness and force. In the following section we outline a general model which addresses a few of the problems relating to the distinction between formal and informal organization.

A general model of formal and informal organization
Our general model of social organization is based on the following propositions:

(i) In any given social action setting, multiple, intersecting social rule systems are likely to be activated. This occurs often in connection with some agents or groups trying to impose one system to the exclusion or marginalization of others. The social action settings which are the objects of 'organizing' are partially bounded arenas within which social groups, coalitions, and various interests meet, struggle, and negotiate. The result is invariably a complex, and partially 'negotiated' order (Strauss et al., 1963). Typically, multiple organizations are found within a defined action setting. The competing or incompatible rule systems make for complexity and for the likelihood of conflicts, including conflicts veiled in patterns of deviance and strategies of deferential opposition.

(ii) Often, in any given setting one rule system may have legal or official status, that is the legitimate right to be imposed by actors responsible for introducing or maintaining the system, e.g. the managers of a business enterprise or of a government agency. In general, modern administrative systems are characterized by a 'legitimate' authority — owners, top managers, administrators as well as others who may be delegated the authority by those holding primary authority — who prescribes many of the organizing principles, rules and regulations, division of labour, etc. (see Table 11.1).

(iii) As numerous organizational studies show, no system manages to either fully organize social action or to fully exclude other systems, even in the case that one system enjoys exclusive legitimacy and the backing of the state. Certain agents, possibly including a well-defined leadership and staff, introduce or utilize informal rule systems in the setting. These entail organizing principles, rules, standards or norms and ways of rewarding compliance or punishing deviation from the rules. Thus, participants are to a greater or lesser extent also subject to at least one regime other than the formal one (Litterer, 1969).

Given the unfeasibility of total exclusion of all systems except for the formal regime — and given differences in values and norms as well as particular interests among participating actors and groups — non-formal organization(s) are pervasive. No single factor or explanation can be found, as diverse studies and examples show:

A. People recruited into a formal organization carry into it general rules systems relating to their status, social conduct, modes of relating to others, social strategies, etc. Some may establish 'local cultures' on the basis of such rule systems. Salaman (1980:132) refers to Rose Giallombardo's study of the informal social structure among inmates of a women's prison. Giallombardo shows how organizational roles relate to the wider society. They are not understandable merely by reference to the isolated, closed organization. The system of roles observable among the female inmates, although naturally centred upon the problems and conditions of imprisonment, is directly related to extra-organizational sex roles.

B. Members of the organization are parts of other networks and organizations, both within the formal organization and outside of it: families, communities, professions, political groups and movements. Within the organization there are class cleavages (owners/managers versus workers); cleavages between professional and occupational groups with differing functions, power and resource control as well as social paradigms based on their training and their roles in the organizations.[87]

Numerous sociological studies of factories and other workplaces show that workers set up and conform to group norms restricting production — work quotas — at the expense of their own higher earnings or the satisfaction of their supervisors. In addition, informal status hierarchies and leadership patterns develop, countervailing and providing a basis of challenge to those formally designed and supervised by management (Scott, 1981; Roethisberger and Dickson, 1939; Whyte, 1956).

Mouzelis (1967:102,160) observes in this regard:

Members of a workgroup cannot disregard management rules and orders without risking formal (as well as unofficial sanctions). On the other hand, the group may 'restrict output', establishing norms determining the proper amount of a day's work (not too much or too little). The group member cannot disregard group rules without suffering the ensuing unofficial sanctions.

By such rules the internal strife and competition between the workers is avoided and group solidarity is increased. Thus, one of the main functions of these informal norms is to allow group members to increase their control over the environment, to be less dependent on management and to be better able to resist any external changes threatening their social and economic positions. Moreover, group life becomes a source of social satisfaction and emotional stability for the individual. In that sense it increases workers' satisfaction and lowers absenteeism and turnover.

Group/status formation within organizations or inter-organizational networks serves to manipulate rules as means of enhancing group prerogatives and independence from every direct and arbitrary interference from those higher up. But as rules can never regulate everything and eliminate all arbitrariness, areas of uncertainty always emerge which constitute the focal structural points around which collective conflicts become acute and instances of direct dominance and subordination re-emerge. In such cases the group which, by its position in the occupational structure can control the unregulated area, has a great strategic advantage which is naturally used in order to improve its power position and ensure a greater share of organizational rewards.[88]

C. Members of an organization form social relations, groups, and internal organizations which take on identity, leadership structure and norms of their own. Neither the most systematic rule regime nor stringent management ever succeeds in eliminating such relationships and fully structuring and regulating the social actions and interactions of organizational members. In particular, not all sources of authority and sanction are controlled, nor does the formal allocation of power among positions in the organization occur precisely according to the formal purposes or management interests. Actors in their assigned positions use their assigned positions, including control rights and resources at their disposals, in ways not intended. In particular, Lindblom (1977:24–6) writes:

Authority, both direct and oblique, can always be extended to gain powers beyond the original grant... The East India Company, given certain authority to do business in India in the Seventeeth Century, extended that authority until it became the actual government of parts of India... A political machine is an authority structure built on an extended use of prior authority. The public works official uses his authority over city contracts to extract, in exchange for a benefit, a grant of authority from each of the men who will constitute the core of his machine. Each then uses the benefit granted him to win concessions of authority from a subordinate group around him.

Members of an organization often gain *undesigned sources of sanction and power,* in connection with emergent opportunities, personal capabilities, or strategies they pursue. In addition or in connection with such informal organization, they develop interpersonal loyalties and norms, which limit or reorient their predisposition to adhere to formal rules and authority. Indeed, the informal structures become valued in themselves for the (alternative) power and influence possibilities they offer, and the loyalties and solidarity they provide. Such vested interests are predisposed to resist and, on the basis of the informal organization, to effectively sabotage the attempts of managers and supervisors to fully enforce formal rules.

Sometimes informal groups and networks emerge in particular forms to buffer individuals and subgroups from the experience of subjection to domination, harsh controls, or impersonality of formal organizations, to provide countervailing strategies and collective support.

D. Members of the organization often create rules and procedures with which to better perform their formal assignments (Dalton, 1959; Litterer, 1969)).[89] Litterer, among others, has pointed out that the design of formal organizations cannot take into account everything necessary to complete the technical aspects of a task or position assignments. He observes (1969:162):

> Consequently, in order to do the work assigned to him, a person frequently has to add many things that are not called for in the formal organization plan, additions which may require him to obtain the support and assistance of other people (Roy, 1964).

Generally speaking, we find two fundamental reasons why 'informal' rules and entire rule systems may be observed even in settings where 'formal systems' have official or legitimate status and exclude other systems. The explanations are formulated in terms of two principles, *the principle of bounded rationality* and *the nonexclusivity principle.*

The principle of bounded rationality

A regime is never complete unto itself. As argued earlier, any rule system requires in its implementation situational analysis, interpretations, and adaptation to the concrete situation where it is to be executed. Action settings vary in time and space. In the latter case, variation is observable in rule interpretation and implementation, arising from situational factors. Participants also adopt rules and innovate with a view to complementing the formal system. Organizational settings change in time, in connection with the introduction of new technology and techniques, changes in participants or relationships among participants, leading to innovations in practices and in the rules.

In general, even if an organization or family of organizations is governed by a given regime (or very similar regimes), and the membership generally supports the regime, rules of an 'informal' nature are invariably introduced in order to improve their performance. These innovations — let us assume for the moment that they are motivated within the formal framework — arise in relation to concrete action problems and changes in, or peculiarities of, the action setting (the adaptation principle). Burns and Stalker (1961), Perrow (1979), among others have stressed that basic 'organizing principles' are typically adapted to different environments or changes in environment. Also, as we discuss later (Chapter 12), inconsistencies and contradictions in social rule systems motivate the initiation of new rules, or the formation of new systems, etc.

The principle of insufficient exclusivity

Action settings are embedded in larger social structures and are partially open to the introduction of unofficial or informal rule systems which are not derivations of, or fully compatible with, the official or formal system. In other words, the official or formal systems — and the agents of power enforcing it — are never able to fully 'close' the action setting to which they apply, excluding other systems. Of course, exclusivity is a matter of degree, some settings being governed much more stringently and effectively by the official or formal regime than others.

One of Weber's great insights was to show some of the conditions under which a high degree of exclusivity and domination was accomplished through the rational–bureaucratic principles of organizing. *In practice, however, complete exclusivity and domination is rarely or never achieved, certainly not over any extended period of time. Multiple regimes structure and regulate social action and interaction in any given sphere — even one where a particular regime enjoys legal–rational or official status.* However, the extent of exclusivity and the coherence of the multiple rule systems applied in a given setting will vary. In some instances, the 'multiple action logics' are more or less compatible, in part because they have emerged from a single cultural frame. In other instances, competing or incompatible logics obtain. The actors in the situation experience contradictory directives, ambiguity, and uncertainty. Conflicts are more likely.[90]

In this sense there is a continual politics to social organizing. Those with legal or official power try to impose on others the regime or variants of it which they represent. At the same time, subordinate members to varying degrees resist, attempting to increase or retain areas of discretion. Actual organizational structure is the result of struggles, negotiations, and adjustments between potentially opposed groups.

We have stressed that actors in organizations do not simply passively conform to role-sets and organizational procedures. They reinterpret, creatively reformulate, and replace or ignore organizational rules and procedures. In some cases, they do this because they believe that they improve performance by doing so. Such behaviour is more likely among members who are involved in or identify with the performance of the organization. They adhere to the basic organizing principles and purposes set down by those who dominate the organization.

Reinterpretation, reformulation and transformation of formal rules and procedures also arise in connection with instances of class and group struggles, for example in work places between worker or status interests and the managers or administrators of the organization. As Salaman (1980:140) points out:

> This notion of organizational members pursuing interests when they interpret and define proper or appropriate behavior, rather than merely performing roles has the advantage not only of relating organizational events to *larger societal processes*, but it also draws attention to the possibility of group rather than merely individual (role) conflict.

Conclusion

We have formulated in this chapter the principles of bounded rationality and insufficient exclusivity to explain why multiple, intersecting social rule systems arise, even in action settings where a single, formal system with a legal or official status is intended to exclude or dominate the others.

One explanation is technical in character, based on the limited rationality of any given rule system; the other is social or political. Actors interested in or engaged in a sphere try to introduce, activate, and develop systems other than the formal. The principle of bounded rationality explains why even for actors adhering to a single legitimate regime, they will be motivated to adapt rules as well as to introduce additional rules. The second principle explains the appearance of 'informal rule systems' in terms of the tendency for actors to introduce additional rule systems which are 'irrelevant' or 'incompatible' with the official or formal system in the relevant action arena. In a certain sense, the principles are offered as explanations of why multiple rule systems are activated and govern action in a given sphere or arena, even when ideology and an elite advocate a unitary system.

The emergence of informal, including deviant operative, rule systems arises in part because the designers of the formal or official systems fail to take into account the concrete problems of implementation, conflict, power and negotiation which arise in organized social life. They may be ignorant of the action settings to which the formal system is to apply. Or, for political or ideological reasons, they simply ignore such conditions. The gaps between 'theory and practice' in social organization develop and persist because there are extremely weak feedback, interpretative–evaluative and social learning linkages. (Improved linkages could contribute to institutional innovations reducing discrepancies.)

As discussed in this chapter, various factors contribute to discrepancies between the public, official rule systems and the informal systems operating in practice:

(i) the multiplicity and variety of concrete action situations and problems which agents engaged in the sphere of action must contend with and which result in 'innovative deviation' from public official systems.

(ii) new problems arise — or in some instances the environment itself changes — confronting those involved with problem situations which they must try to solve practically. Often there is no possibility, either politically or within an acceptable time frame, to reformulate the public, official rules. The solutions organizational participants come forth with — ad hoc, pragmatic rules — reflect not only the types of problems with which they must contend but the frameworks of knowledge, interests and resources they bring to bear on the problems'.

(iii) rule systems applying in a particular sphere — or specific sub-sets of rules — may be contradictory. Such contradictions are often resolved in pragmatic ways where the particular actors involved take into account the relative power of different interests supporting the various rule systems, or the visibility of the activity in question, etc.

(iv) those involved locally have differing interpretations, strategies, and styles in implementing the official rules. They compete and struggle with one another. Group dynamics, conflict and conflict resolution often play a more important role than the formal content of the 'public rule system' concerning which rules are operative.

(v) even in ideal circumstances, those engaged in implementing official rule systems are confronted with local norms, power networks, and social agents that compel them to 'negotiate' with their environment. This results in adaptation and reformulation of the official rules.

These and related factors point up the variety of ways that informal rule systems may develop either as an intelligent adaptation and even a refinement of official rules and/or as forms serving purposes and interests other than those embodied in the formal system. Through an examination of the emergence and development of informal operative rule systems in public agencies, we can better understand the underlying logic and the often counter-intuitive behaviour of such agencies.

Elsewhere (Burns and Tropea, 1985) we take up such problems in connection with analyses of criminal justice systems in the USA. We show that the 'public' and 'backstage' rule systems derive from the different demands on a public administration: on the one hand, it is expected to uphold laws and even non-legal norms. This is its 'public image'. On the other hand, it (or its officialdom) is expected to carry out certain tasks, solving concrete situational problems as they do so: prevent crime, arrest offenders, process them and make judgements on them.

The divergence or incoherence between the concrete tasks and the demands of public image derives, in part, from the division of labour between 'public officials' and the 'public servants' who must carry on. It is also institutionalized in the separation of rule-making and rule-reformation from rule-implementation. Often, there is no public forum for bringing 'theory into dialectical contact with practice'. Weak feedback linkages are particularly characteristic of hierarchical systems where there is a division of labour between those who deal publicly with obtaining resources and legitimation and those who work with the concrete everyday problems and tasks for which the organization is responsible. Subordinate actors or 'the operatives' are often those who introduce or develop 'informal rules' in order to solve practical problems which the shapers of formal systems ignore or miss in order to realize their own particular interests and values.

Typically, local or subordinate actors lack the power resources to change the formal or official rule systems. Even the 'top dogs' may be in no position to openly ignore or oppose the official rules. Hence, the common pattern that adaptations and reformulations of official systems in practice are carried out surreptitiously. The unofficial, implicit or unwritten rules become widespread and equally as important, if not more so in some instances, than the official rules.

Following chapters on multiple rule systems
and conflict
The following chapters apply rule system theory to the analysis of

administrative structures, their contradictions, and reformations. Chapter 12 examines multiple rule systems in the energy policy sphere of local government in Holland, pointing out contradictions in these systems and some of the consequences they have. We also point out certain meta-rules local authorities use to resolve contradictions between different rule regimes originating in central government agencies. Chapter 13 describes and analyses a complex administrative system for planning and managing hydro-power development in Norway. We identify some of the structural features of the administrative system including the institutionalized strategies whereby those controlling the system are able to dominate peripheral groups, even in the face of dissatisfaction and opposition. Of particular interest here are processes whereby counter-institutional and counter-cultural rule frames emerge in opposition to the administrative complex, destabilizing it and contributing ultimately to its restructuring. (Chapters 15 and 16 also deal with multiple, partially contradictory rule systems anchored in different social groups whose members interact with one another in policy-setting arenas.)

12

Local public administration as an arena of conflicting rule systems

Tom R. Burns and Reinier de Man

Introduction

In this and the following chapter we present case studies which illustrate several of the concepts introduced in the last chapter: multiple rule systems, formal and informal rule systems, conflicts between groups or organizations with vested interests in different systems, and meta-rules or institutionalized strategies to resolve conflicts between initially incompatible rule systems.

This chapter examines local government in Holland, focusing on energy policies and programmes, as a setting where agents governed by multiple regimes meet and come into competition and conflict. Politics, coalition formation, and negotiation characterize these local arenas. In some cases, local government authorities, using informal *'meta-rules'*, resolve the dilemmas, contradictions and cross-pressures which they encounter. They do this in ways not anticipated or intended by those agencies at the national level who formulate and reformulate the 'relevant' rule regimes. In other words, local government practice — in this case concerning energy conservation — diverges substantially from the formal policies and regulations formulated at the central level. In general, the conventional model of two or more levels of government does not fit the behaviour of government found in our studies. At the local level, where administration (or 'the implementation of policies') is supposed to take place, policies are made. Politics is the real name of the game.

Energy conservation policy versus established rule systems

The Dutch housing sector. Administrative segmentation, multiple rule systems, and the development of local, informal rules are interrelated aspects of the institutional arrangements of government. These may block or re-direct policy measures. In the Netherlands, government efforts to bring about energy conservation in new housing led to just such blockage and re-direction, as we show below.

The implementation of housing policy in the Netherlands is concentrated at the local administrative level, the municipality, local government ('Gemeente'). As a result, specific decisions on energy quality (insulation, heating equipment, etc.) are also taken at this lower administrative level. Obviously, these decisions are made under a great number of nationally defined boundary conditions. Leaving the middle-level ('Provincie') out of consideration, a two-level administrative model is obtained, at least for European type unitary states (see Figure 12.1).

FIGURE 12.1
The conventional two-level model of government

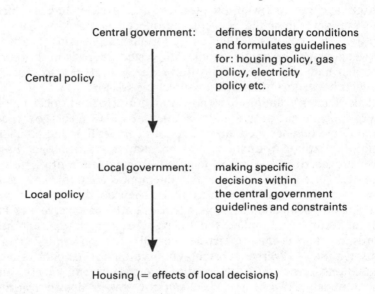

Central policy — Central government: defines boundary conditions and formulates guidelines for: housing policy, gas policy, electricity policy etc.

Local policy — Local government: making specific decisions within the central government guidelines and constraints

Housing (= effects of local decisions)

Our research suggests, however, that the model is very poor in describing and analysing the actual regulative processes with regard to housing. On the one hand, the conventional model suggests that:

• Central government acts in a unified manner. It imposes unbiased, non-contradictory, operational rules at the local level.
• These rules leave a well-defined space for local policy to fill.
• These rules are well-known and fully understood at the local level.

The reality is different:

• Central government itself is institutionally divided. Agents advocating different goals and different rule systems compete for influence.

- These systems often leave little or no space for local policy. In some instances the rules may prescribe more than is consistently or practically possible on the basis of existing resources.
- The local actors often lack elementary knowledge of many centrally defined rules.

Consequently, we propose a different regulative model, one more consistent with both empirical facts and theoretical considerations. Given the segmented character of the central government institutions, the 'local' level is considered *an arena for different institutional claims, e.g. claims from the electricity institutions and claims from the housing and building institutions, each based on its own coalition, power base and rule regime.* Local policy, in that case is nothing more, and nothing less, than the process by which the different institutional claims are selected, negotiated, linked or denied by local government actors. This process is by no means chaotic, there are regularities in it. It has its own logic, follows its own rules. Local level agents develop their own rule regime, consisting, to a great extent, of strategic rules for handling rule systems of the different institutions. These systems are indicated in Figure 12.2.

FIGURE 12.2
Multiple rule systems and the local arena

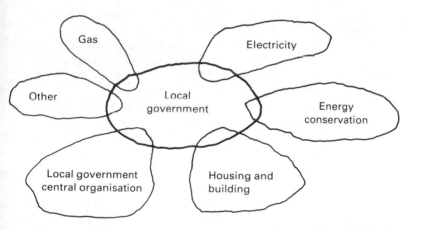

In Figure 12.2 central government departments are not indicated, rather *institutional segments,* i.e. associations of a variety of state, semi-state and private organizations and groups. Local government in this model is not just a lower level in the administrative hierarchy. *It is the meeting-place or arena where institutional claims meet.*

Energy efficient housing:
A complex of institutional claims and rule regimes
Energy efficiency in housing can be established by two means or a combination of these: improving the thermal properties of the house or improving the efficiency standards of the heating equipment. The technical solution of this energy problem entails the enactment of a number of different rule-systems, connected with the various relevant institutional spheres:

(a) Construction in the housing sector is governed by a vast and complex regulation system. Its main elements are related to financing, rent calculation, subsidies and quality control.

(b) Changing the type of heating equipment, or even the type of energy carrier (from oil to gas, from gas to city heating systems), brings at least two institutional segments into the arena: the gas segment and the electricity segment. The rule regimes of these segments embrace a variety of tariff-structures, grid-connection conditions, safety standards and controls, etc. The rule regimes also contain calculation methods for defining the advantage of one energy carrier or heating system over the other.

(c) Demands for achieving a high degree of energy efficiency are usually made by other institutional agents than those mentioned in (a) and (b). These claims come from new, only partially institutionalized, networks of environmental groups, innovative technical and social entrepreneurs (see Baumgartner and Burns, 1984).

(d) If the promotion of energy conservation and energy efficiency at the local level means the design of new administrative structures and procedures, these will be influenced by the institutionalized rules for local government administration.

(e) There are a number of other institutional segments which appear on the local stage, once energy efficiency problems are solved. The financial situation of a local government, for example, is heavily dependent on central government's decisions in this respect (Ministry of the Interior).

The rule regimes governing housing
In Holland the housing rule-regime is tied to an extended *neo-corporatist network of private interests* (building companies, finance, labour unions etc.), and semi-state and state organizations. Such networks stabilize the relations between government policy and private business strategies. Industry accepts a high degree of state

regulation because of the many advantages stabilization offers for construction and housing 'markets'. Business interests themselves have a considerable influence on the form and the content of these regulations which actually leads to a form of 'self-regulation' (see Zald, 1978).

In the housing sector, the government financed and subsidized social housing ('sociale woningbouw') sector of rented houses is the most regulated sector of all. The housing sector primarily serves a social goal, i.e. providing cheap homes for low income groups. Financing is achieved through low interest state loans (with 100 percent coverage), and rents are kept artificially low. These rents do not have any relation to actual exploitation costs but are calculated as a low percentage (between five and six percent) of the total building costs per dwelling. As a result, rents only cover half of the real exploitation costs. The difference between economically acceptable rents (as defined by another regulation) and real rents is paid by the government as a subsidy to the owner, in this case a legally defined public organization. As a result, the government's main concern is the control of building costs. This is accomplished through setting maximum values for building costs per dwelling as well as through the establishment of a number of incentive systems. One of these incentives is a rule by which the 'rent percentage' (the rent as a percentage of building costs) increases as the building costs increase (given the size of the dwelling).

Obviously, there is no guarantee for the quality of such housing. In a classical market higher quality would give rise to higher rents. In this system, rents are administratively linked to building costs.

An example may help point up this linkage. Table 12.1 shows a part of the table for calculating rents on the basis of total housing costs and number of 'living units'.

Energy conservation investment may result in an augmentation of this rent percentage so that the rent increases proportionately more

TABLE 12.1
Calculation of rents

Building costs in 1000 Dfl	Number of living units		
	3 (%)	4 (%)	5 (%)
100	5.3	5.2	5.1
101	5.4	5.3	5.2
102	5.4	5.3	5.2
103	5.5	5.4	5.3
104	5.5	5.4	5.3
105	5.6	5.5	5.4

than the building costs.[91] *Such a rate structure results in negative sanctions against energy conservation.* On the other hand, it encourages conservation measures which entail financial efforts outside the total building costs. For example, it favours measures taken by the utilities as opposed to those which are administratively included in the total building costs (de Man and Van Rossum, 1984:53–65).

The rule on the maximum allowed building costs acts also as a barrier to energy conservation measures. The cost-effectiveness of energy conservation measures is not taken into account. As a result, total living costs are not minimized. The rules steer building costs, not living costs. Cost-effective energy investments are blocked or constrained due to the limitations on building costs.

FIGURE 12.3
Building rules and cost structure
(Single unit in multi-unit structure)

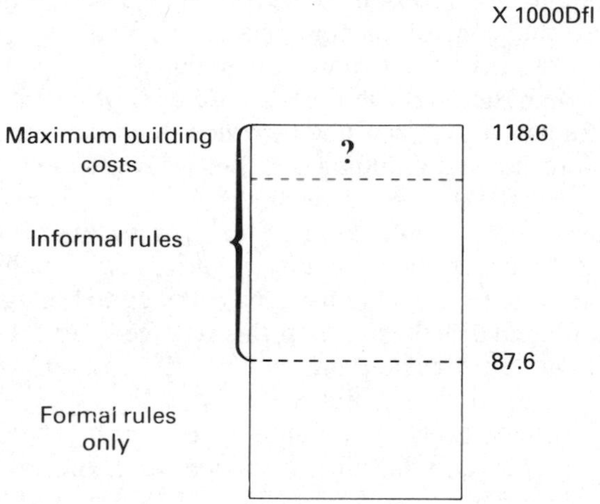

X 1000Dfl

Maximum building costs — 118.6

?

Informal rules

87.6

Formal rules only

In 1982, the maximum building costs, for a certain type of dwelling, were Dfl 118,600. Applying the minimum prescribed formal regulation, it was not feasible to build a dwelling for less than Dfl 87,600. In principle, there remained some Dfl 30,000 available for allocation. *However, in practice, the amount available was much smaller, because of the many informal rules governing house construction.* That is, many aspects of housing, although not formally included in the building code or in other regulations, were important parts of *established building practice.* Central heating and tiles in the bathroom, to mention two examples, are such elements of construction practice. Moreover, they reflect concepts of suitable housing in Holland and, indeed, are part and parcel of established life style. Consequently, the actual allocation possibilities for energy conservation are much more limited than what appears to be possible on the basis of an assessment of the formal rules alone. A serious proposal for major energy conservation in the housing sector would require a systematic analysis and reformulation of building norms, including the many informal and unwritten rules.[92]

Energy is only a very partial, but growing, concern to the decision makers in the housing sector. After the 1973 energy crisis, the energy requirements, in terms of the k-parameter (heat conductivity of walls etc.), were changed in the direction of a somewhat better insulation prescription. In 1978 a second improvement of the k-parameter was introduced in the building code (mbv). After 1978 no further changes were made, in spite of considerable pressures from a variety of groups and organizations in Dutch society. The increasingly difficult financial situation made the government cautious in introducing new quality prescriptions which could cost money.[93]

Energy supply and the impact on housing energy policy
In the decision making process on energy efficient housing, the agents of different energy-supply institutions have important impacts. Their rule systems contain a variety of regulations relating to, among others:

• conditions for connection to the gas, electricity, city heating systems (in terms of safety regulations, financial conditions, etc.)
• price setting of energy carriers, influencing the relative attractions of energy supply forms and energy conservation efforts
• evaluation rules for investments in energy conservation. These rules differ widely between the different supply sectors

In the Netherlands, the main energy form for house heating is natural gas. Coal, electricity and oil are negligible. There is but one serious competitor for gas: city heating. City heating systems deliver warm water to the client. The heat is supplied by electricity plants or by industries with waste heat. As demand for city heating does not necessarily equal the availability of these heat sources, additional heat-generating units are necessary. These units use either gas or oil in the case of a diesel-unit. See Figure 12.4.

In the decision-making process leading to the choice between gas-heating and city-heating systems, two institutional segments and their respective rule regimes are involved: the gas sector and the electricity sector. For simplicity, we only consider the situation where an electricity plant is the main heat source and we ignore the

FIGURE 12.4
Energy flows related to house heating (Netherlands):

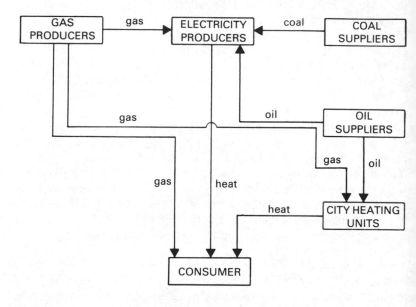

less common situation where industrial heat is involved.

Gas. Natural gas is not only the most important energy source in the Netherlands, but the economic rent obtained from the national and international gas trade is an indispensable part of Dutch government finance. In 1981 gas revenues were more than 19 billion guilders, of which 13 billion guilders were related to gas exports (2.2 guilders = approximately 1 dollar). This financial interest in natural gas implies that a policy for energy conservation may lead to a reduction of government income. This is certainly not a positive incentive for ambitious energy conservation plans. The same situation occurs at the lower administrative level. Local governments obtain a certain amount of income through their public utilities. Energy conservation programmes may reduce this income. On pp. 251–3 this will be explained further.

Gas prices, especially relative to prices of other energy sources and to costs of efficiency improvements, are a very important element in the decision processes on energy-efficient housing. The current prices, the expected prices and the type of evaluation rules define to a large extent the decisions to be taken. The Law on Gas Prices (Wet Aardgasprijzen, 1974) defines the roles of the different institutional actors (see Figure 12.5).

FIGURE 12.5
Gas institutions

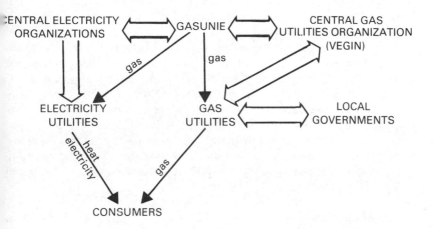

All major gas transactions in the Netherlands are made by Gasunie. Gasunie buys indigenous and imported gas from the oil companies and sells it to large consumers, electricity companies and gas utilities. The prices are settled between Gasunie and its clients, within the framework of the Law on Gas Prices. The government (Ministry of Economic Affairs) acts as a third party and has veto-power over the contracts between Gasunie and its clients. The mentioned law requires that gas prices are equal to market prices of alternative energy carriers. The government distinguishes between two market segments:

(a) *The small consumer market.* Here the only alternative to natural gas is heating oil for domestic use. Gas prices should reflect an equivalence to this type of oil on a caloric basis. This is the rule for so-called domestic fuel oil parity: HBO-parity principle.

(b) *The large consumer market,* including electric utilities. The alternative to natural gas is a heavier and cheaper type of fuel oil. Gas prices are defined on the basis of the so-called industrial fuel oil parity (stookoliepariteit). As the industrial fuel oil has a lower quality and is cheaper than the domestic fuel oil, prices on the large consumer market are accordingly lower. Consumer gas prices are settled in a negotiation process between Gasunie and the central representative of the gas utilities, the VEGIN. Gasunie sticks to the HBO-principle (see (a)) and is supported by the Ministry of Economic Affairs. On the other hand, the VEGIN aims at lower gas prices in order to avoid conflicts between gas utilities and consumers that would result from rapid price increases. The result of VEGIN's resistance to gas price increases has been a lower gas price than would have been defined on the basis of the HBO-parity principle. (Small consumer prices, between 1972 and 1982, increased from 12.1 cents to 46.9 cents. On the basis of the HBO-principle the 1982 price should have been 67.6 cents.)

The negotiation between VEGIN and Gasunie is basically over consumer gas prices and not over the prices paid by the gas utilities to Gasunie. The latter price is defined on the basis of a second set of rules, the so-called gas price margin regulation. The price to be paid by the gas utilities is the consumer gas price minus a margin. The utilities need this margin for covering their exploitation costs (capital costs, operating costs of the gas distribution system) and, eventually, for making a moderate profit. This gas price margin regulation is settled in a separate negotiation process between VEGIN and Gasunie.

City heating

City heating systems obtain their heat from electricity generating plants and some additional heat generating units. In that case, city heating is closely connected to the electricity institutions and their sector specific rules. The main alternative to city heating is the direct consumption of gas. This explains disagreements between city heating institutions and the gas institutions concerning gas prices and the rules for evaluation of city heating systems. The city heating institutions (i.e. their nation-wide institution VESTIN and the electricity institution KEMA) accuse the gas institutions of formulating rules for price determination that lead to unfair competition. The city heating companies, for example, pay small consumer gas prices for their auxilary heat generating plants, instead of the more favourable industrial gas prices. The city heating institutions also argue that the gas price margin regulation leads to a high comparative advantage of direct gas use in relation to city heating. They say that energy conservation could be achieved by more favourable conditions (in terms of prices) for city heating. The gas institutions strongly disagree. Their argument is that the electricity institutions pay unfairly low gas prices in comparison to the gas utilities. Moreover, they argue that city heating, although justified on the basis of the energy conservation goal, is only promoted in order to improve the financial situation of the electricity companies.[94]

Deciding on city heating investment consists of planning under a *high degree of uncertainty*. The gas price, a dominant element in the cost-benefit analysis, is particularly uncertain. Yet, for the calculation, a gas price scenario for the whole exploitation period is assumed. The administrative solution to this problem is that the Ministry itself defines the long-term gas scenario that serves as a basis for the cost-benefit analysis. However, the long-term gas price scenarios tend to be revised suddenly and unpredictably over time. The official forecasts for gas price developments have become substantially lower over the past five years.

Another interesting feature of these cost-benefit analyses is the influence of engineering bureaus on the outcome of the analysis. Various bureaus, with special ties to the relevant institutional segments, apply different rules. *In this case, the rules are disguised as neutral technical and economic analyses, which they are not.* There is a strong normative element in these analyses. It turns out that cost-benefit analyses made by the central electricity organization (KEMA) are systematically more in favour of city heating than those made by the engineering bureau of the central gas organization (VEG-gasinstituut). This difference is a result of systematic differences in the various technical and economic assumptions underlying the analyses. Consider, for example, the two parameters indicated below.

	KEMA (electricity)	VEG(gas)
1. peak heat demand	lower	higher
2. gas price increase	higher	lower

A higher peak heat demand implies the construction of a pipe system with higher capacity. As the principal costs of city heating derive from capital costs, this is negative for city heating. A lower gas price makes direct heating by gas more attractive, but it hardly has any influence on the costs of city heating.

The differences between KEMA's and VEG's parameter choices are consistent with vested institutional interests. The 'electricity world', which is responsible for and promotes city heating, is much more positive toward city heating than the gas world.

Energy conservation
In the complex, segmented system with its various games, it is difficult to identify unambiguously the institutional sectors which favour energy conservation. Traditionally, energy institutions were predominantly supply-oriented. Systematic attention to demand control (energy conservation) had failed until recently. After the energy crisis of 1973, a growing institutionalization of the energy demand side took two forms:

• a slow reform within the existing institutions

- pressure on the existing institutions from the outside, exerted by environmental groups, anti-nuclear groups, consumer organizations
- the formation of organizations which become partly institutionalized within the established institutional networks

Within the established energy institutions, the orientation is still supply-side oriented, but there is a growing attention to energy conservation in the gas and electricity organizations as well as in government departments. The Ministry of Economic Affairs has special units for carrying out energy conservation programmes. The gas and electricity organizations promote, seemingly against their own commercial interests, more efficient energy use. Also the Ministry of Housing is in favour of energy conservation, but is *very careful to avoid promoting technical solutions which involve economic risks*. As a result, the Housing Ministry's emphasis is more on promoting energy conserving behaviour than on changes in housing design or heating equipment.

More ambitious, in this respect, are certain 'outside' groups and organizations. Their rules for deciding on energy questions are more in favour of overall energy conservation. The great public awareness of the importance of energy conservation is, in part, a by-product of the anti-nuclear issue in Holland. In the early seventies, the nuclear debate presented itself as a coal–uranium dilemma. The anti-nuclear movement, not willing to be caught in such a dilemma, concentrated on the demand side, thus avoiding a debate on two unattractive supply alternatives. In the Netherlands, this demand side debate was institutionalized in the 'Public Debate on Nuclear Energy' ('Maatschappelijke Discussie over Kernenergie'). (See de Man and Rossum, 1984.) The results of this public procedure were not satisfactory for the anti-nuclear and environmental groups. However, it played a definite role in institutionalizing a focus on the demand side (conservation) of the energy problem. It also stimulated a consensus formation process between a variety of groups, and it stimulated the establishment of a moderate but growing contact between this energy conservation network and administrative agencies at both the central and the local level. The centre of this network is the Energy Conservation Centre ('Centrum voor Energiebesparing'). This combines a strong anti-nuclear ideological orientation with extended engineering expertise in the energy field. The Centre is, so to speak, the engineering bureau of the anti-nuclear and environmental movements and the counterpart of the engineering bureaus of the gas and electricity institutions. The Centre gives advice on such matters as local energy saving projects, combined heat and power (co-generation), city heating and so forth. The principles and rules which underlie the Centre's calculations are ideologically biased toward conservation options.

Other institutional claims
Apart from the above mentioned claims from the housing, the energy supply, and the energy demand (that is, conservation) sectors, there are a variety of other claims on the local level concerning housing and energy conservation decisions. For brevity, we limit ourselves to the role of the nation-wide organization of Dutch municipalities (Vereniging van Nederlandse Gemeenten, VNG). This organization has a double function. It defends the local administrative interest at the central political and administrative level and it gives advice to its members, the municipalities, on financial and administrative matters. This advice is specially important for the smaller municipalities. The VNG published advice on the organization of local energy conservation policy in 1979 (VNG, 1979). A large number of municipalities adopted the organizational structure which was proposed in that advice. This structure entails an Energy Conservation Steering Group and a number of technical Working Groups on the relevant energy conservation issues. In the Steering Group, all the relevant internal administrative sectors are represented, such as the gas utility, the housing department, the financial department, the public relations department, etc. For technical advice, technical experts from the gas or electricity institutions are invited to join the Steering Group. In practice, the local gas utility often plays a dominant role, in that, for example, the chairman is at the same time the gas utility's director.

The complexity of formal systems and the consequences for the local rule regime

Local policy as a problem
Decision making at the lower administrative level involves many different, often complex and contradictory rule regimes. Rule complexity and inconsistency present special problems as well as opportunities to the local policy maker. Contradictions arise between different rule regimes, in particular the dilemma of choosing, for example, between evaluation rules found in different institutional spheres. In a practical decision situation, the problem is generally solved by selection and simplification of the rules.

   Local decision-makers try to solve problems arising from rule complexity and contradictions and to make use of inherent opportunities. They do not do this in a haphazard way. They apply their own (meta-) rule regime, which entails the institutionalized ways of handling the competing or conflicting rule regimes of different institutional spheres.

In the following discussion we shall confine ourselves mainly to the housing rule regime. The complexity of the rule regime has already been mentioned:

- the detailed regulations on finance, subsidy and quality.
- the rapid change of many rules, creation of new ones, abolition of rules.
- the absence of checks on consistency.

The administrative answer to this complexity is the application of a set of informal meta-rules, i.e. rules for applying or not applying particular rules or rule sets and replacing formal rules with informal, often unwritten rules.[95]

The rules-in-use are independent of the official rules
It is often said that the relatively low standards for home insulation as prescribed in the national building code (see p. 244ff) present a barrier to energy efficient housing in the Netherlands. This is only partly correct. Many local governments, or at least the building and housing sectors within those governments, apply rules which set much higher standards than officially required. These rules are often part of an unwritten operative system.

Competing rule regimes and local choice
At the local policy level, a variety of institutional interests compete for influence. In our terminology, the local rule regime applies to the selection or reconciliation of a variety of not fully compatible rule regimes. This is pointed up by the problem of competing evaluation rules utilized in the gas and electricity sectors as well as those advanced by adherents to energy conservation. If we consider the local administrative level as the 'stage' where the different institutional actors play their games, local policy is, in these terms, a matter of adequate 'stage management'. Its rule regime contains rules about *who* should appear on the stage *during which phase of the decision process.*

This local rule regime for 'stage management' is very often based on the standard structure which has been designed by the central organization of Dutch Municipalities (VNG), and on a number of unwritten rules by which the local gas utility is given an important role in energy conservation policy. Important gas representatives become members of the Energy Conservation Steering Group, and the gas utility is given an additional task to promote energy conservation. Not only is the local gas utility involved but the central gas institutions and their rule regimes become major factors in 'local policy'. In one of our case studies, we found that efforts to turn the gas utility into a general energy utility resulted in a situation *where the general energy problem was transformed into a gas problem!*

A more active form of 'stage management' is found in the case planning and public decision-making concerning city heating and passive solar energy in the Municipality Haarlemmermeer. In a drawn-out decision process (1973–1984) the community finally opted for passive solar housing designs and opposed a city heating project. This process followed a number of steps. (1) 1973–1977. The electricity company (at the provincial level) developed a plan for a large heat-pipe system, intended for city-heating. New districts of Haarlemmermeer were to be connected to that system. (2) 1978–1981. The local government of Haarlemmermeer wanted to control the developments. A City Heating Group was set up, in which, apart from local and provincial actors, central gas and electricity institutions were represented. The engineering bureau of the central electricity organizations prepared a preliminary cost-benefit analysis which favoured city heating. There was no substantial opposition to the city heating plans until 1981. (3) 1981–1984. By this time there had emerged growing attention to alternative means for conserving energy. Pressure from the energy conservation proponents resulted in the commissioning of a study on the possibilities of 'passive solar'. The study was paid by the government funding an organization for solar research. The organization was sympathetic toward energy conservation goals and had relations with energy conservation groups and organizations mentioned earlier. Passive solar, from that moment on, became a serious competitor to city heating. At the same time, a more elaborate cost-benefit analysis on city heating was published by the electricity organization KEMA, which remained positive toward the city heating option. At the time, the municipal council was doubtful about the need for a city heating system and was, therefore, critical toward the expected positive outcomes reported by KEMA. Without a more detailed follow-up of this study, no decision on city heating could be taken, according to the council. In the meantime, the study on passive solar energy yielded very favourable results supporting the advocates of passive solar (and opponents to city heating). After long and cumbersome discussions and negotiations, a follow-up study on city heating was commissioned to an independent engineering bureau rather than to one of the energy institutions. In the new study, the financial results of a city heating system were found to be much less favourable than in the KEMA analysis, but nevertheless favourable.

This came as a bit of a surprise to the City Heating Group, who had asked the engineering bureau to use less optimistic assumptions. Nevertheless, the city heating project was considered unfeasible by the City Heating Group, when the set of additional cost factors which had not been taken into account by the engineering bureau were considered.

The formal decision against city heating was taken in early 1984. An additional incentive for this was the sudden change of the long term gas price scenario of the government. This was the final blow to the project, a project whose planning began in 1973.

In the third stage of the decision process, a coalition of city officials initiated 'stage management' in order to prevent city heating from being accepted. This entailed (a) replacing the electricity organization KEMA by an independent engineering bureau; and (b) placing the conservation oriented institutional network on the stage, and thereby introducing another set of evaluation rules.

Finally, we should note the situation where there is no possibility to exclude a certain rule regime in advance, but where many different rule regimes are simultaneously applied to the same decision process or situation. Such an example is found again in the Haarlemmermeer case study. The negative decision on city heating was coupled to a positive decision on passive solar designs. This meant an additional constraint on spatial orientation and the use of space in general.

Overall, several incompatible spatial constraints on energy planning could be identified in Haarlemmermeer. For instance, the introduction and development of passive solar energy entails the activation of a variety of rules and regulations: (i) the central government's rule on the required green space per dwelling; (ii) rules for maximum land costs per dwelling; (iii) norms for street structures (in order to prevent monotony); (iv) rules concerning maintenance of the old polder structure; (v) government norms on public transport; (vi) rules controlling street costs and orientation of front doors.

Applying all these rules leads to more equations than unknowns. In practice we expect that the more stringent economic rules are likely to be sustained, whereas the others will be weakened or completely ignored. This suggests, in fact, a very bleak future for passive solar energy, although none of the major actors would agree that this is intended.

Central policy and local freedom
The studies reported here point up some of the basic problems

relating to the effectiveness of central government policies and freedom for local action.

Among policy-makers and the broader public it is generally believed that greater regulation invariably implies more control. However, as the analysis suggests, an increase in the number of rules formulated at the central policy level may contribute to *decreasing* central control. Local implementation often involves a variety of negotiations over rules, implementation games, etc. *Attempts at increased central regulation may bring about a net loss of control.* This may occur in two ways:

(i) The increase in rules increases control in policy field X, at the same time that it adds to policy complexity as a whole so that central control over policy fields W,Y,Z, etc. is weakened.

(ii) Even control over policy field X can be weakened by adding more rules which ostensibly are intended to increase control over X.

A loss of control by the central level implies enhanced freedom for the local level and, potentially, enhanced local control over policy. As our material suggests, the complexity of the central rules and the competition between several rule systems (and their institutional segments) creates opportunities for effective local initiative. Whether these opportunities are exploited or realized depends on three factors: (1) the extent opportunities are perceived; (2) the resources available to local policy-makers; and (3) their political skills.

On the basis of these considerations, it is not obvious that energy conservation policy in the social housing sector is best achieved through central prescriptions, for instance more demanding norms in the building code. Provided that the motivation and the expertise are available at the local level, local policy-makers may realize such a policy better with *decreased* central regulation.

The analyses reported here have considerable implications for the study of politics, policy and implementation. In our model of local administration, the local level is an arena for different institutional interests and their associated rule systems. This makes the local level — in the formal framework of relatively centralized states the level where central policies are supposed to be implemented — the political level *par excellence*. The formal policy structure and the actual world of policy-making represent two different worlds. This theme is explored further in the following chapter.

13
Hydro-power administration in a changing world: Industrial growth, environmentalism and centre–periphery struggle in Norway

Tom R. Burns and Atle Midttun

Introduction

This chapter examines the structure and dynamics of an institutionalized system of public domination: hydro-power planning and administration in Norway.[96] Norwegian hydro-power has a long history and its study provides a number of interesting insights into institutional dynamics and the interplay between political, economic and organizational factors.

At its peak in the 1960s, the hydro-power decision-making and planning system emerged as an integrated segment with well-defined participants, clearly specified rules for its organization and planning processes, and relatively well-defined system boundaries vis a vis its environment.

The hydro-power system in this period was the core of an expansive electro-chemical and electro-metallurgical industry which played a dominant role in the national economy. System development was based on a close cooperation between public and private interests. The state had gradually taken over the main part of hydro-power construction and cooperated with dominant private interests in the industrial sector.

The state-owned Norwegian Watercourse and Electrical Authority (NVE) was at the centre of this system. The central decision-making procedure in the NVE system was the giving of concessions to hydro-power projects.

NVE was administratively supervised by the Ministry of Industry (and after 1978 the Oil and Energy Department); it was, therefore, also subject to review by the Industry Committee in Parliament. Enjoying substantial support from private and state industries, the NVE system could mobilize substantial economic resources and political legitimacy. It was able, therefore, to exercise considerable control over its environment and to secure a stable and expansive development for itself.

Hydro-power projects have substantial impacts on the social and physical environments, hurting the interests of some and disturbing the values and social orders of others, in the latter case, for example, Lapp and other local communities. For this reason, the Norwegian authority pursued strategies to dominate and stabilize its environment (and in this sense the study suggests a number of interesting parallels to Selznick's well-known study of TVA (1953), although we do not intend to compare the two studies in this context).

Early on, NVE operated under a mandate — and general political legitimacy for its projects — from the Norwegian Parliament. This, combined with economic compensation as well as incentive funds to individuals and communities, respectively, sufficed in the early post-Second World War period to assure domination and the successful implementation of its plans.

As questioning and criticism increased during the 1960s, NVE pursued a number of new strategies, in particular introducing reforms in the planning process which increased the opportunities for participation of 'legitimate interests' in planning and preparation of projects. This strategy, a form of partial cooptation (Selznick, 1953), did not entail rights to participate in decision-making but only possibilities for these peripheral groups to provide information or to express opinion. The participation of 'legitimate' peripheral groups was to serve as a sounding board for centre initiatives. It also provided channels for persuading peripheral groups and for allowing them to participate in informal, weak forms of negotiation.

A key idea in our analysis is that the maintenance and reproduction of administrative domination over affected actors and groups in its environment depend on:

(i) *cultural hegemony,* whereby an elite or its ideology successfully define values and norms for peripheral groups and potential opponents, that is, their 'interests' and objectives are successfully defined within such a framework.

(ii) *organizational hegemony,* whereby an elite or established institution provides the organizing principles and procedures for public decision-making and administration, in this case relating to hydro-power projects, and these are accepted by peripheral groups and potential opponents.

(iii) *resource control,* including access to economic, political and expert resources whereby an elite can buy off, punish, or delegitimize peripheral groups and potential opponents.

When one or more of these conditions fail to obtain, a system of administrative domination will be destabilized, often leading to reform and even transformation. Opportunities open up for critical examination of and negotiation about the rule regime itself and the rules of the game — rather than about specific project features.

In this chapter we map out the basic structure of hydro-power planning, a rule system complex designed to give concessions to technically and economically feasible hydro-power projects. The complex specifies appropriate participating actors, their various roles, their rights and obligations vis a vis one another, and the procedures and 'rules of the game' of hydro-power planning and decision-making.

We examine the growth in tension and opposition to hydro-power projects during the 1960s and 1970s and the reforms which resulted. The reforms were attempts at adjusting to pressures consistent with the basic organizing principle and purpose of the system. By the late 1960s, nonetheless, hydro-power projects were subject to ever-increasing questioning and challenge, particularly from environmentalists and traditional economic interests such as those associated with farming, fishing and reindeer herding.

We go on to examine the case of a hydro-power project, which evoked organized opposition, eventually leading to the most serious societal confrontation in post-War Norway. The system of administrative domination of hydro-power planning and administration was seriously threatened. The background to the conflict, its course and outcome are examined.

In our analysis of the administrative system, we consider factors such as power and legitimacy which underlie acceptance of or obedience to a regime, or to its destabilization and restructuring.

We then describe the on-going transformation of the system and several of the major forces currently contributing to this development.

The Norwegian hydro-power planning system:
An historical overview

Hydro-power development was already a focus for industrial and financial interests in Norway at the turn of the century. Until the end of the First World War, the country saw a boom of investment in this sector, culminating in the political decision to regulate such activities and to secure watercourses against foreign investment and exploitation. This political process began before the end of World War I. From the 1920s hydro-power development stagnated. A new boom did not take place until after World War II.

After the War, hydro-power was viewed by political leaders and those involved with economic policy-making as a means to build up industry and to contribute to economic growth. The role of the state was organizationally, technically and financially central (see Figure 13.1).

The state's authority, NVE, consisted of four directorates: Through its *State Power Utility,* NVE initiated and developed almost all large-scale hydro-power projects in Norway after the Second World War. Sometimes these projects were joint ventures with private and municipal interests. At the same time, NVE's *Watercourse Directorate* was responsible for granting or refusing concessions to build hydro-power facilities and for balancing hydro-power interests against other local and national interests. Through its *Electricity Directorate*, NVE was responsible for the regulation of distribution and setting of rates and for energy planning and forecasting. A fourth directorate handled administrative, legal and economic matters. Some opposed incorporating in the same organization the regulatory agency and the hydro-power developer. However, this viewpoint never gained support, either politically or administratively.

The Board of NVE ('Hovedstyre') consisted of members of parliament except for the General Director. In view of the fact that hydro-power production came to account for almost 10 percent of Norway's GNP (by 1970), NVE became a very important and powerful institution in post-war Norway.

It had political legitimacy. It had access to state monies and support from industry. It employed hundreds of Norway's best engineers. It was in a position to mobilize considerable human and material resources, both in preparing hydro-power and electricity project plans and executing them.

The only major conflicts around hydro-power in the immmediate post-war period were (1) those concerning the allocation of electricity between general consumption as opposed to industrial consumption and (2) the export of electricity to Denmark and Sweden. These conflicts were largely resolved in favour of industry and Norwegian nationalism, respectively. Stress was placed on the development of Norwegian energy intensive industries: electro-metal (light metal and alloy) production and the electro-chemical industry (fertilizer production, among others). Norway became one of the largest producers of aluminium in the world (the second largest producer in Europe after West Germany and second to Canada as the largest exporter in the world).

The 1950s and early 1960s saw the occurrence of some conflicts around hydro-power projects. These concerned distributional issues, namely, questions about whether the payoffs of hydro-power projects were to be distributed between, on the one hand, regional and national interests and, on the other, local communities affected by the projects. Communes complained that the 'concession fee' (based on electricity output of a project) was set too low and that it was not adjusted relative to general price developments. Criticism was also directed at the way in which the fee was set for particular

FIGURE 13.1
Yearly production of electricity 1937–1975, by producing organization

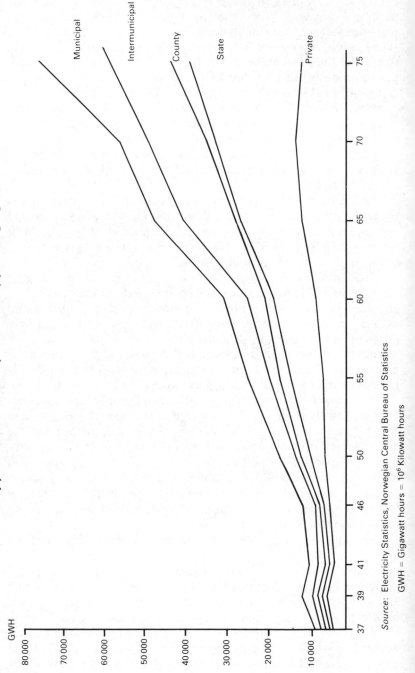

Source: Electricity Statistics, Norwegian Central Bureau of Statistics

GWH = Gigawatt hours = 10^6 Kilowatt hours

projects (Parliament determined the maximum level). Communes demanded an adjustment of the fee. However, such an adjustment would have meant substantial changes in the distributional structure. The income accruing to local communes in earlier projects would have been substantially increased. The Department of Industry and NVE, backed by hydro-power interests, resisted these proposals on the basis of considerations of precedent as well as of cost.

Another proposal was to establish for each hydro-power project an 'economy fund' in order to compensate for the general burdens such projects imposed and to develop the local economy. NVE and the Department of Industry were opposed. However, the Industry Committee of Parliament and Parliament supported this measure because they were concerned about the political issue of the distribution of hydro-power gains between local communities and regional/national interests. At the same time, such funds provided means to deal with special conflicts and to assure greater flexibility in negotiations with local communities. Such funds were established for all new projects (from 1960).

During the 1960s and early 1970s more and more 'affected interests' and representatives of such interests were brought into the planning and decision-making process. This development was consistent with the general democratic principle in Norway and the other Scandinavian countries, that *those groups affected, particularly economically, by a policy, programme, or project should be consulted and given opportunities to communicate their misgivings and, if feasible, allowed to suggest adjustments or simply given compensations.* However, such consultations were typically organized in such a way as to avoid disruption of the basic planning and decision-making process. Essential information about local opinion and demands would thus be forthcoming to the planners. They, in turn, could, through persuasion, negotiation and side payoffs assure the success of their plans.

From a situation in 1950 when few local administrative units and traditional business interests were involved in project planning, an increasing number and variety of actors became engaged (see Table 13.1). Agricultural interests, both at the local and county levels, participated already in the 1950s, but had a much more substantial role in the 1960s and 1970s.

Also, land and water resource interests came increasingly into the picture: land owners, forest owners, fishing and hunting interests. And territorially anchored political and administrative authorities — from the local communes and county representatives — became more numerous and prominent.

In the 1960s not only were those connected with the traditional

TABLE 13.1

Involvement of authorities and interests in concession cases, 1945–80

Period	1945–60								1960s												1970s								
Project number	1	2	3	4	5	6	7	8	9	10	11	12	13	14	15	16	17	18	19	20	21	22	23	24	25	26	27	28	29
Hydro-power Developer	•	•	•	•	•	•	•	•	•	•	•	•	•	•	•	•	•	•	•	•	•	•	•	•	•	•	•	•	•
Municipality	•	•	•	•	•	•	•	•	•	•	•	•	•	•	•	•	•	•	•	•	•	•	•	•	•	•	•	•	•
County Authority	•	•	•						•	•	•			•		•		•	•		•			•			•	•	
Log-rollers Association								•										•								•	•		
Local Fish and Game Association													•			•						•	•	•			•		•
Property Owners			•	•	•	•	•		•	•	•	•	•	•	•	•		•	•	•	•	•	•	•	•	•	•	•	•
Municipal Forest Agency									•		•		•	•	•	•				•			•	•	•			•	•
Municipal Land Agency				•					•	•	•		•	•	•	•			•	•	•	•	•	•	•			•	•
County Electricity Authority					•	•							•		•	•				•				•			•	•	•
County Farm Agency									•	•			•	•	•	•	•	•	•	•	•		•	•			•	•	•
County Fishing Authority									•	•			•		•	•		•	•	•	•	•	•	•	•	•	•	•	•
Lapp/Reindeer Association						•	•	•	•	•	•	•	•																
County Authority												•	•	•					•		•	•	•		•		•	•	
County Fish and Game Agency														•	•	•	•	•	•	•	•	•	•	•	•	•	•	•	•
County Recreation Agency													•			•	•	•	•	•	•	•	•	•	•	•	•	•	•
Business Association														•									•						
Local Tourist Association													•		•		•				•		•	•	•		•	•	•
Central Tourist Association																	•						•				•	•	•
Public Demonstration													•	•	•	•	•	•			•				•		•	•	
Public Utility							•		•		•											•		•		•			•
County Forest Agency																							•						
Municipal Wildlife Agency																													
Local Farmers' Association																•	•	•			•			•				•	•
Central Fish and Game Association																•	•			•	•				•		•	•	•
Municipal Recreation Agency																						•							
Central Environmental Protection Agency																				•				•	•			•	•
Central Farmers' Association																				•	•								
Local Environmental Protection																				•				•	•			•	•
Municipal Regulator of Mountain Areas																												•	
Research Institutions																								•					•

economy (farming, fishing, forestry) highly visible, but other groups affected by hydro-power development and regulation appeared on the scene: the Norwegian Tourist Association, the county recreational commissions, hunting and fishing sport interests and their respective local governing bodies.

By the late 1960s and early 1970s, environmental interests were also more and more prominent and, ultimately, became involved in major controversies around hydro-power projects proposed in this period: In the mass media, the Norwegian Nature Association particularly stood out, as the counter-pole to the hydro-power development interests. However, environmetal and nature interests encompassed national hunting and fishing associations, local recreational authorities as well as environmental protection and local culture protection interests.

These organizational developments were paralleled by increasingly critical opinions toward hydro-power projects on the part of those routinely consulted about proposed projects, that is communal and related authorities, land and water users, and other directly affected interests (see Tables 13.2 and 13.3).

At the end of the 1960s several large projects evoked substantial discussion and opposition. In one case, the 'Nea Hydro-power project', the Trondheim Electricity Company obtained a concession in 1968 in spite of strong protests from Trondheim's Tourist Association and a number of scientific institutions in the area. About the same time, Oslo Light Company was met by substantial opposition to a hydro-power project from the National Tourist Association, State Recreational Council, State Environmental Protection Council and the Urban Affairs Department. There was considerable discussion and debate in the mass media, which continued after Parliament made its decision in 1969.

Not before 1970, however, did hydro-power development lead to open physical confrontation. This occurred in connection with 'the Mardöla Affair'. The principal force behind the opposition was a newly established activist organization (Coordination Group for the Protection of Nature and the Environment). This group, employing civil disobedience methods, tried to block road construction around the project site. They were eventually removed by the police. The conflict captured the attention of the mass media and set the stage for the highly tense climate around hydro-power plans in the 1970s.

One of these planning projects was Alta, to be discussed later. The conflicts around Alta during the 1970s were the culmination of transformations in the socio-political context of hydro-power planning and decision-making. The conflicts began already in 1970 when

TABLE 13.2
Affected interests' assessments of proposed projects

	Time Period		
	1945–59	1960s	1970s
Project construction acceptable with or without minor objections	68%	52%	31%
Major objections to projects or totally unacceptable	32%	48%	70%
Total	100% N = 53	100% N = 185	100% N = 180

TABLE 13.3
Municipal Council judgements on hydro-power proposals

	Time Period		
	1945–59	1960s	1970s
Approve the project proposal either with no objection or only minor reservations	65%	58%	35%
Express major objections or disapprove altogether	35%	42%	65%
Total	100% N = 20	100% N = 48	100% N = 17

large demonstrations were organized, opposing the flooding of a symbolically important Lapp village in the Alta area. Later in the 1970s, when parliamentary action was finally taken on Alta, large protest meetings, demonstrations, and political mobilization took place, both locally and nationally. Eventually, there were hunger strikes, civil disobedience, and 'camp-ins' in front of the House of Parliament.

The challenge from environmental and other interests during the late 1960s and 1970s led to legal and administrative reforms. Favourable rules were instituted relating to the involvement of environmental and other affected interests in concession treatment of projects. The Watercourse Regulation Law of 1969 (Paragraph 4a) stated that the regulative agency should take into consideration 'general interests which would be affected' by hydro-power projects. Interests mentioned were those associated with 'environmental protection', 'recreation', 'science', and 'cultural heritage'. The Law and, in particular, paragraph (4a), were uncontroversial at the time.

The legal changes — and related reforms in regulation — became the backdrop for disagreements and conflicts within the state administration, when, for instance, the newly established environmental protection (and resource) administration challenged hydropower plans and proposals. Thus, in the Alta case (and that of Saltfjell/Svarti), the Department of Environmental Protection supported the Norwegian Nature Association's opposition to NVE's project handling and interpretation of environmental protection regulation. They saw NVE's behaviour as inconsistent with the Watercourse Regulation Law. Thus, within the state administration, *there emerged controversies over interpretation of the law.* At the same time, a related conflict emerged concerning the competence of different authorities (and the interests which they represented) to define and interpret the situation. In particular, the Environmental Protection Department sought to countervail the analyses based on technical/economic rules and regulations by more ecologically oriented principles (environmental protection regulations served this purpose). Of course, NVE sought to limit the use of such principles and, in general, to minimize serious consideration of ecological matters.

Administrative reforms and changes in concession procedures occurred also through judicial action. One initiative, an innovation in the Norwegian context, was taken by the Norwegian Nature Association. The Association fought in the context of the Alta case to obtain greater participatory rights in hydro-power planning and decision processes.[97]

In this case, the Association did not raise the question of its right to participate in compensation processes (see note 97), but only about its competence, as an 'interest', to bring the State (NVE) before the courts on grounds of inappropriate or inadequate administrative handling of hydro-project(s).

The Association was duly declared a competent interest by the court system (ultimately, the Supreme Court) with the right as an agent to bring the State to court for administrative mistakes or mishandling of cases. Moreover, the courts recognized that a claimant may have a legally legitimate interest and right to initiate court action *even if* the outcome of the case has no direct significance for its own position. This decision represented a major shift in the rules of the game and made even more problematic, future hydro-power projects.

Finally, as pointed out earlier, the establishment of the Department of Environmental Protection, its recruitment of legal and economic competence as well as other experts (from the natural sciences) increased its authority and power to challenge and to make uncertain each and every hydro-power project. Such changes, along with the emergence of a major new resource base, petroleum, and the new, powerful institutions and agents connected with it, set the stage for the decline of NVE and the initial transformation of the entire hydro-power planning system (see also Chapter 16).

The organization of hydro-power planning and decision-making
Decision-making in hydro-power construction has a long tradition and is a highly regulated process in Norway. The rules of the formal concession framework distinguish three phases:

- The planning phase, which is administered initially by NVE and later in the phase by the Oil and Energy Department (OED) (before 1978 the Department of Industry had OED's responsibility). This phase is broken down into sub-phases of planning, application, investigation and evaluation.
- The political decision phase, where OED submits its recommendation to Parliament, whereupon Parliament makes the final decision.
- The implementation phase, in which the hydro-power decision is carried out, including the legal settlement of claims for damages to 'disturbed interests'.

Figure 13.2 maps the actors, activities and transactions of the formal concession process. The process takes place within a given set of institutional settings. These settings and the organizing principles and rules which regulate them, are relatively well-defined and stable. Nevertheless, they undergo change, at times slowly and almost imperceptibly, other times rapidly and very visibly. Such changes will be discussed later.

The formal concession framework consists primarily of rules organizing activities and transactions in the economic, administrative and judiciary spheres. The technical administrative preparations, planning and assessments are formally separated from political processes and decisions. Local interests participate in the sense that they obtain information about plans and 'express their views' on a number of occasions: first to the developer, then to the Watercourse Directorate, and (in the case of communes and relevant departments of government) to the Oil and Energy Department (OED). Also, the Board of NVE and the Parliament's Industry Committee carry out investigations of their own to ascertain the opinions of local communities and interests. Environmental interests are allowed to participate both directly through hearings as well as through their spokesmen in the administrative system, the Ministry of Environmental Protection.

The various opinions are supposed to be recorded, organized and presented along with NVE's (and in a later version OED's) preparation of the case and recommendations. The expected outcome of such a process is a *well-formulated plan for a hydro-power development*, where the conditions under which building and production will be carried out are specified. Appropriate adjustments in the plans are supposed to take into account the criticisms of environmental groups and to minimize the costs and damages to local interests. The court proceedings at the end of the process cannot affect the decision, already taken by Parliament. The sole aim of these proceedings is to decide on compensation to individuals directly affected by the project.

Let us examine more closely the major social decision and bargaining spheres composing the Norwegian hydro-power planning complex.

The administrative and economic spheres

A hydro-power construction project is initiated by a developer who must apply to the concession authority (Watercourse Directorate, see below) for permission to carry out the development. In Norway before 1940 private companies were the prevalent developers. Since then public utilities (state, district, or municipal) have dominated hydro-power development. As a rule, the State Power Utility (SKV) in NVE, alone or in joint venture with municipal or district power companies, is the developer of larger projects such as Alta.

The economic and administrative spheres are combined in this case rather than treated separately because NVE has tended to be the entrepreneur (SKV) in the largest projects, as well as the concession authority (Watercourse Directorate).

The decision-making process for hydro-power development is based in the public administrative system. The key actor in this setting, NVE or more precisely its division, the Watercourse Directorate (VDD), considers the application of the developer, carries out investigations, and makes recommendations to the Ministry of Oil and Energy (OED). A number of public administrative organs are asked to make statements at different points in the process. Included here are ministries, such as those of Environment, Farming, and Fishing, as well as several organs at the county and municipal levels. In most instances, OED simply passes the case on, without major alteration, to the Parliament for final decisions. (For developments of less than 20,000 HP, and without serious conflicts,

FIGURE 13.2
Formal model for decision-making in hydropower construction:
spheres, activities, actors

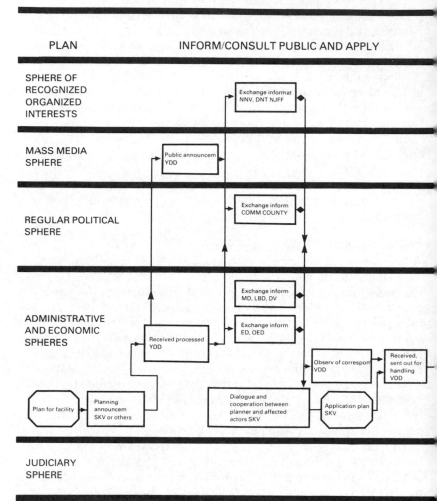

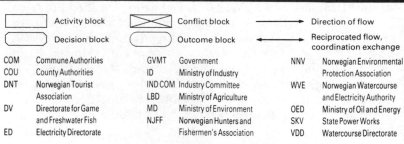

(Figure 13.2 continued)

(Figure continued on next page)

ADMINISTRATIVE DECISION

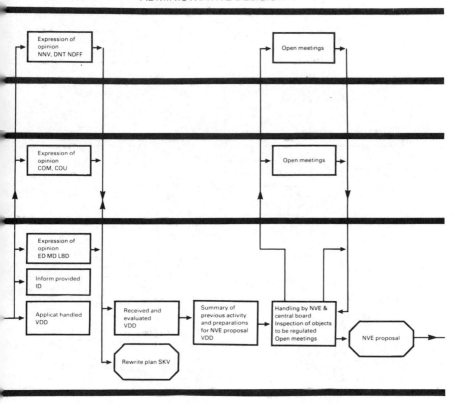

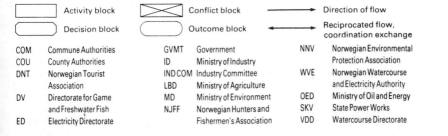

(Figure 13.2 continued)

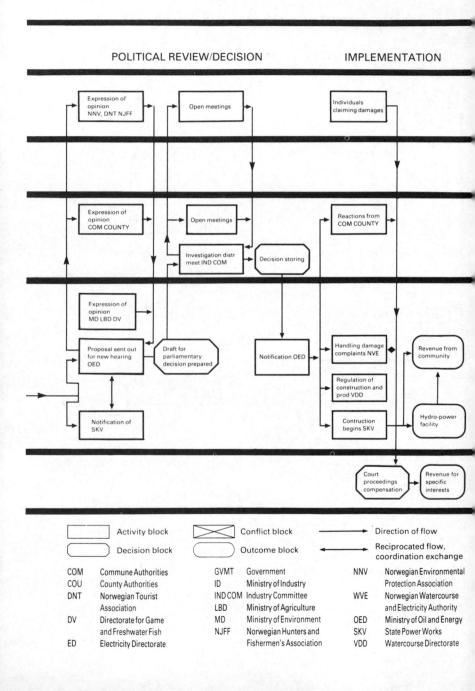

POLITICAL REVIEW/DECISION   IMPLEMENTATION

Expression of opinion NNV, DNT NJFF	Open meetings	Individuals claiming damages
Expression of opinion COM COUNTY	Open meetings	Reactions from COM COUNTY
	Investigation distr meet IND COM	Decision storing
Expression of opinion MD LBD DV		
Proposal sent out for new hearing OED	Draft for parliamentary decision prepared	Notification OED
Notification of SKV		

Handling damage complaints NVE — Revenue from community
Regulation of construction and prod VDD
Contruction begins SKV — Hydro-power facility
Court proceedings compensation — Revenue for specific interests

	Activity block		Conflict block	⟶	Direction of flow
	Decision block		Outcome block	⟵	Reciprocated flow, coordination exchange

COM	Commune Authorities	GVMT	Government	NNV	Norwegian Environmental Protection Association
COU	County Authorities	ID	Ministry of Industry		
DNT	Norwegian Tourist Association	IND COM	Industry Committee	WVE	Norwegian Watercourse and Electricity Authority
		LBD	Ministry of Agriculture		
DV	Directorate for Game and Freshwater Fish	MD	Ministry of Environment	OED	Ministry of Oil and Energy
		NJFF	Norwegian Hunters and Fishermen's Association	SKV	State Power Works
ED	Electricity Directorate			VDD	Watercourse Directorate

the government may take the decision without parliamentary approval.)

Regular politics
According to the formal rules, a hydro-power development proposal, after administrative handling, is transferred to the political sphere. First, it is considered at the ministerial level, before being submitted as a proposition to Parliament. Initially the matter is referred to the Parliament's Industry Committee. The latter carries out hearings — some repetitions of the hearings which NVE and OED have carried out — and makes its recommendations to Parliament. The latter makes the final decision in plenary session.

Mass media sphere
In the formal framework mass media are assigned the role of conveying information to large publics who may be interested in a hydro-power project. For example, NVE announces in local newspapers the intentions of a developer to plan a hydro-power development. The function of the mass media is as a transmission belt of information and messages, not as a forum for mutual exchange of viewpoints and debate, a source of interpretation and analysis, or a means for mobilizing people for action.

Sphere of recognized, organized interests
In connection with investigations of a hydro-power case, there are a number of organizations and affected interests which should be contacted by the developer or NVE and asked to express their viewpoints (after 1970 this becomes an explicit part of the planning phase). This concerns especially local economic interests such as farming, fishing, reindeer herding. But more recently ideal or value-rational organizations such as the Norwegian Nature Association have been heavily engaged in a number of cases (Midttun, 1986).

According to the formal rules, these interests are supposed to provide administrative organs with information about how they or the interests they represent, would be affected by the proposed plan. They are not expected to take initiative by raising claims of their own.

Judiciary sphere
The implementation phase of a hydro-power development case takes place in part within the judiciary sphere. Here cases are handled strictly formally, with clearly specified conditions, rules defining participation rights and procedures to be followed. The judiciary sphere is normally involved in damage assessments made

after a decision concerning a project has been reached by Parliament. (Recent developments around the Alta case have shown that the judicial sphere can be used to voice a wider range of claims. This is discussed later.) Through judiciary processes, damages to affected recognized interests, individuals and firms are compensated. Such an arrangement serves, of course, to channel and regulate opposition until after the formal decision has been taken. It plays therefore an important role in conflict resolution and legitimation of the collective decision process.

The formal process, although complicated, is relatively well-specified and systematically organized. The high degree of institutionalization reflects the long-established history of these processes and the desire to carefully regulate the multiple interests likely to show concern and to become involved in the process. In a certain sense, *the rule system is designed to de-politicalize hydro-power planning and decision-making as much as possible.* Politics is brought in only after the planning phase in order to approve or legitimize the plans and informal decisions made earlier. It is not intended that 'paraliamentary review and decision' should lead to serious debate and collective decision-making with uncertain outcomes.

Figure 13.2 represents the *formal organization* of Norwegian hydro-power planning and decision-making using the method of social decision flow-chart (Burns and Midttun, 1985, 1986).[98] *This is the rule regime which most cases in Norway have followed more or less closely from post World War II until the 1970s,* in awarding hydro-power concessions. Of course, as pointed out earlier, there have been alterations and reforms in the system all along, especially rule changes so as to widen the range of interests included. Since the late sixties, however, a few cases have deviated radically from the formal design. One of these cases, Alta, the most controversial case of its kind in Norway, is mapped out and analysed below. The formal framework was seriously destabilized, and decision-making about Alta took the form of irregular politics and escalating confrontations between authorities and opponents. The latter often acted totally outside the domain of the formal concession framework.

The Alta process
The Alta-Kautokeino riverway originates deep in the Western part of Northern Norway (Finnmark). The source river Kautokeino flows slowly through plains past the Lapp (Ame) villages of Kautokeino and Masi into two lakes. At this point the river changes character completely. It cuts through mountains in great rapids
.

toward the sea, through the largest canyon in Northern Europe, reaching the Alta valley and finally the North Sea. Salmon spawn profusely in the Alta region, making Alta a rich fishing area, not only for commercial fishing but for sport fishing.

NVE launched plans in the late 1960s to exploit the Alta- Kautokeino watercourse for hydro-power, including the creation of a large reservoir at the Lapp village at Masi. The 'Alta case' proceeded for more than 12 years, a process surrounded by great uncertainty and conflict. Even though Parliament decided twice (1978 and 1980) on construction, plans were not implemented until 1981.

Local interests, including Lappish minority groups and fishing and farming interests, strongly opposed the project. The Alta case also generated considerable conflict within the administrative system. Alta construction plans were revised a number of times reducing the hydro-power output by more than 50 percent (from an initial 1400 GWh). Conflicts over interpretation of due process arose between different ministries and especially between the Ministry of Environment and NVE. Also local and environmental interests questioned the legal basis for the administrative and political decisions, a matter taken before the courts.

Alta provoked widespread political debate in Norway. The parties with a 'green orientation' and environmental interests saw the case as an opportunity to question formal procedures and rules for making decisions on questions of environment and resource management. They also found opportunities to raise basic questions about the character and development of modern society.

In 1970, 1978 and 1979 local mass meetings and demonstrations were held to protest against the construction plans. In 1970, the residents of Masi, a small Lappish community which would have been forced to move by the dam construction, succeeded in persuading Parliament to take this part of the project out of the hydro-power plans.

In the summer and early Fall of 1979, civil disobedience actions took place. Local inhabitants and Norwegian environmental groups blocked the construction of a road up to the site for the planned power station. Police were called in and arrests made, without however succeeding in clearing the way.

The irregular political activity culminated with a 'camp-in' demonstration by a group of Lapps in front of the parliament building in Oslo in the Fall of 1979. The effect of this act, widely covered by the mass media, on public opinion eventually forced the Government to halt implementation of the decision to build the Alta dam.

In 1980, when the Government decided once again to go ahead with the construction, major confrontations took place between construction opponents and a massive (for Norway) contingent of 600 police concentrated by the Government at the building site. The police lived on a ship anchored in Alta harbour, and were transported by military trucks to the construction site where large numbers of hearty Norwegian protestors camped during mid-Winter 1980–81. The protestors offered passive resistance (many were shackled together, and had to be cut loose from one another). No obvious physical violence took place. The struggle to block the hydro-power project ended in failure. Construction was taken up again and is expected to be completed in the latter half of the 1980s.

The Alta struggle, while failing to achieve its specific aims, contributed to a major restructuring of the hydro-power planning system. The aim of the reorganization and reorientation has been to anticipate and avoid hydro-power projects in the future which could evoke mobilized opposition. In this sense, the Alta protest appears to have assured the preservation of a number of Norway's remaining water resources.

In order to describe and analyse the Alta decision-making process, an additional sub-system, which we refer to as the sphere of irregular politics and counter-institutional activity, must be added to the set of institutional spheres making up the formal system. In addition, the scope and character of the mass media sphere must be redefined.

Irregular and counter-institutional politics
With the concepts of irregular and counter-institutional politics, we give a name to a number of rule governed activities such as 'folkmeetings', demonstrations, actions and civil disobedience, which fall *outside of regular political and interest organization activity in Norway*. We have chosen to set these activities off under a separate sub-system in order to mark the dissimilarity between these types of political activity and those of regular politics, traditional interest organization activity, and government functioning.

Irregular politics and counter-institutional activity are characterized by a relatively large degree of openness in the possible definitions of issues and problems and a limited degree of formal organization, at least initially in 'movements'. (This is particularly noteworthy in a neo-corporatist society such as Norway (Andersen, 1986; Midttun, 1986)). The resources and skills here differ also from those commonly used in the administrative and regular political spheres. The two most important ones are the ability to effectively mobilize social networks, and to organize actions and events which have symbolic value for participants and which also gain the attention of the mass media and the general public.

It should be apparent that these activities are structured by rule systems, *with political rules of the game excluding — at least in the Norwegian context — the use of violence.* Those involved in mobilizing and organizing also appeal to, and gain their legitimacy from, certain norms and principles, such as general 'democratic rights'. Groups have a right to form, to try to persuade and mobilize other Norwegian citizens who accept the 'political rules of the game', and to try to advance or to protect their legitimate interests through influencing the political process.

Mass media and opinion formation
In general, the Norwegian mass media have supported established institutions and their policies. Occasionally, they may point out some of their failings and weaknesses. In almost all instances of hydro-power developments since World War II, the mass media have backed the decisions of central elites (i.e., to build).

These tendencies are countered, however, by the predisposition of the mass media to seek out for news coverage conflict-filled and dramatic events. Demonstrations and civil disobedience are types of events which attract the attention of the mass media. If the initiators or organizers of these manage to avoid being labelled as extremists, then the publicity in the mass media may result in their viewpoint being communicated and discussed before a large public. On the other hand, if the actions are successfully presented as extremist or undemocratic, then the mass media can contribute to a weakening of support for peripheral groups. Gitlin's study (1980) suggests that the mass media do not simply cover a story but play a large part in creating it. In deciding how to 'frame' a movement and even determining what aspects are newsworthy or should be highlighted, the media can represent it as thoughtful, or inflammatory, as worthy of attention or of dismissal.

In concluding our presentation of institutional spheres important to hydro-power planning and decision-making in Norway, we should stress that the characteristics of spheres may change during the course of decision-making as a result of actors intentionally or unintentionally transforming the social rule systems governing spheres. They may change the rules and procedures governing transactions within and between spheres; new actors may be included or old ones excluded, new types of activities and transactions may be introduced and developed.

Structural comparison of decision-making processes
A structural comparison of the formal procedure and the actual

FIGURE 13.3
Process-structure summary of the formal system

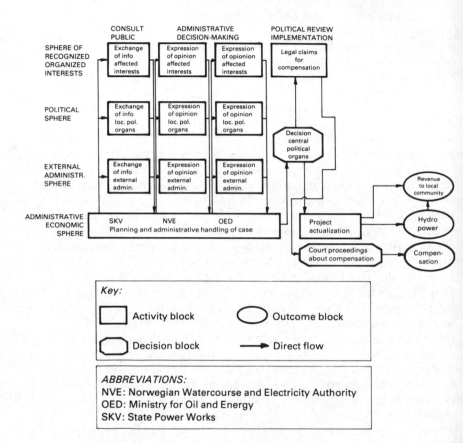

historical development of the Alta case reveals systematic differences. These are pointed up in Figures 13.3 and 13.4 (Figure 13.3 is a substantial condensation of the flow-diagram in Figure 13.2).

Several striking contrasts and related observations emerge from such comparisons.

(i) The Alta process was extremely complex and 'disorderly'. This contrasts with the orderly process — the relatively well-defined coordination between spheres, processes and actors — spelled out in the formal scheme. The latter characterized most post-war hydro-power cases.

(ii) Conflict was not kept *within* the bounds of the formal system.

FIGURE 13.4
Process-structure summary of the Alta affair

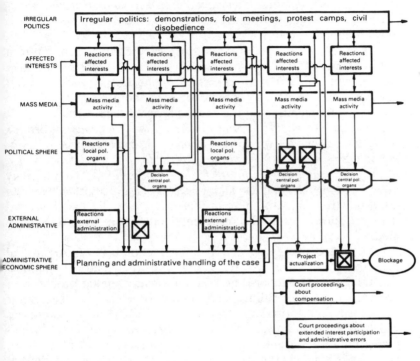

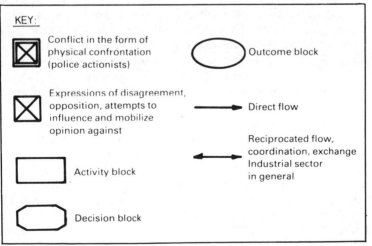

KEY:

⊠ (double box) Conflict in the form of physical confrontation (police actionists)

⬭ Outcome block

⊠ (single box) Expressions of disagreement, opposition, attempts to influence and mobilize opinion against

→ Direct flow

☐ Activity block

⬌ Reciprocated flow, coordination, exchange Industrial sector in general

⬡ Decision block

Opposition, for instance, was not limited to expressions of opinions and claims for compensation for losses. Rather, the *opposition was collectivized and expressed itself through direct actions and demonstrations, and in spheres other than those where administrative initiative prevailed.* Irregular political and mass media processes came to play prominent roles.

(iii) As a result of irregular political pressures and attention from the mass media, *Parliament was drawn into the process at a much earlier point of time than the rules of the formal model would indicate.* They were also forced to intervene at the start of the implementation phase, contrary to the formal framework.

(iv) *The mass media did not simply serve as a transmission-belt for NVE, as presumed in the formal framework, but became a transmitter of the messages of the opposition, a forum for debate, and a means for mobilizing support for the opposition.* The interplay between irregular politics and mass media processes played an important role in Alta. For instance, large public meetings and demonstrations received considerable attention from the mass media.

(v) The Alta process involved the interaction between the formal processes (to which NVE, OED and the national political leadership tried to adhere) and the informal, irregular processes of opposition, counter-culture and counter-organization. The latter entails opinion formation, mobilization and influence processes which took place *outside the spheres of control of the actors dominating* the formal framework. This alternative movement entailed: (1) *mobilization* where action groups were established, and alternative definitions of problems and demands were formulated, (2) *irregular and counter-institutional initiatives,* in that action groups openly opposed the authorities and organized and demonstrated against them, (3) *conflict escalation and illegal action* (civil disobedience) where action groups resorted to illegal actions to block the Alta development after the decision process was formally closed by the parliamentary decision.

(vi) The irregular and counter-institutional activities of the opposition impinged on, and interacted with, the formal process. Settings, and actors in those settings, who were not formally recognized or whose rights to participate and influence the decision-making in any real sense were extremely limited, became involved in and played an important part in the process of challenging the formal decision-making and implementation processes. These peripheral actors consisted of traditional economic interests such as local farmers, fishermen and reindeer herders (Lapps). Also, idealist interests such as environmental groups and zero-growth advocates were involved in the irregular and counter-institutional movement. These were found particularly among urban youth and service occupational groups outside industry, including government.

(vii) Quite clearly, the opposition managed in a number of instances to break NVE's and OED's monopoly over the social decision process. These latter actors were unable to prevent the emergence and spreading of alternative definitions of the situation, mobilization of opinion and resources around these, and the alteration or obstruction of the regular processes.

(viii) Through irregular and counter-institutional politics, the opponents to hydro-power development managed to block project implementation, at least temporarily. The decision process went on for more than 10 years (as compared to an average time period of five years for post-war hydro-power decisions). The reconsideration of the matter in Parliament (1978–80), and the consideration given by the courts to the case, were major achievements of the opposition.

The critical developments making up the Alta process may be seen as a product of conflict between two opposing 'rationalities': one to develop the river for electricity production, the other to preserve it more or less undisturbed. These movements were active in different spheres and generated a complex, global process within Norwegian society. The forces for development were based in the established administrative and political structures, having legitimate initiative and access to major power resources (administrative, technical, economic, and political) in these settings. The other movement, in opposition to the first, lacked equivalent legitimation and access to power resources. Given this unequal distribution, the opposition resorted to a variety of stratagems to gain influence in two spheres, namely mass media/public opinion formation and irregular politics, where they had some chance to mobilize support and resources and eventually to win influence in the regular political sphere. The opposition successfully activated social networks, articulated an alternative interpretation and argument, and utilized mass media to gain attention and to transmit their appeals. Also, effective use was made of channels to established structures and actors where there were sympathizers and 'fellow travellers' (e.g. the Ministry of Environmental Protection'). While 'the Alta affair' seemed 'disorderly' to the planners and administrators responsible for hydro-power projects, there was, in a certain sense, an order. The struggle was played out *within the complex of rule regimes characterizing the larger Norwegian political culture and institutions.* At the same time, new strategies and organizational innovations were introduced, particularly by the opponents to the hydro-power development. These contributed to 'opening the hydro-power planning system' and to generating uncertainty about project fate and, ultimately, the future of the entire system.

The social organization of public domination and movement-induced destabilization in a democracy

We have found it useful in the analysis of Norwegian hydro- power planning and decision-making — and the Alta case in particular — to group major actors and spheres into two classes, *Centre and Periphery* (Galtung, 1971; Baumgartner et al., 1986). These refer to a *relation of domination: unequal control over resources, differences in values and social organization, and differential patterns of social mobilization and action.*

(i) The *centre* or 'industrial complex' in Norway is committed to economic growth. Within this complex are the employers' association, labour unions, the Labour Party and the Conservative Party, and key government ministries such as the Industry Department. From its ranks come initiatives and support for industrial projects such as major hydro-power developments as well as initiatives for the recent North Sea oil exploitation. The complex dominates the major spheres within which hydro-power plans are proposed and processed, namely the economic, administrative and political.

(ii) The *periphery* consists, within the Norwegian context, of traditional economic interests (local farming, fishing, reindeer herding); other local interests (tourist and recreational interests, commune and political party interests) as well as ideal interests such as environmental groups. These diverse peripheral groups respond to industrial initiatives, for instance hydro-power projects, with varying degrees of support and opposition.

In the Alta case, multiple peripheries and multiple centres could be identified. For instance, periphery groups were made up of Lapps, environmentalists and local non-Lapp people. These came to form an important but uneasy coalition. At the same time, as we indicated earlier, the Centre was no monolith. Within the government, agencies such as the Department of Environment Protection had a number of unofficial supporters of the opposition movement. Nevertheless, for purposes of the analysis here, we shall speak about 'centre' and 'periphery' as homogeneous collectivities, stressing as we do so that this is an over-simplification. Our aim here, however, is to focus (1) on the divergence between Centre and Periphery and (2) on the linkage between Centre patterns of domination and Periphery innovations in strategic thinking, organization, and action.

The interaction between Centre and Periphery occurs on the level of *socio-cultural framework* as well as *social organization.* Sustained domination requires that the Centre successfully induce or persuade the Periphery to accept its cognitive-value framework and its organizing principles and rules. This concerns, for instance, questions of how strategic decision-making and major projects in society should be organized and carried out, and for what purposes. Under conditions of stable domination, the formal concession framework functions more or less as it should. That is, it leads to hydro-power decisions, including compensations and negotiated side-payments to local interests and communities for 'any losses that may be incurred'.

Planning and administrative activities according to the Centre's formal system become problematic whenever Periphery groups manage to organize and oppose the Centre's cognitive-value framework as well as its principles of social organization, planning and control. An organized Periphery collectively defines the situation differently; for instance, they offer alternative or opposing formulations of legitimate uses of natural resources. They organize themselves and act in ways which are not envisioned in the planning rules and procedures. This generates uncertainty and instability. Decisions can be substantially delayed or blocked and lead to different outcomes than those envisioned by Centre actors. Additional groups and issues may be drawn in and serious conflict escalation can occur.

Thus, from the perspective of our framework, the implementation of the formal planning and decision-making framework in a concrete instance depends largely on the activation and maintenance of Centre–Periphery domination.

In any analysis of the stability or instability of a particular social order, one may consider a number of different features of the relevant rule systems and the concrete settings in which these apply. We propose to concentrate on questions such as the following:

(i) To what extent are organized groups and networks on the Periphery who wish to participate and influence decision-making on hydro-power development *recognized legitimate agents,* individuals or collectives, with rights to participate in the planning process?

(ii) To what extent does the *cognitive and value framework,* activated or developed by Peripheral actors, lead to appropriate or inappropriate demands (in area, scope, level, etc.) in relation to hydro-power plans, compensation, and other aspects of such planning?

(iii) To what extent do Periphery actors, in order to influence the decision-making, engage in *appropriate organizing and group formation,* and avoid mobilizing resources and initiating action in spheres other than the formally prescribed one(s)?

(iv) To what extent are *activities, strategies, techniques* and other means used by Periphery actors appropriate or acceptable in the formal planning process?

In the Alta case, Periphery groups came with 'inappropriate' innovations: definitions of the situation, cognitive and value frameworks, forms of organization, and strategies. The groups embarked on rather radical innovations, in part because they experienced their negotiation possibilities as blocked and the decisions arrived at through the formal framework unacceptable. They managed to shift the controversy into new arenas, drawing in additional actors and issues. Thus, there emerged *systematic and open conflict between Centre and Periphery groups*. This challenged not only the institutional framework for hydro-power planning but the very system of domination itself.

Below we develop the ideas outlined above in the form of *two models of social structure and social process*.

One model presents the conditions under which the formal decision-making framework is likely to be implemented, as has been the case in almost all Norwegian hydro-power decisions in the post-war period. This entails, above all, situations where the Periphery accepts the Centre's cognitive-value and organizational frameworks, for whatever reasons they do so. The reasons may range from a deeply established predisposition to obey state authority, loyalty to the 'political rules of the game', the promise of substantial gains, or liberal economic compensation for all losses, or various combinations of these factors.

A second model represents the conditions under which the formal system is disrupted and breakdowns occur, giving rise to an Alta-type process. This entails, above all, a rejection by Periphery groups of cultural and organizational forms consistent with the formal system, and the activation or creation of non-compatible forms backed by organized power.

Model I: Realization of the formal decision design
The realization of the formal decision-making scheme is likely to occur whenever the Centre is able to gain adherence to its cognitive-value framework and principles of social organization. Selvik and Hernes (1977) make a point of the fact that hydro-power construction is, in a certain sense, a *routine affair* for the planning and administrative authorities, while it is *a new type of situation* for local and many Peripheral groups. *They are at a disadvantage when it comes to the formulation of separate cognitive models of the situation, and the establishment of adequate social organization to*

maximize the protection of their interests.

Some characteristic features of the cognitive-value framework of the Centre are as follows:

- industrial and economic growth orientation
- adherence to established formal rules and procedures
- stress on orderliness and on types of rationality (e.g. rational–legal) which generate and maintain orderliness

Typical Centre rules of social organization are (see Figures 13.3 and 13.4):

- formal or rational–legal systems of domination with Periphery actors 'participating' in strategic decisions, if at all, only in marginal ways and at predetermined points
- formally specified procedures
- ordered and linear case-proceedings

According to the formal decision-making framework, the main activities and processes take place within the set of institutional spheres largely controlled by Centre actors with Periphery actors playing only secondary or auxiliary roles (see Figures 13.2 and 13.3 indicating the institutional spheres relevant to formal decision-making). Periphery actors are presumed to accept to a greater or lesser extent the cognitive framework, rules of organization, and concession procedures advocated by the Centre.

This acceptance is based on the authority and expertise of Centre actors and their institutions as well as the economic and other advantages which they are able to provide Periphery actors. This implies that:

- Periphery actors accept the rules and procedures of the concession model
- they adhere to a 'definition of the situation', including acceptable interests or motives, such as 'privatized interests'
- they voice claims that can be handled within the scope of the model, namely economic compensation for losses and damages, decided by a compensation court
- they participate compliantly, that is according to the rules designated by the concession framework
- they pursue individual strategies rather than collective strategies when seeking compensation for damages and in expressing dissatisfaction with, or criticism of, a hydro-power project

As noted earlier, *the main activities,* according to the formal decision model, take place within institutional spheres controlled by central actors, that is within the domain of the industrial complex.

The main communications and processing of information take place within Centre planning, administrative, political, and legal institutions. Periphery actors typically express their opinion and make proposals only when asked.

The outcome, hydro-power construction and generation of electricity, primarily realizes the purposes and ambitions of Centre actors. Of course, Periphery actors receive incentives and compensation in terms of concession revenue (to local communities) and minor specific compensations through the court system (this legal process only determines how damages are to be compensated; as pointed out earlier, it does not influence the actual decision about whether or not the project should be realized).

A general characteristic of the formal model is therefore *the asymmetrical but complementary relationship* between the two sets of actors and their respective spheres of activity. Centre interests dominate the planning process while Peripheral interests are more or less fitted into this scheme of things. To the extent that conflict occurs, it is *institutionalized and handled within Centre-controlled settings.*

Model II: Major deviance from the formal decision design
Substantial deviation from the formal design is likely to occur whenever Centre–Periphery domination — which the institutional set-up for hydro-power planning presupposes — is eroded or transformed. Such restructuring can be traced to specific socio-political processes and innovations. In the Alta case, key peripheral groups developed a set of attitudes, values and perspectives incompatible with Centre cognitive-value and organizational frameworks. Moreover, they gradually came to refuse to play the Periphery role envisioned in the formal set-up.

Characteristic elements of the Periphery's emerging cognitive-value framework in the Alta case were:

- value-rationality, stressing environmental and non-economic values, over those of economic growth and industry; important local and community interests did not feel that the destruction or disturbance of farming, fishing, herding and community practices could be compensated by economic means
- insistence on claims that transcended the limits of the formal procedure and rules
- re-definition of the case in terms of collective problems, e.g. local rights and Lappish minority-rights, calling for collective solutions, not acceptable within the formal framework
- questioning of fundamental constitutional rules, such as the right

of Central authorities to overrule local decisions, as in cases where the local communes are by and large opposed to hydro-power construction
- affirmation of rights to civil disobedience in defence of basic values and democratic rights
- the general shift in values and attitudes about large-scale technology and industrial facilities as well as environmental protection questions
- the growing national support and mobilization opposed to construction of Alta

Periphery actors experienced concrete problems which they believed could not be solved within the formal framework, that is, they desired a radical reduction or elimination altogether of the Alta hydro-power project. In such situations, actors either must give up their objectives or try to change features of the situation to enhance their capabilities to realize those goals. The latter entails developing new collective strategies as well as possibly changing the rules of the game.

Peripheral actors' re-definition of their problem situation viewed from a perspective other than that of the Centre actors thus sets the stage for new types of social organization and strategic action. Strategic and organizational developments, which of course are coupled, were initiated on Peripheral actors' premises and tended to transcend the established formal framework.

Hence, in addition to developing a cognitive-value framework, influential groups of the Periphery developed forms of counter-organization, which were neither integrated in, nor compatible with, the organizational structure maintained and used by Centre actors.

Characteristic features of Peripheral social organization were:

- formation of collective agents such as the 'action groups' which were not legitimate actors according to the formal concession framework
- alliance formation, for example between several locally affected interests, and between such interests and Lappish and environmental interests on the national (and even international levels) and the development of new power bases and strategies of action
- the organizing of mass civil disobedience and symbolic actions totally outside the concession framework

Through the development of counter-institutional perspectives, deviant organizational forms and strategies, Periphery actors managed to draw in new participants and to gain support for their perspective on the problem. This self-amplifying process played a major role in the developing incompatibility between Centre and Periphery, and in the erosion of Centre–Periphery domination. The incompatibility between Centre and Periphery was, at the same time, accentuated by the open conflict between them. In part, the conflict contributed ultimately to cognitive closure among Periphery actors. The Centre's definition of the situation and interpretations were more and more rejected in favour of perspectives articulated and developed among Periphery actors. Similarly, Centre rules of social organization were more and more rejected as Periphery actors developed their own organizing principles. As 'communication' and 'negotiation' between Centre and Periphery became blocked, conflict escalated.

By protesting against the formal rules and procedures of the economic/administrative and regular political spheres and by successfully initiating processes governed by other rules within new social contexts, Periphery actors both increased their influence over the decision-making process and managed to partially delegitimize the formal system as the locus of authority and decision-making about Alta.

As a result of irregular politics, such as civil disobedience, and through successful attraction of mass media and public opinion interest, *new conflict arenas emerged.* The distribution of power and resources in favour of Centre actors in the formal framework was countervailed by Periphery actors' ability to exploit new institutional settings where the distribution of power and resources between Centre and Periphery was less unequal.

A side-effect of the successful enlargement of the conflict arena was a partial loss of legitimacy of the formal institutional set-up. Central actors pursued two counter-strategies here. One was to try to reinforce the regular rules and procedures, to get the process back on track, ultimately by sheer force (the use of police), when necessary. Another strategy was to try to defeat Periphery actors by engaging in public debate and by using the mass media. Apart from the fact that merely engaging themselves defensively in such contexts was de-legitimizing, Centre actors had no monopoly in resources such as skill and effectiveness in public debate, and thus they enjoyed no particular advantage in these public arenas.

Redesign and transformation
The major confrontations during the 1970s and early 1980s, the increasing questioning, and the development of collective strategies for effective challenge to hydro-power projects made it more and more obvious that radical changes would have to be made in the

planning system. Besides highly visible struggles with large numbers of demonstrators and police involvement, other developments threatened to destabilize further the established planning system and to make highly uncertain the prospects of future hydro-power projects. The Department of Environmental Protection increasingly used its legal mandate, and the 'political noise' around the Alta case, to strengthen its jurisdiction over environmental aspects of hydro-power construction.[99] Other destabilizing developments involved the courts. Administrative procedures and decisions had been challenged by the environmental movement as well as Lapp groups not only through political channels but through the judiciary. This strategy was an innovation in the Norwegian context.

At the same time, powerful new government agencies appeared on the scene in connection with North Sea oil developments, in particular the Oil and Energy Department. The latter took over responsibility from the Ministry of Industry for hydro-power matters as well as general energy issues. This set the stage for new alliances and games, specifically between those in the Oil and Energy Department, the Department of Environmental Protection, and the Department of Finance. Although these agents had different interests, they shared a common desire to weaken the established power of NVE.

These various developments resulted in initiatives to substantially change the rule regime for hydro-power planning. A number of different proposals were advanced. One suggested breaking up NVE and distributing the responsibilities to other agencies. Another far-reaching proposal entailed giving the Department of Environmental Protection responsibility for formulating a 'comprehensive plan' for dealing with potential hydro-power projects in the future. The latter proposal is presently being tried. Each of several hundred such projects is subject to a systematic environmental impact analysis, along with the usual economic and technical analyses carried out by NVE. The impact analyses include surveys and assessments of local affected interests in order to determine the 'socio-political feasibility' of each project.

The Department of Environmental Protection is engaged in ranking the projects according to economic/technical criteria as well as socio-political criteria. Its proposal is to be reviewed and approved (or altered) by Parliament. Following this step, top ranked projects may commence with the established concession/review process as described earlier.

At the present time, one can see the rough contours of a transformation of the hydro-power planning system, where the purposes and organizing principles of industrial interests are being merged with new environmental and resource management interests. Along with changes in key actors, decision-making procedures and organizational structure, the 'system boundaries' are being expanded and redefined (Midttun, 1986). The re-organization can be seen as the outcome of a power game as well as a strategy to prevent (or to minimize) environmental impacts and to preclude major societal confrontations in the future.

Through these innovations in planning goals and rules of organization, the Department of Environmental Protection has gained greater control over hydro-power planning, ostensibly at the expense of the traditional hydro-power segment. The 'comprehensive plan', however, is controversial and it remains to be seen if it will pass through Parliament without serious and effective counter-challenges from industrial and hydro-power interests.

Conclusion

We have suggested that, during a long period of post-Second World War history, the 'industrial complex' in Norway dominated Peripheral groups such as those involved in traditional economic sectors as well as the environmental movement. Decisions about the allocation and use of natural resources such as land and water were made in accordance with the specific goal of industrial expansion. The industrial complex was prepared to exploit to the fullest natural resources, and to introduce technologies or technology systems such as large-scale hydro-power facilities which have major impacts on their natural and social environments. The values and interests of some Peripheral groups were violated in connection with the growth projects.

The domination of the 'industrial complex' was based on (1) the ability of core actors in this complex to 'define the situation', to legitimize its goals (such as growth, economic gain), and to mobilize technical, economic and legal expertise; (2) the institutional centrality of actors oriented toward industrial development and their control over strategic economic and political resources.

Our study has pointed up that, despite the great inequalities in power, the system of domination was destabilized because: (1) Peripheral groups, including the environmental movement, 're-defined the situation' in their own terms and developed a collective counter-interpretation and analysis — in a word, an alternative cultural framework; (2) Peripheral groups established and developed their own organizing principles, mobilized resources, and opposed institutionally the industrial complex and its plans for the Alta hydro-power development. A key element in the relatively effective opposition to the 'industrial complex' — and its project plans — was the formation of a coalition between local opponents (often on grounds of economic and cultural interests in the area) and national environmental movements (with more 'ideal interests'). *All of this was possible within a more or less well-functioning democracy.*

The development of hydro-power planning in Norway in the post-war period illustrates the formation, reformation, and (initial) transformation of a complex, and in this case powerful, administrative system. Partly by design and explicit policy, partly as a consequence of critique and struggle, new rules and organizing principles were forged. These provided new action opportunities and strategic power capabilities for some groups of agents, particularly new actors such as the Department of Environmental Protection and the Oil and Energy Department as well as the Norwegian Nature Association. Such actors could in turn exploit their positions to extend or to re-direct an initial development. In this way more radical transformations in rule regimes are brought about, pointing up the dynamic interplay between formal structures and political processes.

IV
EXPERTISE, TECHNOLOGY AND SOCIAL ORGANIZATION

14
Technology and technique, social action and rule systems

The Church welcomes technological progress and receives it with love, for it is an indubitable fact that technological progress comes from God and must lead to him.

Pope Pius XII (1876–1958),
Christmas Message, 1953

We are well aware ... that the future of man and mankind is threatened, radically threatened, despite very noble intentions, by men of science. And it is menaced because the tremendous results of their discoveries, especially regarding the natural sciences, have been and continue to be exploited — for ends which have nothing to do with the prerequisites of science, but with the ends of destruction and death.

Pope John Paul II, Speech before UNESCO,
2 June 1980. (Both quotations from Coppock (1984))

The complaint that we have become slaves of the machine or of technology is similar. Despite science-fiction nightmares, machines have no will of their own. They can neither invent nor produce themselves, and cannot compel us to serve them. All decisions and activities they carry out are human decisions and activities. We project threats and compulsions on to them, but if we look more closely we always see interdependent groups of people threatening and compelling each other by means of machines — the technical thing-in-itself is never the source of the compelling force and hardship to which people are subject; these are always caused by the way people apply technology and fit it into the social framework.

Norbert Elias (1978a: 24–5)

Introduction

In this chapter rule system theory is used as a point of departure to develop an analytical language for investigating the social character of technology, where technology is viewed as a major component of social action and as a signficant factor in the structuring of modern social organization.

Winner (1983) has also proposed such a broad perspective on the analysis of technology, in discussing 'fabrication', 'the activity through which homo faber strives to erect a durable home on earth':

> Arendt understood that activity of this kind involved the combined work of artists, craftsmen, historians, poets, architects, engineers and constitution makers... I am suggesting that it is now useful to think about technological design features in roughly the same way that the legislators of the ancient world or the eighteenth-century philosophers pondered the structural characteristics of political constitutions. Technologies provide frameworks of order for the modern world. As such, it now makes sense to try to understand the forms of authority, justice, public-good, and freedom that their order entails.

We present only a sketch of what we believe can eventually be developed into a framework for describing and analysing technology and technological development in modern society (see Baumgartner and Burns (1984) and Burns (1985)).

In conceptualizing technology in its social context, we concentrate on the following:

(i) *Technology is treated as a component or integral part of social action.* It consists of physical artefacts used in purposeful activity, where such activity is structured and regulated by one or more rule systems. The use of technology results in impacts, intended and unintended, on the social as well as the physical environments. For instance, an energy supply system produces more than 'energy'. It provides employment, it draws capital and other resources away from alternative uses. It has a variety of effects on the environment, in the case of fossil fuels some very negative effects, as we have slowly come to recognize.

(ii) *Technology as physical artefacts used in purposeful action presupposes social rule systems as well as practical, situational knowlege relating to their production and use.* The relevant rule systems include descriptive rules about characteristic features and performance properties of a technology as well as evaluative and action rules. Specific rules — a grammar of the use of the technology — are followed in order to increase the likelihood that action based on the technology is appropriate (e.g., legal) as well as effective. Symbolic/expressive activities, such as musical performance, the communication of status, and the expression of affection (where tools and special techniques are employed) also entail following certain rules and procedures. Of course, creativity in the use of technology entails breaching the conventions of 'normal' or 'proper' usage.

(iii) *Technological development is linked dialectically with rule system changes.* On the one hand, rule systems orient, select and structure technological developments, constraining certain possibilities and providing opportunities for others. On the other hand, technological innovation and development evoke changes in rule systems governing the activities in which the technologies are used. As Winner suggests (1983:262):

> A deceptive quality of technical objects and processes — their promiscuous utility, the fact that they can be 'used' in this way or in that — blinds us to the ways in which they structure what we are able to do and the ways in which they settle important issues *de facto* without appearing to do so. Thus, for example, the freedom we enjoy in the realm of 'use' is mirrored in our extreme dependency upon vast, centralized, complicated, remote and increasingly vulnerable artificial systems.

Technology is intimately connected with social action and interaction. At the same time, social activities involving technology are organized and, to a greater or lesser extent, institutionalized in complex socio-technical systems. Knowledge of technology and socio-technical systems presupposes knowledge of social organization and, in particular, of the rule systems governing socio-technical systems. This essential knowledge, among other things, distinguishes technology from natural science, as discussed later.

We shall explore properties of technique as well as certain interlinkages between 'scientific knowledge' and technique. Technique is defined as a type of production or rule knowledge, whether it concerns steel-making, politics, or love-making.

Technological innovations evoke opportunities and pressures to change established social rule systems. But since organizations and societies vary in their institutional and socio-cultural make-up, the context of innovation varies and, therefore, the types of opportunities, challenges, and 'tensions' generated in connection with technological innovation. We shall explore the interplay between social structure (rule regimes) and social forces (activity/technology complexes), where they constrain one another as well as stimulate changes in one another. This has been one of the persistent themes in the book thus far.

Established technological areas, such as pharmaceuticals and building construction have long been governed by elaborate (and multiple rule systems). Even these areas periodically undergo dramatic technological changes. Entirely new technologies and production techniques enter the field. Professional groups (for example, pharmacists or architects) may mobilize to establish or maintain a monopoly of technology control in their area of competence and production (drugs and building design, respectively). Their strategy may be to try to keep out certain innovations from the practice of their field or to obtain monopoly control over them.

Both strategies are illustrated in our discussion on the regulation of medicines in Sweden.

Before tackling the major problems of this chapter, we discuss briefly concepts and definitions relating to technology, technique, and socio-technical system.

Technology, society and social rule systems

The production and use of tools and technical aids is found in all spheres of human activity and in all historical periods. What differs today from several thousand or even several hundred years ago are the scale and structure of complex tool use,[100] the rapidity with which new tools are developed and put into use, and the scope and intensity with which innovations in tools impact on and transform social life.

Even the broad concept of 'industrial revolution' fails to encompass the variety and scope of technological revolutions which have shaped, and continue to shape at ever-increasing rates, modern society. These are, among others:

- new power sources, new techniques of metallurgy and machine-making; the widespread use of machines in economic production (the technological revolution proper)
- the revolution in communications: ships, railroads, telephone, telegraph, satellite and tele-communications (see Rosenberg, 1982:246)
- writing (and eventually the printing press) and the clock are other essential innovations the former for its role in recording; accumulating and codifying rule systems as well as revolutionizing communications among human groups; the latter for providing the technological basis for precise timing and coordination among large numbers of people (often located in different solar-time regions).
- the revolution in social organization and administration (especially the development of means to extend it over national and international areas). This would not have been possible without transformations in communications. In connection with this, W.I. Sussman points out, 'In large measure, the office and the office building are products of the new communications; they are unthinkable without the telegraph and telephone, typewriter and business machine, the elevator and the railroad'
- the revolutions in thinking, education, research and technical change

Such technological developments, successfully organized and administered in socio-technical systems, brought immense improvements in productivity and in the wealth of nations and transformed the conditions of human life (Rosenberg, 1982:246).[101]

The social scientific study of technology focuses our attention on major forces shaping and reshaping modern society and also on the complex interplay between human socio-cultural systems and 'systems' of the natural world. Rosenberg, drawing on Marx, argues (1982:39):

> Technology is what mediates between man and his relationship with the external, material world. But in acting upon that material world, man not only transforms it for his own useful purposes (that is to say, 'Nature becomes one of the organs of his activity') but he also, unavoidably, engages in an act of self-transformation and self-realization. 'By thus acting on the external world and changing it, he at the same time changes his own nature.' Technology, therefore, is at the center of those activities that are distinctively human. For technology comprises those instruments that determine the effectiveness of man's pursuit of goals that are shaped not only by his basic instinctive needs, but also those formulated and shaped in his own brain. 'A spider conducts operations that resemble those of a weaver, and a bee puts to shame many an architect in the construction of her cells. But what distinguishes the worst architect from the best of bees is this, that the architect raises his structure in imagination before he erects it in reality. At the end of every labor process, we get a result that already existed in the imagination of the laborer at the commencement.

Clearly, from such a perspective technology is eminently sociological, both in view of the social processes shaping socio-technical systems and of the impact that technological innovations and developments have on society. Technology does not belong to 'technicians' and 'technocrats' in the same way that a science, such as physics, belongs to its professional community.

Contemporary sociology has had relatively little to say about technology and technological change, even if sociology emerged in connection with the industrial revolution. Weingart (1984:115) points out:

> Technique, technology, or more generally artifacts have had no systematic place in Sociological Theory since the modern theory of action superseded Marx and Durkheim.

In general, the language and analytic framework which sociology and the other social sciences have available to investigate and analyse objects, physical artefacts, and the physical world are at present very limited. Moreover, there is considerable conceptual and analytical confusion around such notions as technology, technique, tools, technical systems. 'Technology' in particular may refer, among other things, to (Bereano, 1976; Hummon, 1984;

McGinn, 1978; Margolis, 1978; Rosenberg, 1982; Schon, 1978; Mitcham, 1978; Weingart, 1984): (i) objects or artefacts themselves, (ii) knowledge or know-how about producing or using the artefacts, and (iii) the entire system of artefacts, knowledge, and organizational/institutional arrangements around the production and use of artefacts.

Below we introduce some basic terminology, making distinctions and formulating concepts which will be used in later sections.

Technologies are physical tools of action, extending human powers
Technologies are artefacts (tools, machinery, equipment, buildings, etc.) which extend the capabilities of human action and are, therefore, sources of power (Schon, 1978; Hummon, 1984; Margolis, 1978; McGinn, 1978).

Artefacts of technology — tools, instruments, machines, equipment, buildings — are to a great extent used instrumentally, that is to achieve certain objectives or to solve certain problems, where improvement in performance (speed, quality, reliability, etc.) can be ascertained.

There are also artefacts such as objects of worship and symbols which are not used in human action in such ways, i.e. where instrumentality is not readily apparent (Mitcham, 1978).

In considering technology in connection with social action, we find it useful to distinguish between the artefacts themselves, the activities involved in managing and using them, and the social rule systems and key principles governing their management and use. The same artefact may serve, on the one hand, as an instrument to effectively achieve certain product-making or object-transforming effects and, on the other, as a symbol of authority or even worship: for instance, a sword. Nevertheless, the two rule systems and their related practices correspond to different 'social forms', with quite distinct logics. One is oriented to material effects, possibly as part of a technical system. The other is oriented to structural effects, maintaining or reinforcing a social relationship. The two logics may be fully compatible or complementary, but not necessarily so.

Technology control and use is governed by social rule systems
Technologies as physical artefacts are, of course subject to the laws of nature. At the same time, human agents make up social rules about their use: who controls the technology, its uses and benefits (or pays for some of its impacts); who uses it under specified circumstances; how it is to be used; for what purposes; under what conditions; where and when. Technology from this perspective should be examined in the fabric of everyday actions and inter-

actions in which human actors participate and from which they derive meaning (Winner, 1983:258).

Socio-technical systems

The social organizational aspects of technology in social action have been stressed by Rosenberg (1982:247–8):

> Technologies are more than bits of disembodied hardware. They function within societies where their usefulness is dependent upon managerial skills, upon organizational structures and upon the operation of incentive systems. In addition, of course, a high payoff to the transfer of technology will depend upon the compatibility of its factor proportions requirements with those prevailing in the specific country or available nearby. It may also depend upon the quality of the country's natural resources — the phosphorus content of its iron ore, the richness of its copper ores, the sulfur content of its coal. Thus, the successful transfer of technology is not a matter of transporting a piece of hardware from one geographic location to another. It often involves much more subtle issues of selection and discrimination, and a capacity to adapt and modify before the technology can function effectively in the new socio-economic environment. Even apparently minor differences in resource quality, for example, may necessitate major alterations in the technology — as has often been the case for technologies involving chemical processes. These caveats, based upon widespread nineteenth-century experiences, are intended to suggest that the successful transfer of technology depends greatly upon the specific domestic circumstances of the recipient country.

The social organization of technology/action leads us to the concept of socio-technical system. Such a concept becomes particularly useful when one considers complex, large scale technologies such as factory systems, nuclear power, electrification systems, and so forth. Such systems consist, on the one hand, of complex technical/physical structures which are designed to produce or to transform certain things and, on the other, of social institutions and organizations designed to structure and regulate the operations/activities. The sub-structures may be owned or managed by different agents; the knowledge of these different sub-structures may be dispersed among different occupations and professions; different social networks, organizations, and institutions may be involved in the construction, operation and maintenance of sub-structures. The problem of establishing and maintaining a socio-technical system becomes one of linking together these different social and physical structures into a more or less integrated, operative or functioning whole (Baumgartner and Burns, 1984).

Technologies, including massive physical structures such as buildings and dams, entail the application of social rule systems governing the control and use of the technology. This point of departure allows us to develop the notion that innovations in rules formulated or developed in connection with the introduction and use of a new technology may not 'fit in', or be compatible with, existing social (and physical) structures.

Incompatibilities between a new technology and established or conventional socio-technical systems and social structures are overcome by 'change agents' and 'entrepreneurs' through the mobilization of resources and the exercise of social power (Baumgartner and Burns, 1984; Burns, 1985). In this way new socio-technical systems are established or old ones are transformed. Such structuration will not take place if the actors motivated to introduce and develop a new technology cannot mobilize the necessary social power and other resources (capital, expertise, infrastructure, legal rights, political support, etc.).

Some technological innovations or socio-technical developments require rule changes in, for instance, production, financial, administrative, political, educational and scientific spheres, among others. The success of a new technology or socio-technical development will depend on whether entrepreneurs and change agents in the different areas can form alliances or networks across spheres in order to bring about such multiple sphere and inter-sphere rule changes. In the absence of sufficiently powerful change agents or networks of these, the technological innovation will be aborted or seriously delayed. Some impediments arise as collective expressions of vested interests and 'critical assessments' on the part of groups who mobilize in order to block undesirable technological developments, such as nuclear power.

The history of the development of socio-technical systems (such as the factory as well as hydro-power, electrification, and nuclear systems) point up that the socio-structural and political problems are as much a challenge — and an area of great innovation — as the purely technical. Laudan (1984:91) stresses this point:

> Entrepreneurs need technical skills, but in order to design systems on this scale (electrical systems, etc.) they have to employ many other skills as well, economic, social, and political.

Thus, the problems of control, organization, and management in the extension of human action through the use of tools have entailed *qualitative shifts — and new orders of magnitude* – in going from hammer, knife, hut and fire to modern machines, buildings and nuclear power plants. The modern organization of major socio-technical systems — whether in capitalist societies or communist societies – has entailed *the separation of most participants from the processes of design, organization, management and control of these systems.* Such structuring processes are in the hands of relatively small elite groups. Of course, designers and producers in many instances, but certainly not consistently, shape and develop such systems according to their perceptions of the needs or demands of users and potential users as well as in terms of their own interests and organizing principles.

Technology and science
The link between science and technology is a complex one. Some researchers see it as a close, hierarchical relationship: science is the basis of technology; technology is applied science (e.g. Bunge). Others see the relationship as one of mutual interdependence (e.g. Rosenberg in some of his writings). Still others see it as a very loose connection, with technology and technological development enjoying in many areas a high degree of autonomy from science (Rosenberg (1982); our position in this chapter).

The discussion here will be necessarily brief. Our basic theses are the following:

(i) Science is one of the bases of technology. However, more knowledge than that of science goes into the creation and development of technology. Of course, the scientific content of technology varies from case to case (obviously, the scientific input into such technologies as nuclear power and bio-technology is extremely high whereas it is much lower and less necessary in the production of wood products, clothes, and simple machine tools. At the same time, as Rosenberg (1982) and others have argued, technological innovations and developments stimulate and even make basic contributions to scientific knowledge.

(ii) Technology entails non-scientific elements because of its integration into human action and social organization, for instance, production and consumption activities. It is fitted into practical, cognitive, material and institutional structures. *Therefore, it contains types of knowledge which are entirely social, political and cultural.* Basic science has a more purely 'cognitive character', knowing rather than doing (Layton, 1972). (Of course, technical knowledge consists of analytical knowledge as well as operative knowledge.) Its 'truths' need not necessarily be fitted into the social world as it is organized and functions.

(iii) In general, the social rule systems governing scientific and technological knowledge and activity differ. There are differences in aims, methods, and bases of legitimacy. In a word they represent different social forms of activity. McGinn (1978:195–6), referring to Nietzsche, writes:

For Nietzsche, science, a different form of human activity, constitutes an essentially Socratic optimistic and would-be triumphant approach to dealing with the problematic nature of the human condition, as opposed to, say, the consolatory approach implicit in the tragic world view. Science, Nietzsche claims, places something akin to an absolute value on truth and assumes that life can be made meaningful by understanding it through rational, intellectual means.

As a different way of appropriating the world, technology, with its animating Promethean Geist, is also optimistic and assigns a kind of categorical value to 'technological progress'. The predominant spirit informing post-Renaissance technological activity, a spirit liberally fueled by its remarkable successes, assumes that, ceteris paribus, the human condition can only be ameliorated and rendered more meaningful by ongoing technological progress (i.e. improvements in the knowledge or resource or methodological sectors of various technologies).

The belief that there is a rational solution to human problems reflects the concept of reality which science and technology share. However, science entails the systematic development of descriptive rules and principles, including scientific generalizations and 'laws', and the procedures to formulate, test, and elaborate such rules. Technology, on the other hand, consists of a rule framework stressing *knowledge of the world which can be used in action, in producing or doing something and, in this sense, is eminently practical.* Weingart (1984:121) stresses this point:

> The property of technology which it shares with action in the concrete world is its uniqueness; the 'diversity of practical conditions' (context dependence) require 'unique methods', namely experiments on machines at real scale and under realistic conditions

Thus, technology is not 'applied science' but much more complicated, at least in a social science perspective. Obviously, applications of science have played a great role in the development of aircraft, rockets, etc. On the other hand, technical developments such as the steam engine led to the progress of scientific knowledge.

Although science and technological knowledge, considered on an abstract general level, can be thought of as generated by a common process of rational problem-solving, they differ in fundamental ways as social forms and forms of knowledge (Laudan, 1984:10). As pointed out earlier, technology, in contrast to science, is a part of socio-technical systems with concrete activities and social organization which have a direct impact on people's lives. People react to technological developments in ways that they only rarely react to science. A substantial part of science is 'autonomous' in this sense.[102] Political reactions to 'scientific ideas' or results do occur in the modern world, as the contemporary histories of fascism, communism, and religious fundamentalism demonstrate. These reactions occur *largely on ideological grounds.* Science and its theories come into conflict with religion and ideology about Nature, Man, and Society, but *do not have direct, concrete impacts on social* life, people's conditions, and their concrete relation to nature and to one another, in short on *power relations.* Technology and technological development have practical, direct impact and often evoke concrete struggles.

Technique, types of knowledge and effective action

'Tools' and 'technologies' presuppose a certain operative knowledge on the part of users, that is the socially formulated rules and procedures which specify how activities employing the tools are to be performed. Such 'technique', understood in a general way, pervades all spheres of human activity.[103] As Weber has pointed out (1968:65):

> The 'technique' of an action refers to the means employed as opposed to the meaning or end to which the action is, in the last analysis, oriented. 'Rational' technique is a choice of means which is consciously and systematically oriented to the experience and reflection of the actor, which consists, at the higher level of rationality in scientific knowledge. What is concretely to be treated as a 'technique' is thus variable... Then the 'meaning' of the concrete act (viewed from the larger context) lies in its technical function; and, conversely, the means which are applied in order to accomplish this are its 'techniques'. In this sense there are techniques of every conceivable type of action, techniques of prayer, of asceticism, of thought and research, of memorizing, of education, of exercising political or hierocratic domination, of administration, of making love, of making war, of musical performances, of sculpture and painting, of arriving at legal decisions. All these are capable of the widest variation in degree of rationality.

Technique is a type of 'social technology'. It may but need not entail the use of scientific knowledge, whether the activity concerns steelmaking, love-making, or political action. *Technique refers to a rule set* governing the execution of certain activities in an effective or proper way within a defined sphere or complex. That is, it relates to *action* not technology *per se.* While technique is obviously important in the production and use of technology — where 'proper' or effective techniques should be followed — it covers a much broader range of social activity, as Weber suggested.

Each of us has certain procedures — techniques — for starting our cars, setting our watches, operating washing machines, making still photographs or moving pictures, among others. Many of the specific rules of the procedure are followed to assure desired effects. We believe — on the basis of our own experience or the advice of persons we consider knowledgeable — that failure to by-and-large follow the procedures would in most cases result in malfunctioning: the motor of the car fails to start or operates less effectively (a 'sour motor'); the photographs do not turn out or are blurred.

Such rule knowledge is a pervasive part of daily life in technologically advanced societies. Typically, the mass of people who follow these procedures are not the ones who have discovered or formulated them. Often they know little about the mechanisms — and even less about any underlying scientific theories — of motor cars or internal combustion, watches, washing machines, cameras. They simply learn the procedure — indeed, they must learn the procedures if they are to make effective use of the machinery of everyday life and 'to carry on'.

Earlier we examined techniques of social organizing and collective decision-making (Chapters 10, 12, and 13). In the following discussion we illustrate briefly the character of technique as production rules, drawing on recent research on high-carbon steels. The discussion compares ancient techniques with modern ones, pointing up that similar results may be obtainable with vastly different conceptions of what one is doing and why a technique works.[104]

Swords and armour made from Damascus steel were the stuff of legends, by the time of the Crusades. Sherby and Wadsworth (1985:94) in an article in *Scientific American* point out, 'For centuries thereafter they remained objects of fascination and frustration for European smiths, who tried in vain to reproduce consistently the distinctive damask, or surface pattern.' Sherby and Wadsworth examine the mystery of Damascus steel, its hardness as well as toughness (as opposed to brittleness).

One reason European smiths had so much difficulty, according to the authors, may have been that they were accustomed to working with low-carbon steels which have a higher melting point. Following 'normal steel-making procedures' would result in Damascus-type steels crumbling under the blows of the iron-forger's hammer at white-hot temperatures (temperatures which low carbon steels tolerate).

The scientific knowledge essential to understanding steel-making has been available for some time, even if the techniques for producing different types and qualities of steel are still being developed. Sherby and Wadsworth point out (1985:94):

> The basis for a complete scientific understanding of Damascus steels was not established until the turn of the century, when a series of investigators worked out the phase transitions steel undergo as a function of temperature and carbon content. Even today, when the iron-carbon phase diagram is well known, the art of Damascus swordmaking is a patentable discovery under American law.

The authors refer to a variety of historically recorded procedures used in heat-treating Damascus blades. These often gave considerable weight to considerations that seem immaterial to the modern engineer (1985:98):

> For instance, some smiths insisted that swords be quenched in the urine of a redheaded boy or in that of a 'three-year-old goat fed only ferns for three days'.

They refer to a detailed, lyrical description of a hardening procedure which was found in the Balgala Temple in Asia Minor (1985:98):

> The bulat (Damascus steel) must be heated until it does not shine, just like the sun rising in the desert, after which it must be cooled down to the color of a king's purple, then dropped into the body of a muscular slave ... the strength of the slave was transferred to the blade and is the one that gives the metal its strength.

Sherby and Wadsworth interpret the instructions as follows: Heat the blade to a high temperature, presumably above 1,000 degrees C ('sun rising in the desert'), then air-cool it to a temperature of about 800 degrees ('king's purple'). Finally, quench it in a warm (37 degrees) brinelike medium.

According to Sherby and Wadsworth (1985:99), the Balgala procedure would result in a sword which is hard but also too brittle to withstand the impact of a blade that has been heated to only just above 727 degrees before quenching. Such a blade would be tough as well as hard.

The authors claim, with some reservations, to have re-discovered the lost art of Damascus steel-making. Using knowledge of ultra-high carbon steels, they present a procedure which produces a steel 'strikingly similar to that of Damascus steel' (1985:99):

> First we heated a small steel casting, whose carbon content was 1.7 percent to a temperature of 1,150 C (light yellow) for 15 hours. The prolonged heating dissolved the carbon and produced a very coarse austenite. Next the casting was cooled at a rate of about 10 degrees per hour. The slow cooling allowed a coarse, continuous cementite network to form at the austenite grain boundaries.
>
> Finally we reheated the casting to 800 degrees C and rolled it, reducing its height by a factor of eight. This step, which simulated forging, stretched the grains in the rolling direction and broke up the carbide network. When the steel was etched with an acid that attached the iron matrix preferentially over the carbide, a damask was visible to the unaided eye. The microstructure of the casting was strikingly similar to that of Damascus steels.

They also succeeded in developing a procedure to make superior ultra high-carbon steels that lacked a damask (1985:99):

by rolling the casting as it cooled from 1,100 degrees C through the austenite-plus-cementite phase. The mechanical working refined the austenite grains and caused the cementite to precipitate out of solution as fine, uniformly distributed particles rather than as a coarse network. Thus, the finished steel bore no surface markings.

Such damask-free ultrahigh-carbon steels are stronger and more ductile at room temperature than conventional automobile steels. Furthermore, they are superplastic (that is, they behave like molasses or semi-molten glass) at temperatures of 600 to 800 degrees C. As a result they can be shaped with precision into complicated objects, such as gears, with a minimum of expensive machining and by-processing methods that are adaptable to mass production. This suggests they might find wide industrial application.

This case illustrates the social formulation and use of technique, in particular, production rules and procedures. Also, it points up the linkage between scientific knowledge and technique. Science provides *descriptive rules* about processes, effects of conditions or variables such as temperature, chemical treatment and so forth. Technique entails know-how: procedures to follow in producing an effect or an object. Technique, as in this case, may make use of scientific knowledge of the properties of high-carbon steels. However, the scientific knowledge was not essential to the discovery and development of the technique, such as the making of high-carbon steels. Following Rosenberg (1982:143ff.), one might make the distinction between the deductive methods of science and the experimental/practical methods of technology. However, technology also consists of ad hoc theories and operative rules which 'work, even if the reasons for this are not known scientifically' (Rosenberg, 1982:143).[105]

Technology, social rules and power
Technologies are instruments of social action with consequences. As with social action generally, human agents develop and apply elaborate rules around their use: knowledge rules, value and operative rules. Indeed, the design of technologies presupposes certain social rule systems on the part of those who use them. At the same time, technologies such as machines are 'systems of action' *incorporating rules in their design* (see Perrow, 1979). In this sense, a technology, even a simple technology such as a door key, entails an institutional frame, implicit social rule systems to regulate the use of the key in locking and unlocking one or more doors (where principles of property rights, technical rules, informal rules agreed on by friends and neighbours, as well as a number of unwritten rules operate).[106]

The introduction of new technologies and the formation of socio-technical systems entail more than setting up and using new machines and other physical artefacts. They entail social re-organizing and the making of new rules as well as the adaptation, transformation or replacement of old ones.[107] Effective use — or even any 'suitable use' of the technology — requires in most cases some minimal knowledge and utilization of operative rules. Indeed, the design of the technology presupposes knowledgeable, compe-tent users — that is, human agents who have or can acquire the necessary competence.[108] The design presupposes, in particular, that users or potential users know or can learn essential operational information about the technology, its performance characteristics, strong and weak features, and so forth. They should also possess certain general as well as particular values concerning treatment of the technology, its utilization as well as its maintenance. Finally, users must learn specific rules and procedures of operation, main-tenance and repair. Of course, some technologies, such as those for mass consumption, are designed so that minimum knowledge is required to be able to use them effectively. The 'grammar of use' may be no more than a few rules about which buttons to push, when to push them, and precisely how to do so.

In other words, there exist *cultural and institutional infrastructures* around technologies and technology-action complexes. Tech-nological development entails transformations of this infrastructure. In order that a new technology be used effectively — to accomplish those things that it has been designed to do — certain cultural and institutional changes are required. These may be difficult to bring about, both because of political opposition as well as because of high uncertainty associated with radical restructuring with its unpredictable consequences. Mismatches or incompatibility between technology design and social infrastructure explain in part why technology transfer to the Third World countries from the First World so often fails (Baumgartner et al., 1986).

Even in developed countries, we see many instances of misma-tches between new technologies and the socio-technical systems into which they are introduced. Often there are political struggles associ-ated with such mismatches.[109] Those actors (such as engineers and managers) who wish to introduce and make more efficient use of the technology push for changes in the organization of production, occupational structures, and production norms. Employees, labour unions, and professions/occupations with vested interests or values in the established structures, resist those efforts.

That these struggles may result in radically different outcomes is well-known from comparisons of the introduction of new tech-nologies in diverse countries; or from the introduction of the same technology in different sectors of the same country, e.g. the public sector and private sectors with a very traditionally oriented management and/or labour force in contrast to dynamic sectors with managements and possibly a labour force ready to rapidly introduce and to exploit the new technologies. Such variation also is found between companies in a single branch.

The point is that, on the one hand, the introduction and development of new technologies entail changing established rule systems. On the other hand, those with vested interests in, or value commitments to, these systems may struggle to maintain them. The structuring and restructuring of socio-technical systems has impacts, sometimes of a radical nature, on everyday actions and interactions. In this regard, Winner (1983:251, 254) stresses:

> Technologies are templates which influence the shape and texture of political life. Thus, the construction of any technical system that involves human beings as operating parts amounts to a partial reconstruction of social roles and relationships. Similarly, the very act of using the kinds of machines, technologies and systems available to us generates patterns of activities and expectations that soon become 'second nature' to us. We do indeed 'use' telephones, automobiles, and electric lights in the conventional sense of picking them up and putting them down. But our world soon becomes one in which telephony, automobility, and electric lighting are forms of life in the sense that life would scarely be thinkable without them... Yet if the experience of the past two centuries shows us anything, it is certainly that technologies are not only aides in human activity, but also powerful occasions for reshaping that activity. In no area of inquiry is this fact more important than in our own discipline, the study of politics.

Through using technology in concrete and practical activities, actors acquire new experience, they learn and change. They revise their situational analyses as well as their operative rule systems relating to the activities in which the technology is employed. Technology's dialectical interplay with human action gives occasion for the restructuring and transformation of rule systems underlying the institutional arrangements and culture of society.

The fundamental decisions about technological design, introduction, and development are largely in the hands of relatively small elite groups (technical, economic, and socio-political). These influence, out of all proportion to their numbers, the lives of the vast majority through the impact of technological development on social life. Indeed, in some instances the survival of mankind, or at least life as we know it, is at stake.

This power is an abstract power, in a certain sense more formidable than the power of those controlling traditional forms of violence or means of production.

This is pointed up by the revolutions in micro-electronics and communications. Robotization and computerization, in particular, promise, among other things: to transform within decades occupational structures and employment conditions; to intensify control over work life; to extend the bureaucratization of organizational life and social life generally; and to enhance the possibilities for central access to and control over vast amounts of information and social intelligence. Let us for the purposes of discussion, concentrate only on transformations of occupational structures, work life and employment conditions.

In a recent review, Draper(1985:46) argues that major parts of the industrial working class will disappear as a result of robotization: welders, painters, machinists and toolmakers, machine operators, inspectors and industrial assemblers (without any guarantee that the transformation will automatically create new jobs for the men and women it displaces) . Estimates in the USA and England indicate substantial *net elimination* of jobs (in the US, for instance, 1.7 jobs on the average in day-time plants were eliminated per first generation robot, and 2.7 on the average in round-the-clock plants. Second-generation units are expected to result in a much larger net elimination, to be followed by third, fourth, and fifth-generation robotics). This development may, over the long run, be compatible to some extent with an ageing population whose active part is also declining. In the short to medium run, however, the workforce will not decline, and new jobs in services are not likely to be created fast enough to absorb those made redundant by robotics. Indeed, some fear the impact of office automation even more than they fear robotization of industry (Draper, 1985:51; Leontief and Duchin, 1985 suggest that three quarters of a million managers and five million clerical workers in the USA may find themselves technologically unemployed by 1990).

Concerning the transformation of industry — and the conditions of employment in industry — Draper (1985:46) concludes, 'If we pretend that this transformation will automatically create new jobs for the men and women it displaces, we will probably end up with a vastly expanded underclass, not a vastly expanded pool of computer programmers.' Draper and others point out that *robotics is specifically designed to cut the need of labour. Moreover, it is not designed to deal with the formidable problems of finding jobs for or preparing industrial workers for white-collar work.* Shaiken (1985) stresses that, unlike other technologies which increase the productivity of a worker, the robot actually replaces the worker. That is the primary purpose for building robots (Scott, 1985; Draper, 1985). Draper (1985:46) argues:.

Besides, as T.A. Heppenheimer, one of Minsky's contributors points out, they 'didn't get bored, take vacations, qualify for pensions, or leave soft-drink cans rattling around inside the assembled products. They ... would accept heat, radioactivity, poisonous fumes, or loud noise, all without filing a grievance.' Furthermore, they could work round-the-clock without malingering, going to the toilet, or blowing their noses, and were therefore more productive than any human worker, and one man or woman could often supervise several robots. The increase in output per hour was potentially enormous.

The robotic revolution which penetrated the automobile industry — and has contributed to 'a generation of practical experience' and the development of a knowledge base that helps cut costs and the risks of failure — is rapidly being extended to other areas. The electronics industry has undergone a major transformation, in that robots are already widely used to assemble finished products (Draper, 1985:48):

About nine tenths of Apple's Macintosh computer, for example, is assembled automatically — in part by equipment purchased from IBM. This astonishing feat is of deep importance. Welding and painting occur in many industries but the assembly of machines and other products is much more widespread, and it accounts for the largest single share of industrial workers and manufacturing costs. The experts agree that by the middle of the next decade it will be the most important application in robotics. In the meantime, assembly already occupies nearly 20 percent of the robots in Japan, where some electronics manufacturers claim that they have auto-mated one half to three quarters of their assembly operations. ... Not long ago the tomato growers of California hired 40,000 migrant workers a year to pick their crop. Then they started using a robot called the Tomato Harvester, and by the start of the 1980s they required only about eight thousand laborers to pick a crop three times as large. This was a fairly difficult application, too, for the modern commercial tomato, although hard, is less hard than most of the objects that robots manipulate, and tomatoes in general tend to be irregular in shape and to grow at unpredict-able locations on the vine.

The area of robotics, as so many other areas, is dominated by large companies and networks of engineers and research institutes. The major producers are Unimation (owned by Westinghouse), General Electric, Fanuc of Japan in a joint venture with General Motors Robotics, along with Bendix, Renault, Volkswagen, United Tech-nologies and IBM (Draper, 1985). Draper (1985:48) suggests:

These large companies are making such investments because they know something that the rest of us do not. They know that whatever may be happening at any particular moment, robotics, like the steam engine and electricity, is destined to be part of an industrial revolution. This Third Industrial Revolution will fuse design, manufacture, and marketing into a single stream of information that will eventually permit us to automate just about anything we do not want to do ourselves.

Robotics is only one part of a complex of technological revolutions which have begun — and will continue — to transform work, occupational structures, employment conditions, consumption patterns, leisure, and whole societies.

Technological change and politics:
Limitations and possibilities of intervention

Different groups and interests in society are likely to perceive and evaluate technological innovations and developments in different ways. Precisely because many technological innovations and developments have practical, concrete impacts on work and social life, people's conditions and opportunities, and their relations to nature and to one another, they often evoke concrete struggles — on micro as well as macro levels — about their introduction and impacts.

Conflicts may arise between those supporting a new development and those opposing it, or at least certain features of it. The ways in which groups and interests in society respond will in part determine the rate of development, the ultimate success of the enterprise, and the extent of any damage on the physical and social environments from the development.

Since the 1960s there has been growing concern about the impacts of technological innovation and development on the environments in which we live and on the quality of life. Changing perceptions and evaluations of nature and social life have emerged with respect to resource limits, pollution, work life and employment, as well as other areas of social life. This has affected the willingness of emergent, strategic groups in modern society — green movements and organizations struggling for pollution control and protection of the environment — to accept unrestrained technological development. Some of the consequences of such development have only become widely recognized or known in the past few decades. Social movements and institutions have emerged to push, not necessarily successfully, new demands and considerations relating to modern technologies and their development.

Social learning about, and the increasing politicization of, technological development has led more and more to the recognition that:

(i) Technological innovations and the development of sociotechnical systems may not only produce positive, intended effects but also negative consequences for the environment, for working conditions and employment, and for social life generally, many of these impacts unanticipated or unintended.

(ii) The benefits and negative impacts may be experienced in different time frames. The immediately obvious costs may appear quite small in comparison with the intended benefits. But in the case of complex socio-technical systems, the process of social learning and assessment of consequences may be a long, difficult enterprise. As Martino (1972) has pointed out, it is the unintended (and often unanticipated) consequences which frequently show up as costs, but which have not been considered at the outset. By the time they are recognized, the technology is all too well entrenched (with vested interests and an organizational and physical infra-structure), and it appears impossible or far too costly to replace it (that is, the problem of apparent irreversibility).

(iii) The benefits and 'costs' of technologies and technological development are usually distributed unequally among groups and segments of society — as well as other generations, for instance, leaving a heritage to future generations of depleted resources and a polluted, unattractive environment and shattered community structures.

(iv) Individuals, groups, organizations, and social movements may react to the impacts of modern technologies and technological developments. This may be in response to distributional effects, to environmental damage, to the depletion of resources and pollution, to the loss of jobs or meaningful work, or to the declining quality of the work environment or everyday life. Some citizen or interest groups react also on grounds of 'due process' or the principle that they should be able to participate in and influence the decisions and developments affecting their lives and the lives of their children.

In democratic societies, the general public and public interest groups have certain rights to participate — directly or indirectly — in major decisions and to influence change, such as those relating to the introduction and development of major new technologies. Of course, such decisions may be made to a greater or lesser extent through 'markets' or through decision-processes, internal to an industry or key consumer groups. But even 'markets' are subject to public scrutiny and regulation.

New values, greater political awareness, and social learning about technological change — and its potential impacts on the environ- ment — have made it increasingly difficult (at least in the European democracies), to simply propose and introduce so-called tech- nological solutions to many of the problems and challenges facing modern society. Tough questions are raised in some instances. In today's world there are normative and political pressures to con- sider non-economic and non-technical goals and values in the assessment, choice and development of technology. One such con- sideration concerns the extent to which a technology or family of technologies is 'environmentally friendly or compatible'; or the extent to which it will improve work life and conditions of employment. Technology need not be selected and developed in order to realize maximum increases in productivity or economic gain. Selection and development may be guided by 'qualitative considerations'. This is likely to become more and more the case in the future.

Much of the discontent and conflict relating to modern technologies and their development result from a failure of planners and policy-makers to allow affected groups to express their diverse values and concerns *early in the planning stage at a time when decisions may be more readily reversed or reformulated in quite different ways.* This is particularly important in the case of projects and developments which are on a *large-scale and have long timeframes.* Of course, involvement of currently active groups is no guarantee against future problems and crisis. New groups may emerge. Some established groups or unorganized citizens may come to change their viewpoints about or assessments of a development. However, early public discussion and genuine attempts to determine what developments appear not only technically/economically feasible but politically and culturally feasible would be a major step in the right direction.

This is consistent with the principle advanced here that *technological development is a social learning process as well as an enterprise in the collective structuring of social life.* In the course of such processes, social agents, individuals, groups and organizations, acquire knowledge and reformulate their goals, strategies and engagements. New concepts, shifts in values, and changes in the relevant 'rules of the game' and social institutions will be reflected sooner or later in the technological development. Often these changes occur at a slower pace than the more purely technical or engineering changes and, occasionally, only after prolonged and costly struggles. The 'feedback' associated with technological development is characterized not only by delays, distortion and confusion, but by barriers (including attempts at creating 'oblivion'). Thus, social learning and assessment and a more human and environmentally considerate shaping of the future may be partially blocked. Social science research has the *potential* to shed light on such barriers and to facilitate social feedback and learning. This might contribute to humanizing — and ecologizing — technological development to a greater extent than is the case at present.

It can do this in part by contributing to the identification of unarticulated interests and emerging groups as well as providing an empirical basis for dialogue and debate between opposing interests.

This is not to suggest that conflict can be eliminated, only that it can be better institutionalized and grounded on more systematic knowledge, allowing possibly for more creative dialogue and democratic policy-making.

Regulation of medicines and medical techniques

The historical study of any family of technologies which have an apparent impact on social life points up the dialectic between technical developments and the rule systems, including policy systems, organizing and regulating the production and use of the technologies. Drawing largely on Swedish material, let us examine such processes in the regulation of medicines and medical techniques.

Medicines and drugs. Lilja (1984:26) points out that legislation and regulation relating to medicines and drugs had its origins in Frederik II's laws for the 'Two Sicilies', formulated between 1231 and 1241 (for a general historical background, see Sonnedecker (1974)). The major principles in this regime were: (i) pharmacists' activity should be distinguished from that of physicians; (ii) pharmacies should be inspected and controlled by the authorities; (iii) pharmacies should produce and sell medicines of satisfactory quality; (iv) authorities should decide the location of pharmacies and their prices.

Lilja (1984), among others, argues that the development of the rule regimes regulating medicines occurred in this time period, the thirteenth century, in part because of the growth of medical training in Southern European universities. For example, it was possible to study medicine at Paris University from 1205. The university, the students and the authorities were interested in distinguishing between physicians with university education and those lacking such education.

Already in the first medical statutes, university educated physicians were given a professional monopoly within their areas. This was a natural development, but it also had consequences for the making, interpretation, and implementation of rules regulating medicines. University educated physicians enjoyed the *initiative in rule formation governing the production and selling of medicines.*

Lilja points out in a discussion of developments in Scandinavia (1984:26):

> Frederick II's legislation was the basis for the comprehensive medicine laws which were enacted for Denmark and Norway 1672 and for Sweden and Finland in the course of the 1688 medical ordinances. Collegium Medicum (later the Medical Board) was established in 1663 by four university educated physicians in order to safeguard their professional interests. The Collegium Medicum took the initiative to formulate the

medical ordinances in cooperation with the king and his council. Legislation aimed, among other things to do something about the unorganized (disordered) selling of medicines at squares and markets. The selling of pharmaceuticals should be limited to the pharmacies, which in turn were to be controlled by the authorities. In practice, this control came to be exercised by physicians through inspections of pharmacies.

Nevertheless, the selling of medicines outside the pharmacies continued, despite regulation. According to Lilja (1984), the control of medicines in Sweden remained based on the 1688 ordinances up until 1913. The education of pharmacists however changed greatly during this period: from having been a craft education, it came more and more to be oriented to natural science chemistry.[110] The rapid development of chemistry during the 1800s provided the technical possibilities to control the content of medicines through chemical analyses. There was increasing discussion and debate about the control of medicines: questions concerning combining medicines, the great variation in doctors' manners of prescription, as well as issues of medical training (questions which are still of concern today).

Parallel to these professional developments, a revolution in manufacturing was going on. By the end of the 1800s, there had emerged a significant manufacturing and selling of medicine-like substances outside the pharmacies. Through advertisements in newspapers, it was possible to achieve widespread dissemination of information about preparations. The manufacturers wished to have much freer medicinal legislation, basing their arguments on liberal ideas about the limited role of government in the economy. On the other hand, the pharmacies were highly critical of the growth of medicine sales outside the pharmacies and pointed out the often exaggerated claims in the announcements of the new preparations.

Initially, Parliament was unprepared to help the pharmacists do something about 'the illegal sale of medicines'. The Pharmaceutical Society eventually established a private agency to monitor and analyse medicines sold on open markets, engaging for this purpose the Department of Medical Chemistry at Uppsala University.

The price and quality of the medicines were compared to the products offered by the pharmacies; their contents were also analysed and compared with the claims for cure announced in the advertisements. Results from these studies were used in campaigns against open market medicine sales. These initial efforts at 'social regulation' were eventually taken over by the state and an agency of state medicine control was established (1913).

The enactment also of the statutes for pharmaceutical goods in 1913 was intended to deal with the illegal selling of medicines outside pharmacies. However, the legislation did not control the manufactured preparations which were sold in pharmacies. During the 1920s, the sale of industrially manufactured preparations increased dramatically in the pharmacies themselves. These preparations were even marketed with the help of advertisements and flyers.

Again, the owners of pharmacies took the initiative in establishing 'private control' of manufactured preparations. The Pharmacies Control Laboratory was organized. In Norway, the government, upon the initiative of the pharmacy owners, required the registration of all industrial preparations (1928). Six years later such registration was introduced in Sweden.

As increasing numbers and varieties of medicines appeared on markets, regulation of medicines developed further, with close collaboration between the pharmacy (and profession) representatives and the government. This system was somewhat modified after the Second World War, as norm-setting and regulation became increasingly influenced by international developments. In part this had to do with technical developments: measurement and production methods discovered internationally and diffused through industrial countries became the point of departure for establishing new norms. The cost and health consequences of such norms were rarely discussed in the professional literature. In recent years, however, adherents of natural medicine and representatives for the medicine industry have more and more taken up the question of how such norms and regulations should be determined. In part, this relates to what appears to be increasing problems of legitimacy.

The 'politicalization of medicines' in the 1960s has entailed increased influence and regulation by government, at the expense of professional groups. As a result of the Thalidomide catastrophe in Sweden (Thalidomide was the sedative which resulted in foetal abnormalities; it had been widely prescribed in Sweden), the public and politicians demanded that new methods should be developed and applied in order to increase the security of medicine distribution and use. This entailed, above all, the requirement that all registrations of new drugs be accompanied by data on toxicity animal tests as well as systematic clinical investigations.

Lilja (1984:31) points out that a variety of controls have been introduced and developed: (i) the licensing of importers, manufacturers and sellers; (ii) reporting of clinical tests; (iii) registration of medicines as well as reporting of 'natural medicines'; (iv) tests of preparations; (v) reporting side-effects; (vi) control of marketing; (vii) price and cost controls; (viii) prescription requirements and other limitations on selling; (ix) information to health care personnel and the public.

The study of rule-development and regulation relating to medicines points up that: (i) rules regulating medicines were established initially to buttress university educated professionals (physicians) in their struggles for legitimacy with other 'physicians' and 'practitioners'; (ii) technological developments of new medicines evoked attempts at maintaining or extending control, particularly by the professional groups, medical doctors and pharmacists, most threatened by the 'industrialization of medicines and medical preparations'. In Sweden, these professions gained control over the distribution of medical products, including, of course, those requiring prescription; (iii) at the same time, the bi-effects of new drugs and the greater use of a variety of drugs has led to increasingly elaborate rules and controls about the conditions under which and how new drugs will be introduced and dispensed. This has entailed the development of an elaborate administration with its own vested interests in laboratories, data banks etc.

Increasingly, concern is directed at the concrete use of drugs in medical care. There are indications that more systematic data will be collected — and analyses carried out — on the actual use of drugs. This can be expected to lead to new types of regulations, for instance, specifying and standardizing treatment programmes for high-incident illnesses. In Sweden, at least, the 'treatment programmes' for high-incident illnesses appear likely to be decided and planned at the county level, whereas today these are largely specified and carried out through physician networks. Approved drugs, marketed by the industry, are adopted by physicians who follow the industry's guidelines, possibly modified on the basis of *professional judgement or local experience.*

Artificial insemination and the Swedish act of 1985.[111]   The technology of artificial insemination has been available for some time and widely used in animal breeding. The extent of its use in human groups before 'official attention' was given to the matter would be of considerable interest in the study of 'innovation processes' and the cultural and institutional factors facilitating or inhibiting them.[112]

Artificial insemination as a remedy for dealing with involuntary childlessness was adopted by American and French doctors as early as the 1860s, primarily in the form of artificial insemination by husband. Artificial insemination by donor (AID) is known to have been practised in Sweden at least since the 1920s.

Approximately 2,000 insemination acts (sociologically, a complicated and organizationally fascinating phenomenon) are performed annually in Sweden, resulting in somewhat less than 300 babies per year out of a total of around 90,000 (in 1982, some 230

AID babies, and 40 babies resulting from artificial insemination with the husband's sperm, were born).

Interest in artificial insemination has grown rapidly in recent years — not only as a technology for treating involuntary childlessness but as an issue of public policy. In most countries these activities are almost totally exempt from statutory and official controls. Sweden is the first country to pass comprehensive legislation on artificial insemination (effective from 1 March, 1985).[113]

The Swedish Parliament first took an interest in artificial insemination at the end of the 1940s, when a Government commission was appointed to investigate the matter. In 1953 that commission presented draft legislation on artificial insemination. The draft, which only applied to AID, was based on the then prevailing principles that childbirth was both the duty and wish of women and should take place within wedlock. Among other things, the proposed legislation laid down the rule that the identity of the donor must be withheld from the prospective parents. Moreover, it should not be possible for paternity proceedings to be brought against the donor. In other words, the woman's husband was deemed to be the child's legal father.

These proposals were never enacted. Ewerlöf suggests (1985) that the influence of the powerful anti-legalization lobby, which included religious groups, may have played a role. At the same time, there were Swedish children available for adoption and cases of artifical insemination were a rarity at that time. Legislation hardly seemed warranted (Ewerlöf, 1985:4).

As artificial insemination became an increasingly established method of remedying involuntary childlessness, the demand for legislation became correspondingly more apparent. Swedish law offered no protection whatsoever for AID children. According to the law on parentage in Sweden (The Code of Parenthood), a husband who had consented to his wife or female cohabitant being inseminated with sperm from another man could at any time and with no limitation file proceedings with a court to establish that he was not the child's biological father. The seriousness of this problem was made all too clear in a case decided by the Swedish Supreme Court in March, 1983. In the course of divorce proceedings, the husband petitioned the court to rule that he was not the father of an AID child, and therefore should not have to assume responsibility for the child.

The father's claim was allowed. The child was left with no legal father. After the divorce, the ex-husband was excused from paying a maintenance allowance. Several similar cases were subsequently brought before Swedish courts, causing widespread popular indignation and a vigorous debate in the news media.

The new legislation on artificial insemination makes Sweden the first nation to adopt a comprehensive approach to the matter (Ewerlöf, 1985:8). The underlying principle is that having children is *not* an unconditional human right and that activities of this kind should therefore only be permitted on condition that the child will be able to grow up in favourable conditions. The aim is that AID children should acquire full 'respectability' and a status which can be compared, for example, with that of adopted children.

The new law lays down the principle that a man who has consented to his wife's or cohabitant's insemination with sperm from a donor must be deemed the child's legal father. The socio-legal definition of this complex social situation is as follows. The 'adopting father' may *never* abrogate his responsibility. The donor, on the other hand, will *never* incur any responsibility for the child.

AID is sanctioned for women who are married or living in quasi-marital relationships. It is intended to help families prevented by the man's infertility from having children in normal ways. On the other hand, the legislation *does not permit single women or women living in lesbian relationships to make use of the method.* This latter rule was introduced on the basis of arguments about 'the child's best interests'. Child psychiatrists and child psychologists argued that a child needs both father and mother figures. The argument went that a child, having to grow up with only one parent, has correspondingly less chance of developing under favourable conditions. Ewerlöf (1985:6) points out that this provision in the legislation has not met thus far with major protests. The Left Party Communists (VPK) and 'a couple of women's organizations' have objected. Otherwise, the principle was 'more or less unanimously endorsed'.

The new legislation made it the task and professional responsibility of the physician to examine the insemination couple medically and to select a donor. The physician is also required to ascertain whether AID is advisable in view of the insemination couple's 'psychosocial circumstances'. The law stipulates that the donor must be in 'good mental and physical health', must not be suffering from any demonstrable hereditary disease, and must be of 'normal intelligence'.

The law requires that the written consent of the woman's husband or cohabitant be obtained *before making use of the AID method.* The record of the consent is kept by the responsible physician. The husband or man is entitled to revoke his consent up until insemination. Once this event has occurred, the man is irrevocably responsible by law for any child which may be born as a result of the artificially produced insemination.

The new legislation affirms the importance of parental frankness and honesty toward the child. However, the law does not require that the parents tell the child about its origins, although there were some who advocated this. On the other hand, the legislation does provide opportunities for children to find out about their origin. This provision was introduced to 'safeguard the child's best interests' (Ewerlöf, 1985:6). Children expressing a desire for information about the identity of the donor are allowed to eventually gain access to hospital records concerning the donor. 'But the child must be sufficiently mature not to suffer harm as a result of this information, and as a general rule this means that he or she must be in late teens. Hospital information should not be released without the child first having an interview with a social worker or similar representative (Ewerlöf, 1985:6).

The legislation lays down that, out of consideration for the donor, hospital information on the donor can not be divulged to the child's parents or to any third party.

The legislation on insemination proscribes the *import* of frozen sperm into the country without first obtaining permission from the National Board of Health and Welfare. The law also makes the commercial performance of insemination punishable by fines or imprisonment. Such punishments are also to be imposed for supplying sperm for insemination purposes inconsistent with the Insemination Act of 1985. This provision is aimed at prevention of what Ewerlöf (1985) refers to as 'uncontrolled insemination activities'.

The dynamics of regulation. The rule systems structuring and regulating a field never cover all contingencies, particularly major innovations or their impacts. In the discussion of artificial insemination of humans, the laws concerning 'paternal responsibility' were invalidated (or led to what were considered by part of the public as outrageous outcomes). *In general, major technological innovations typically lead to a complex of problems, which established rule systems cannot deal with.* Initial attempts at solution will be 'ad hoc' and unsystematic, therefore difficult to anticipate. Coherent structuring and coordination become increasingly difficult, except in exceptional circumstances. Negative unanticipated as well as unintended outcomes are likely to result.

Under such circumstances, some actors, professional groups or organizations may try to come to grips with the complex of problems associated with technological innovation by institutionalizing more 'appropriate' organizing principles and reforming rule systems. These are intended to regulate the technological development as well as the production and use of the technology. In some instances, the intent may be to strictly limit or even prevent the use or further development of the technology (such as dangerous chemicals, drugs, or nuclear power).

Established rule systems not only influence the selection and development of technologies in the areas of activities where the systems apply. They may also become 'shackles', blocking particular developments, at least as viewed by advocates. Or, from the viewpoint of opponents, these serve as strategic resources with which to prevent undesirable or catastrophic outcomes. *Thus, processes of technological innovation and development often revolve around struggles to change or to maintain established rules regulating the technology or areas to which the technology is or might be applied.* Success in reform or in establishing a new rule complex may enable the successful, further development of a technology or family of technologies, with a variety of gains for some groups, not only producers, and possibly losses for others, particularly third parties.

Of course, rule systems — even intelligently formulated and well-designed systems — rarely determine the technological development. To a greater or lesser extent they only steer and possibly limit it. There is a continual interplay between 'social structure' and 'the processes of technological innovation and change'.

Conclusions

In this concluding section, we shall outline several questions suggested by the conceptualization of technology and technological development suggested by social rule system theory.

(i) Technology development is both conditioned by social structure and conditions it. In the former case, established institutions, professions and elite groups tend to select and develop technologies consistent with their positions of power and authority as well as their conceptual frames and ideologies. Such technological development is observable, for instance, in the areas of energy supply, mass (and now satellite) communications, and the organization of automated process- and batch-production systems.

At the same time, technology developments — such as those associated with the formation of an information society — have *unintended and, to a great extent, uncontrollable consequences:* the transformation of the economy, shifts in strategic functions of society including the relative decline of industry and the emergence of service and knowledge economies, the growth in social power of certain private and public white-collar groups associated with these transformations, and the societal struggle over income distribution in an economy which is stagnating as well as undergoing technological transformation.

The micro-electronic and communications revolutions, in particular, entail the use of new technologies in production as well as in consumption. These become instruments of function as well as of social power and social status. Some class and status divisions are deepened, others transformed. Computer illiteracy promises to be as serious a handicap as language illiteracy.

(ii) Often the more disruptive and damaging impacts of technological development lead governments, at least in democratic societies, to intervene and to try to regulate the development. Through evoking such 'regulative responses', techological development generates not only the direct rule transformations associated with its production and use, but indirect transformations: legislation, policy reformulations, other rule changes which are introduced through political and administrative processes.

Paradoxically, in the modern welfare states of Europe and North America, there is considerable insecurity and alienation today: (a) because technological transformations alter work and employment conditions as well as life styles, family and community relations and (b) because political–administrative responses to the impacts of technological development generate new and often confusing laws, regulations, and agencies, an entire complex, to regulate the development and to deal with some of its negative social and environmental impacts. *Hyper-change and over-development result.*

A new logic or rationality should be a major aim — certainly over the long run — of the philosophy and policies concerning technology development. The new logic should be more transparent to the general public and policy makers, in part simpler and more coherent. *It should be aimed at establishing 'preventive policies and measures' rather than the vast hodge-podge of curative policies and measures which so characterize the current logic.*

(iii) Consciousness about the implications of technology choice and development has grown and, in our view, will continue to grow. The processes of technology design, introduction and management are being made — and should continue to be made — more transparent. Such knowledge should enable better information spreading and an improvement in public debate and, indeed, public influence over technology design and development in the future.

15

A modern oracle and politics: Studies in energy forecasting

Tom R. Burns, Tormod Lunde, Reinier de Man and Atle Midttun

Introduction: The social organization of energy forecasting

In this chapter we examine the social organization of energy modelling and forecasting, focusing on case studies we have carried out in Britain, Holland, and Norway. (See Baumgartner and Midttun (1986) for a more comprehensive treatment.) The organization includes professional networks within which prognosis models are produced, maintained and developed.

The discussion (1) identifies certain modes of transaction between model-builders and forecasters and policy-makers and, in particular, examines the diverse roles that models and their ouputs play in policy processes; and (2) suggests what these modes may imply for (i) the structure and dynamics of model-building/policy transactions and for (ii) the integrity and internal discipline of model-building professions.

A public policy system is a rule regime with a formally or informally specified set of actors (see Chapters 12 and 13). These are members of professions (economists, engineers, modelling experts, and so forth) and organizations such as professional associations, research institutes, state agencies and ministries. The environment of the policy system consists also of actors and potential actors: other government agencies, political parties, interest organizations, communities, mass media, and the general public. Some of these are engaged in model-building and forecasts in one form or another. This is especially the case of some professional groups, research institutes and interested government agencies.

Forecasting — referring here to a general concept covering model-building, model use, and the making of forecasts and scenarios — is a technical activity. Our main concern here is to examine the transactions between technical experts or groups and a political or policy-making community — to consider their different rationalities and forms for producing and using knowledge and for making decisions. This will lead us into a consideration of the political functions which forecasting may serve. The formulation and interpretation of models, such as energy models, entails the use of certain rules and techniques. The models themselves consist of descriptive rule systems representing certain features and structures of social and physical systems. The rules of the model transform inputs (data, information) into outputs. Model rules determine the types of inputs required and the types and forms of outputs. The transformative and interpretative rules of the model, whether they are formulated as a series of general rules or a system of simultaneous equations, correspond to the practical social rules governing the sphere of social action and transforming 'inputs' into 'outputs'.

Forecasting requires extensive assessments and the exercise of judgement in the 'grey zone' of selecting and organizing data and in model construction before the models become operative and before they can be used to generate forecasts. Cultural, socio-political and institutional factors influence the forecasts and policy measures adopted. Typically they are not an explicit part of the models. Such factors exert their influence partly through exogenously determined variables, partly through structural parameters within the models. In the former case, determination of the values of exogenous variables entails political decisions. In the latter case, the parameters were estimated on the basis of time series. A period of time has to pass before a change can be incorporated into the models through a re-estimation of the relevant equations. In some instances the changes may be so substantial that a reformulation of parts of the model may be required. In both these cases, a *variety of decisions are required — which provides opportunities for political and ideological influences to affect the selection of interpretations addressing ambiguities, the choice of techniques and procedures, and decisions about when model changes should be made.*

Of particular interest to us in this chapter are: (1) the interaction between technical, possibly scientific rules of validity, modelling and interpretation, on the one hand, and political consensus-building and acceptation rules, on the other; (2) the political and institutional factors which influence the selection of modelling rules, techniques, and professional groups; and (3) some of the major political uses of forecasting.[114]

Technical models for producing prognoses are the core technology of a modern prognosis-making system. Control over the core technology is a major power base in the system (Thompson, 1967; Pfeffer and Salancik, 1978). Since the structure of the model determines which input data are required for the making of prognoses, the technical structure of the model determines the form and content of information requirements and the external dependencies of the prognosis-making organization.

Control over the technology also makes it possible to decide — or to influence the decision — when to publish prognoses. Thus, a prognosis-making institution can influence and/or legitimize political decision-making by releasing or withholding information pertaining to strategic decisions.

At times, alternative models based on different paradigms and model technologies may be available simultaneously. However, since established criteria of goodness-of-fit for prognosis models do not exist, the choice between alternative models is determined typically according to professional status and authority and/or political power.[115]

In Section 15.2 we examine case studies of Holland and the UK. Section 15.3 presents the case of Norway where the relationship between model-builders and policy-makers changes rather dramatically over time (the struggles and transformations described in Chapter 13 provide part of the context for the changes). Finally, we make some concluding remarks.

The studies of this chapter point up the normative and political biases which may enter into model-building and forecasting. They also suggest the role technical elites may play in defining social reality or — perhaps more typically — in supporting and legitimizing the definitions set forth by policy-makers. Indeed, this is one of the purposes of forecasting.

A modern oracle and the interplay between technology and politics

The problem: Energy prognoses and policy-making
During the 1970s in Britain, Holland and Norway, as in many other countries, energy modelling programmes and the number of energy forecasts grew substantially. Initially, expectations about the importance and value of these efforts for energy planning and policy-making were high. Practical results were, however, disappointing:

(i) The predictive power of the models turned out to be very low. Large and complicated models did not result in prognoses substantially better than very simple ones.

(ii) The use of energy models, forecasts and scenarios with respect to highly politicized questions such as nuclear energy and coal-fired plants (and in Norway, hydro-power facilities) proved to be highly controversial, rather than contributing to 'objective considerations of future possibilities and limitations'.[116]

By the end of the 1970s policy-makers and policy analysts, including modellers, realized that the role of energy forecasting in practical policy-making differed significantly from the role of what some envisioned as 'scientific objectivity' (de Man, 1986).

The case of the Netherlands
The political context. Political decisions in the Netherlands are made in large part according to the neo-corporatist state model (concerning such models, see Schmitter, 1979; Streeck and Schmitter, 1984; de Man, 1986; Teulings, 1985). The central core of the government is relatively weak, and policies are prepared in large networks involving state institutions and private interests. The dominant policy style is consensus formation through extended consultation and negotiation procedures (Dutch: 'overleg'). This makes pure technocracy an exception rather than a rule: technical and scientific advice is generally but one of the legitimation grounds for a decision. The weight of technical and scientific advice relative to other legitimation grounds is established in an 'overleg' process. Even the content of such advice is often subject to negotiation.

The energy context. After World War II the Netherlands industrialized considerably. This explains in part the high growth in energy consumption between 1945 and 1970. Until the early 1970s, nuclear energy had a top priority. In the years after the War, it was believed that nuclear energy was the technological solution to the energy problem. Two developments substantially altered this expectation.

(1) In the early 1970s the resistance to nuclear power grew. Experiences in the USA gave some legitimacy to questions and doubts directed at technological and economic arguments supporting nuclear energy.

(2) Large quantities of natural gas were discovered in the Netherlands (and its off-shore waters) in the early 1960s. The Dutch situation changed from that of an importer of energy to that of a net energy exporter.

As a result of these circumstances, a number of nuclear projects were cancelled in the early 1970s. A compromise was reached between the ambitions of the nuclear energy industry and its critics. This became official with the publication of the 1974 Government Energy Paper (Energienota, 1974). The Paper projected only three nuclear plants of 1,000 MWe to be built before 1985. Because of a failure to achieve consensus in the parliament and the broader policy networks, this plan was never implemented. The decisions were repeatedly postponed. One procedure for postponing the nuclear decisions was the government-organized 'Public Debate on Energy', which took place between 1981 and 1984. In the debates, energy forecasts — formulated as energy scenarios — played an important role.

The Dutch energy scenario game. The Dutch energy scenario game — that is, the social process in which energy scenarios were

formulated, more or less influenced and utilized by the government
— was played by two groups of players: the establishment
institutions, on the one side, and the critical groups and organizations, on the other (de Man, 1986). In 1976, public officials, the
proponents in the debate, published two long-term energy scenarios
for the Netherlands. The opponents, a coalition of anti-nuclear and
environmental groups, responded with the publication of a low
energy scenario, which projected for the year 2000 only half of the
official projected energy demand. Attempts to have this low energy
scenario accepted by the government almost succeeded. The
Ministry of Environment would have financed a further scientific
elaboration of the study, if not for the fierce resistance from the
Ministry of Economic Affairs, which is responsible for energy
policy.

Despite this failure, the Public Debate on Energy provided the
critics with opportunities to advance their views and demands. As a
result of pressure from parliament, the government decided to fund
scientific work to develop a low energy scenario, along with more
traditional energy scenarios. We cannot provide here a detailed
description of the way the low energy scenario was developed. The
main features of the energy scenario game that played a decisive
role were as follows:

(i) The official funding of the low energy scenario implied some
increase in influence of, at the same time a loss of independence for,
the opponents to the establishment perspective. The research work
was carried out in continual interaction with the official policy
institutions.

(ii) The opportunity provided by the government to establish
contact between opponents and the official institutions, stimulated
the critics to form a closed coalition. This coalition managed to
exclude the development of any other low energy scenario. (This
points up the way in which neo-corporatist arrangements stimulate
the organization and integration of sector interests.)

(iii) The scenario work entailed considerable negotiation.
Exogenous variables of the model calculation were not defined on
the basis of methodological or theoretical considerations but on the
basis of political acceptability. For example:

- A commission defined a list of 'free' and 'fixed' parameters. Fixed
  parameters were not allowed to be changed in the calculations.
  This excluded a range of interesting issues from the debate. The
  oil price development, for instance, could not be examined.
- Other parameters were not 'determined' but 'negotiated'. The
  technical possibilities of energy conservation were negotiated

between representatives of the Ministry of Economic Affairs and the critics.

• At a certain stage of the energy scenario game, employment became a central issue. The proponents of high energy conservation argued that their policy line would solve a substantial part of the unemployment problem. A commission decided that unemployment would be an exogenous parameter, fixed and the same for all scenarios.

(iv) The latter negotiations resulted in a slight upward revision of the total energy demand projection for the low energy scenario. The numerical values in the conventional scenarios became much lower than the conventional scenarios made years before, in large part because of lowered expectations about economic growth, but in part also because of the increased stress on energy conservation.

(v) The overall impact of the low energy scenario on official policy was small or negligible. Through the processes of negotiation and consensus formation, the Dutch 'alternative model' was 'adopted'(coopted) and its radical implications were emasculated in the processes of negotiation and political acceptance.

The case of the United Kingdom
The political context. The UK context differs greatly from that of the Netherlands. The structure of political decision-making is less preoccupied with consensus and more purely technocratic in character. In such a political context, we found that scientific work, such as energy forecasting, was less subject to negotiation than was the case in the Netherlands.

The UK energy context. The energy context of the UK is also very different from the Netherlands. Energy resources are ample and growth in energy consumption has been low. Britain's energy problem entailed making the transition from a coal energy economy to a multi-fuel energy economy rather than finding new supplies for rapidly growing demand. The transition implied serious conflicts between the different nationalized fuel industries, all fighting for their share in the energy supply. Britain has a long established nuclear industry with a relatively good safety record. This is one of the reasons why the British nuclear debate is not only different but more moderate than in many other countries, where the technology was newly introduced in the 1970s. Of course, in England, as in many other OECD countries, there are a large number of anti-nuclear and environmental organizations opposed to the construction of nuclear power plants. In contrast to the Netherlands, however, nuclear energy is scarcely a parliamentary issue. Nuclear policy is not fundamentally questioned by either the Labour or the Conservative Party. The capability of environmental and anti-nuclear groups to exercise influence through regular political or administrative channels is very weak, if non-existent.

The UK energy scenario game. The main features of the UK energy scenario game are presented briefly below (in the same categories used in the presentation of the Dutch energy scenario game; for full details of the history, see de Man (1986)).

(i) Long term energy forecasts did not play any substantial role in the UK before the second half of the 1970s. This motivated Gerald Leach in 1979 to carry out his low energy study. Leach took a moderate position in the energy debate. He was not categorically opposed to nuclear energy, and he did not represent any group or movement. On the other hand, the scenarios of the Friends of the Earth and the National Centre for Alternative Technology, developed directly after the Leach scenarios, did represent the perspectives of critical groups. These scenarios are comparable to the Dutch low energy scenario. The low energy scenario work was financed by the government, as in Holland. This was a consequence of the policy of the then Secretary of State for Energy who funded the opposition, quite exceptional in British politics.

The official funding of low energy scenarios entailed one restriction. The research work should be carried out by qualified people and by respectable institutions.

(ii) The *sustained interaction* between model-building groups and government institutions, so prevalent and important in the Netherlands, is not observed in the UK.

Also, the closed coalition of critics of official policy, such as appeared in the Netherlands, is not observed in Britain. This is explainable both by the absence of neo-corporatist policy and networks and the low status of nuclear energy on the political agenda in Britain. The internal cohesion of the critics is low in Britain because of the lack of opportunities to make effective ties with official institutions and to exercise influence by mobilizing allies as well as other forms of support. The lack of cohesion and forms of coordination is illustrated by one example: The Friends of the Earth presented strong arguments against a major role of electricity in their scenarios. On the other hand, the National Centre for Alternative Technology assumed a central role for electricity.

(iii) Negotiation between low energy scenario builders and the official institutions was virtually absent. As a result, the low energy scenarios were clear and honest representations of the various opposition standpoints. They did not make compromises with official policy. This points up both the conceptual strength and the political weakness of these scenarios and their sponsors. The high figures for biomass energy in the Friends of the Earth scenarios, for instance, made these scenarios completely unacceptable to other than the environmental groups.

(iv) In the British case, unlike the Dutch case, the low energy scenarios made in the scenario game were maintained. There was no upward revision due to negotiations. On the contrary, the scenario game resulted in the presentation of a more extreme environmental standpoint and, as a result, a loss of credibility.

(v) The low energy scenarios failed to have any substantial impact on British energy policy.

The energy scenario games for the Netherlands and the UK show two distinct modes of transaction between model-builders and policy-makers. The Dutch case suggests how political views of both the establishment and the critics were brought into direct negotiation. Both views penetrated the official forecasts. Stable, intermediary networks between critics and the establishment were formed. However, they were outside the realm of core policy networks. The consensus reached in the Public Debate, that is in the temporary organization set up for the debate, was therefore somewhat isolated from the main policy-making and did not have an immediate effect. The networks, which developed in the course of the Debate, could have an influence in the longer run, but this remains to be seen. The UK case exhibits, on the other hand, a 'marketplace' of ideas with no negotiation between the establishment and various political groups setting forth alternative energy scenarios. One may conclude that both in the UK and the Netherlands, the process of policy-making and modelling contributed to reproducing the prevailing styles of policy-making.

Comparing the two cases more systematically (see Table 15.1), we observe a marked difference in the logic of the forecasting and policy process, but, nonetheless, a great similarity in the final policy outcome of the process. This suggests that forecasts do not 'feed into' policy, so much as policy objectives define the requirements of forecasts. On the other hand, the case of Norway, which we shall shortly discuss, reveals a complex interplay between model-builders and policy-makers.

The organization of modelling in Norway, which is discussed in the following section, went from a situation of model monopoly closely linked to official energy policy-making, anchored in the hydro-power planning and administrative apparatus, to a situation of competing models. Two of these were anchored in contending policy visions: that of the industrial complex and that of the opposing environmental networks. Eventually, one model emerged

TABLE 15.1
Comparison of Dutch and British cases

	UK	Netherlands
Boundary conditions		
Type of policy-making style	Pluralist	Neo-corporatist
Energy context	Nuclear issue low on agenda	Nuclear issue high on agenda (until 1983)
Process		
Negotiation between critics and official institutions	Virtually absent	Present
Consensus among critics	Small	Great
Scenario construction	In freedom and isolation	In interaction with offical institutions
Outcomes		
Degree of consensus reached	Low	Considerable
Building up intermediate networks between 'establishment' and 'critics'	No	Yes
Immediate effect on policy formulation	No	No
Reproduction of prevailing political style	Yes	Yes

as hegemonic, even though, as this book goes to press, the energy policy sphere itself remains split between the 'industrial complex' and the 'green complex'.

The politics and transformation of a modern oracle:
The case of Norway

Introduction

Energy prognoses have played a prominent role in energy policy-making and planning in Norway. Up until the mid-1970s and then again after 1979, relatively well-defined rules governed the social organization of energy modelling and forecasting. The rules specified who was responsible for energy policy-making, who was to order and coordinate the production of prognoses, who was to build models and produce prognoses, and how such prognoses were to be linked to policy objectives and formulations. Until 1978 the Ministry of Industry had the formal responsibility — with the Norwegian Watercourse and Electricity Board (NVE) having practical responsibility — for energy policy-making and the production of official energy consumption forecasts in Norway.

Until the oil crisis of 1973, a subdivision within NVE (the Norwegian Watercourse and Electricity Board) controlled the making of prognoses. These 'definitions of reality' served to reinforce NVE's powerful administrative and economic position in Norwegian energy policy-making and planning (see Chapter 13).

Following the 1973–74 crisis, there emerged energy problems and issues which NVE could not deal with. Because NVE's prognoses missed actual developments very substantially, it became vulnerable to challenge. New critical actors, associated with the environmental movement, along with scientific entrepreneurs entered the scene. As a consequence of the failure of NVE's prognoses, a number of research institutes started to develop alternative models to that of NVE. This was partly on the initiative of several leading economists, partly on that of the Ministry of Environment.

The development went as follows: Economists (as opposed to the engineers at NVE) in the Ministry of Finance who had responsibility for macro-economic planning in Norway wanted to increase the ministry's control over the government budgetary process. To do this, they needed to reduce their dependence on the authority and power of NVE. At the same time, the Ministry of Environment which represented interests fundamentally opposed to those of NVE — environmentalist rather than growth-oriented — also wanted to take control over prognosis-production away from NVE.

A period of 'model competition' followed. However, it should be stressed that NVE was the only institution which had a fully operative energy model, of course a very important technology in the 1970s. Therefore, it was able to maintain its authority and substantial power in policy-making until 1978/79. Ultimately, a new model — and institution for modelling — triumphed, and monopoly was re-established in Norwegian energy forecasting.

The new model, called EMOD, became operative in 1978/79. It was a version of MODIS, the world-renowned input/output model used in macro-economic planning in Norway (the model had been developed by the first winner (shared) of the Nobel prize in economics along with other leading Norwegian economists). MODIS had been adapted to represent and analyse energy demand and the impact of price and other macro-economic factors on demand. The new model was developed in the Central Bureau of Statistics, by the Ministry of Environment, along with the Ministry of Oil and Energy and the Ministry of Finance. The common perspective integrating these ministries emphasized economic allocation of resources. The economics profession (as opposed to NVE engineers) played a central role in the modelling process itself. With an operative model of their own, these ministries were able to outmanoeuvre NVE. In 1978 the responsibility for the production of official energy forecasts was transferred to the newly established Ministry of Oil and Energy. This reorganization along with the successful operation of the EMOD model assured a major shift in authority and power relationships relating to energy forecasting. NVE became a peripheral actor in the system (as did a number of research institutes which had been active in the mid-1970s during the period of 'model-competition').

In the following section we shall examine modelling and forecasting in Norway from an historical and social organizational perspective.

The politics of model selection and development
Energy forecasts in Norway up to the end of the 1960s were undertaken in an organizational milieu with a strong technical orientation. The Ministry of Industry was politically responsible, but the forecasts were developed, as pointed out earlier, by a division within NVE. The forecasts were based on information obtained from local electricity companies, boards coordinating electricity and local electricity consultants. Assumptions about economic growth were provided by the Ministry of Finance. The organizational structure of Norwegian forecasting during this period is presented in Figure 15.1.

The NVE forecasts used relatively simple model rules, befitting the engineers who were reponsible for forecasting. They involved simple trend extrapolations.[117] NVE collected and aggregated county-level forecasts independently determined by the regional electricity-supply organizations. Moreover, the generation and flow of data were under the exclusive control of actors within the electricity-supply system. Their interests in and evaluation of the energy demand situation completely dominated the forecasting process. The initial changes in this setup came already in 1969 with the Ministry of Finance's formulation of the 1970–1973 Longterm Programme and later planning documents. Here a more detailed division of economic sectors was included in the models and the energy-use in each sector was forecasted on the basis of the economic growth expected in that sector.

Knowledge of the total production and the relation between production and energy-use in each sector allowed a forecast of its energy consumption. Specific factors relating to energy-consumption in each sector were also included. The electricity

FIGURE 15.1a
The institutional structure behind early energy forecasts in the 1960s

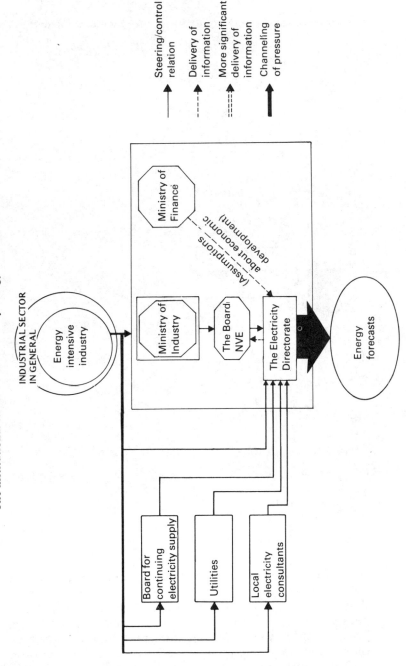

FIGURE 15.1b
The institutional structure behind forecasts for the Energy Report in 1970

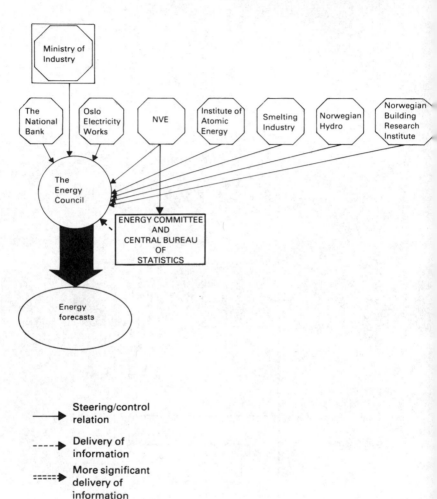

Steering/control
relation

Delivery of
information

More significant
delivery of
information

consumption in each sector was also specified. This was estimated
on the basis of the division of the total energy consumption between
different energy-carriers. This was the first time that the relation
between energy consumption and economic development was
brought explicitly into the forecasting process. Energy prices — and
their impact on consumption — were not yet included, however.

One of the consequences of this development was that NVE and

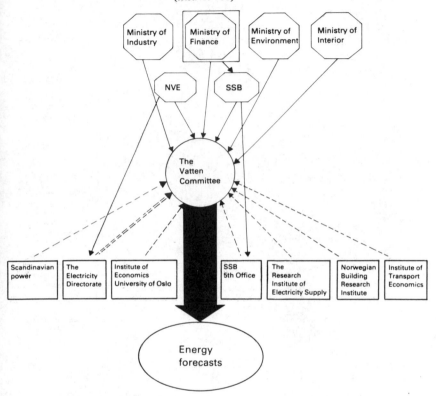

FIGURE 15.1c
The institutional structure behind the forecasts of the Vatten Committee
(mid-1970s)

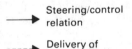

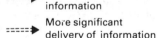

SSB = Central Bureau of Statistics

→ Steering/control
relation

----► Delivery of
information

=====► More significant
delivery of information

the energy-supply organizations lost their monopoly over information in energy-forecasting. The new techniques presupposed data on economic development within different sectors and thus established the basis for a link between the electricity forecasts and general macro-economic planning in Norway. This link did not become an institutional reality until the oil-crisis in 1973/1974, when NVE together with the Central Bureau of Statistics (SSB) initiated the

FIGURE 15.1d
The institutional structure behind forecasts for the 1980 Energy Report

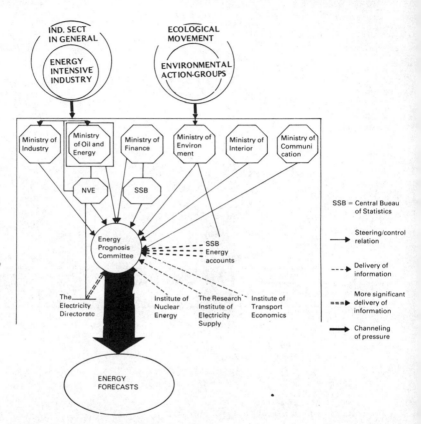

development of so-called 'after-models' to the macro-economic models used by the Ministry of Finance. These models make use of energy-consumption coefficients for each sector for which energy forecasts were generated. This allowed the estimation of energy consumption once the gross production of the sector was known, hence the term 'after-models'.

The coefficients for energy use already illustrate the grey zone between science and politics. The size of the coefficients depends to a large extent on the rules determining the time-period used for estimation. This provides opportunities to influence the forecasts by selecting an estimation-period which gives desirable forecasts.

The forecasting method used with the 'after-models' did not differ basically from that used for the preceding model generation under NVE's control. The principal difference was that the number of explicitly defined sectors was increased and the sector definitions closely matched those used in the government macro-economic planning models. The energy models thus came to depend directly on data generated by these models under the control of the Central Bureau of Statistics (SSB) and the Ministry of Finance. (The increased dependence of energy modelling on macro-economic models did not change with the multiplication of energy models which took place in the mid-1970s. All the energy models except one were closely linked to existing economic models. This dependence provided the backdrop for the high degree of integration of energy and economic modelling in the late 1970s.)

There were other changes in the energy forecasting system. In connection with the Energy Report of 1970 (St. meld. nr. 97, 1969–70), an Energy Council was established by the Ministry of Industry to supervise the forecasting activity. The Council initiated investigations and also developed new models in cooperation with the Central Bureau of Statistics. As pointed out above, energy forecasts were now linked more closely to the government's economic models. The new organizational arrangement is represented in Figure 15.1.

The re-organization involved no more than simply adding a new council and a research group (at SSB) to the setup with key established actors in the forecasting system, NVE, and the Ministry of Industry. Also, the Energy Council had a solid representation of industrial interests, particularly energy-intensive industries (alloy and light metal producers as well as the major fertilizer producer — at that time, Norway's largest company Norsk-Hydro), with strong links to hydro-power construction and a commitment to economic growth. The influence of this interest group was mirrored, for example, in the estimation of future energy use for the energy-intensive sector. The industry's own wishes, based on heavily subsidized tariffs, were included in the forecasting models without modification.

Thus, even though new econometric techniques had been introduced, and new pricing principles such as setting the price of electricity at long-term marginal cost were discussed, the eventual forecasts did not deviate substantially from those made by NVE. It should be pointed out that the emerging environmental movement (see Chapter 13) had not as yet shown an interest in forecasting. This was to change, ultimately, with radical consequences for the Norwegian energy forecasting system.

The establishment of a new energy committee, 'The Vatten Committee', in the mid-1970s marked a break with earlier regimes. Organizational structure and formal mandate as well as forecasting results pointed this up. The task of the committee was to discuss *energy saving measures* and to examine the impact of such measures on energy consumption as represented in electricity forecasts. The committee was appointed by the Ministry of Finance. Besides NVE and the Ministry, the Ministries of Environment, Local Government and Labour, and the Central Bureau of Statistics were represented. As Figure 15.1 indicates, the Vatten Committee made use of a number of modelling institutions for its forecasts. Indeed, its work initiated a social learning process which developed energy knowledge and competence in energy-modelling in several of these institutions. The 1973/74 oil crisis and the subsequent energy debate had a direct impact on forecasting assumptions and the resulting forecasts. The committee arrived at forecasts that showed considerably lower electricity consumption than anticipated according to NVE forecasts (see Figure 15.2).

The tendencies toward more conservative energy prognoses, manifested in the organization and work of the Vatten Committee, continued in the formation of the 'Energy Prognosis Committee'. This was created in connection with the Parliamentary Energy Report (1980), but was to become a permanent organ. The inclusion of the new Ministry of Oil and Energy and the Ministry of Transport complicated the picture somewhat. However, the core development in connection with the work of this committee was the achievement of an operative energy model, the EMOD-model based in large part on the Norwegian macro-economic input/output model. The EMOD-model was developed by the new Resource Accounting Group of the Central Bureau of Statistics, with the backing of the Ministries of Environment and Finance.[118]

The group was physically and organizationally located in the centre of the general economic planning and forecasting system. It was therefore much better connected to major institutional powers than any of its competitors, including the NVE model.

Control over forecasting had by now shifted in large part, although not entirely, from NVE to the Resource Accounting Group. The model-building teams of EMOD and NVE's 'after-models' were the only research teams directly represented on the committee. These groups were also indirectly represented through the Central Bureau of Statistics, the Ministry of Oil and Energy. The choice of the two modelling teams was part of a political compromise where representation on the committee and centrality in the institutional structure were more important than technical issues or scientific competence.[119]

The committee chose in the end to use the EMOD model for all except the service sectors where the NVE 'after models' were preferred. It had to make a number of other controversial decisions concerning, for instance, the choice of exogenous variables and their values, provided by the modelling teams. Some of the variable values were simply handed down from ministries. This was the case for assumptions about future oil prices (provided by the Oil and Energy Department) and those concerning exchange rate and international trade developments (provided by the Ministry of Finance). One of the most strategic decisions concerned the choice of energy demand elasticities with respect to energy prices. Given the enormous instability of the data it was empirically very difficult to estimate these coefficients. (Recall the price developments of the 1970s. Using pre-1970 data did not help solve the problem, since it was unlikely that elasticities for a period with relatively stable and much lower energy prices were valid for the 1980s.) In the context of such high uncertainty, normative and ad hoc assumptions played a substantial role in the assumptions and analyses of the committee (the work of other economists suggested elasticities substantially different from that ultimately assumed by the committee (-0.2) and one leading economist argued openly that they had been set too low).

Given the composition of the committee, its dominant interests, and the assumptions that went into the forecasting models, it is not surprising that the forecasts of electricity consumption were considerably lower than those of NVE (see Figure 15.2).

The shift of control over forecasting from the hydro-power sector with NVE in a dominant position to an institutional network with the Central Bureau of Statistics in a leading position was closely associated with the introduction of economic concepts and techniques of modelling.[120]

At the same time, the environmental and budgetary authorities shared common interests in supporting this development since both wished to gain greater control over hydro-power planning and investment policy, respectively. The Ministry of Finance — with its overall responsibility for economic policy and planning for the public sector — wanted to increase control over the economy in general and over coordination of long-term policy-making and planning in different sectors, including energy. They sought to do this by imposing more systematic and economic criteria on investments and resource use generally. The Ministry's limited capabilities prior to the full operation of EMOD were indicated by controversies around electricity forecasts in Autumn, 1978. New forecasts, based on assumptions about declining economic growth, were made in NVE but were kept secret during political discussions and decisions in Parliament dealing with controversial hydro-power projects. Even

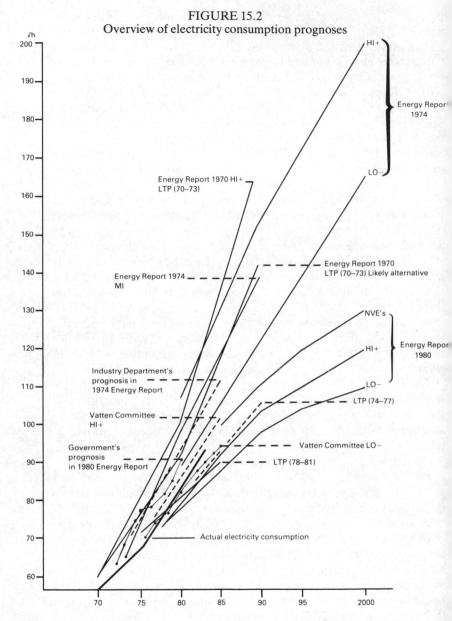

FIGURE 15.2
Overview of electricity consumption prognoses

KEY:

LTP = Long-term programme of the government   MI = Middle alternative
LO− × Lowest alternative   TWH = Terawatt hours = 10⁹ Kilowatt hours
HI+ = Highest alternative   SSB = Central Bueau of Statistics

the Ministry of Finance failed to gain access to these forecasts and, finally, had to prepare their own, using the new EMOD model.

The interest of the Ministry of Environment in the development of a new energy forecasting paradigm should be apparent from the discussion and analyses of Chapter 13. One of its goals – pushed by its constituencies — was to reduce energy consumption and, thereby, the rate of hydro-power development. The alliance with the Ministry of Finance not only gave it much greater weight in inter-governmental politics vis a vis the Ministry of Industry (and NVE) but enabled it to advance arguments based on economic concepts and principles rather than having to rely mainly on ecological ones. Under the Norwegian conditions of heavily subsidized electricity rates, the application of rigorous economic criteria would lead, it was reasoned, to reduced expansion of hydro-power. In the eyes of the environmental movement, the Ministry did not go far enough in establishing an energy policy based solely or largely on ecological grounds.

The normative choices and political judgements which influenced the development of energy models in Norway did not simply affect relations in the technical community (communities). They concerned matters of utmost economic and political importance to Norway. The choice of model was closely connected with the selection of modelling groups, their particular professional perspectives, and differing interests in hydro-power construction. At the same time, since models are based on different assumptions about reality, for instance physical and economic features, they also imply different policies and measures. Pricing is a typical measure suggested by an economic model, while changes in the regulations for house construction and production processes are more natural political tools if one derives policy measures on the basis of a physical model.

The impact on energy demand forecasts of political, organizational and professional developments described above is striking. As Figure 15.2 indicates, the Vatten Committee's forecasts in 1975 differed substantially from earlier forecasts. The Committee's high forecast is approximately half way between earlier forecasts and those made subsequently by the Energy Prognosis Committee (Baumgartner and Midttun, 1986). The forecasts published by the latter committee for the Parliamentary energy report follow more or less the path outlined by the Vatten Committee. However, they set the break point in the energy demand growth rate as late as 1990. The forecasts made by NVE included in the same report are also lower than its earlier forecasts, but higher than the Committee's high and low curves. Moreover, NVE envisioned an acceleration in the growth of energy demand after 1995, in contrast to all other forecasts made by the Committee.

Economic and political changes in Norway, parallelling those in many other industrialized countries during the 1970s, explain the downward revision in energy demand forecasts (see Baumgartner and Midttun, 1986). Economic growth assumptions were continually lowered as time went on and slow economic growth persisted. The energy-price impacts of the oil crisis set in question the future of Norwegian energy-intensive industries. These industries remained internationally competitive because they had access to heavily subsidized electricity. But these (hidden) subsidies were increasingly criticized as the 1970s progressed. Ultimately, a decision was made to set a maximum quota of cheap electricity which could be used by the energy-intensive industries. This would obviously limit future demand from the industry. The general commitment of the government to make energy conservation an important policy goal had an impact on energy forecasts, particularly in the charged political and professional context which we have described. Politically, the decisive factor in generating lower energy-demand forecasts was the emergence of an ecological movement which managed to introduce into the public debate an alternative model of societal development, entailing economic growth rates lower than those in the past. The socio-cultural values underlying this movement were institutionally anchored within the government in the Ministry of Environment (established in 1972). This change in administrative structure both reflected and accelerated the ongoing shift in political priorities in Norway. Power was redistributed among administrative bodies as well as within political parties. At times, these changes led to open political confrontation between environmentalists and the 'industrial complex', supported by various ministries and professions. The attempts to reduce energy-demand forecasts gave rise to some of these conflicts as well as resulting from the overall struggle.

Modes of organizing modern oracles and the politics of modelling
Our theoretical perspective indicates three types of factors which should be investigated in studies of expert/policy-maker interactions:

(1) institutional regimes and socio-political processes which are decisive in the selection of modellers, modelling milieus, and ultimately the techniques which these utilize.

(2) the modelling principles and techniques; data bases and norms and procedures which prominent groups of modellers and modelling institutes make use of in building and developing models.[121]

(3) the prognosis model(s) consisting of a system of rules organizing/selecting input data, determining limits of variable values and parameter values, processing input data and generating prognoses as outcomes, which to varying degrees and in varying ways feed into policy processes.

Our studies of energy forecasting suggest: (1) the activities of modelling and policy-making may be linked institutionally in several different ways, and (2) the dynamics and development of these linkages may vary considerably.

The socio-political and institutional context plays a decisive role in the selection of the modellers and (directly or indirectly) the model-building techniques. The rules of consensus-building and political acceptance may also influence the forecasting process. At the same time, the modelling forecasts contribute to varying degrees to support the dominant definitions of social/physical reality and, thus, the interests and power of powerful groups in the larger institutional framework, including the professional groups involved in modelling.

In the Norwegian and Dutch case studies we found specific, established relationships between policy-makers and one or more modelling groups. Relatively well-defined transactions took place between modellers and policy-makers, with particular forms of discourse and negotiation. Even here the relationships may vary substantially, depending on the relative authority and power of the modelling community (communities). In addition, the linkages may be very intimate and involuted or entail relatively weak couplings. For instance, those between modellers and policy-makers were intimate in Norway and Holland, whereas they were relatively weak in Britain (Baumgartner and Midttun, 1986). The 'autonomy' of modellers in Britain both reflected and reinforced the strength of scientific norms and practices and, at the same time, their distance from the policy process. In Norway, in spite of intimate interconnections, scientific norms could be sustained to some extent by virtue of the very considerable authority of the Norwegian econometric modellers and their model, which ultimately became the basis of the energy forecasting model.

In preparing and formulating energy policy in Norway, policy-makers interacted intimately with modelling technicians. These groups of actors were governed by two different social rule systems — or action logics (Karpik, 1982; Wittrock, 1986). In particular, criteria of evidence, argument, and the legitimacy of decision-making differed in these systems. Incompatibilities and dilemmas were dealt with, in part, through the application of meta-rules and through socio-political negotiations.

Drawing on our earlier analyses of stable institutional forms, we can distinguish three institutionalized modes of organizing the transactions or mediating processes between modelling groups and policy-makers in our case studies (see Figure 15.3). The mode of exclusive administrative control (as exemplified in Norwegian energy modelling at NVE) has parallels in the German case, discussed briefly below. However, the Norwegian and German politics of modelling were entirely different. In Norway, the challenge to exclusive administrative control of energy forecasting came from *within* the government and entailed *inter-agency politics*, eventually with the triumph of the agency with established (econometric) modelling competence. In Germany, there emerged an *outside challenge* to administrative control of forecasting. A brief examination of the German case can shed further light on the mode of organizing and the dynamics of modelling/policy-making relationships.[122]

Energy forecasts in Germany were carried out largely by economic institutions at universities under the supervision of the Federal government. The forecasts were closely connected with the energy programmes of the government (especially nuclear programmes). They entailed mere trend extrapolation and served as a basis for legitimizing energy policy. This was the only legitimate energy forecasting. The government apparatus successfully excluded other perspectives and maintained its integrity during the 1970s and early 1980s (the period when the restructuring described for Holland and Norway was going on).

Nevertheless, an arena emerged *outside the government* in the German Parliament[123] in the form of the *Enquete-Kommission* (1979–1980, under the Chairmanship of the Social Democrat Reinhard Ueberhorst). This development was a direct response to the anti-nuclear movement and the increasing politicization of energy policy in Germany. Alternative perspectives were included in the Commission's membership and deliberations, a political acknowledgement of the anti-nuclear movement as well as the more encompassing social movement of 'The Greens'. Note that, in contrast to Holland, the opposition was *not* brought into government consultative bodies. On the other hand, they became in Germany part of the overall political process, possibly with longer term and more radical impacts.

The parliamentary arena did not directly affect the government organization of forecasting and policy. However, it did shape public discussion. It also appears to have contributed to the implicit understanding today in German politics that energy forecasts cannot be used as a legitimizing basis for energy policy. Counter-forecasting,

FIGURE 15.3
Transaction modes between technical/applied science
groups and policy-making/administrative agents

ORGANIZING MODES;

KNOWLEDGE ⟩ ─ ─ ─ ─ ─ ─ ⟨ MEDIATING FORMS ⟩ ─ ─ ─ ─ ⟨ GOVERNMENT
PRODUCING   POLICY-MAKING
GROUPS OR   (I) market (England)   ACTORS AND
NETWORKS   AGENCIES

                       (II) networks and
                             inter-organizational
                             ties (Holland,
                             Norway)

                       (III) exclusive
                             administration
                             (Norway,
                             Germany)

based on other than official sources, has become a resource in the political arena.

Our case studies suggest substantially different patterns of conflict, conflict resolution, and political development.

There are three general ways in which model development may come about, depending on socio-political processes and the institutional set-up, which our case studies also illustrate:

(1) Models may develop incrementally under the control of a single actor. New descriptive and interpretative rules are added gradually to the existing descriptive rule system. In some instances, a partial restructuring of the descriptive rules may be carried out. In Norway the NVE model during the early period and the EMOD model today illustrate this process.

(2) Models may develop through successive replacement where, for instance, a new modelling technique or a new actor with a new model replaces the one previously controlling the technology. This occurs through socio-political and/or professional shifts. In the cases of Norway and Germany, forceful counter-movements and institutional actors emerged which supported new types of models, tech-

TABLE 15.2

Patterns of modelling development

England: Market organization of forecasting

Marketplace pluralism: ————————→	Marketplace pluralism
competing institutes accepting contract research or with network ties to socio-political groups	
(relatively high variance among models in methods assumptions, and forecasts)	(high variance)

Holland: Network/inter-organizational negotiation

Political/organizational —→	Cooptation and ————→	Convergence
pluralism	consensus-building	
(high variance)		(low variance)

Norway: Inter-organizational politics

Model and administrative—→	Competition and political—→	New monopoly (with
monopoly	struggle within inter-organizational networks	different location, methodology, and profession)
(low variance)	(high variance)	(low variance)

Germany: Political counterposition

Government ————————→	Formation of a political —→	Countervailing forecasting
administrative selection and control	arena outside government	capabilities in political system; official forecasts no longer able to legitimize policy; they ceased to be made
(low variance)		(high variance)

---

niques and interests. This led eventually to a transformation of the energy modelling arena and, in the case of Norway, to major revisions of official energy prognoses.

(3) A situation of competing models may emerge, where the models are based on somewhat different assumptions (possibly even methodological principles) and offer different policy options and future scenarios. Such developments occurred in Norway during the middle phase and could also be observed in Britain, Holland at a very early stage, and West Germany today.

The various patterns of modelling development in our studies are summarized in Table 15.2 (Germany is included so as to extend our comparative perspective).

Political and professional games around model-building and model-use in policy research and policy processes typically remain hidden from the public (Germany may possibly have become an exception in this respect). Technical language, mathematical formulations, and statistical judgements form an almost impenetrable shell of technical or scientific objectivity, which also masks the presence of political biases and judgements. Public critics find it difficult to make an issue of or to politicize 'modelling', 'forecasting', and research. These questions are further examined in the following chapter.

16
Science and practical action: Studies in competing logics

Tom R. Burns and Reinier de Man

Introduction: Competing logics

Max Weber (1919) argued that values, for instance political values, should be kept separate from scientific activity. However, in instances where scientists interact with practitioners and policy-makers, the boundary between scientific research and practical action is difficult to define precisely and to maintain. This is particularly the case with applied and policy research, which is the focus of this chapter. These encounters may give rise to a great deal of ambiguity and conflict.

We have seen in the preceding chapter ways in which the discipline of modelling has been subjected to political and ideological influences, subverting some of the technical and scientific norms of model-building.[124]

This chapter continues our exploration of the interplay between two or more social rule systems, or *logics of action* in concrete organizational or inter-organizational settings.[125] Here we are interested in the case where one social action logic or family of logics, that of science, encounters that of practical or political action. In some cases only one system or set of coherent systems applies, what Wittrock (1986) refers to as unitary logic settings (see related discussion, Chapter 11, pp. 213ff. For instance, political rules of the game prevail, possibly for legal or normative reasons. Or the rules of science prevail because the decision-setting clearly entails highly technical and scientific considerations which legislation or policy-making is simply intended to back up.

Many applied and policy research settings are characterized by *multiple, diverse logics* (Wittrock, 1986). Other things being equal, participants experience such situations as ambiguous, confusing, and conflict generating, unless, that is, they develop shared meta-rules indicating which logic is to prevail or they formulate a new synthetic logic, thus transforming the situation into one of unitary action logic.

In applied and policy research, where scientists interact with practitioners, the motives and actions of the researcher are subject to non-scientific norms and influence, in part because he or she is dependent on, and therefore open to the influence of, other types of actors in the various phases of research activity. A researcher may even be tempted to actively engage himself or herself in the political game of trying to persuade, influence, or countervail other actors. In sum, researchers in applied science settings are faced with multiple reference groups: the research community, including institutions of higher education and research; the groups of practitioners or policy-makers (often there are several groups or agents, some having incompatible conceptions of and demands on applied researchers).

Some of the dilemmas and problems of applied research are pointed out in a recent investigation of 'treatment research', that is research on treatment programmes, such as physical and mental therapy. The author, Stina Johansson (1985), found that the scientific norms and methodological demands of a scientific community often clash with treatment norms prevailing in the settings where treatment programmes are carried out. As a result, the norms of science are vulnerable and may even be undermined in settings where research interacts with treatment.

One of Johansson's studies entailed an investigation of a research project evaluating an experimental psychiatric programme at a county hospital in the town of Luleå, in northern Sweden. The practitioners used psychodynamic theory in their therapeutic work. The researchers, on the other hand, utilized a framework based on class analysis and 'materialistic psychology'. During the course of the research, confrontations occurred between the two professions. In the planning phase, they struggled for influence over the orientation and norms of research. The researchers managed to establish their autonomy from the practitioners, the latter disengaging themselves from the research activities. This led ultimately to ethical problems in the relationships of the practitioners to their patients, upon whom the research impinged.

During the research phase itself, different ethical systems could be observed to be in conflict: the procedures and methods of the researchers threatened the professional duty of the practitioners to care for, and to assure the integrity of, patients. At the end of the project, a power struggle re-emerged around the question of how to use the results.

Johansson also examined a number of dissertations in the area of treatment research at the faculties of medicine and social sciences in Swedish universities. In several cases the researchers chose to assume much greater responsibility and authority than the norm of independent research would indicate. Unreported alliances formed.

Many researchers worked professionally at the same place where they carried out their investigations. Indeed, such association between researchers and practitioners was often essential for achieving acceptance on the part of other practitioners and patients. In some cases the researchers behaved more like instructors or teachers than independent investigators. In those cases where researchers were detached, Johansson reports the occurrence of disturbances in therapeutic processes.

Table 16.1, comparing the norms of research with the operative norms in treatment research and therapeutic communities, summarizes Johansson's major results. Treatment research has an intermediate position between scientific investigation and therapeutic practice. Many important decisions concerning treatment research are made in the arena where research interests, professional interests, and political forces meet and at times come into conflict. Such decisions concern, among other things, the definition of a competent agent, definitions of suitable research problems, and determination of when, where, and how research shall be carried out. In the case of treatment research, Johansson found that publishing rules and the control of research quality were under the influence of agents outside the research community.

The differences in the regimes of pure scientific research and treatment research reflect, of course, the fact that treatment research, besides any ambition it has to develop knowledge for itself, is supposed to aim at finding more effective and humanitarian treatment methods. These practical considerations, particularly when research is carried out in concrete treatment settings, serve to influence the ways in which data is collected, handled, and published.

Table 16.1 points up that, while researchers and professional therapists may share a general frame of 'scientific rationality', they operate with different social paradigms specifying the purposes of their activities and operating methods. Moreover, they have different definitions of the 'objects of study' as well as contrasting procedures for dealing with 'these objects'.

Even more disparate are the social paradigms governing, for instance, scientists, on the one hand, and politicians or practical policy-makers, on the other. Clark and Majone (1984:7–8) suggest that, in general, professions or groups in different roles use diverse criteria to evaluate scientific activity and this explains in part some of the misunderstandings and conflicts which arise when, for instance, applied science meets politics:.

An academic statistician, a company expert and a Congressional staffer

TABLE 16.1

Comparison of social rule systems of science, treatment research, and treatment professions

	Modal norms of science research	Operative norms of treatment research	Operative norms of professional therapy
Who defines competent agent?	The research community and its educational and research institutions. Formal and informal certification	The research community in negotiation with different interest groups	Professional association, networks, and schools. Formal and informal certification
Who defines research problems?	The researcher in critical interaction with research community	The researcher in strategic negotiation with sector interests, administrators, and professional groups, including research community	The therapist and professional networks
What value placed on adherence to research procedures and norms	Methodological and theoretical aspects of research problems of primary importance	Practical relevance, of major importance	Treatment process and objectives as well as professional development of primary importance. Adherence to research, research procedures and norms secondary
How: rules for collecting and using data	Rules of good scientific procedure. Data ultimately owned by members of the research community. In principle, unrestricted search for truth	Uneasy combination of research logic and professional ethics Professional/client confidentiality; data may not be used for investigations other than the defined project	Laws and ethical principles designed to protect the integrity of the patient with respect to the collection and use of relevant data. Choice of methods and procedures accordingly

Table 16.1 (*continued*)

	Modal norms of science research	Operative norms of treatment research	Operative norms of professional therapy
When should research activities take place?	Whenever research results optimized. In principle, any time	Ambiguous and decided in negotiations between interest groups, administrators, and professional groups	Research should not take place when it disturbs either treatment processes or patients or threatens patient integrity or professional/client confidentiality
Where (what treatment settings)?	Wherever research results optimized. In principle, any place or setting	Ambiguous and decided in negotiations, as above	Research should not be conducted in 'sacred' or highly sensitive settings
Rules for publishing results	Publish each and every verified result. (Also, rules for giving credit for prior research and against plagiarism)	Obligation to be careful with descriptions and quotations from patient data and treatment processes	Determined by norms of professional/client confidentiality and patient integrity, often backed by legislation
Who controls the quality of research results?	The research community as ultimate judge	Ambiguous with multiple judges: interest groups, administrators mass media, and research community	The therapist, and possibly professional networks, and the patient or patient's family

will use different criteria to evaluate a study on the coincidence of cancer deaths and particular occupations. Their conflicting judgements of the study will not be resolved by reference to less uncertain or more clearly presented data. *Required instead is a mutual comprehension of the different critical perspectives being employed.*

That different critical appraisals are arrived at by people in different roles is not a bad thing as such. It may simply reflect different needs and concerns of different segments of society, or different degrees of freedom in making certain key methodological choices. So long as the judgements leveled from the perspective of one particular role are not presented or misinterpreted as judgements relevant to or speaking for all possible roles, we have a healthy state of pluralistic criticism. Difficulties begin to arise when this neat partitioning of roles and the criticism voiced from them begins to break down. Unfortunately, such breakdowns seem more the rule than the exception in actual practice.

Rule system theory focuses attention on the particular modes of organizing transactions between applied scientists and those in non-scientific roles in policy settings, the dilemmas, confusion, and conflicts arising in these transactions. In the following section we discuss briefly general notions of rationality and legitimacy as suggested by social rule system theory, focusing on certain relevant features of applied science and policy-making. We go on to discuss some of the implications of our analysis for policy and applied research.

Science and politics

The close coupling of much scientific activity to politics has become typical of the modern world, the outcome of sustained efforts to harness science to national political interests — interests not limited simply to military considerations. Wittrock in a recent book points out the importance of this development and some of the dilemmas and tensions this has engendered (1984:8):

> During the 20th century and particularly after the Second World War, governments have increasingly tried to link up science to national aims and public policies as well as to tap it as a source of economic growth. The role of applied science as a commodity and tool has brought the scholarly world infinitely greater resources in the period after the Second World War than ever before in its history. But it has also tended to undermine its identity and its guiding norms. The translation of science into power, policy and wealth can more adequately be described in terms of processes of bargains than of threats. But the bargains have involved a Faustian element. They have not only provided sufficient leverage to permit large-scale research projects. The entrepreneurs and 'condottiere' which epitomize these undertakings do not conform to the noble norms of an international scientific aristocracy, and the cherished value of openness has been intimately linked to the existence of such an aristocracy. Instead, competition between short-lived project groups is conducive to disruptions in the free flow of information and to efforts to exclude others from it. ...
> Sheldon Rothblatt observes that 'the marketability of science' and 'the desire of powerful industrial states to employ science in the service of national aims ...may virtually be accepted as constants, and scientists have always been in two minds about it'. However, in the last two decades efforts have been intensified all over the Western world to use research as a limitless factor of production to promote growth and to pull economies out of slump and stagnation, as a cure-all guide to policies for social betterment and welfare, and as a rational basis for policies to trim bureaucracy and increase efficiency. Not only may these efforts have highlighted an inherent tension in an established pattern of accommodating universalistic norms and particularistic commitments in modern universities and research institutions. These efforts have also revealed tensions and inconsistencies in many of the fundamental conceptions underlying science policies of recent years.

In modern society, public decisions are made according to one or more legitimation criteria, including that of scientific validity. These consist of rules and principles for assessing the rationality of a decision. Referring to the 'Will of God' or to 'destiny' is illegitimate in modern, Western societies. A decision can only be justified in terms of its contribution to legitimate objectives, its knowledge base and likely effectiveness, and its compatibility with law or administrative procedure.

Two general types of principles for assessing the legitimacy of social decision-making have been distinguished by Simon (1977)(also, see Kickert, 1979). The first type refers to the *content of the decision* ('substantive rationality'). Such legitimation principles are based on technical sciences, economics, and other branches of systematic knowledge. The principles define if a decision is consistent with, for instance, economic or technical knowledge. The second type refers to the decision-making procedure ('procedural rationality'). The organizing principle of parliamentary decision-making, for example, defines what decisions are legitimate in terms of the *procedure that is followed,* irrespective of the rationality of the outcome. A parliamentary majority decision for building nuclear plants or hydro-power facilities may be *politically and legally rational at the same time that it may conflict with other rationality principles.* For instance, the decision is judged to be economically, security-wise, or environmentally unsound.

The various rule systems applied to the social process of organizing and legitimizing public decisions are neither fully consistent nor complete. They leave play for negotiation and political games among those involved in the transactions, particularly in cases where different legitimation bases are activated. Economic reasoning may lead to the conclusion that, for example, investment in alternative energy sources or in conservation provides for greater returns than continuation of nuclear investment programmes. On the other hand, the decision to continue with the nuclear programmes may be entirely consistent with procedural rules for decision-making and planning in parliamentary democracy: parliament and the political leadership have expressed their will in a formal decision, namely legislation. Yet another principle for legitimizing the decision might be based on the degree of general public acceptance: thus, while a decision may be formally legitimate according to the institutionalized rules of parliamentary democracy, resistance to the decision from citizen groups and local communities may be so high that the decision cannot be effectively implemented. In such a case general acceptance, although formally not a valid legitimation base in a parliamentary democracy, may become another criterion for choosing or justifying decisions (see: Offe, 1983).

In sum, public policy-making and planning typically entail the activation *of multiple legitimation bases,* which are coupled to different institutional segments of society and professional groups (see Chapters 12 and 13). These bases have different rationalities, consisting of systems of rules for evaluating decisions, before, during and after decision-making and implementation. They do not, however, present unambiguous and clear-cut recipes for making or justifying decisions. The contradictions between different rationalities and the ambiguity of rationality rules open the way for conflict, various types of negotiation, and political games. Such games may lead to the activiation or formulation of 'meta-rules' for handling competing rule systems, a notion which shall be discussed later in this chapter (see also Chapters 12 and 17). Clark and Majone (1984:33) observe:

> Two overriding questions asked regarding policymaking in open societies are its efficacy in solving practical problems and its responsiveness to popular control. As C.E. Lindblom remarks, however, these questions lead to 'a deep conflict [that] runs through common attitudes to policymaking. On the one hand, people want policy to be informed and well analysed. On the other hand, they want policymaking to be democratic... In slightly different words, on the one hand they want policymaking to be more scientific; on the other, they want it to remain in the world of politics'.
>
> The results of scientific inquiry performed in policy contexts is a potential source of political power. The question therefore arises, as it does regarding any source of power, of what constitutes its legitimate use. In appraising efforts to provide usable knowledge through scientific inquiry we must therefore finally consider criteria of legitimacy.

'Scientific' analyses and results are often used in modern society as a basis on which to justify or legitimize public decisions, a pattern that many studies of the relationship between policy-oriented research and public policy-making point up. Clark and Majone (1984:35) stress this function, pointing out:

> The social uses of science have always had something in common with the social uses of religion. And in the two decades following the Second World War, modern science took on a most religious-looking numinous legitimacy as an unquestioned source of authority on all manner of policy problems.

Science can be conceived as a social rule system (including methodological rules and procedures) for defining the rationality of a proposition, conclusion or decision. The rule frame is maintained and developed by 'scientific communities'.[127] Different scientific paradigms (and the institutions in which they are embodied) imply different rule systems. Scientific knowledge may be an important factor in some public decision processes, whereas it fails to have any substantial impact in others. In part, scientific paradigms have to compete with other rationality bases and with each other. On the one hand, substantive scientific rationality may compete or clash with legal and normal forms of rationality, as in political or legal settings where 'unscientific' concepts of 'evidence', 'truth', 'analysis', and 'logical argument' are also valid. On the other hand, two or more scientific paradigms may compete with one another in areas related to policy-making, such as monetarism and Keynesianism.

The influence possibilities — and in general the role of science in policy-making — tend to vary according to the policy problem and properties of the policy process.[128] In relatively simple and orderly decision-making processes with clear goals and well-defined participants, one may readily apply clear-cut, established rules — although these need not necessarily be scientifically based — in making decisions and in justifying the decisions made. In complicated decision processes, where goals are ambiguous and where there are a large number of participants with substantially different institutional affiliations and legitimation bases, scientific rationality would have to compete with other legitimation bases. In such a situation, some or all of the interests may try to mobilize scientific analyses and conclusions, to support their positions. In some instances, science becomes a common factor, a universal basis of legitimacy. It serves, then, as a context-independent means for 'determining truth'. (Whether or not this is justified in all instances, it nevertheless has a concrete effect on consensus-building and policy-making). Between the case where scientific clashes with political authority and the case where all participants in the decision setting accept the authority of expertise as a basis on which to define and assess policy options, there are varying combinations and grades.

Clark and Majone (1984), drawing on Wildavsky and Tannenbaum (1981), provide an illustration of the complex interplay between researchers and politicians — and also some of the ways in which biases may enter into scientific judgements. The case concerned scientific advice on the question 'What is the size of America's remaining oil and gas reserves?' (1984:9–11,18):

> The NRC (National Research Council) showed that serious scientific studies of the question had produced estimates spanning an order of magnitude, and that government (U.S. Geological Survey) estimates tended to be two to three times the size of industry estimates. The NRC itself concluded that the most reasonable estimate was less than half the

most recent USGS figure, and only slightly larger than those proposed by industry experts.

In the course of a Congressional inquiry, one NRC committee member admitted 'Estimates of future supplies of oil and gas are so dependent upon unknown scientific factors and unknown environmental and political factors as to be almost unknowable.' Clark and Majone (1984:10–11,18) observe:

These 'almost unknowable' estimates were nonetheless published to three significant figures by the NRC with no uncertainty ranges. How were the particular NRC values arrived at? According to another NRC committee member, 'from our point of view, we thought it advisable ...to accept more conservative estimates, thinking that most of the Geological Survey estimates are relatively high, and most of the oil company estimates relatively conservative.' As Wildavsky and Tannenbaum ask in their review of the case, 'This is science?'.

Congress wanted 'a number,' and the National Research Council therefore gave them 'a number,' even though committee members acknowledged in their testimony that it was little more than guesswork — i.e. nothing like the consensually certified knowledge that its trappings and origins implied. Similar examples, of which perhaps the most notorious would involve the willingness of scientists to deliver cost-benefit assessments of long-term and large-scale environmental changes, could easily be cited.

Clark and Majone quote an NRC committee member, 'We thought it advisable ...to accept more conservative estimates...' They go on to conclude (1984:18):

It is clear that there existed virtually no overlap in the critical criteria underlying the three different evaluations of the oil and gas studies. Whatever more fundamental disagreements may have existed regarding the worth of the studies, most of the conflict in the hearing room can be traced to the different critical standards being employed by different critics.

In general, as Clark and Majone stress (1984:3–4):

Study after study gleefully demonstrates that scientific inquiry in policy contexts is shot through with 'fatal' methodological flaws, 'hidden' biases, erroneous data, or trivial intent. To cite only some of the most readily accessible examples, works by Ida Hoos, D.B. Lee, and Gary Brewer delivered the flow critical to early social system studies; Quade and Cline to military analysis; Ackerman and Fiering to water resource management; Hutchinson, Loasby and Henry for economic forecasting; and Arthur and Sanderson for systems studies of Third World development. The publication of Donella Meadow's *Groping in the Dark* has left the global modeling community in such scholarly rout that only the military seems willing to fund it. Most recently, *Policy Sciences* has entertained its readers with an 'exposé' of the shortcomings of IIASA's analyses of energy policy.

They add, however (1984:4), 'Missing is any indication that good scientific inquiry in policy contexts might have more appropriate objectives than trying to emulate either pure science or pure democracy.' In practice (Clark and Majone, 1984:1)

> Scientific inquiry cannot discover most things policy makers would like to know. Much of what it does discover remains uncertain or incomplete. How, then, is would-be-scientific knowledge any more reliable a guide to policy than other forms of knowledge, prejudice, or propaganda? Moreover, in practice experts often disagree on what science knows and on what the knowledge means for policy. But if the knowledge produced by science is not consensual, what special claim for hearing has it in a world of multiple opinions and biases?

Clearly, the misapplication or abuse of science in policy processes puts up for stakes the future legitimacy of scientific knowledge as a policy input (and even science as a major social institution).

Scientific and political logics
Below we schematically present and compare the social rule systems of science and politics, as bases for the structuration and legitimation of human activities dealing with information, evaluation, and decision-making. We also discuss meta-rules for handling inconsistencies between scientific and political rule systems, and important interaction patterns between scientists and policy-makers.

I. Scientific rule system[129]
Science, as Merton (1976:32–3) has pointed out, appears as one of the great social institutions, coordinated with the other major institutions of society: the economy, education and religion, the family and polity. Like other institutions, science has its normative subculture: a body of shared and transmitted norms, values and principles designed to govern the behaviour of those involved in the institution. The norms and standards define the technically and morally allowable patterns of behaviour, indicating what is prescribed, preferred, permitted, or proscribed.

Merton stressed that a scientific community does not have a single, perfectly consistent set of norms.[130]   Since our aim here is to consider inter-institutional inconsistencies and conflicts between different professional groups, we shall largely ignore contradictions and conflicts within scientific communities. That is, we intentionally stress the 'unitary logic of science', recognizing that the institution of science does not constitute a fully consistent social rule system.

One of the most important aspects of scientific activity concerns the validity of arguments. The rules for such validation are contained in methodology and scientific paradigms. A proposition or argument is considered valid ('true') if it is made in accordance with such rules.[131]

In general, scientific statements are to be formulated, and validated according either to procedures of logical argument and/or to support of empirical data (where empirical evidence should be obtained, organized and presented according to established methods and procedures in the discipline). The core rules and procedures of a scientific discipline, including those of an informal nature learned through practical research experience, give identity to the scientific enterprise.

Certain rules, which are quite common in everyday social life, are excluded: for instance, there is no voting on arguments because the majority may well be wrong, neither is there negotiation over arguments. The truth cannot be negotiated as a compromise between two opinions. In the actual practice of science, such negotiation and compromising goes on, as seen in polemics, coalition-formation and politics within scientific communities (an indication of the important distinction between 'theoretical ideal' and 'practice'. However, negotiated settlements and compromises *relating to the 'content of science' cannot be professionally or publicly legitimized, even if such behaviour does go on).*

Scientific knowledge and analyses may serve as inputs into policy and planning processes. As inputs, they contribute to collective processes of defining and organizing 'images of reality' and programmes of action. In such ways, they influence problem definitions, solutions proposed, and the perceived legitimacy of proposals and policies.

II. Public acceptance rule system

The public acceptance rule system has in many ways a logic or rationality contrary to the scientific rule system. It largely serves two purposes: to make decisions politically acceptable and to reduce conflict between different parties in the decision process. 'Scientific truth' is not the central issue in defining and constructing social reality in everyday political or social life. *The acceptability of a certain reality to the different parties with their particular interests is of much greater importance.*

The great differences in the logics of action based on rule systems I and II are pointed up in the use of language and forms of communication. In system I, ideally one uses explicit language in terms of well-defined concepts, clear methods and unambiguous results. As a reflection of the level of uncertainty about their validity or reliability, one qualifies statements or makes probabilistic statements. On the other hand, rule system II often entails the strategic use of vague or equivocating statements as well as contradictory formulations in order to *actually maintain or increase ambiguity.* The ambiguity is required to avoid conflicts and to maintain a basis for acceptance or negotiation between the different parties. At the same time, politicians or practitioners often want from scientists clear, unequivocating statements in order to support their arguments or proposals. However, scientific requisites are usually not readily consistent with such political requirements.

'Reality and truth' are in system II *negotiable in a certain sense,* where the negotiation aims at group or public acceptance and conflict resolution. At the same time, policy-makers often know that a current false statement about social phenomena, at least by scientific standards, may become true by pronouncing it true (Merton, 1957; Henschel, 1978; among others):

Statement *P* ⇒   Authoritative ⇒   Influence ⇒   Statement *P*
is false   (e.g. scientific)   on social   is true
                   pronouncements   action

As a result of such strategic opportunities, scientific and, in general, technical 'truths' and arguments become political resources that can be and are used in gaining acceptance for a policy or programme and 'making a difference in the world'. But the logic of 'making truth' differs from the logic of 'discovering truth'.

Another field of differing behaviour concerns the publication of data. Rule system I presupposes great openness, whereas rule system II usually implies highly selective barriers for information transfer. Open exchange of information could easily result in conflicts or blocked positions that are difficult to handle. Often policy-makers want to have full access to certain scientific knowledge, as a strategic resource in their games and actions, but oppose its publication in the belief that their competitors or opponents would gain accordingly. Thus, withholding or releasing information becomes a strategy in its own right, legitimating and de-legitimating policies and public decisions.

The social rule systems of science and politics entail two distinct action logics and rationality types. They seldom occur in pure form. They should be seen as *sociological ideal-types.*

Conflicts between them in the realm of policy research and policy-making tend to be handled by meta-rules. The latter reconcile incompatible or contradictory rules, by, for instance, ignoring or changing rules (see also Chapter 12). This is indicated in Figure 16.1.

III. Meta-rules for handling I and II
Scientific validity and social or political acceptance may well be consistent. When both rule systems are activated at the same time, which is not unusual in the case of many policy processes, *institutionalized strategies may be available to handle problems of potential inconsistency.* Solutions are worked out through various sociopolitical games based on a set (usually incomplete) of *informal rules for unifying, negotiating and modifying the original rules from I and II* (de Man, 1986). The rules for scientific research are partly compromised (such as freedom of information) and partly applied only formally and symbolically, *whereas informal rules serve the actual and hidden purposes of the research and conclusions.* (Pseudo-scientific arguments are used sometimes for purposes of achieving political acceptance and the legitimation of particular policies and decisions.)

Or, the scientific rules are formally activated and applied for purposes of policy exclusion/selection and producing/maintaining a certain definition of reality. For example, in a certain policy context, a well-tested and respectable econometric model is proposed as a basis for policy analysis. The proposal and supporting arguments take the form of scientific statements. However, the underlying purpose of the argument is to prevent problem definitions and solutions — other than those which can be handled by the model — from entering the political arena (Baumgartner and Midttun, 1986).

Rule systems I and II *both contain rules for information selection and organization.* Scientific theories and methods (I) are selective in that they consider or deal only with relatively well-defined aspects and parts of 'reality'. On the other hand, processes oriented to the political acceptance of decisions imply information selection and organization according to the particular rules of political expediency and compromise. Controversial or conflicting information is often avoided in the pursuit of consensus, for example, concerning problem definitions and formulations of strategy space. Thus, the rule systems of science and of politics both exclude and select, *but they do so on different grounds and in different ways.* (Even scientific paradigms differ from each other in this respect.) Nevertheless, points of convergence may occur, providing policy-makers with an opportunity to exploit *scientific exclusion and selection rules for their own political or government purposes.* Scientists are not disinclined to try to use such points of convergence for their own professional (and personal) interests. In particular, support of a scientific group or community is exchanged for public funds with which research institutes and schools of thought are established and developed.

The meta-rule(s) reconciling the apparently conflicting rule systems (I and II) rest on a more general principle: In many policy research settings, scientific selection rules are appealed to and formally applied, whereas the *dominant or prevailing informal rule(s) belong to system II.*[132]

In any case, when policy-makers and scientists meet, they negotiate — or have previously negotiated with each other — about compatible working rules. (Such negotiations take place after or in conjunction with policy-makers selecting scientists or research groups with whom they feel comfortable on the basis of either their professional styles and/or ideology.) Obviously, such information and negotiation games are asymmetrical in terms of the actors' knowledge, modes of outcome analysis, and strategy.

FIGURE 16.1
Rule system inconsistency and meta-rules

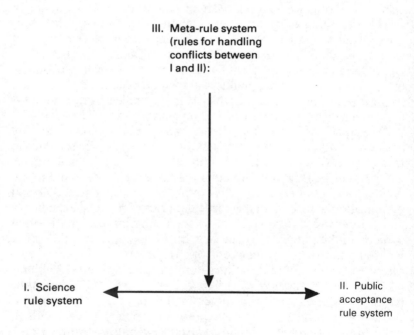

III. Meta-rule system
(rules for handling
conflicts between
I and II):

I. Science
rule system

II. Public
acceptance
rule system

Dilemmas of policy and applied research
The interplay between scientific and political rule systems is usually apparent in the case of most interactive or participatory policy

research, consultancy, and applied social science in general. Such research embraces both rule systems possibly along with meta-rules for combining them.

Analytically, one may distinguish several types of relationships between scientific communities and policy-makers (see Baumgartner and Midttun, 1986). In an extreme case the community has no dealings or communication with policy-makers or other actors influencing policy processes. In some cases the relationship may be a diffuse one, where, for instance, one or more research groups make predictions or forecasts which they report through publications and mass media presentations. To the extent that actors important to the policy process receive this information and act on it, the predictions would be of political importance — they would make a difference. More intimate and established forms of exchange and coordination between experts and policy-makers have been examined in this and the preceding chapter, in some instances pointing up ways in which 'expert knowledge', including scientific knowledge, may be compromised.

Policy research governed largely by scientific rules would be most likely in instances where: (1) science has a well-established legitimation basis in society, the relevant scientific community is strongly cohesive and committed to the integrity of scientific rules, and (2) either the research community is largely segregated or buffered from policy-makers, their games and exercise of power or the policy process itself entails relatively unambiguous problems with minimum controversy (non-partisan). Under such conditions, the modal products of research would be methodologically governed and knowledge-based statements or analyses relevant to policy related phenomena, possibly with an indication of feasible policy alternatives for achieving given goals.

In the case of 'policy research' dominated by 'the logic of political acceptance', the aim is more one of reaching consensus among the decision-makers involved concerning the definition of the situation and appropriate strategies or courses of action to deal with it. The validity criterion is that of political acceptance, not that of 'scientific truth'. Different validation procedures are possible: in a democracy, majority rule applies in one case, while in another unanimous decision-making applies along with various systems for negotiation between majorities and minorities. *Consensus decision-making, negotiated outcomes or majority vote do not imply scientific validity.* Such procedures give rise to 'politically defined realities' which serve a useful public function but do not necessarily stand up to the methods and standards of modern science. Of course, the authority of science may contribute to defining social reality and determining certain modes and results of analysis. *And these in turn can lead to policies and actions that make a difference in the 'real world', for better or for worse.*

In general, policy research faces a number of pitfalls:

● Much academic policy research, carried out in spendid isolation according to conventional scientific rules and procedures, is not accessible or acceptable to policy-makers. This may be the typical case. On the other hand,

● When policy research is primarily designed to contribute to consensus formation, the research may largely serve to legitimize policies, not to elucidate substantive issues.

● The stress on consensus formation may put in jeopardy scientific norms and quality. In the extreme case, the research simply contributes to the formation of 'myths of policy science'.

Political acceptance is, of course, a legitimate goal of policy research in democratic societies. A variety of research methods have been developed for the purpose of increasing the likelihood of consensus formation. For example, interactive (or participatory) policy research methods deliberately include both scientific and acceptance rule systems in the research design.

Forms of interactive research are, among others, Delphi-methods for consensus formation among experts, different types of reference-group policy research, and scenario-analysis conducted in public discussion. Other innovative institutional forms should be explored with the involvement of policy researchers and their research institutes as well as policy-makers engaged in policy processes (Clark and Majone, 1984:39).

The contradictions and dilemmas inherent in engaged policy research can and should be made more explicit. The autonomy — and integrity of scientific norms — are essential, if such research is not to simply legitimize official policies. In the absence of adequate scientific discipline and rationality, scientists engaged in public policy research may serve, even unwittingly, to provide unsound policies with the 'halo' of science. At the same time, they contribute over the long run to undermining their own legitimacy (as a number have certainly done in the making of energy policy (Baumgartner and Midttun, 1986)).[133]

One would hope that the sociology of science, and in particular of policy research, will contribute to making more transparent the power of scientific elites in modern society and to increasing the level of self-knowledge and self-discipline within scientific communities.   The role of applied science in policy-making and public debate should be more precisely delimited, thus reducing the abuse of scientific authority in political life and assuring the continued legitimacy and support of science, including the social sciences, in modern society.

17

Conclusion: Principles of social organization and the structuration of modern, Western societies

Tom R. Burns and Helena Flam

Basic principles of modern culture
In this book we have examined the structure and dynamics of a few major types of social organization in modern society:

- markets
- formal organizations including government
- wage negotiation systems
- socio-technical and expert systems
- planning and policy-making systems

Although the studies reported here have been fragmentary and selective, they provided opportunities to elaborate several of the key concepts and principles of social rule system theory and to indicate the scope of the theory:

- social actors, groups, organizations and movements are bearers as well as makers and reformers of rule systems
- social agents cooperate, conflict, and struggle with one another in forming, reforming and implementing rule systems
- the restructuring or transformation of social rule systems results from power shifts, major changes in ideology and values, and sustained performance failures in strategic areas of social life. Such restructuring is observable in changing patterns of social action and interaction, and, indeed marks transitions between regime periods or phases
- the rule regimes corresponding to major types of economic and political institutions: (a) consist of certain classes of rules which make up a structure (that is, rules do not simply have arbitrary relations to one another) and (b) organize and regulate social interactions in the social settings to which the regimes apply (however, they do not determine behaviour, since human action is situationally conditioned by physical, biological and ecological factors as well)

And perhaps most importantly, social rule system theory identifies

366

two fundamental social processes for systematic investigation and analysis:

(1) *the formation and reformation of social rule regimes,* entailing the social processes of formulating, excluding, selecting and ordering rules in relation to one another.

(2) *the implementation of social rules.* Implementation processes entail rule interpretation, situational analysis, the use of tools and resources, practical behavioural skills and in many instances, the mobilization of power and authority to enforce social rules.

In this concluding chapter, we attempt to place these fundamental rule processes in their proper context — to suggest their characteristic forms in modern Western civilization.

In previous chapters, we have examined several characteristic mechanisms for legitimate social rule formation and re-formation in Western societies. Not surprisingly, some of these mechanisms had already been given a theoretical cast by Weber: expert, rational–legal and democratic rank among them.

In Weber's view, the two interrelated components of modern rationality, 'expert rationality' and 'rational–legal organization', would surely and systematically crowd out traditional, spontaneous (and charismatic), and other modes of rule formation not governed by the 'double star' of rationality.[134] Zetterberg (1983:2–3): drawing upon Weber, writes:

> Rationality organizes the multiplicity of human thoughts into systems. Rationality also organizes the vast repertoire of human behaviour into unified institutions.
>
> Rationality will not become mankind's destiny without opposition. Weber believed it would be no more beloved than 'an iron cage in life's enchanted garden.' When the philosophies, plans, and utopias that imbue our lives with meaning fail to explain injustice, need, loneliness, suffering, death, we are drawn to charismatic ideologies and leaders, ideas and personalities whom we think have the ability and the calling to provide us with solutions. But charisma occasions only temporary interruptions in rationality's triumphant march forward.
>
> With the passage of time, charismatic prophets are succeeded by popes, and revolutionaries become administration. In other words, the process of rationalization also absorbs charisma, by turning it into routine. In the long run, charismatic doctrines are not effective roadblocks against rationality.
>
> The development of rationality in its twin configurations — the systematization of ideas and bureaucratization of activity — leads to a 'victory for reason', which in our culture means the victory of technocracy. Weber was not elated by the prospect. He predicted that development would move toward petrification, 'an icy cold polar night.' As early as the first decade of the 1900s, in his study of the Protestant ethic and capitalist spirit, he characterized the typical individual of the twentieth century: 'a heartless expert, a spineless pleasure seeker.'

Although Weber viewed the future of 'life's enchanted garden' with pessimism, he nevertheless saw democracy as a modern expression of charisma. In his framework, democracy was singled out as the only institution capable, in principle, of slowing down the triumphant march of rationality and, in particular, of its organizational embodiment, bureaucracy.

As we shall argue at greater length below, the interplay between these modes of legitimate social organization has led to the emergence of new, modified rationalities, incorporating selected elements of the old ones. Furthermore, we suggest — the leading theme in our conclusion — that the 'iron cage' of modern rationality has so many compartments and Houdini passages that, in fact, some freedom is still left to move within and beyond the boundaries which it imposes.

Somewhat in contrast to Weber's fears, then, we argue that even in highly regulated, 'neo-corporatist societies' — where his pessimism would appear to be most warranted — democracy, activated and mobilized by peripheral communities and social movements, is still alive. Democracy has not succumbed yet to the dulling forces of rationality and bureaucratization. It continues to serve — albeit in new forms and arenas — as a basis for an ongoing struggle with political domination, Moreover, the structural incoherence in Western societies is sufficiently high to leave a considerable freedom of choice among various rule regimes, including the most modern forms — rational–legal organization and technical expertise.

Our cautious optimism, however, is time-and-space limited. Unqualified optimism would appear naive or foolish, indeed, in a world dominated largely by 'elitist–liberal' and dictatorial systems with powerful technical, military and industrial interests, and only influenced sporadically by peripheral groups, or regional and social movements with alternative visions of social organization.

Modern rule formation
Social rule formation as a fundamental human activity involves *power and knowledge:* (i) the activation or mobilization of power to formulate or reformulate social rules and (ii) the application of knowledge in rule formation and interpretation processes. The first concerns the social agent or agents who have the power or authority to establish social rules structuring an area of human activity, and the second concerns the knowledge or expertise applied in the course of formulating, reformulating, and selecting rules. In the modern world, these activities are typically organized rationally,

according to formalized or rational–legal principles and the systematic application of expert knowledge. Let us briefly discuss these characteristic features.

Mobilization of power and authority in modern rule formation. The activation or mobilization of power or authority to formulate and establish social rules is found in all social groups, organizations, and societies. However, the institutional forms or culturally specific strategies for organizing these processes vary across cultures and over time. In modern, Western societies, there are three institutionalized modes or strategies for organizing rule formation: *rational–legal , democratic, and negotiative–contractual.* These culturally specific forms enjoy wide legitimacy and play a *predominant role in official or public rule formation and reformation in modern society.* This is not to say that other modes play no role. As we have argued in Chapters 11, 12 and 13, various types of 'informal' social organization, activated and maintained by peer and other group processes, are also an important feature of modern society.

(1) *Hierarchical, rational–legal organizations,* such as judicial systems and administrative bodies, constitute one type of institutionalized frame for authorizing and legitimizing rule formation. Authority and power to form, interpret and reform rules are vested in positions in a hierarchy, occupied by persons with requisite expertise and/or having at their disposal staffs of experts. In general, modern organizations are characterized by both the employment of experts and consultation of outside expertise , which are regularly exploited in the process of rule formation.

(2) *Democratic forms,* including election procedures, constitute another institutionalized mode for activating and legitimizing power and authority in rule formation and reformation. Democratic procedures of rule formation are widespread and are particularly closely associated with the public sphere, especially the election of political leaders. However, the application of the organizing principles of democracy is not limited to the public sphere, since many private organizations, firms, associations, and clubs are governed — or claim to be governed — by such principles.

Representatives of organizations, associations, parties, or communities gain approval and legitimation of rule formation and reformation through the mobilization and counting of votes, a quantitative indication of support. Mobilization itself, generally speaking, is not peculiar to our times. It is found in all social groups, organizations, and communities in cases where rule formation is a more or less public or visible process and the support of key actors or groups is considered essential to insuring the success of rule formation and, ultimately, implementation.

However, systems for vote calculation and the organization of mass democratic mobilization, as instruments of collective decision-making, are particularly characteristic of modern, Western societies. In many instances, simply following these procedures assures legitimacy. Thus, although electoral participation in many nation–states is notoriously low, encompassing between 30 and 60 percent of all voters, the electoral process itself, if it is carried out in accordance with the procedural rules, seems to suffice for legitimizing the election of leaders and their decisions about new rules and rule systems.

(3) *Negotiative–contractual forms* constitute a third mode of organizing social rule formation. They involve *social forums and networks*, including inter-organizational and inter-corporate networks, where social agents negotiate and exchange. Such negotiations may result in more or less binding agreements or contracts, specifying the rules which are to govern an area of activity, common undertaking, or interaction among the parties to the agreement. The processes of rule formation in such networks are often governed by well-defined procedures, which in some instances are essential, if not sufficient, to the legitimacy of contract outcomes themselves.

Technocracy in modern rule formation. Social rule formation in the modern world is characterized by the systematic application of knowledge. In more traditional societies, 'wisemen', 'elders', 'those who know', etc. were the sources of this knowledge. Weber understood 'traditional authority' in such terms.

In the modern world, the formation of rules for social action typically entails the mobilization and application of *'expert'* knowledge. We have come to understand 'expert' as someone who possesses *systematic, specialized, and certified knowledge* of, for instance, law, engineering, management, marketing, medicine, and so forth. But this modern-centricity should not blind us to the high level of expertise which elders and wisemen possess in traditional, but even in modern, societies and which is mobilized and used in interpreting old rules and formulating new ones. Their expertise is based on accumulated (unwritten) knowledge of group or community rule systems.

Institutions and the general public in modern societies usually find such forms of expertise archaic and 'inadequate' for their times and problems, precisely in that they are not sufficiently imbued with technical and scientific knowledge. For this reason also, even religions tend to give way to the march of science and technocracy, precisely in those areas where systematic, rational knowledge is available and defined as relevant.

The mobilization and application of impersonal, professional 'expert knowledge' constitutes the prevailing logic of rule formation in Western civilization and is especially important to the modern state, capitalist enterprises, but even voluntary associations. In a certain sense, the principle belongs to the unwritten constitution of modern Western societies, playing a central role in organizing social life. It is a cultural template and a basic strategy for social organizing and public social action (see Swidler (1986) concerning the notion of strategies for organizing social action).

Enforcement and implementation
The major institutional form for organizing and enforcing social rules is through formal organization. Such organization is limited in scope, excludes non-relevant systems from the sphere of action, and follows certain rational–legal principles and procedures in implementing and/or enforcing rules. (See Chapters 11 and 13.)

Generally speaking, rules formed on the basis of administrative authority, a negotiated contract between legitimate agents, or electoral backing, enjoy widespread legitimacy in modern society. Legitimacy is reinforced whenever the rules are believed to incorporate expert knowledge. Legitimacy substantially reduces 'enforcement costs' (North, 1981; Burns et al., 1985). However, several important qualifications are called for, pertaining to the conditions under which rules are modified, opposed, or rejected.

Complexity and contradiction in modern culture
The three prevailing modes of rule formation in modern society — rational–legal, democratic, and negotiative–contractual — are not necessarily compatible. In many instances, *they lead to contradictory specifications of acceptable rules and organizing principles.* Thus, the rules formulated by an organizational authority, possibly on the advice of technical expertise, may contradict the rules advocated by leaders who are supported through democratic mobilization. Or the rules agreed on in a contract, such as labour contracts, which have negative consequences either for the parties involved or for third parties, may result in a social movement which, through democratic mobilization of support, countermands rules agreed in the contract, or even restructures the contractual relationship itself (as has occurred historically in the case of certain types of labour contracts).

One typical 'contradiction' is that between democratic, administrative, and contractual types of rule formation, on the one hand, and the principle of technocracy on the other, for instance:

(i) expert proposals are countered by the claims or demands of those enjoying democratic support

(ii) the proposals of professional experts contradict proposals of those having administrative authority or power to actually decide on the formulation, interpretation, and implementation of rules

(iii) experts stand opposed to the parties to a contract, who wish to form and interpret in their own terms the rules to which they agree

In addition to tensions and conflicts of the sort indicated above, the incoherence among expertise systems, and also within such systems, contributes to producing a much less 'rationalistic', well-ordered society than Weber anticipated.

(1) Expert culture is not a single coherent culture. There are multiple types and forms of systematic knowledge and expertise in the modern world. Although cooperation among different types of experts and the integration of knowledge essential to complex undertakings is commonplace, they also compete with one another — and are used selectively and strategically by major agents — in the processes of rule formation and reformation. In general, different types of expertise contend with one another both about substantive issues and about suitable or correct organizing principles and rules relating to the application of knowledge in social action.

Even within a single discipline, there are often contending schools and groups, which make for a much less monolithic and domineering expert group than Weber appears to have envisioned.

(2) Indeed, with the intensification of professional/expert education, corporate group formation, and professionalization, the modern world is faced with multiple and often competing perspectives: for instance, the legal, the economic, and the environmental, among others.[135] Social differentiation is anchored in distinct normative and epistemic bases and diverse action logics. From this perspective, the problem of the fragmentation of modern society appears much deeper and more involuted than that simply identified with the obvious division of labour. A great number and variety of limited purpose organizations and institutions make and implement rules, and participate in other rule-making settings, where they represent their own particular interests and make use of relevant, but very narrow expertise. For better or for worse, a high level of coherence and integration of social life is unlikely, or at least would entail very high costs.

(3) Political struggle and movement — and charisma in the sense of possessing authority to question established systems and to pro-

pose new systems or radical transformation of the old — have not disappeared, as Weber seemed to fear. Their scale and intensity, particularly as countervailing forces to modern rationality, seem however, to vary considerably over time.

(i) Regional, ethnic and peripheral communities oppose, effectively resist, and upset the rationalization process. Even a well-established administrative system, which for years effectively dominates its environment, may suddenly find itself challenged by new actors and coalitions of previously dominated groups (as examined in Chapter 13). Furthermore, while class struggle has been highly institutionalized and regulated in all democratic, Western countries, such regulative orders are rarely problem-free and still experience serious crises (a major theme in Chapter 10).

(ii) Many important processes of knowledge formation and power mobilization take place outside the established, institutionalized arrangements where 'modern rationality prevails'. Not only do irregular, non-standardized and ad hoc areas of social action — particularly in informal networks and communities — continue to operate and develop, but new arenas and unconventional groups emerge. 'Charisma', as Zetterberg suggests (1983), is not only attributed to individual leaders, but also to entire groups and movements (such as the 'Greens' in West Germany; see below) which advance new visions and organizing principles for the social order.

(iii) 'Value rationality' continues to inspire social action and to play a role in rule formation and reformation, in part because modern rationality fails to adequately explain or address suffering, death, tragedy, and injustice, not to speak of the threat of nuclear catastrophe. Moreover, the 'principles and core rules' of society are not limited simply to the formal, rational ones, but also encompass core rules of an informal, diffuse character, that are maintained, reproduced, and developed in communities and networks of human agents. Here we have in mind 'moral' or 'common sense' concepts and principles of property, authority, duty, justice, love and solidarity. These may be reflected to a greater or lesser extent in the formal, legal and administrative structures of a modern society, but may also contradict them in many important respects. Such contradiction makes for tensions and struggles between the proponents and opponents of particular forms of rational–legal, democratic, and negotiative–contractual rule regimes, for example between those advocating 'highly regulated markets' and those struggling for 'market freedom', or more 'natural' concepts of justice and equality as opposed to legal or administratively operating concepts of justice and equality.

Rule system formation in the modern world

The problem of rule proliferation in modern societies
A modern society is structured and regulated by a vast number and variety of social rule systems and rule system complexes. Many of these in the twentieth-century nation–state are of a legal and administrative character. Albrow (1971:353) observes:.

> The facts of an immensely increased amount of legislation, the dominating role the official plays in the framing of this legislation, the extent to which it has been found necessary to allow wide areas of discretion to officials in implementing legislation, to permit the drawing up of rules which shall have the force of statute, and the increasing degree to which this legislation penetrates the fabric of social life, are facts common to industrialized societies. The official, through his experience of this complexity and through his training, must take an increasingly prominent position. The public, in either humble or influential positions, or through organizations and interest groups, increasingly makes contact with administration and attempts to bring influence to bear directly upon officials and not through the mediation of the elected representatives.

In general, most members and groups command only a limited knowledge of, and have very little engagement in, rule formation and rule enforcement in major spheres such as the economic and the governmental in modern society. Their most active participation, if any, occurs in areas in which they are employed or practically involved (work life, community affairs, specific political issues or campaigns). Otherwise they are typically ignorant of major parts of most of the macro rule systems of modern society: family law, inheritance law, corporate law, employment and tax laws, environmental and resource management laws and regulations, pension rule systems, etc. Of course, most are probably familiar with a few general principles and/or a few practical rules sufficient for their own immediate purposes and dealings with some of these institutions. At the same time, common citizens and groups, in contrast to elite actors, lack the resources to obtain substantial, systematic knowledge about major rule system complexes in modern society and their far-reaching consequences. Even elite actors find it difficult to gain an overview or to substantially alter old rule systems or to establish entirely new ones.

Even in small countries such as Norway or Sweden, thousands of laws have been passed since 1945, with each law often containing many rules and regulations.[136] In addition to legislation, there are the manifold regulations which typically build on a legislative act or rules contained in such an act. Some of these are very narrow in focus, dealing, for example in the case of Norway, with the North

Sea petroleum sector, hydro-power construction, or energy matters generally. Others relate to taxation, family and work life with more or less direct impacts on most citizens and their welfare.[137] Significantly, specialization in rule formation and implementation is both a general, institutionalized strategy to master (or cope with) rule system developments in modern society and a structural factor contributing to the further elaboration and cumulative formation of rule system and system complexes. This is a major cause of the fragmentation of modern life. Various specialists concentrate on the rules, regulations and regimes relevant to their segment, or sub-sub-segment. Even in small countries, there are thousands of specialized public councils, committees and boards and multi-level governments. Interest organizations of various types lobby and, in some instances, participate in these institutions, some of which may be semi-official, in order to protect or advance their interests in the rule-making and rule-implementation processes in sectors relevant to them. These organizations themselves narrowly specialize and concern themselves as much with rules of procedure as with substance, ignoring vast areas of modern social activity which are of little or no apparent relevance to their interests.

The problem of structural incoherence in modern societies
The prodigious differentiation of modern society enables, on the one hand, the systematic development of particular rule systems, including their 'rational' elaboration. On the other hand, it hinders or, possibly, makes unfeasible any comprehensive or holistic overview. Paradoxically, society becomes 'more and more regulated' and apparently rational — in the sense of mobilizing expertise and applying systematic knowledge to specific rule-making and rule-interpretation processes — at the same time that many of its citizens and leaders lack a sense of an overarching social order and rationality in the whole.

A modern society is made up of highly differentiated spheres and segments, each with a characteristic set of social organizations, agents, and types of social activity. Examples are the political and economic spheres as well as particular segments within each of these spheres, for instance within the economic sphere the car, steel and computer industries or segments linking up spheres, such as the hydro-power segment in Norway.

The various actors involved in societal subsystems have quite diverse mandates and functions: business leaders or public administrators and their organizations, relevant labour unions, legislative bodies, courts, political leaders and political groups, other interest organizations, mass media, etc. Contradictory knowledge bases, methodologies, definitions of the situation, and modes of organization characterize the particular sub-system where relevant policies are formed and social action organized. Each sphere or segment is governed by laws, policies, and administrative procedures, and other types of formal and informal rule systems.

Spheres and segments typically combine different organizing principles. For instance, the sphere of democratic government consists of hierarchical organizing principles (state bureaucracies, leadership structures within parties and parliamentary bodies) combined with non-hierarchical ones (democratic procedures and elections, inter-party negotiations, cabinet negotiations). Thus, one can distinguish bureaucratic appointment systems from democratic or egalitarian procedures (e.g. the selection of political leaders by voting). Also, while politicians along with peak organizations or major investors are largely preoccupied with policy-making, and follow certain consultative and democratic procedures in making decisions, policy-implementation is often organized bureaucratically.

Similarly, the economic sphere consists of markets, enterprises, industrial and commercial unions, along with networks of various types. Even a business enterprise is not simply organized on the basis of property rights and the power and authority which such rights enable, but entails administrative principles, accounting procedures, socio-technical systems, and much more (Burns et al., 1986).

In general, a major sphere or segment of activity in society is made up of a *set of inter-linked institutionalized social relationships* (along with non-institutionalized and ad hoc social arrangements). The overall social organization combines both hierarchical and non-hierarchical, personal and impersonal, each structuring and regulating social transactions in the sphere.

Quite clearly, such 'complexes' making up a major sphere or sub-system of society need be neither systematic nor consistent. The degree of coherence (or incompatibility) is an empirical variable. Also, institutionalized complexes may be relatively 'tightly organized' or characterized more by 'loose couplings'.

Social actors and movements are actively engaged in trying to deal with concrete, everyday problems of fragmentation and incoherence, arising from the involuted differentiation of modern society and the frequent encounters between contradictory logics of social organization which tend to generate ambiguity, social uncertainty, and conflict. In these efforts, actors often make use of meta-organizing principles and meta-rules. In some cases they institutionalize new, higher-order or meta-systems in order to cope with contradictions and to integrate societal sub-systems. (One such system is discussed below.) Modern society has no single designer nor an overall, coherent design. There are multiple sources of organizing principles, rules and policies, many of which compete with and contradict one another. The pressures for change are many and varied. Diverse rule-making groups and institutions pursue their own particular interests, visions, and modes of knowledge development. Coordination and integration among different rule-making processes, and the agents involved, tends to be weak. We refer to this condition as *structural incoherence*. Of course, the degree of effective integration and coordination varies from country to country and sphere to sphere (see later discussion).

Our main proposition is that multiple rule-makers (and rule-interpreters and -implementers) are located in different parts of societal structure, in different class positions, in different institutionalized segments, with different roles, resources at their disposal, and interests. They cooperate (forming temporary alliances or more permanent networks or organizations), but they also struggle with one another to maintain, adapt, or reform major rule systems. *These processes result in patterns and cycles of structural incoherence. Incoherence is partly regulated through established modes of conflict resolution and social integration established in any given modern society.*

Patterns of structural incoherence and integration

Utilizing the concepts of structural incoherence and modes of organizing social integration, we suggest a few theses on modern society.

Thesis I. Structural incoherence is more characteristic of peripheral spheres of society than core spheres. Considerable structural incoherence arises when multiple rule-makers (and interpreters) produce diverse rules or rule systems within a given sphere without coordination or organized integration. This is typical of many peripheral spheres of modern society, involving or dealing with resource weak groups: those in marginal occupations and professions, the elderly, the destitute, unorganized workers, criminals, etc. Rule inconsistency and contradictions prevail in the administrative and legal spheres where these groups constitute the 'clientele', except in cases where *a powerful group or profession within or outside the sphere manages to shape a coherent rule system complex governing the sphere.*

On the other hand, core spheres such as corporate ownership/ production/banking/economic policy are, in general, not allowed by dominant economic interests to undergo substantial incoherent structuration in Western nation–states. Such a development would result in economic failure or collapse and/or substantial losses for those with vested interests in a particular type of integrated capitalist system.[138] Indeed, the economic system is continually monitored, investigated, and analysed in order to ascertain ways in which performance can be improved through rule changes or innovations (including 'deregulation'), and to identify sources of declining performance (e.g., declining investments, declining productivity, etc.). Laws are changed (e.g. tax laws), policies are introduced or shifted, and new programmes are established to assure more effective economic functioning.

This is not to imply that law-making, policy-formulation, and administration do not interfere with economic function and, in some instances, cause performance decline. But, in contrast to peripheral spheres, such developments in core spheres typically become matters for systematic investigations, debate and policy reassessment. Corrective measures are tried. Laws or policies, for instance environmental laws, are toned down or are not enforced; corporate taxes are reduced or other favourable changes are introduced in economic policy.

The point is that the core spheres of the capitalist economy — ownership/production/banking/economic policy — are not allowed to develop a high degree of structural incoherence and low performance capability comparable to the conditions obtaining for peripheral systems as, for example, criminal justice (Burns and Tropea, 1985). [139]

This tendency characterizes modern Western capitalism not only because business interests are powerful and have many different channels through which they influence legislative and administrative processes of rule-formation and rule-implementation. Other powerful groups — politicians, policy-makers, administrators, labour leaders — also have a stake in ensuring that capitalist institutions are maintained and function more or less effectively. This convergence of interests makes for constantly renewed efforts to ensure institutional coherence and functional effectiveness. The core sphere features the ideology, the structure of economic and political power, and the institutional arrangements dominating modern, capitalist societies. In sum, structural incoherence is a matter of degree in modern Western societies. Great structural incoherence co-exists alongside considerable structural coherence of core spheres.

Thesis II. The articulation and structural incoherence of peripheral spheres varies among modern, Western societies. In general, neo-corporatist systems experience a lower degree of such incoherence than pluralist systems. In any social system, priority is typically given to one or another of the principal modern forms — rational–legal, democratic, and negotiated–contractual — for organizing rule-making, -interpretation, and -implementation, and dealing with social conflicts in connection with such processes.

Two of the most characteristic principles for organizing rule processes in democratic societies are those associated with 'pluralism' and 'neo-corporatism' (Andersen, 1986; de Man, 1986). Note that both systems entail 'elitist democracy', that is the domination of rule processes by elites within the frame of democratic nation–states. Other organizing principles are represented in different forms of dictatorship.

The Scandinavian countries, Holland, Austria and Belgium represent cases of relatively tightly organized systems, with considerable regulation of social tension and conflict, in particular in relation to social rule formation and policy processes. Countries exemplifying primarily pluralist principles, with circumscribed organized regulation of social tensions and conflict, are Britain and the USA.

Since our research has dealt largely with neo-corporatist systems (Holland, Norway, and Sweden), we focus here on their characteristic organizing principles, referring to elite-pluralist systems, largely for emphasis. Characteristic features of these two principles for social organization are presented in Table 17.1.

Rule-formation and implementation in neo-corporatist systems is, for the most part, organized *multilaterally*, while it is more typically *unilateral and bilateral* in pluralism.

Neo-corporatist type of social organization is exhibited in tripartite or multipartite institutions, the consultative and collective decision organs for representatives of, at least, capital, labour and the government. Such 'organs' are not simply an *'additional'* sphere. Rather, *they provide an institutional frame on another level.* In particular, they deal with the interfaces — and contradictions — between, for instance, 'state' and 'market' and the agents representing these. Within this institutional frame, rule-formation and regulation processes take place on the *meta-level* in relation to 'market', and 'state' on the object level.

In the multilateral consultations and decision-making of neo-corporatism, even actors representing more peripheral interests often become involved, although the extent and quality of involvement varies considerably. Indeed, this is a distinctive feature of the system: the incorporation of peripheral actors, after they have mobilized, in the rule-formation process, even where it concerns core areas. In this way, peripheral institutions — and key groups in

TABLE 17.1
Pluralist and neo-corporatist systems of social organization
and decision making

Neo-corporatist		Pluralist
1.	Multi-lateral consultation and decision-making. More inclusive involvement in rule-making, rule-interpretation and implementation	1. Unilateral and bilateral decision making. More exclusive involvement in rule-making, rule-interpretation and implementation
2.	Institutionalization and regulation of interorganizational relationships, conflicts, and conflict resolution. That is, regulated according to norms of fairness (not only procedural, but substantive) In general, high degree of rule formation and regulation	2. Minimum formal institutionalization and regulation of inter-organizational relationships, conflicts, and conflict resolutions. State simply guarantees associational freedom and contractual rights In general, low degree of rule formation, and regulation
3.	Norms of 'compromise', mutual benefit, fairness	3. Norms may or may not be prominent, but in any case are vulnerable
4.	Organizational or societal power is important but mediated by rules, including distributional norms. Social power based also on appeal to key or core norms	4. Organizational or societal power is extremely important in specific transactions. Compromises may be followed as a strategy, fairness may also be followed as a strategy. But shifts in bargaining power are followed rather quickly and dramatically by shifts in strategies
5.	Relatively high predictability and certainty under normal conditions in both core and peripheral spheres	5. Relatively low social predictability and high uncertainty in peripheral areas; relatively high in core spheres

these spheres — have opportunities to express their opinions about, and to try to prevent or reduce negative, unintended impacts on their own spheres. As ultimate veto groups, they become involved in the rule formation process. The involvement itself provides incentives for those from a particular periphery sphere to coordinate their assessments and strategies. That is, mobilized groups are disposed to function as a 'segment', thereby not only enhancing their influence on core sphere decision-making, but providing an organizational basis for more coherent structuration of the sphere (or segment) in which they are engaged. The institutionalization of multilateral consultation and decision-making, along with segmentation of peripheral spheres, tends to reduce or assuage the problem of incoherent structuration in modern society.

The elaborate consultation and negotiation among key affected groups and interests, even substantially weak groups, contrasts with the relatively few opportunities the latter have to make their voices heard in a pluralist system. In the latter, economic power, political weight, including relative lobbying strength are the keystones to effective rule formation and implementation. These are occasionally countervailed by mobilized organizations, political parties, or mass demonstrations and result in elite concessions, some of which are withdrawn once mobilization subsides.

Several earlier chapters dealt with neo-corporatist systems and the multifaceted problems with which these systems are ridden. The problems in neo-corporatist systems are of a different character than in pluralist systems. Peripheral groups feel, in many instances, that they have been coopted or have been inadequately taken into account. The system presupposes ideologically — that is, as a right — such 'taking into account'. There may be revolts and re-negotiation about the terms of participation, including the rules and organizing principles for consultation and negotiation.[140] This is the social logic.

The structural and development features of the two organizing principles, pluralist and neo-corporatist, are suggested in Figure 17.1.

Actor-structure dynamics in social continuity and discontinuity

From the perspective of rule system theory, social organizations — communities, formal organizations, networks, and societies — are continually being reproduced and modified. In some instances, the modifications are substantial, entailing shifts between, or transformations of, core organizing principles and regimes (that is, the rational–legal, democratic, negotiative–contractual, and technical organizing principles in modern societies). Actors themselves are actively involved in these processes to determine which regime or regimes are to govern a sphere of activity or social process. Agents with vested interests struggle to maintain established systems or to limit changes in them. Others, often with diverse motives, engage covertly or openly in modifying or transforming the systems.

Thus, through their transactions, social agents maintain, modify or transform rule regimes which shape 'structural constraints' and 'opportunity structures'. However, even in periods of radical change, they never start from scratch. They cannot choose a completely different system with *alternative futures,* since their point of departure is always an on-going socio-cultural system in which they are embedded and which conditions their actions and transactions.

FIGURE 17.1
Neo-corporatist and pluralist type systems of structuration

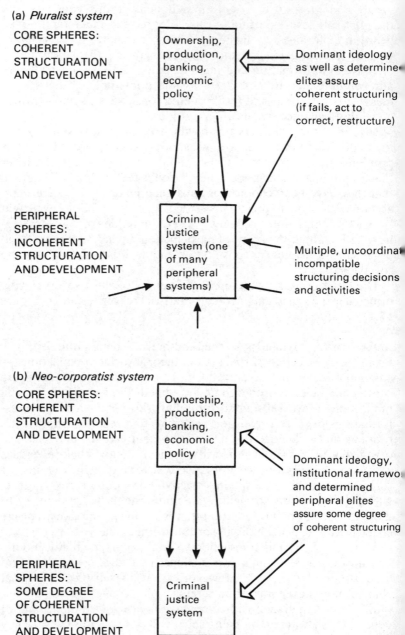

(a) *Pluralist system*

CORE SPHERES:
COHERENT
STRUCTURATION
AND DEVELOPMENT

Ownership, production, banking, economic policy

Dominant ideology as well as determined elites assure coherent structuring (if fails, act to correct, restructure)

PERIPHERAL
SPHERES:
INCOHERENT
STRUCTURATION
AND DEVELOPMENT

Criminal justice system (one of many peripheral systems)

Multiple, uncoordinated incompatible structuring decisions and activities

(b) *Neo-corporatist system*

CORE SPHERES:
COHERENT
STRUCTURATION
AND DEVELOPMENT

Ownership, production, banking, economic policy

Dominant ideology, institutional framework and determined peripheral elites assure some degree of coherent structuring

PERIPHERAL
SPHERES:
SOME DEGREE
OF COHERENT
STRUCTURATION
AND DEVELOPMENT

Criminal justice system

FIGURE 17.2
The structuring of social systems
(cf. Archer, 1985)

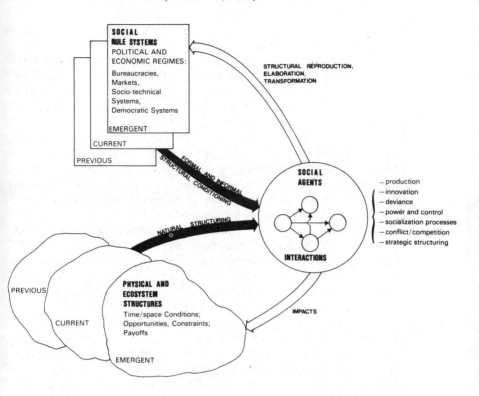

Rather, they evolve a future through praxis, experiment and learning, conflict and struggle.[141] The rationality of choice is not a 'goal rationality' but a *process rationality, the balancing of human order and freedom.*

Social interaction takes place in concrete settings usually with more or less established social rule systems defining agents, rights, obligations, access to resources. The structural conditioning of social action and interaction also depends on physical circumstances, which (given available technology) make for a given resource availability and the shaping of action constraints as well as opportunities. Structural conditioning of social transactions is not determining. It is typically contradictory and problematic (Wardell and Benson, 1979), as we have suggested in this and earlier chapters.

Two major sources of contradictory conditioning may be identified: *socio-cultural incoherence and system or functional incompatibility*. We shall briefly discuss these, in summarizing the analyses of this book.

Socio-cultural incoherence

Such incoherence arises whenever social agents try to apply multiple, contradictory rule systems to a social activity or sphere of action. The contradictory systems are a result of various social agents or groups formulating and developing them for different purposes, using different methods and strategies.

Furthermore, in a modern, differentiated society, the development of, and education in, multiple rule systems is often carried on more or less autonomously in relation to particular spheres or segments of social activity, e.g. law, administrative theory and practice, research and development programs in various techniques. For instance, in our studies we have found that multiple, more or less inconsistent, social rule systems are formed and reformed in connection with major societal cleavages as well as in specialized, largely autonomous segments. *The systems — in the absence of socially established meta-rules and principles of integration, synthesis, or compromise — generate ambiguity, uncertainty, and conflict among agents adhering to them in varying degrees.*

Contradictory, multi-rule formation is particularly characteristic of class and other group struggles, as manifested in the major political and economic arenas as well as 'shopfloors' and at other places of work where such struggles take place (as discussed in Chapters 8, 9 and 10). Several instances of conflicts around rule regimes and rule formation, arising from sustained social opposition or major societal cleavage, have been presented in earlier chapters: class and status groups struggling around the formation and reformation of wage negotiation systems; social movements, government bureaucrats, and experts struggling around the use of water and land resources ('hydro-power developers' versus 'environmentalists' in Norway); technical experts and politicians struggling about professional integrity and roles in policy-processes.

Whenever actors try to apply multiple and contradictory rules in the absence of operative meta-rules, their patterns of social activity tend to be unstable.[142] Rule system incoherence provides opportunities for some agents to restructure rule systems to their own advantage or in ways consistent with their vision of social order. For other actors, the incoherence gives rise to efforts to maintain particular regimes in which they have vested interests or which correspond to their image of social order. Their efforts often entail strategies to alter or reform rules in minimal ways. The struggle between those striving to innovate and restructure and those seeking to conserve established structures is a universal pattern in social life.

Functional or system incompatibility
A second major source of contradictory structural conditioning arises from alterations in action conditions. For instance, the social organization or specific rules of a system are found to be lacking certain productive or desirable capacities in organizing and regulating social action and interaction in relevant action settings. In a certain sense, social organization does not 'fit' the concrete action conditions, action processes, or technologies and resource dispositions obtaining in historically given situations. Under these conditions, actors are inclined to introduce rule innovations and, ultimately, to reform or transform the rule systems constituting social organization. (Rule system innovations, possibly resulting from political processes, also give rise to mismatches between rule systems and specific action settings.) Key points here are the following:

(i) *An established social rule system or complex of systems cannot be successfully applied to new problem situations or to old problems in a new context* (although this may have to be discovered through trial and error). As a result, major actors or groups move to reform or to replace the rule system, because they perceive net gains to be realized through such rule system restructuring.[143]

(ii) *Radically new technologies and techniques are introduced and developed,* motivated by the apparent advantages these offer in economic production, communication, or warfare. The introduction of substantially new technologies and innovations often contradicts the rules of established social structures. In this way, social agents — through their innovations in technique and technology — change the conditions of their actions, often unintentionally. (Comprehending and regulating the very new or the unknown is highly problematic.)

(iii) *Social learning and innovation* associated with coping with rule ambiguities and contradictions in concrete social activities lead to the formation of new principles and systems of rules. Such processes are also exemplified in the codification of laws and regulations, the systematization of sciences and mathematics, and the professionalization of occupations.

(iv) *Alterations in rule systems are often unintended consequences* of concrete action problems and activities, including those where actors struggle and negotiate about interpretation and implementation of rules. In general, the interplay of multiple rule systems, in social contexts where there is no meta-rule system to resolve ambiguities and conflicts, weakens or confuses the enforcement and long-term maintenance of rule systems.

(v) *Value and ideological shifts alter the interpretation* of, adherence or loyalty to, and development of social rule systems.

(vi) *Changes in environmental/physical conditions* affect action opportunity and outcome structures by altering resource availability and distribution and the size of social groups struggling over resource distribution.[144] These, in turn, evoke innovations in, and transformation of, operative social rules, in part because social agents cannot (or are unwilling to) implement and reproduce established rule regimes, under the changed environmental/physical conditions.

Developments such as those indicated above often lead to the emergence and development of new groups, social interactions, and resource control mechanisms which do not fit the initial assumptions and formal institutionalized relationships of established regimes. Shifts in values, patterns of authority, or resource control make it difficult for those committed to the established regimes. They are faced with trying to maintain these regimes against the will of new powerful groups, advocating rule reforms or entirely new regimes.

To conclude: the rule regimes and regime complexes corresponding to major types of social organization are likely to undergo reformulation and transformation under conditions where: power shifts and social control failures occur among established groups adhering to differing organizing principles and regimes; new social agents or coalitions — movements, classes, professions, parties or political elites — emerge, advocating new organizing principles and regimes and possessing sufficient social power to introduce these; the core technologies or resource base of established rule regimes are substantially altered. The basic modes of organizing social rule formation — rational–legal, negotiative–contractual, and democratic along with the principle of technocracy — are core components of Western civilization. These modes, with deep, historical and cultural roots, have been progressively developed and extended to most areas of social life, replacing in some instances, in other instances incorporating or making peripheral, traditional forms of social organization such as family, neighbourhood, and local community.[145] At the same time, modern Western societies — with capitalist organization of production and markets, the nation–state, and political democracy — consist of contradictory modes of social organization, contributing to the creative thrust and sustained dynamism of Western societies (Collins, 1986).

Contradictions among the organizing modes — and between them and more traditional or emergent forms of organization — have provided a powerful, internal source of dynamism. Individuals, groups and organizations, representing or espousing different organizing modes struggle with one another to maintain and develop the particular modes they represent or espouse. Nonetheless, there are socially regulated limits to such struggles. They have typically been carried out within an overarching ideology and institutional framework legitimizing the plurality of organizing modes and regulating conflicts among the contending forces (see Chapter 6). Conflicts occur without eliminating groups or the organizing modes they espouse. Coalitions are formed between and among agents in such a way as to maintain a certain power balance. Adherence to an overarching framework and to 'rules of the political game', which is essential to conflict resolution, have probably been reinforced, in many instances, by the development of national identity as well as by network ties and solidarity among elites representing or espousing the different organizing modes. Finally, the general effectiveness of the modes, in their various mixes, in dealing with problems associated with the formation and development of industrial society in Western nations has undoubtedly contributed to their legitimation, stabilization and reproduction (Burns et al., 1986).

Modern social organization, as we have sugggested in this book, is characterized by a high level of differentiation and complexity, technological and scientific development, and exploitation of natural resources, including land, water, energy sources, etc. Some of these developments have meant increased effectiveness and welfare, and a general easing of the human condition, while others (environmental pollution, resource depletion, and arms development, among others) have been largely harmful and, possibly, even disastrous for the human species in the long run. Looking globally, we see pockets of human dignity and reason; but also despotism, torture and cruelty. (Standards of morality are changing but this does not necessarily entail improvements. We have little perspective, either on the distant past or on the long-term future.) Today, nuclear war threatens the extermination of life as we know it. As of yet, we have no viable, foolproof social organization to deal effectively with this threat.

Since the early 1970s, economic shocks and political destabilization have confronted Western nations, and even more so Third World nations, with a complex of problems: energy and other raw material price shocks and volatility; environmental threats; challenges to public authority; erosion of the international monetary order which threatens a global banking crisis; escalating militarization, to name just a few. Nations of the world are presently in the difficult process of analysing their structural faults and action limitations and of exploring possible new forms of social organization. In the past, wars have been one of the major mechanisms for radical restructuring of societies and international systems, although this has not usually been the intention of the war-makers, nor the desire of new rule-makers.

To avoid war, new principles of socal organization and institutional order, particularly on the international level, will have to be worked out. This implies, of course, new rule system complexes. The challenge — not an entirely new one in human history — is both practical and theoretical.

Notes

1. The development of social systems (and their institutions) depends to a substantial degree on two basic dialectical relationships: (I) the relationship between human societies and nature, or the physical and biological environments on which societies depend; and (II) the dialectical relationships among social agents and their frameworks for social organizing. Mankind's necessary dependence on the natural environment create the circumstances for the environment to shape human structures, through shaping to some degree, human action and interaction possibilities and experience. But, in turn, human consciousness and activity shape and reshape the natural environment, often in unanticipated and unintended ways.

2. At the same time, we suggest a few of the ways in which rule systems not only organize and pattern social activity but structure social experience and, in general, contribute to the construction of social reality.

3. The framework shares several features with the meta-theoretical and ontological contributions of Giddens(1976, 1984): the concept of knowledgeable agents, their active engagement in rule processes and the reproduction and transformation of social structure, the duality of structure, the recursive nature of human activity, unintended consequences of human action, among others. In contrast to Giddens' work, however, the framework provides the basis for a programme of systematic, empirical research and the tools to formulate general models and subtheories of particular types of social organization and the processes whereby they are formed and reformed. This feature of the framework is demonstrated in Parts Two, Three, and Four of the book.

4. Abridged versions of Chapters 1 and 2 appear in Ulf Himmelstrand (ed), *Sociology: The Aftermath of Crisis*, Sage Publications, London, 1986.

5. Allardt (1972) and Etzioni (1970) refer to voluntaristic and collectivistic approaches, while Wallace (1969) refers to the subjective/objective distinction which is not quite the same thing. Wallace (1969:6–7) suggests:

> The difference between these definitions of the social correspond to the difference between the Newtonian and the Weberian definition of 'action'. Newton's definition of mechanical action was entirely in terms of external observables... Weber took exactly the opposite view by asserting that bodies' social action is so far distinguishable from mechanical action as to be definable only in terms of their internal states. 'Action is social ...', Weber said, 'by virtue of the subjective meaning attached to it by the acting individual.'

6. In a world threatened by nuclear destruction, technological revolutions and prolonged economic crisis, what happens in sociology associations and university departments hardly deserves the title of 'crisis'.

7. See Burns et al. (1985) and Baumgartner et al. (1986) for comprehensive treatment. The theoretical approach draws on and attempts to develop concepts of modern systems theory and cybernetics (Ashby, 1957; Boulding, 1956; Miller, Galanter and Pribram, 1960; Deutsch, 1963; Buckley, 1967; Etzioni, 1968) and game

theory (Luce and Raiffa, 1957; Rapoport, 1960; von Neumann and Morgenstern, 1953) as well as Marxian theory and research. Also see Archer (1985).

The approach offers a powerful set of new theoretical/methodological tools in sociology and the social sciences generally (and has a number of linkages to developments in modern mathematics, artificial intelligence, expert systems, and cybernetics which cannot be examined in this context. See Alker (1980, 1981), Johnson (1983), and Burns et al., (1985).

8. Our model (drawing on Simon and others) stresses imperfect information and knowledge in human decision-making and action.

9. One may investigate and analyse rule regulated social action, and its performance and distributional effects *irrespective* of the background of the rules and their meaning to the actors involved (Allardt, 1970; Gellner, 1960:170–2).

10. Social agents may or may not be aware that they cause a shift or transformation in their conditions and, ultimately, in their social systems. For instance, peasants and/or their lords clear forests from their lands or use agricultural techniques which bring about radical soil erosion and climatic changes. These reduce the agricultural productivity of the land over the long run. The population and its institutions may be ultimately unsustainable (at least on the basis of an agricultural mode of production).

11. A great many sociologists and other social scientists have followed Weber's lead, but relatively few have attempted to elaborate and develop theoretical concepts of rules and rule systems in systematic ways. Among those who have worked systematically with rule concepts, although in very diverse theoretical and methodological traditions, are Alker et al. (1980, 1985), Cicourel (1974), Giddens (1984), Harre (1979), and Harre and Secord (1972). (In Scandinavia, Allardt (1972) and Segerstedt (1970) have given serious attention to social rules in sociological analysis.)

Although these attempts have been fruitful in many ways and offer useful tools for social science research, they have not, as yet, become a major part of mainstream social science, and sociology in particular.

12. Among the major contributors to the development of social rule system theory are: first and foremost, Max Weber (besides his standard works, see his *Critique of Stammler* (1977); Hayward Alker, Jr (1980, 1985), Burns et al.(1985); and Harre and Secord (1972), Harre (1979), Giddens (1984) and Cicourel (1974).

13. This is our point of departure to specify a finite set of rule categories underlying all social institutions structuring and regulating social relations (See Chapter 7).

14. Here one is interested in understanding *(Verstehen)* the ways in which specific actors organize their activities and make choices, what meanings and values they give to their actions, what alternative choices and meanings are available in, or are excluded from, the rule frames with which they operate.

15. Descriptive, evaluative and prescriptive rules are socially produced and reproduced means to deal with uncertainty, arising in social life, in part as a result of the bounded rationality of human beings. They answer basic questions: (i) factual questions such as 'At what temperature will iron melt?', 'If a material consists of iron, is it true that it will burn at around 275°C?'; (ii) value questions such as 'Is it good (or right) to continue to expand welfare benefits on the basis of increased taxes?' ; (iii) prescriptive questions such as 'Should we follow procedure A or B in dealing with this research application?', or 'Should we establish regime A or B to govern international monetary flows in the future?'. To be more precise: *Descriptive rules* entail factual or descriptive formulations about the past, present, or future: What happened, what happens or is likely to happen under certain conditions? Where? When? How? Why? Who is involved or affected? The rules are socially

formulated and communicated in descriptions or statements about, for example, how a market or an economy functions, how a school system or a government agency operates, or how certain types of social agents behave. Socially produced and reproduced descriptive rules refer to objects, states of the world, agents, activities, events and developments. They categorize the world, making socially important distinctions. They also include statements about regularities or patterns, along with rules of interpretation and inference, for instance: all As are Bs; should anything be A, then B; or Y is a function of (X1,X2,...Xn). The more formal, systematic forms of such knowledge are found in science. These may be in the form of declarative rules, scientific generalizations, or 'laws' specifying causal structures. In all areas of social life, participants have 'models', even if only rough and unsystematic ones, making distinctions and indicating causal relationships. Descriptive rules can be expressed as: *If* <conditions x,y,z,... >, *then it is so that* <proposition>.

Socially produced descriptive rules or generalizations, such as 'under most circumstances human beings act to find pleasure and to avoid pain' often serve as knowledge components in human choice and action. Nonetheless, they are analytically distinct from evaluative or action rules, even if descriptive rules are used extensively in the execution of action rules. *Evaluative rules* concern those things which should be valued, or which should be pursued in life, in a sphere of activity, or in a specific social relationship or organization. Such rules may also indicate the converse, namely what should be avoided, opposed, or destroyed. Examples of socially defined 'valuables' are salvation in heaven, the pursuit of wealth, a free press, a functioning democracy, specific democratic procedures or particular welfare programmes. 'Bads' are 'hell', poverty, insecurity, a declining or fettered press, an oppressive government or anti-democratic practices. Evaluative rules, specifying what is desirable or undesirable, have the form: *under* <conditions k,l,m...>, *assign values to* <categories>.

'Categories' refer to objects, agents, activities, events, states of the world, and developments which are socially distinguishable in cognition and language, and to which differential valuations are assigned. *Action or prescriptive rules* consist of instructions and 'know-how' about how to respond to certain problems, conditions, or situations or how social decisions and activities should be organized or coordinated: what to do, how to do it, where one should do it, when, and with whom. In other words, such rules consist of norms, procedures and prescriptions for socially correct or effective action. For instance, traffic rules, legal as well as informal rules, provide instructions about how motorists should behave in defined settings, such as a traffic intersection. There are rules and principles indicating how meetings should be conducted, votes taken, or decisions reached in political or administrative settings. General organizing principles, laws, and 'rules of the game' fall under this heading. In general, an action rule can be characterized as follows: *if* <conditions a,b,c,..> , *then do* <action or procedure>. The conditions may be implicitly or explicitly specified, for instance indicating when and where the activity or decision is to be carried out. The rule may be formulated in a number of ways: 'Do not do x'; 'Do x to obtain such and such a result'; 'Under these conditions, you may not do this or that'. Combinations are of course possible: 'These activities are allowed, those are forbidden'.

16. That is, the shared rule system in a social relationship orients the action of each in terms of the system and the action of each takes account of the other. Weber suggests (1968:26–7): The social relationship thus consists entirely and exclusively in the existence of a predisposition (a term preferable to probability) that there will be a meaningful course of social action — irrespective of the basis of this predisposition..

17. Eisenstadt and Curelaru (1977:57) stress the point that social rules provide a basis for mutual predictability among actors, a meaningful framework for long-term rights and obligations among people, that is, continuity and the foundations of *mutual trust.*

18. One can make a general distinction between socially based inducements to rule-following and intrinsic and self-motivated inducements (see Chapter 4). Also see Weber (1968) and Etzioni's theory of compliance based on normative, remunerative and coercive types of power (1975).

19. Social rule systems in modern society are often imposed, enforced through remuneration and/or coercion. As Perrow (1979:82) points out about bureaucracy :

> For Weber, authority in bureaucracies was rational–legal authority, a type of domination based upon legally enacted, rational rules that were held to be legitimate by all members. The rules were either agreed upon or imposed. The fact that members accepted the legitimacy of the authority in no way altered the fact that rules could be imposed and coercion lay behind them.

Of course, in practice networks of social controls (in many instances with considerable redundancy) operate to assure a high level of acceptance or adherence to social rules in many social systems.

20. Actors try to impose social rules or rule systems on themselves as well as others after being convinced of their rightness, correctness or appropriateness for structuring and regulating their behaviour. A system 'fits' or appears compatible with personal experience as well as deeply felt values or norms. This implies that classes of actors who share a few very social principles along with common experiences are likely to develop or adopt rule systems compatible with this background.

21. *In general, compliance with some socially diffused rules provides its own rewards, partly by increasing the probability of successful or effective interaction with others* (enabling, for instance, coordination among participants), with machines, or with the physical environment, and partly by reducing uncertainty in social situations.

22. Rule system theory is, in large part, compatible with the various modelling traditions and their languages. However, the theory implies several reservations about the use of quantitative modelling found in, for instance, path analysis, econometric and system dynamic studies.

'Causal modelling' in social science, as developed and applied up to now, is most appropriate as a *representation of social relationships and processes under conditions of a stable rule regime.* The descriptions and analyses can offer insight into complex structures and even dynamic properties of social systems, provided relevant feedback processes are taken into account. *Regime changes imply, however, new model relationships and dynamic properties.*

From such a perspective, multi-variate causal models are partial tools for representing and analysing social phenomena governed largely by relatively stable social rule systems in more or less well-defined contexts . Certainly, as the best researchers know, one should be genuinely sensitive to the limitations of such models and use them diagnostically. Path and regression analyses, in particular, may serve as descriptive statistics, techniques useful in specifying and describing *performance systems* under particular temporal and social structural conditions (see Chapter 10).

23. As Weber (1968:32) pointed out:

> Economic action, for instance, is oriented to knowledge of the relative scarcity of certain available means to want satisfaction, in relation to the actor's state of

needs and to the present and probable actions of others, insofar as the latter affects the same resources. But at the same time, of course, the actor in his choice of economic procedures naturally orients himself *in addition* to the conventional and legal rules which he recognizes as valid, that is, of which he knows that a violation on his part would call forth a given reaction of other actors.

24. Role, although one of sociology's central concepts, remains a relatively underdeveloped, unspecified concept (Andersson, 1986). Social rule system theory, as this and later sections suggest, offers a useful point of departure to define and specify role in terms of ordered systems of rules or grammars.

25. Of course, this factor would play less of a role in the case of young people who were faced with the opportunity of a choice and starting more or less from scratch in learning one or another social rule system.

26. Allardt (1972:6) points out the importance of traditions in social patterning. These may be considered rules to which people adhere more or less unreflectively and routinely. Yet, as Allardt suggests, traditions may be fragile and easily changed once people are motivated or induced to do so. Of course, traditions backed by powerful social sanctions are a different case altogether than those which are simply habitual in character.

27. Lindblom (1977:21–3) points out concerning the contemporary erosion of family authority over children that a parent 'must wheedle, cajole, entreat and bribe, exercises that require time and money. Thus, the marginal costs of controlling their children has risen very high, sometimes so high that they give up trying'.

28. Ideological support is established through child and adult socialization as well as more obvious, formal systems of propaganda. Moreover, since core principles and rules typically will have wide and diverse impact on various rule systems and social forms which make up everyday life, they are difficult to change. In general, there are established vested interests prepared to resist changes in them. Also, there may be wide-spread reluctance to changing organizing principles and rules which represent considerable cumulative knowledge and innovation. Indeed, procedures are often established to impede or make costly changes in such organizing principles and core rules.

29. Weber states (1968:53):

Domination (Herrschaft) is the probability that a command with a given specific content will be obeyed by a given group of persons. The concept of power is sociologically amorphous. All conceivable qualities of a person and all conceivable combinations of circumstances may put him in a position to impose his will in a given situation. The sociological concept of domination must hence be more precise and can only mean the probability that a command will be obeyed.

If it possesses an administrative staff, an organization is always to some degree based on domination. But the concept is relative. In general, an effectively *ruling organization* is also an administrative one.

30. Albrow (1970:39), examining domination in an administrative order, according to Weber, writes:

The most important aspect of the administrative order was that it determined who was to give commands to whom. Administration and authority were intimately linked. Every form of authority expresses itself as administration. Every form of administration in some way requires authority, since its direction demands that some sort of power to command is vested in someone.

31. Our conceptualization of domination in production organization entails an

extension and specification of that of Weber (1968). See Chapters 7 and 11.

32. Invariably there are conflicts and struggles in and around any given role concerning its definition or design and its relationships to other roles. However, roles are not only a locus for tensions. They also provide various action opportunities, some of them institutionalized, to resolve tensions and to innovate.

In part, actors in their particular roles and role networks negotiate and renegotiate their 'local circumstances' in everyday activities: on 'shopfloors', 'homefloors' and other settings for concrete transactions. Under some conditions, the tensions and conflicts become more open and macro in character. Groups, organizations and social movements engage in meta-level processes concerning the structure and function of institutionalized arrangements in which roles are embedded, for instance the contemporary struggles concerning the relationships between men and women. These questions take us far beyond the problem of 'persons' and 'roles' and the various personal ways individuals experience and cope with the problems and opportunities which their social roles — as parts of larger social structures — present for them.

Questions of this type are the focus of the studies and analyses of Parts II, III, and IV: human agents engage in forming and reforming institutional frameworks — rule regimes — with specified roles, role relationships, configurations of rights and obligations, distribution of resource control and opportunities for gain and power accumulation.

33. Disagreements and conflicts arise not only in connection with contradictions in rule systems to which different social agents adhere. They occur also because agents obtain inconsistent data or interpret the same data in incompatible ways. On the basis of inconsistent data or interpretations, they come to contradictory conclusions about available options, effective or correct action, the likely outcomes of alternative courses of action, and so forth.

34. In discussing early Christian communities, Pagels (1983) provides a striking example of structural sources of disagreements, arising from disparate, incompatible rule regimes affecting everyday life. The story concerns a spouse who has converted to Christianity, while her partner remains pagan. The wife finds her husband blocking her Christian duties and everyday patterns of worship. The husband acts as one of Satan's agents in hindering her from compliance with obligations and rituals, according to Christian discipline. Although she intends to participate in morning worship, her husband makes an appointment with her to meet him at the baths at dawn. If there are feasts to be observed, her husband arranges for a dinner party on the same day. Her pagan family insists that she attend immediately to family business. On the other hand, her Christian 'family' requires her to care for its members (Pagels, 1983). The case points up the social tensions arising when two disparate and inconsistent rule regimes, borne by different actors, impinge on a sphere of social activity, in this case family life and relationships. It also suggests the extent to which Christianity at one time must have been experienced as a new basis on which to organize one's life, to form or develop new social relationships, and to feel meaning in life.

35. (See Kitschelt, 1985.) The following discussion does not reflect the historical complexity or national specificity of the relationships and systems we shall discuss.

36. In some cases, there may exist an overlap between class and status group identity: the owners/managers of capital may consist of members of an ethnic or religious group which claims superiority over that of working class groups, but even in such cases either class or status action or both can emerge as aspects of power struggles.

37. Rule system theory presumes that binary oppositions are conceptualized and

institutionalized through *concrete historical processes in any given society*. This holds, even if some dimensions in an abstract sense are *universally experienced* in human groups, for instance relations of domination. As we show later, such distinctions are expressed in deep ordering principles of social grammars, making up the cultural realms of society.

The outcomes of binary structural choices in the historical development of social grammars find expression in the design of social rule systems and the procedures used in their application. *This theoretical principle is opposed to Levi-Strauss' structuralism* (1963) in that: (i) The rules of binary opposition are not inherent givens in all perceptions of the world by the 'human mind'. Rather, they are learned and developed, adapted and transformed in part through concrete social transactions, including political struggle. (ii) Moreover, the rules of transformation whereby contradictions are dealt with and possibly resolved are not inherent in human minds. They are part of culture, learned, transmitted, and developed. Similar rules of transformation can be traced to parallel discovery and innovation as well as to processes of diffusion. Of course, the range of possible transformation rules may be strictly limited by the constraints of the human mind and the technologies which it is capable of creating.

38. Of course, the participants may experience ambiguity in some settings, for instance because a grammar cannot or is not followed closely, or one or more participants try to create or to exploit ambiguities.

39. DeVille (1985) argues that purely competitive markets, as formulated in economic theory, are logically impossible: (1) either one postulates completely independent, undifferentiated agents in the market with purely selfish interests and no social coordinating mechanisms — where such a system leads to chaos; (2) or one postulates at least one social coordinating mechanism, for instance, 'the auctioneer', and the market is no longer purely competitive the way it is defined in theory. Therefore, competition as a concrete social process entails organizing rules. On the other hand, in economic theory, social rules are the negation of competition!

40. A market governed by a minimum of social or political regulation would entail, nonetheless, a regime established and maintained by social agents, possibly against the will or interests of other actors. 'Natural markets' — what might more precisely be referred to as purely network markets — are largely marginal to modern economies. They are mainly of historical or comparative interest (e.g. in the studies carried out by anthropologists of 'markets' in traditional societies or contemporary studies of illicit markets (see Chapter 9)).

Market transactions — particularly complicated, long-term deals — depend on social trust and the absence of malfeasance. But, as Granovetter (1985:484) has argued, this state is unlikely when individuals have neither social relationships nor an institutional context, as in an artificial 'state of nature'.

41. As we discuss later, some rules emerge as *unprescribed strategies*. Those involved, for instance, adapt to particular action conditions such as high uncertainty or the propensity of others to adhere to agreements, or to resist temptations to exploit weaknesses of others. Given a certain shared culture and a common 'problem situation', market actors arrive without extensive coordination or communication at more or less similar 'rules of thumb' and 'strategic principles'. These may spread through processes of diffusion.

42. As we suggest elsewhere, the state may establish market rules in the general interest.

43. Historically specific institutional arrangements affect the capacity of various groups and organizations to exercise influence over rule formation and regulation of

markets. For example, the USA with a large internal market remains highly decentralized due to the independent powers of states, courts, and Congress. Consequently, a wide variety of points of access are available, thus offering opportunities for more independent and bilateral action on the part of particular groups and interests. The situation is very different in highly centralized political systems (e.g. Britain and France) as well as neo-corporatist systems (such as Sweden, Holland, and Austria). In the latter systems, the points of access are not only more limited but the density of agents engaged at these points is higher. As a result, market rule formation involves multilateral negotiations and decision-making. (See Chapter 10 on the Swedish model of wage negotiations.)

44. One might presume that markets, as conceptualized in the 'competitive model', are generally open to those who have products (apples or tomatoes) to sell and to those who have means (money or barterable goods) with which to make purchases. Markets, however, vary considerably in terms of legal and extra-legal rights to participate. Such participation rules have substantial impacts on supply and demand and, therefore, prices. Accordingly, the rules may become the locus of struggle and political games, such as the rules governing access to the restaurant, hotel, taxi, or liquor business. As suggested above, the rules regulating the zoning of land and real estate in urban areas are often strategic parameters in local politics.

45. The argument can be developed further by considering along with monetary payoffs non-monetary gains and losses. For instance, in the medical area one would want to examine closely the coalition between doctors and the producers of medical technology oriented toward pushing advanced medical technology. These inter-organizational coalitions — and their strategies — often lead to investments and lines of development which seem to be of very limited benefit generally, and in some instances harmful, to patients. However, they boost the professional development opportunities and income of doctors and producers of technology.

46. In some instances, there are social rules, including laws, requiring participation. For example, employees are required in some nations to participate in private insurance schemes (automobile insurance, house insurance); or those wishing to apply for a driver's licence are required to take driving lessons.

47. Of course, in the case of consumer markets, such as food, clothes, and shoes, where in affluent societies the stakes are not particularly high, the rules for consummating a transaction are relatively simple. On the other hand, those governing automobile or property sales, such as the purchase of a house or apartment, are elaborate, with a series of steps, investigations, certifications, before 'final settlement' is reached.

48. Some market rules may be 'neutral' in the sense of safeguarding the interests of both market partners as well as third parties.

49. Leblebici and Salancik (1982) point out that if the number of contracting parties is small and they are known to each other, there are not likely to be strong incentives to develop a formal institution for organizing transactions or an inter-organizational agency to regulate such transactions. Of course, there would be informal and tacit rules governing the transactions. They argue (1982):

> However, if there is a large number of potential parties and a rapid turnover of participants, a guarantor who facilitates the exchange process and regulates the behavior of the parties is highly advantageous in reducing uncertainty, distrust, and transaction costs.

50. Social rules restricting entry are only one — but a very fundamental factor — blocking or inhibiting entry to a market. Other factors, well known to economists, are:

(1) Possible suppliers lack the capital, technical expertise, market knowledge and contacts and believe that acquisition of these lie beyond their capabilities or would entail major risks.

(2) Fully capable suppliers do not enter because they perceive no economic incentive to do so. Paradoxically, stricter exclusion principles often make market entry more attractive, since prices will be higher. Indeed, the state may institute more stringent rules, precisely to attract capable, likely-to-succeed suppliers. Moreover, the in-group of sellers is motivated to support the exclusion rules, the organizations enforcing them, and their solidarity vis a vis potential intruders as well as opponents to the market exclusion rules.

51. Aggregate supply may be limited also by the institutionalization of rules which divide the market up among suppliers. This might be coupled with full exclusion of additional suppliers. The 'rules of the game' for this market would likely be more favourable to sellers than one where most sellers qualifying to various tests may engage themselves.

This is another way of referring to 'the division of labour' as organized and regulated in market systems. Thus, doctors make sure, often with legal backing, that 'potential competitors' such as nurses and 'non-scientific' medical practitioners do not provide certain types of services which only 'qualified physicians' are allowed to provide. At the same time, nurses may provide certain 'nursing and ancilliary services', and 'their market' is protected from 'less qualified or non-certified' practitioners. 'Non-scientific' or 'non-Western' medical practice is tolerated marginally.

52. On the other hand, rules standardizing, e.g. building materials, generally reduce transaction costs (by facilitating information gathering and comparison of products) and enable greater economies of scale. Of course, standardization may be premature, locking the development of production and products in non-optimal lines (that is, limiting or excluding the possibility of exploring and elaborating alternative lines of development). See Burns (1985).

53. Of course, as we suggest later, ideology and moral sentiments are a two-edged sword. Whenever the state tries to organize and regulate markets and market developments in ways which clash with established ideology and the moral sentiments of a community, the administrative costs of enforcing a market regime become very large, and enforcement often fails in any case.

54. South Africa would provide excellent (and tragic) illustrations of some of these processes. At the same time, there are certainly tendencies in areas for opportunism and the breaching of exclusion rules.

55. For a community of drug addicts, the demand curve will be highly price insensitive over a considerable price range, this range depending on their income level or affluence. Once prices approach the limits, for most of them, of their capacity to pay (let us assume for the sake of argument that this capacity is based on legitimate income), the slope of the demand curve would tend sharply upward. However, shifting into successful illegal activity would enable drug addicts to reduce the slope in the upper region.

The example is not an entirely hypothetical case. It points up the complex relations — and problems of effective social control — around highly necessary or attractive goods.

56. For upper status members of society, the loss of status resulting from exposure as a drug-dealer might serve to inhibit involvement. However, this would scarcely serve to restrain some lower status members and outsiders of society. Even substantial prison sentences fail as a major deterrent, provided the possible gains from illegal

activity are very substantial (as they are in many countries) and there are reasonably good chances of escaping detection or conviction. In general, a jail sentence does not possess the same sanctioning power or social consequences for many lower class members and outsiders as it does for middle and upper class members of society. Middle class law-makers often fail to appreciate this sociological principle.

57. The debiting of administrative enforcement costs will, in most instances, have an impact on marketing functioning and prices. For our purposes here, three cases can be distinguished: third parties such as the state pay, sellers pay and buyers pay. In practice of course, the costs may be allocated with a variety of mixes.

(i) *Third party payment.* We refer to third party payment when the costs of market rule enforcement are borne by third parties, for instance, the government (ultimately, taxpayers). We see this in the regulation of industries such as trucking, the airlines or the aircraft industry. In modern Western societies all or most formal labour markets are publicly regulated.

For whatever reason, third parties such as the state bear the costs of enforcing market exclusion rules, the consequence of which is that the impact of these rules on prices is minimized. Of course, the price increases arising from restricting supply or from imposing regulations and procedures which raise transaction costs remain. In general, systems where buyers and/or sellers bear the enforcement costs have a greater impact on prices, other things being equal.

(ii) *Enforcement costs borne by sellers and/or buyers.* The sellers, for instance their branch association, are debited enforcement costs. The actual enforcement of the rules may be carried out by third parties such as the state which charge a fee or impose a special tax.

The likely effect of such debiting will be to raise the price of the product(s) sold on the market. In other words, sellers — all of whom are obliged to make a contribution or to pay a tax — pass on the additional costs to buyers. Thus, ultimately buyers bear the costs (see later discussion on this being a negotiable matter in competitive markets).

The enforcement charge or fee may, indeed, be imposed directly on buyers. However, the official selling price need not reflect or contain these fees.

Whether buyers or sellers bear the enforcement costs, prices of the market products will tend to be increased accordingly, other things being equal. (Perfect competitive theory would predict that competitive pressures would tend to generate the same result.) At the same time, the incentives to engage in illicit transactions, that is to breach exclusion rules, are increased. These incentives are indicated by the differences between price levels on the legal market and (potential) price levels on illicit markets minus the expected costs to deviants for being apprehended (or avoiding apprehension).

58. Information processes and communication tend to operate differently in illicit markets than in legal ones. This is particularly the case in the learning of informal norms and the procurement of relevant market information about potential buyers and/or sellers. Zaltman and Wallendorf (1979) point out:

> Given that the potential buyer knows that the exchange is in violation of the norms which are legally enforced, and that the buyer has still decided to engage in such an exchange, he or she must find a supplier and learn the norms of the subculture in which the exchange takes place. Unlike most other products, the consumer searching for a stolen television set or heroin cannot look in the Yellow Pages. The supplier of illegal products and services therefore has a more difficult time getting information to the potential first-time consumer. Much of the infor-

mation comes through friends and acquaintances who are also part of the sub-culture. For instance, one's friends are usually the first source of supply for illegal drugs. Once the buyer and seller have found each other, what is the negotiation pattern? Since they are both violating a norm (although the seller's violation is considered more serious as discussed earlier), how do they come to trust each other? In illegal transactions, the buyer must ascertain whether the other person is actually a seller. Also, the seller must ascertain whether the other person is a potential buyer or a potential enforcer of the societal norm (for instance, an undercover police officer). There is a norm of mutual evaluation which is not usually present in fully legal transactions.

These efforts by the seller to assess who the buyer is will vary, depending on the intensity or severity of the negative sanctions which could be invoked by authorities if the seller were discovered. One thing the seller must do as the intensity of the negative sanctions increases is to selectively market the illegal products or services. The seller wants potential buyers to know about him or her as a supply source; however, the seller does not want enforcement authorities to know of the illegal exchanges. Controls on information will increase relative to the negative sanctions for violating the crime. The severity of negative sanctions will also affect the efficiency of distribution channels in getting illegal products to consumers without being visible to enforcement authorities.

59. Some suggest that illegal exchanges constitute a large sector of the economy. For instance, in the case of the USA, Zaltman and Wallendorf (1979) refer to estimates that in 1973 the resale of stolen goods amounted to $16 billion. They add that not only do the illegal exchanges themselves constitute a large segment of the economy, but that large expenditures are also made on efforts to enforce the laws associated with such practices as resale of stolen goods, illegal gambling, drug trafficking, and so forth.

60. Actors may build up — inductively so to speak — a social organization without a general framework to guide them. This would occur in the absence of an overar-ching institutional framework (with core organizing principles). Such cases arise in entirely new areas of social action or in the aftermath of a crisis of confidence in which an existing framework is rejected by major actors.

61. The separation of bargaining about rules governing work and those governing wages meant, as Katz stresses, that in practice wage rule bargaining and agreements were not influenced by the consequences of shop floor work rules (affecting pro-ductivity) and vice versa. Since wage rules were rigidly applied, and there was no explicit consideration of the link between wage setting and the short-run employment consequences of wage levels, the system as a whole became poorly adapted to the emerging crisis and the challenge of the Japanese automobiles in US car markets during the 1970s. Given the substantial growth in the industry earlier, there had been no clear indications that wage rules along with independently determined work rules (ignoring productivity consequences) would lead to employment losses. At worst, they might lead to some reduced employment growth in relatively poor performing companies such as American Motors.

In the crisis of the 1970s, rigid adherence to the two main rules governing wage formation — AIF (Annual Improvement Factor) and COLA (Cost-of-Living Adjust-ment) — led to pressures for change, even inside the union from rank and file members who would, as a consequence of the obvious trends, face layoffs and unemployment.

62. Katz argues (1982) that the decentralized bargaining on work rules tended to diffuse plant-level management/labour disputes in that work rules could be determined according to local preferences and adjustments made to local conditions, at the same time that the settlement of wage questions and the tensions around wage issues were negotiated and settled centrally.

63. The question here is whether or not there might be a return at some future date to the old system, for instance, subsequent to substantial improvements in the industry's sales and profitability. After Chrysler's achievement of profitability, the UAW (United Auto Workers) requested a return to the old rules. Management asked, and apparently received, an indefinite postponement of any return.

64. These developments in the wage rule systems generate increased variation in income and employment conditions across companies and subsidiaries in the industry, in contrast to the more uniform patterning which prevailed up to 1980.

65. This, as later 'historic compromises' between capital and a significant but not all-inclusive part of the labour movement, must be viewed in the context of more radical as well as anarchist movements among workers. The latter were perceived as more threatening and unacceptable to employers — and political authorities — than mainline, largely social democratic unions.

66. Sweden's economic performance was generally weak during the 1970s and early 1980s (Turner, 1985). Economic growth and industrial production lagged, the latter even declining during the latter part of the 1970s (Turner, 1985:5). The Swedish export industry suffered a sharp decline in international competitiveness, under the generally prevailing conditions of recession. Falling market shares cut export revenues at the same time that government subsidies, other transfer payments and budget deficits supported indirectly an increased import bill. The result has been chronic deficits in external account (Turner, 1985).

67. There are various explanations of the conflict (see Broström, 1981), which we shall not explore here. One factor was the tactical manoeuvreing of the peak labour market agents in the private and public sectors vis a vis one another. This complex interplay between public and private segments — without the benefit of a framework for negotiation or even deliberation — certainly increased the likelihood of misunderstanding and miscalculation.

68. Analyses of the type presented in this section have been developed independently by Suarez and Golborne (1986); also see Baumgartner et al. (1986), Chapter 4.

69. This is not meant to imply that economic and political forces play no role in the establishment or transformation of a regime or in its stability. Indeed, the analyses of this chapter point up some of these linkages.

70. For instance, in the agreement for 1966, LO introduced a wage development guarantee. The aim was to ensure that groups which did not benefit from wage drift could maintain their levels without the procedure of negotiations-about-exceptions which earlier had been customary. This was in a sense a foreboding of times to come. The struggle over relativities took the form of attempts to establish — or to prevent the establishment of — wage development guarantees. The battle of relativities was well on its way.

71. The sources of our data are indicated below:
Blue-collar wages: The statistics come from different sources. The period 1946–1960 comes from Johnston (1962) and refers to adult men. (1) The period 1961–1963 originates from LO, and the period 1964–1983 has been provided by SAF, both periods refer to all workers. The data refers to the private sector.
White-collar wages: The statistics on white-collar wages have been provided by

SAF. The total can be presented in two ways: first as a raw sum, secondly as a measure standardized for among other variables: age. The data refers to the private sector of the economy.

Economic indicators: Here we present only a few economic indicators: change in GNP (SAF and national income accounts); inflation (CPI, from Statistical Central Bureau and Statistical Yearbook); unemployment (as percent of labour force, from OECD statistics); public employment (Arbetsmarknadsstatistiskårsbok); industry profits (as percent of turnover, from Statistical Central Bureau); change in productivity (SAF); state's balance (as percent of GNP, from Statistical Yearbook); increases in employment taxes or fees (SAF); working days lost in industrial conflicts (Förlikningsmannaexpeditionen); 'wildcat strikes' (working days lost in industrial conflicts, from Förlikningsmannaexpeditionen); white-collar degree of organization (Kjellberg, 1983); relative size LO/TCO (Kjellberg, 1983);

72. One aspect of the problem is the *diversity and inconsistency in norms of distributive justice to which labour market actors in Sweden adhere* (Olsson and Burns, 1986). Differential commitments to distributive norms among various employee collectives become socially and institutionally problematic precisely when considerations of relativities and income distribution are paramount in group or organizational behaviour — as is the case today with a stagnating economy and declining real income. Examples of distributive norms or principles which our research has found to be important among Swedish labour market actors are (see Table 10.2, p.209:

(1) equalization of wages and income ('solidary wage policy'). This principle finds its greatest support in the LO, particularly among those workers in the public sector. Opposition to it is substantial among white-collar groups but even among LO groups, particularly in the private sector.

(2) differentiating wages and income according to degree of 'responsibility'. This principle finds wide support among all employee collectives. Greatest support is, as would be expected, found among white-collar groups. There are not many in Sweden who find the principle inappropriate.

(3) differentiating wages according to performance, such as quantity or quality of output or increases in productivity. Private sector groups support this principle substantially more than public sector groups. In general, the principle does not enjoy the extent of support of the first two.

(4) differentiating wages or income according to education. This principle has relatively meagre support in Sweden, except among the 'academic' white-collar unions (SACO). But even among these, the first three principles are dominant.

These diverse principles of fairness or equity (along with others such as 'seniority principles') appear to enjoy varying degrees of support among different employee groups and labour unions, as suggested by Table 10.2.

Indeed, almost all organizations and their members adhere to more than one principle, but they differ in the priority they give them in practice. Thus, no principle enjoys a clear or obvious hegemony. This contributes to confusion and conflict in collective bargaining as groups struggle over relativities and income distribution guided by quite different principles of distributive justice.

Employers also adhere to particular principles at the same time that they are often in a 'middle role' between contending unions. In some instances, they may try to play labour groups off against one another. Of course, such divisive behaviour as well as pragmatic strategies contribute to destabilization of collective bargaining and activation of the wage carousel.

In sum, in Sweden today there is no commonly accepted principle of distributive justice to determine appropriate relativities among different employee collectives. At the same time, as pointed out earlier, there is at present no organizing principle or concept for collective bargaining around which the key labour market actors can rally or mobilize support.

It should be stressed that there was never a single dominant or hegemonistic principle of distributive justice or income policy, even if SAF–LO agreements in the 1950s and 1960s gave the firm impression that the 'solidary wage policy' reigned supreme, ideologically and in actual policy. In practice, there were multiple principles — and diverse groups advocating and struggling in support of these. (i) Local norms concerning appropriate wage structure and relativities gave cause to considerable branch and local pressures against central SAF–LO agreements and contributed to the substantial wage-drift of Sweden (Burns and Olsson, 1986). (ii) In the engineering sector, and the export sector generally, there were strong norms and pressures to compensate productivity increases as well as qualified workers. Again, this was an important factor in wage-drift (Burns and Olsson, 1986). (iii) In the salaried employee unions there was strong support for the maintenance and development of principles of compensation according to responsibility, expertise, and performance.

Thus, one could find already in the 1960s local unions and employers, national unions and employer confederations for entire industries, and professional groups which did not fully accept the 'solidary wage policy' and centrally determined agreements. These developed institutionalized strategies and, in one way or another, worked against the 'Swedish Model'. The differing perspectives on questions of distributive justice — and opposition to a SAF–LO dominated collective bargaining — emerged in powerful and destabilizing ways in the turbulent 1970s. Thus, opposition tended over time to shift from canalization in more hidden, deviant forms (wage-drift, unofficial strikes) to finding expression in more open, political forms (proposals for introducing new rules or for restructuring the collective bargaining system).

73. Mouzelis (1967) has pointed out the considerable confusion in the literature concerning the formal and informal distinction, and argues that, while the distinction may have been initially useful, it has ceased to be so. In our view, the problem is the lack of a developed theoretical perspective which could point to distinct types of 'informal' rules and rule systems.

74. Spheres of society such as the political, the economic, and the socio-cultural consist of orders made up of sets of distinct social relationships. Thus, the economic sphere consists not only of 'market relations' but of hierarchical production relations and, possibly, negotiation relations where representatives of employers and employees (sometimes with the state involved) negotiate conditions of employment.

75. The settings may be seen also as arenas reflecting cleavages and struggles in the larger society, as Chapters 13 and 15 illustrate (see Zey-Ferrell (1982:183) for similar arguments from a different perspective).

76. Actors also bring into the action setting their own *actor-unique styles and idiosyncrasies*. These, however, do not concern us here. We have chosen the more sociological task of investigating different social rule systems and their interplay.

77. Blau and Scott (1962:5,7) write:

…business concerns are established in order to produce goods that can be sold for a profit, and workers organize unions in order to increase their bargaining power with employers. In these cases, the goals to be achieved, the rules the members of the organization are expected to follow, and the status structure that defines the relation between them (the organizational chart) have not spontaneously emerged in the course of social interaction but have been consciously designed *a priori* to anticipate and guide interaction and activities.

In an organization that has been formally established, a specialized administrative staff usually exists that is responsible for maintaining the organization as a going concern and for coordinating the activities of its members. Large and complex organizations require an especially elaborate administrative apparatus.

78. Weber's ideal type (in this case that of the rational–bureaucratic organization) can be understood in our terms either (1) as a specification of a certain established or institutionalized set of organizing principles and rules or (2) as a description of an ideal system that would be produced by implementing such principles and rules under optimal conditions.

79. Weber points out (1946:196–7):

> The authority to give the commands required for the discharge of these duties is distributed in a stable way and is strictly delimited by rules concerning the coercive means, physical, sacerdotal, or otherwise, which may be placed at the disposal of officials.
>
> The principles of office hierarchy and of levels of graded authority mean a firmly ordered system of super- and sub-ordination in which there is a supervision of the lower offices by the higher ones... With the full development of the bureaucratic type, the office hierarchy is monocratically organized. The principle of hierarchical office authority is found in all bureaucratic structures: in state and ecclesiastical structures as well as in large party organizations and private enterprises.

80. Knowledge of these rules represents a special technical education which the officials possess (Weber, 1946:198). It involves jurisprudence, administrative or business management, or technical training. Weber stressed (1946:198):

> The reduction of modern office management to rules is deeply embedded in its very nature...This stands in extreme contrast to the regulation of all relationships through individual privileges and bestowals of favour, which is absolutely dominant in patrimonialism, at least in so far as such relationships are not fixed by sacred tradition.

81. Weber argued (1946:200–1) that the bureaucratic official, in the purest case, is appointed by a superior authority:

> An official elected by the governed is not a purely bureaucratic figure. Of course, the formal existence of an election does not by itself mean that no appointment hides behind the election — in the state, especially, appointment by party chiefs. As a rule, however, a formally free election is turned into a fight, conducted according to definite rules, for votes in favour of one or two designated candidates.
>
> In all circumstances, the designation of officials by means of an election among the governed modifies *the strictness of hierarchical subordination*... The career of the elected official is not, or at least not primarily, dependent upon his chief in the administration. The official who is not elected but appointed by a chief normally *functions more exactly, from a technical point of view,* because, all other circumstances being equal, it is more likely that purely functional points of consideration and qualities will determine his selection and career... Moreover, in every sort of selection of officials by election, parties quite naturally give decisive weight not to expert considerations but to the services a follower renders to the party boss. ...

Popular elections of the administrative chief and also of his subordinate officials usually endanger the expert qualification of the official as well as the precise functioning of the bureaucratic mechanism. It also weakens the dependence of the officials upon the hierarchy.

82. Weber states (1946:199):

Legally and actually, office holding is not considered a source to be exploited for rents or emoluments, as was normally the case during the Middle Ages and frequently up to the threshold of modern times... Entrance into an office, including one in the private economy, is considered an acceptance of a specific obligation of faithful management in return for a secure existence. It is decisive for the specific nature of modern loyalty to an office that, in the pure type, it does not establish a relationship to *person, like the vassal's or disciple's faith* in feudal or in patrimonial relations of authority. Modern loyalty is devoted to impersonal and functional purposes.

83. Weber specified this 'exclusion principle' in the following terms, suggesting the importance he placed on it: (i) the official is free personally but within the organization he is subject to a single (monolithic) control and disciplinary system. (ii) the member observes only the impersonal duties of his or her positions or office. (iii) the member's position is his or her sole or major occupation. (iv) duties are to be performed impersonally, and therefore not subject to the norms and values of personal, family, political, or other relations.

84. Weber (1946:221,223) writes:

The bureaucratic structure goes hand in hand with the concentration of the material means of management in the hands of the master. This concentration occurs, for instance, in a well-known and typical fashion, in the development of big capitalist enterprises, which find their essential characteristics in this process. A corresponding process occurs in public organizations.

War in our time is a war of machines. And this makes magazines technically necessary, just as the dominance of the machine in industry promotes the concentration of the means of production and management...Only the bureaucratic army structure allowed for the development of the professional standing armies which are necessary for the constant pacification of large states of the plains, as well as for warfare against far-distant enemies, especially enemies overseas. Specifically, military discipline and technical training can be normally and fully developed, at least to its modern high level, only in the bureaucratic army.

85. Perrow (1964) argues that this was not always so because it was better for people or more efficient. Nevertheless, Weber himself stressed repeatedly the importance of sustained organized action, predictability and efficiency of this form of administration and authority (1964:337–8):

The purely bureaucratic type of administrative organization (bureaucracy) ... is from a purely technical point of view, capable of attaining the highest degree of efficiency and is in this sense formally the most *rationally known means of carrying out imperative control* over human beings. It is superior to any other form in precision, in stability, in the stringency of its discipline, and its reliability. It thus makes possible a particularly high degree of calculability of results.

86. For such an organization to operate on a continual basis, it has a more or less stable source of financing, independent of the staff's personal resources: either

income generating activities, as a business enterprise, tax supported activities of government agencies, or voluntary contributions of memberships. Weber stressed the importance of a money economy for the full development of modern bureaucracy (1946:208): .

Even though the full development of a money economy is not an indispensable precondition for bureaucratization, bureaucracy as a permanent structure is knit to the one presupposition of a constant income for maintaining it. Where such an income cannot be derived from private profits, as is the case with the bureaucratic organization of large modern enterprises, or from fixed land rents, as with the manor, a stable system of *taxation* is the precondition for the permanent existence of bureaucratic administration. For well-known and general reasons, only a fully developed economy offers a secure basis for such a taxation system. The degree of administrative bureaucratization in urban communities with fully developed money economies has not infrequently been relatively greater in the contemporary far larger states of plains. Yet as soon as these ... states have been able to develop orderly systems of tribute, bureaucracy has developed more comprehensively than in city states. Whenever the size of the city states has remained confined to moderate limits, the tendency for a plutocratic and collegial administration by notables has corresponded more adequately to their structure.

87. Crozier (1964) in his studies found that subordinates tacitly agree to play the management game, but they try to turn it to their own advantage and to prevent management from interfering with their autonomy. Or, alternatively, the professionals within a bureaucratic organization may seek to maintain wider professional norms of behaviour that foster autonomy and expectations of involvement in shaping the goals of the organization (Thompson, 1980:21).

88. Crozier's study (1964) of power relations in organizations pointed up how one group, for example maintenance workers, could take advantage of an area of uncertainty under their control in order to impose their will on another group, the production workers. Such a relation of domination was strictly informal, and would not be found in any organizational chart or handbook of rules and regulations.

89. Blau (1956) in his study of a public agency pointed out that organizational efficiency and goals could be best served in some instances through unofficial practices and informal personal relations, in contravention of the rules and the formal organizational structure. Formal rules may have to be modified also in the face of technical problems, client demands, the need to maintain good public relations, or morale among workers. Some of these changes may, of course, be incompatible with certain purposes or goals of top managers or policy-makers.

90. Etzioni (1975:460) discusses research which examined the relationships between informal groupings within formal organizations under different compliance conditions. He refers to work by Tichy (1973) which found that normatively organized systems tended to develop informal structures that are integrated to a great extent with the formal structure. Formal relations tend to absorb or shape informal ones. Systems based on coercion (for example, prisons and many hospitals) tend to develop segregated informal structures that control a large sphere of social activities with norms and values opposed to the dominant formal system. Organizations based on remuneration of their members tend to develop informal structures that are integrated and compatible with the formal structures to a greater extent than those in coercive systems. On the other hand, the distinction is sharper and more persistent than in normative types of organizations.

91. Take, for example, a four-unit dwelling costing 100,000 Dfl which would

incorporate energy conservation investments of Dfl 3,300. According to the table, rent percentage changes from 5.2 to 5.4 percent. Therefore, the energy investments lead to an overall increase in rent of Dfl 378.20 of which Dfl 206.60 has to do with the change in rent percentage.

92. Indeed, there are a vast number of such additional regulations, in many instances defining housing standards and quality controls. The most important quality prescriptions are contained in the model building code, 'mbv'. The mbv is used as a condition for acquiring state loans and subsidies. The mbv, listing hundreds of prescriptions relating to materials, construction techniques, and scale, etc., has been developed by the nation-wide organization of Dutch municipalities and is regularly adjusted to changing needs. The adjustment is carried out by a commission in which a variety of private and public interests are represented. Although the building code is not designed by a central government organization, it is used by the central government organization in making subsidies and loans. Other quality regulations, designed by central government, relate to house maintenance. The exact levels of maintenance costs are defined by the central government on the basis of a uniform regulatory code.

The implementation of these regulations in relation to costs, rent levels, and housing quality requires an elaborate administrative organization. In the Netherlands, there are a number of decentralized governmental agencies whose main task is the approval of building plans, rents and exploitation regimes. These agencies apply the centrally defined rules and they negotiate on building plans in early stages of the design process.

The housing rule system is not only complex, due to the great number of regulations, but also rapidly changing, in part due to changes in technologies and, in part, to policy changes. The result is a continuous stream of amendments of existing rules to the local governments and to the ownership organizations ('owning-corporaties'). The problems caused by this complexity and change for the local administrative level are discussed later.

93. Due to the present economic crisis, the basis of the Dutch welfare state is under threat, and so is the highly regulated housing system. Shortage of finance places the housing system under considerable strain. Cost reduction is the most urgent goal of today's housing policy, the main motivating force for rule reform in the housing sector.

94. The institutional network around city heating planning consists of the central electricity organizations, the nation-wide organization of city heating companies, central government (Ministry of Economic Affairs) and the government organization NEOM (Nederlandse Energie Ontwikkelingsmaatschappij, Dutch Energy Development Company) which decides on whether to give subsidies and loans to the city heating company. This decision is made before the construction of the city heating system.

95. In our case studies on energy-efficient housing we encountered a number of interesting examples of such rules about rules, for instance:

(a) *existing rules are simply not considered*
In the Dutch Municipality Kaatsheuvel, we studied a planning process for energy-efficient housing: a small-scale heat-pump system and a high degree of insulation. As a result of additional energy-conservation investments the building costs would rise substantially above the maximum level specified by the government. Those involved in planning in the community considered the rule which set a maximum as merely a formality.

(b) *perceived rules do not in fact exist*
Earlier we mentioned the decentralized administrative organization which takes care of the implementation of the regulations on finance, rents, etc. in housing. Building plans have to be approved by these agencies before subsidies and loans will be assigned. In practice, these organizations are believed to have much more power than they really exercise. Those who make building plans believe that certain plans 'will never be approved' due to hypothesized informal or implicit rules, whereas the responsible administrative agencies state: 'that is none of our business'.

96. Elsewhere Burns (1985) and Baumgartner and Burns (1984) have concep-tualized the social processes whereby such socio-technical systems are built up, defended and developed further by entrepreneurs. See also Hughes (1983) and Selznick (1953).

97. The Association had tried to use the judicial system in an earlier case, that of Aurlund. They sought to be defined as an 'agent' or 'interest' which could participate in compensation decisions, which are made after a project has been approved by Parliament. A split Supreme Court denied them the request.

Here, as in the Alta case which was raised in the courts, the Association raised the issue of how 'affected interests' should be defined, thus affecting participatory (or inclusion) rights.

98. Such a flow-chart consists of a diagram with actors, activities, and transactions registered within a matrix where the relevant set of institutional spheres are represented along one axis and time along the other axis. Phases of social action and interaction are also distinguished. The following modelling rules indicate further content:
1. Define relevant institutional sectors or spheres of social action and interaction.
2. Determine the time sequence of major activities, including decisions and transac-tions, and write a brief descriptive label for each activity. Those activities are selected for inclusion which social rule system(s) designates as key or essential decisions and actions in the overall process. The resulting model may be that defined by the formal rule system (Figure 13.2) or that defined by actual practice (including activities generated by informal rules and the strategic interaction of actors).
3. For each activity note:
    a) activity sector or sphere,
    b) prior activities (with likely linkages to present activities indicated).
    c) participating actors and groups of actors, which are organized by sector or sphere (abbreviations of key participants are listed with each activity and trans-action).
    d) subsequent activities (with likely linkages specified); the direction of flow is indicated by arrows.
    e) reciprocal and interrelated flows and activities are indicated by ⟷.
The technique of decision history flow-chart enables systematic collecting and organizing of large amounts of structure-process data. Through substantive cat-egorization, detail can be reduced and more abstract analyses carried out (compare Figures 13.2, 13.3 and 13.4). The technique also enables a comparison and contrast of decision-flow profiles of different cases. In this way, one can make structural observations and draw analytical conclusions about the patterns of development of social decision processes over time, the activity and transaction patterns across institutional spheres, and the activity and transaction patterns of different actors over time.

The comparative analysis of social decision processes may take different forms according to the analytical perspective and interest of the research. One may, for example, compare social decision-making in different sectors, or at different times in a single sector; or both types of comparisons may be carried out. One may also, as we do later, compare an actual case of decision-making with the formally specified rules and procedures. This becomes the point of departure for efforts to explain conformity and deviation from the formal structure.

The approach utilized here in describing and analysing social decision-making requires collecting various types of data. Data are collected on the actors involved, key activities and transactions as well as processes of social learning and shifts in perceptions and strategies. Methods such as interviews with participants and observers, collection and analysis of public statements and protocols are used. Social organizational data — on relations among key actors and groups of actors and on the institutional settings for social transactions — are gathered through similar techniques. In both cases, particularly in the investigation of social institutions, cumulative knowledge based on previous research is exploited. In settings with a high degree of formalization such as administrative and legal systems, formal specifications of rules and regulations are often available in documents and handbooks. Information about informal and deviant decision-making procedures and rules is obtained through interviews with participating actors and knowledgeable observers.

99. One initiative toward the end of the 1970s, which emphasized environmental concerns in a radical way, was the formation of national parks. The creation of the Hardangervidda National Park entailed stopping two major hydro-power projects which had been planned. The concept of a 'national park', new to Norway, was not, however, institutionalized in the planning process. The Hardangervidda National Park was the result of ad hoc negotiations within the Labour Government at the end of the 1970s, where environmental interests led by the Department of Environmental Protection were counterpoised to the 'industrial complex' led by the Department of Industry and NVE.

100. Lindblom (1977:30) points out that the essential feature of this revolution launched in Western civilization was in putting two resources to work on a scale never before attempted: machines of great variety, made possible by accelerated science and engineering; and coal (and later oil and nuclear energy) as a source of power to run them. He adds, 'Just as the organization of the mines called for organized business enterprises, so also did the man-machine coordination necessary to take advantage of the productive potential of the new machines.'

We not only want to stress the quantitative aspects of the revolution, but the qualitative shifts, in that human beings have been incorporated into complex socio-technical systems designed and managed by others. Moreover, the major tools of modern production, including the know-how and resources to produce and develop tools and techniques, are concentrated in the hands of relatively few persons and agents such as the managements of large, often transnational corporations.

101. But more. All spheres of social life have been shaped and transformed by the industrial revolution and are now undergoing restructuring in connection with the post-industrial revolutions in technology: music/cultural forms, home production and consumption, factory and industry, office production and service production generally, farming, politics and diplomacy, and not least war-making.

102. Discussing the social limits on the application of science to technology, Rosenberg (1982:42) writes:.

Science itself can never be extensively applied to the productive process so long as that process continues to be dependent upon forces the behaviour of which cannot be predicted and controlled with the strictest accuracy. Science, in other words, must incorporate its principles in *impersonal* machinery. Such machinery may be relied upon to behave in accordance with scientifically established physical relationships. Science, however, cannot be incorporated into technologies dominated by large-scale human interventions because human action involves too much that is subjective and capricious. More generally, human beings have wills of their own and are therefore too refractory to constitute reliable, that is, controllable inputs in complex and interdependent productive processes.

The decisive step, then, was the development of a machine technology that was not heavily dependent upon human skills or volitions, where the productive process was broken down into a series of separately analysable steps. The historic importance of the manufacturing system was that it had provided just such a breakdown. The historic importance of modern industry was that it incorporated these separate steps into machine processes to which scientific knowledge and principles could now be routinely applied. 'The principle, carried out in the factory system, of analysing the process of production into its constituent phases and of solving the problems thus proposed by the application of mechanics, of chemistry, and of the whole range of natural sciences, becomes the determining principle everywhere'(Marx). When this stage has been reached, Marx argues, technology becomes for the first time capable of indefinite improvement.

103. Schadewaldt (1979:165–7) points out that the concept of technique in Greek referred to the 'art of production', know-how to produce. This applied to the carpenter, athelete, or musicians:... 'that knowledge and ability which is directed to producing and constructing...the art or skill of the master-builder and more generally, the art of every kind of production.

104. In the case of sexual practices the Taoist conception that retained male semen flows to the brain would not satisfy modern medical knowledge of anatomy and physiology. However, the non-physiological meanings of this interpretation may have been extremely important — as part of a vision of life and the basis for 'self-control' — more so than the scientific knowledge itself, at least in accomplishing social discipline, which is often essential in human sexual practices.

105. Rosenberg (1982:13) observes:

> What is certainly clear and is borne out by the histories of England, France, the USA, Japan and Russia over the past two and a half centuries or so is that a top-quality scientific establishment and a high degree of scientific originality have been neither a necessary nor a sufficient condition for technological dynamism.

106. I am grateful to Bernward Joerges (Wissenschaftszentrum, Berlin) for this observation.

107. The socio-technical systems built up around a major technology such as the motorcar (roads, fuel distributive system, drive-in movies, motels, shopping centres, etc.) make certain actions and transactions possible, at the same time that others become terribly complicated or impossible (Winner, 1983).

108. Engineers and designers are a strategic group engaged in rule formation relating to the design of technology and socio-technical systems. Also important in this connection are those such as managers, engineers and workers who decide on the concrete utilization of technology (and therefore in the implementation as well as reformulation of rule systems relating to new technology use).

109. Engineers, designers, and managers may easily misjudge the ease with which a technology may be 'introduced'. Those who see their occupations or jobs threat-

ened may exaggerate the difficulties. Typically, the outcomes are complicated. However, the point is that, often there is a well-developed politics to technological innovation and development (see Burns, 1985; Baumgartner and Burns, 1984; Baumgartner et al., 1986).

110. The following is based on the work of Docent John Lilja, Institute of Social Pharmacy, University of Uppsala. Among other publications, his 'Läkemedelskontrollen: ett mångtydigt begrepp,' *Svensk Farmaceutisk Tidskrift*, vol. 88, 1984:26–31; 'Det svenska apoteksväsendet 1920–52: Från självständiga apotek till apotekskollektiv', u.m.; 'The Nationalization of the Swedish Pharmacies', u.m.

111. This section is based largely on Göran Ewerlöf's article, 'Artificial Insemination: Legislation and Debate,' *Current Sweden*, no. 329, 1985, The Swedish Institute, Stockholm. Ewerlöf is a district court judge and Secretary to the Swedish 'Insemination Committee'.

112. For studies of technological innovation and development in the areas of alternative energy technologies, see Baumgartner and Burns (1984) and Burns (1985).

113. Neither Sweden nor any other Western countries have statutory provisions concerning 'in-vitro fertilization' (IVF), even though the technique is rather widespread internationally. It is estimated that up to October 1984 approximately 1000 IVF babies had been born in various parts of the world and at least the same number were on the way. These figures refer to cases where an ovum is extracted from a woman's body, fertilized with sperm from her husband or cohabitant and then returned to her body for gestation. In the USA there have also been a few instances of an ovum from a female donor being used.

114. In a certain sense, we consider modelling a political resource, above all in legitimizing a particular policy or political position. See related discussion in Chapter 16.

115. Conventional objective testing of models is unfeasible, in addition, because, among other things, public prognoses and plans have a self-altering character (Burns, 1978; Henshel, 1978, 1982).

116. In many instances, as our case suggests, energy forecasting was used as a political resource in supporting or legitimizing a particular policy or proposal. However, its utilization in controversial areas such as nuclear power planning may lead to widespread adoption, as a result of opponents to a policy or political position also trying to gain access to or control over such a resource. Wagner (1985) suggests that the regular confrontation of expertise and counter-expertise by opposing actors in a policy process leads to questioning of their 'scientificity'. Consequently, scientific or technical knowledge, as a political resource, will tend to be increasingly devalued.

117. Forecasts appeared in the Norwegian Longterm Plans of 1965, 1969, and 1979 for the Norwegian Economy.

118. The energy model-building efforts of this group were part of a larger enterprise to develop resource-accounting systems, a major effort launched by the Ministry of Environment in connection with its commitment to developing resource management policy. Energy-accounting was, however, given priority.

119. The Energy Prognosis Committee contacted all existing energy modelling groups and allowed them to come forward with forecasts based on a common set of assumptions. The Committee's main problem concerned ways of choosing among the forecasts supplied by the different teams. The choice was made largely on a normative basis. Committee representatives admit this.

120. This shift from domination of the hydro-power perspective to economic-and-

resource-oriented milieus and techniques did not immediately affect the hydro-power authority's dominance in the physical and organizational structures of the hydro-power supply system itself. As discussed in Chapter 13, major changes have been brought about here only recently.

121. Such groups have, as the Norwegian and British cases suggest, a certain autonomy and initiative on their own. In Norway in particular the EMOD modellers could draw upon the scientific authority and monopoly of professional expertise associated with MODIS.

The organizational basis of autonomy and initiative in Britain is quite different. There it is based on a modelling institute's non-involvement or very limited involvement in policy processes. A modelling group or institute operates in a marketplace of ideas and research contracts, in competition with other groups and subject to the forces and temptations which such competition may entail.

122. We have not investigated this case ourselves, but it has been systematically studied and analysed (see Diefenbacher's article in Baumgartner and Midttun (1986)). Peter Wagner has been particularly helpful in pointing out contrasting features of the German case relative to our other cases.

123. Other interpretations are possible here, namely that parliament is also 'the government'. In our view, government governs, parliament deliberates, challenges, approves, dissents.

124. Many feel that modelling is not a scientific activity. Our own studies would certainly support this view. Nevertheless, some modellers have had the ambition to make model-building into a more scientific endeavour. This is not a question of absolutes, but struggle over professional norms of autonomy and integrity, as the Norwegian and Dutch cases examined in the preceding chapter might suggest.

125. Karpik (1981) refers to logics of social action on the basis of which individuals and groups organize their thinking, decisions, and action. Wittrock (1986) conceives of policy settings as operating according to one or more modes. In the case of multiple mode situations, incompatibilities arise. In this way he conceptualizes *unitary and diverse logic realms of policy-making*. In rule system terms, the different modes of social action are structured and regulated by distinct social rule systems.

126. In discussing a somewhat similar type of table, Clark and Majone (1984:17) point out:

The very diversity of standards in the table helps us to understand some of the conflicts that arise over the appraisal of science in policy contexts.

127. The emergence and consolidation of these communities can be historically traced. As Boulding (1964:39) observes:

The foundation of the Royal Society in London in the latter half of the seven-teenth century is a crucial date. Here science begins to emerge as an organized subculture. Even then science was still largely a work of amateurs, and the amateur period of science lasted well into the nineteenth century. It is only in the twentieth century that science has become a substantial, organized part of society on a full-time professional basis.

128. The capability of a scientific community to influence public decision-making depends on the specific socio-political context in question, the level of consensus and structure of the community, and the power of its theories. These factors contribute to legitimizing the community as 'scientific' with the competence, and even the right, to make statements about the area of reality to which the science applies.

(1) Theoretical/methodological capabilities. Some sciences, such as the natural and technical sciences, have considerable explanatory or predictive power, whereas others, such as economics and the social sciences generally are unable to provide predictions or explanations of the same quality. Of course, this does not prevent economists, in particular, from engaging in the business of making forecasts and predictions, and this much more extensively and with greater authority than their fellow social scientists. In a certain sense, economists have proved themselves bolder and more adept at exploiting their authority as 'genuine scientists'. To a considerable degree this has depended on the strength of their profession, a factor to which we now turn.

(2) Professional discipline and authority vis a vis the outside/political world. Internal professional discipline and closure serves several important structural functions: (i) it tends to discourage members from making public confessions of the profession's theoretical and methodological failings; (ii) it limits public disputes or disagreements among experts of the profession; (iii) it acts to restrain excessive paradigm cleavages within the profession. Such closure rests not only on internal professional controls but discipline vis a vis the larger world.

The case of economics is again an interesting one. Actual predictive power is often low indeed. However, this is, in part, compensated by the internal discipline of the profession. Sociology and political science, on the other hand, have not apparently managed to discipline their memberships and to achieve closure to a comparable degree.

A shared paradigm, even if of low explanatory or predictive power, can play an important role in establishing and maintaining internal discipline. It also may provide the self-confidence to engage publicly in the forecasting business. The possible parallels with the Greek Oracle and with prophets in history would be worth investigating systematically. (We are indebted to Leon Lindberg in suggesting some of these insights.)

129. We do not assume that the social rule systems of scientific communities are fully consistent and complete. Among other things, there are 'contending schools' within any scientific community. Moreover, there are diverse subsets of rules applying to particular settings of scientific activity: for instance, the rules guiding the 'context of discovery' or of practical research itself tend to differ from those governing the 'context of justification' or presentation of analyses and results (Reichenbach, 1982).

130. The internal contradictions and dilemmas arise in part because the institution of science incorporates potentially incompatible values (Merton, 1976). For instance, the value placed upon originality leads scientists to want their priority to be recognized, and the value set upon humility leads them to insist on how little they have in fact been able to accomplish. Also, Merton identified contradictions between the core norms and value of the discipline and tactical, pragmatic norms having to do with the practical production processes and relationships of power within a discipline. There are also conflicts between sub-communities, schools, and scientific traditions with competing paradigms and methodologies within a scientific community.

131. Boulding (1964:40) argues that the stability of scientific knowledge depends in part on the fact that inferences of science are drawn not from observation but from theories, thus serving to buffer 'the scientific community against the rejection of its inferences or rejection of its messages or observations'.

132. Clark and Majone (1984) argue that meta-criteria or evaluation rules can be found which would allow for a more global and balanced practice of scientific

inquiries in policy contexts. They assume, too optimistically in our opinion, that scientists will to a large extent provide the meta-criteria of 'adequacy', 'effectiveness', 'value' and 'legitimacy'.

In our view, the meta-rules and evaluation criteria are to a large extent 'negotiable', and the actual results will depend on the arguments, authority and power resources which scientific communities can mobilize. In some policy settings their bargaining position may be stronger, more sustained than in others.

133. There has been a general development along these lines, Clark and Majone (1984:35) argue:

> There is still a great respect for learning among politicians and policymakers, but there is also much greater skepticism and suspicion, and the image of objective 'value-free' science and scholarship is severely tarnished (cited from Harvey Brooks). But the unquestioning acceptance of science's legitimacy no longer holds ... What we see then is that the postwar numinous legitimacy of science has been eroded, leaving in its wake a need for a socially negotiated civil legitimacy. Our society's great preoccupation in recent years with 'public interest' and 'critical' science, with hearing procedures and 'independent' assessments, and with demands for 'better' ethical standards of scientific practice reflect both the urgency and the difficulty of those negotiations.

134. The differences between traditional and modern societies concerning the organization of primary modes of social transaction — the exercise of domination, social exchange and collective decision-making — have been defined in sociology with a variety of general terms, which have not only been difficult to operationalize but to develop theoretically in a systematic way: gemeinschaft/gesellschaft (Tonnies); traditional/rational–legal (Weber); folk culture/urban culture (Redfield); sacred/secular (H. Becker); value maintenance/instrumentality. (Parsons) went further in trying to specify dimensions (pattern variables) with which to distinguish the structure of social organization, e.g. affectivity/affective neutrality; collective orientation/self-orientation; ascription/achievement; diffuseness/specificity.

A more precise set of dimensions based on identification and comparative analysis of historically and culturally specific rule processes and forms would be a useful start here. What are the characteristic features, for instance, of the rule-making, rule-interpretation, and rule-implementation processes associated with 'formalization', 'depersonalization' and 'specialization'? What are the consequences in practice? What are characteristic features of social rule systems organizing human relationships formally and impersonally as distinct from other systems (as discussed, in part, in Chapter 11)? In what ways do these different systems reinforce, complement, or contradict one another?

135. The legal profession — as well as the legal system — enjoy a certain degree of autonomy, which entails, among other things, the development of methods and technical procedures for 'legal rule formation, interpretation, amendment, etc.' that may go on to a greater or lesser extent independently of — or only with a loose coupling to — those judicial and government systems where decisions are made about law and its interpretations. Nevertheless, since lawyers are extensively employed in — and serve as external advisors to — these systems, their 'culture' of legal formulation, interpretation, and reformulation undoubtedly exercises a sustained and wide-spread influence.

136. Twining and Miers (1982:294) refer to 326 public general Acts enacted in Britain's Houses of Parliament during the period 1976–81. They add that this

takes no account of the many other rules having legislative effect concerning their interpretation and implementation, which have been promulgated since their enactment.

137. Most citizens have some concern about, but know only a very small part of the complex of laws, rules and regulations governing social security, taxes, housing, food products as well as other important consumer goods such as housing, cars, white appliances, among others, schools, health care, pensions, etc.

138. As suggested earlier, there are also contradictions within a capitalist economy, for instance between segments where these have identifiable organizing principles, dominated by certain types of capitalist interests: mining and extraction, industry, trade, or financial capital.

139. DeVille and Burns (1977) have argued that a capitalist system, which is integrated to a certain degree through regulatory institutions, tends to generate new types of incoherencies which the regulatory institutions cannot effectively deal with, and, indeed, in some cases contribute to self-amplifying incoherence and instability, in a word, crisis.

Structural incoherence, which depends on forces and developments outside the social system and which cannot be dealt with by available regulatory institutions, is characteristic of many Third World countries (Baumgartner et al., 1986).

140. Moreover, even a well-developed corporatist system may experience substantial failure or breakdown when confronted (Andersen, 1986):

(i) with an entire new sphere of activity where established organizing principles appear difficult to apply and where practical knowledge is minimal (often, entirely new rule system complexes may have to be built up and developed).

(ii) with powerful, external agents (e.g. multi-national corporations) that fail to share the neo-corporatist ideology and institutional frame. This sets the stage for deviance and destabilization of the entire system.

141. We are grateful to Les Johnson for suggesting this important idea.

142. Incompatibility and conflicts between social rule systems can be usefully thought of as contradictions between different *social logics or rationalities*. Lucien Karpik has developed and applied in a very powerful way the concept of social logic in organizational and institutional analyses. (See Karpik (1982) and Weiss (1982).)

For instance, instrumentally oriented rule formation contradicts normatively or politically oriented rule formation. On the one hand, the introduction of new production or communication technologies as well as destruction (war) technologies is largely motivated by a desire to improve performance, often leading to changes in social organization, division of labour and knowledge, and shifts in strategic function and power. On the other hand, 'social or value rationality' is driven by a desire to maintain and reproduce social structure, including established status and power relationships, community ties, norms, etc.

143. An established or newly established regime may be confronted with a recalcitrant reality. The regime presupposes capabilities of the actors, resource control, and physical action conditions which do not correspond to real conditions: (i) actors lack the capabilities or motivation to play out their roles according to the regime; (ii) the transaction conditions presupposed by the regime – for instance equality among actors in terms of resource control, knowledge, and authority — are not realized, so that prescribed patterns cannot be implemented; (iii) established interaction practices entail high levels of distrust, cheating, and lawlessness whereas the proposed regime presupposes solidarity, mutual consideration, and law-abiding behaviour. Of course, a regime by stressing certain desir-

able states or patterns may contribute in part to bringing about such patterns, or, at least, preventing extreme forms of the opposite from occurring. This follows from the principle that rules are a factor in the production of social behaviour.

144. Physical changes include natural catastrophes, climatic and geological shifts and alteration of resource bases. Included here are also changes brought about by the impact of human institutions and policies (whether or not the decisive agents are aware of or intend the changes). The depletion of strategic resources (soil and mineral resources, water, forests, fossil fuels, etc.) has been a common feature of the history of human societies. Demographic forces, including developments in food production as well as disease, plague and war, are also important conditioning factors. Again, human institutions and policies affect population increases or decreases. This includes, of course, sanitation and health care but also marriage, sexual, and reproductive practices — all of which are regulated in human societies by social institutions. Such rule systems, however, may be very difficult to manipulate or legislate since they are widely diffused and closely associated with private and local spheres of activity. Like 'physical forces'and global socio-political and economic forces, these social arrangements are often beyond the control of particular social agents or groups, even very powerful ones. Such factors impel social agents to adapt and restructure those rule systems which are subject to their manipulation and reformulation in the sphere or settings on which the factors impinge.

145. In general, social rule systems, which are or become authoritative, command the support or approval of important agents and groups in society: state agencies, the ruling class, elites, the articulate middle class or whoever holds power and wealth (Baumgartner and Burns, 1986: Friedman, 1977). Modern capitalists, agents of the state, and major professions in Western civilization more or less back up or accept modern modes of organized rule formation: rational–legal, negotiative–contractual, and democratic with, in general, the systematic application of 'expert' knowledge.

As argued earlier, legitimate, modern rule formation processes – and the rule systems they produce – have tended to push out, dominate, or compromise peripheral, local, traditional, and 'tribal' systems. Thus, 'managers', 'civil servants', 'lawyers' and other 'experts' replace amateurs, non-experts, 'local' and 'tribal' leaders, or at least dominate them in formally organized settings. The non-modern or peripheral rule-bearers and rule-makers, and their systems, are under sustained pressure to give way – at least publically – to those backed by legal, administrative, scientific and other types of modern authority. Of course, there is small-scale and large-scale political struggle and actor-system dynamics.

References

Albrow, M. (1970) *Bureaucracy*. London:Pall Mall and Macmillan.

Albrow, M. (1971) 'Public Administration and Sociological Theory', *Advancement of Science*, pp. 347–56.

Alker, Jr. H., J. Bennett and D. Mefford (1980) 'Generalized Precedent Logics for Resolving Insecurity Dilemmas', *International Interactions*.

Alker, Jr. H. (1981) 'From Political Cybernetics to Global Modeling', pp. 353–78. In R.C. Merritt and B.M. Russett (eds.), *From National Development to Global Community*. London: George Allen and Unwin.

Alker, Jr. H., T. J. Biersteker and T. Inoguchi (1985) 'The Decline of the Super-states: The Rise of a New World Order?' Paper presented at the World Congress of Political Science, Paris, July, 1985.

Allardt, E. (1972) 'Structural, Institutional, and Cultural Explanations'. *Acta Sociologica*, 15: 54–68.

Andersen, S. (1986) 'Neo-corporatism as a Context for Strategic Adaptation: The Case of the Norwegian Petroleum Sector.' Ph.D dissertation. Stanford: Stanford University.

Andersson, Bo. (1986) *Essays on Social Action and Social Structure. Studia Sociologica Upsaliensia*. Uppsala: Acta Universitatis Upsaliensis.

Archer, M. (1985) 'Structuration versus Morphogenesis'. In S.N. Eisenstadt and H.J. Helle (eds.), *Macro Sociological Theory: Perspectives on Sociological Theory*. London: Sage Publications.

Archer, M. (1986) 'The Sociology of Education' In U. Himmelstrand (ed.), *Sociology: The Aftermath of Crisis*. London: Sage Publications.

Arrow, K. (1974) *The Limits of Organization*. New York: Norton.

Ashby, W.R. (1957) *An Introduction to Cybernetics*. New York: Wiley.

Axelrod, R. (1984) *The Evolution of Cooperation*. New York: Basic Books.

Baker, W. (1984) 'The Social Structure of a National Securities Market'. *American Journal of Sociology*, vol. 89:775–811.

Baumgartner, T. and T.R. Burns (1984) *Transitions to Alternative Energy Systems: Entrepreneurs, New Technologies, and Social Change*. Boulder, Colorado and London: Westview Press.

Baumgartner, T., T.R. Burns, and P. DeVille (1986) *The Shaping of Socioeconomic Systems*. London/New York: Gordon and Breach.

Baumgartner, T. and A. Midttun (eds.) (1986) *The Politics of Energy Forecasting: A Comparative Study of Energy Forecasting in Western Industrialized Nations*. Oxford: Oxford University Press.

Bennett, J. (1964) *Rationality*. London: Routledge and Kegan Paul.

Bereano, P.L. (1976) *Technology as a Social and Political Phenomenon*. New York: Wiley.

Berger, P.L. and T. Luckman (1967) *The Social Construction of Reality*. Harmondsworth: Penguin.

Blau, P. (1956) *The Dynamics of Bureaucracy*. New York: Random House.

Blau, P. and W.R. Scott (1962) *Formal Organizations: A Comparative Approach*. San Francisco: Chandler.

Boudon, R. (1979) *The Logic of Social Action*. London: Routledge & Kegan Paul.

Boulding, K. (1955) *Economic Analysis*, 3rd edition New York: Harper & Row.
Boulding, K. (1956) 'General Systems Theory — The Skeleton of Science'. *Management Science*, 2: 197–208.
Boulding, K. (1956) *The Image*. New York: Academic Press.
Boulding, K. (1964) *The Meaning of the Twentieth Century*. New York: Harper & Row.
Bourdieu, P. (1977) *Outline of a Theory of Practice*. Cambridge: Cambridge University Press.
Broström, A. (1981) *Storkonflikten 1980*. Stockholm: Arbetslivscentrum.
Brögger, S. (1976) *Kärlekens vägar och villovägar*. Stockholm: Wahlström and Widstrand, pp. 67–71.
Buckley, W. (1967) *Sociology and Modern Systems Theory*. Englewood Cliffs, N.J.: Prentice-Hall.
Bunge, M. (1981) *Scientific Materialism*. Dordrecht: Reidel.
Burns, T.R. and G.M. Stalker (1961) *The Management of Innovation*. London: Tavistock Publications.
Burns, T.R. (1985) *Technological Development with reference to Hydro-power, Nuclear and Alternative Energy Technologies*. Berlin, Wissenschaftszentrum.
Burns, T.R. (1986) 'Actors, Transactions, and Social Structure: An Introduction to Social Rule System Theory'. In U. Himmelstrand (ed.), *Sociology: The Aftermath of Crisis*. London: Sage Publications.
Burns, T.R. (1979) *Energy and Society Project Description*. Oslo: Institute of Sociology.
Burns, T.R. (1978) *Prediction, Social Action, and Social Transformation:* Self-altering Processes in Social Life and Their Implications for Social Science Methodology and for Social Planning. Unpublished ms.
Burns, T.R., T. Baumgartner, and P. DeVille (1985) *Man, Decisions, Society*. London/New York: Gordon and Breach.
Burns, T.R., P. DeVille and H. Flam (1986) *The Structure and Dynamics of Capitalism: Actors, Institutions, and Development*. Uppsala: Institute of Sociology.
Burns, T.R. and A. Midttun (1985) *Economic Growth, Environmentalism, and Social Conflict: A Case Study of Hydro-power Planning in Norway*. Berlin: Wissenschaftszentrum.
Burns, T.R. and A. Olsson (1986) *The Swedish Model in Transition: Complexity, Tension and Social Change in a Neo-corporatist System*. Uppsala: Institute of Sociology Report.
Burns, T.R. and J. Tropea (1985) 'The Structuring of Criminal Justice Systems'. Paper presented at the Annual Meeting of the American Academy of Criminal Justice, Las Vegas, Nevada, April, 1985.
Chomsky, N. (1957) *Syntactic Structures*. The Hague: Mouton.
Chomsky, N. (1965) *Aspects of the Theory of Syntax*. Cambridge: MIT Press.
Cicourel, A.V. (1974) *Cognitive Sociology*. New York: Free Press.
Clark, W.C. and A. Majone (1984) 'The Critical Appraisal of Scientific Inquiries with Policy Implications'. Laxenburg, Austria: IIASA Report.
Collins, R. (1986) *Max Weber: A Skeleton Key*. London: Sage Publications.
Commons, J.P. (1959) *Legal Foundations of Capitalism*. Madison: University of Wisconsin Press.
Constant, E.W. (1984) 'Communities and Hierarchies: Structure in the Practice of Science and Technology', in R. Laudan (ed.), *The Nature of Technological Knowledge*. Dordrecht: Reidel

Coppock, R. (1984) *Social Constraints on Technological Progress*. London: Gower Press.

Crozier, M. (1964) *The Bureaucratic Phenomenon*. Chicago: University of Chicago Press.

Crozier, M. and E. Friedberg (1977) *L'acteur et 'Le systeme'*. Paris: Presses Universitaires de France. (1980 edition in English: *Actors and Systems: The Politics of Collective Action*. Chicago: University of Chicago Press.)

Crozier, M. and J-C. Thoenig (1975) 'La regulation de systemes organizes complexes'. *Revue Francaise de Sociologie*, 16:3–32.

Dahl, R.A. and C.E. Lindblom (1963) *Politics, Economics and Welfare*. New York: Harper & Row.

Dalton, M. (1959) *Men Who Manage*. New York: Wiley.

Dam, K. W. (1982) *The Rules of the Game: Reform and Evolution in the International Monetary System*. Chicago: University of Chicago Press.

Deutsch, K. (1963) *The Nerves of Government: Models of Political Communication and Control*. New York: Free Press.

DeVille, P. (1985) 'Socio-economics and Economic Theory: Logical Requirement or Casual Empiricism?'. Presented at the Third International Workshop of the Swedish Collegium for Advanced Studies in the Social Sciences. Amsterdam, 28–30 November, 1985.

DeVille, P. and T.R. Burns (1977) 'Institutional Responses to Crisis in Capitalist Development'. *Social Praxis*, 4:5–46.

Douglas, M. and B. Isherwood (1980) *The World of Goods*. Harmondsworth, Middlesex: Penguin.

Draper, R. (1985) 'The Golden Arm'. *New York Review of Books*. October 24, pp. 46–52.

Durbin, P.T. (1978) *Research in Philosophy and Technology*, vol 1. Greenwich, Conn.: JAI Press.

Edgren, G., K-O Faxen and C-E Odner (1970) *Lönebildning och Samhällsekonomi*. Stockholm: Raben & Sjögren.

Eisenstadt, S.N. and M. Curelaru (1977) *Current Sociology*, 25, (2).

Elias, N. (1978)a *The Civilizing Process*. Oxford: Blackwell.

Elias, N. (1978)b *What is Sociology?* New York: Columbia University Press.

Etzioni, A. (1968) *The Active Society: A Theory of Societal and Political Processes*. New York: Free Press.

Etzioni, A. (1970) 'Toward a Macrosociology', in J.C. McKinney and E.A. Tiryakian (eds.), *Theoretical Sociology*. New York: Appleton-Century-Crofts.

Etzioni, A. (1975) *Complex Organizations*. New York: Free Press.

Etzioni, A. (1985) 'Encapsulated competition'. *Journal of Post Keynesian Economics*, 7:287–302.

Ewerlöf, G. (1985) 'Artificial Insemination: Legislation and Debate', *Current Sweden*, no. 329, 1985, The Swedish Institute, Stockholm.

Flam, H. (1985) 'Market Configurations: Toward a Framework for Socio-economic Studies'. Presented at the Third International Workshop of the Swedish Collegium for Advanced Studies in the Social Sciences, Amsterdam, 28–30 November, 1985.

Flanders, A. (ed.) (1969) *Collective Bargaining*. Harmondsworth: Penguin Books Ltd.

Friedman, L.M. (1977) *Law and Society*. Englewood Cliffs, NJ: Prentice-Hall.

Galtung, J. (1971) 'A Structural Theory of Imperialism.' *Journal of Peace Research*, 8:81–117.

Garfinkel, H. (1963) 'A Conception of, and Experiments with 'Trust' as a Condition of Stable, Concerted Actions'. In O.J. Harvey (ed.) *Motivation and Social Interaction*. New York: Ronald Press.

Gellner, E. (1960) Review of P. Winch's *The Idea of a Social Science*, appearing in *The British Journal of Sociology*, 11, 170–2.

Giddens, T. (1976) *New Rules of Sociological Methods*. New York: Basic Books.

Giddens, T. (1979) *Central Problems in Social Theory: Action, Structure and Contradiction in Social Analysis*. Berkeley: University of California Press.

Giddens, T. (1984) *The Constitution of Society*. Oxford: Polity Press.

Gitlin, T. (1980) *The Whole World is Watching: Mass Media in the Making and Unmaking of the New Left*. Berkeley: University of California Press.

Goffman, E. (1974) *Frame Analysis: An Essay on the Organization of Experience*. Cambridge: Harvard University Press.

Granovetter, M. (1985) 'Economic Action and Social Structure: The Problem of Embeddedness'. *American Journal of Sociology*, Vol. 50:481–510.

Gutting, G. (1984) 'Paradigms, Revolutions, and Technology', in R. Laudan (ed.) (op. cit.).

Haas, J.E. and T.E. Drabek (1973) *Complex Organizations*. New York: Macmillan.

Harre, R. (1979a) *Social Being*. Oxford: Blackwell.

Harre, R. (1979b) *Matter and Method*. Atascadero, Calif: Ridgeview.

Harre, R. and P.F. Secord (1972) *The Explanation of Social Behavior*. Oxford: Blackwell.

Henshel, R.L. (1978) 'Self-altering Predictions', In J. Fowles (ed.), *Handbook of Futures Research*. Westport, Conn.: Greenwood Press.

Henshel, R.L. (1982) 'The Boundary of the Self-fulfilling Prophecy and The Dilemma of Social Prediction'. *British Journal of Sociology*, 33:511–28.

Hernes, G. et al. (1982) *Maktutredningen. (Norwegian Social Power Study.)* Oslo: University of Oslo Press.

Himmelstrand, U. (1986) *Sociology: The Aftermath of Crisis*. London: Sage Publications.

Hirsch, F. (1977) *Social Limits to Growth*. London: Routledge & Kegan Paul.

Hirschman, A. (1982) 'Rival Interpretations of Market Society: Civilizing, Destructive or Feeble', *Journal of Economic Literature*, 20:1463–84.

Hofstadter, D.R. (1985) *Metamagical Themes*. Harmondsworth, Middlesex: Penguin.

Hughes, T.P. (1983) *Networks of Power*. Baltimore: Johns Hopkins Press.

Hummon, N.P. (1984) 'Organizational Aspects of Technological Change'. In R. Laudan (ed.) (op. cit.).

Johansson, S. *Treatment Research: Scientific Norms versus Professional Ethics* (in Swedish). Ph. D. Dissertation in Sociology. Studia Sociologica Upsaliensia, 23. Uppsala: Acta Universitatis Upsaliensis.

Johnson, L. (1983) 'Epistemics and the Frame Conception of Knowledge'. *Kybernetes*, 12:177–81.

Karpik, L. (1982) 'Organizations, Institutions and History', in M. Zey-Ferrell and M. Aiken (eds.). Scott, Foresman and Company, Glenview, Illinois.

Katz, H. (1982) 'The US Automobile Collective Bargaining System in Transition', *British Journal of Industrial Relations*, 22:205–17.

Kickert, W. (1979) *Organization of Decision-making: A Systems Theoretical Approach*. Amsterdam:North Holland.

Kitschelt, H. (1985) 'New Social Movements in West Germany and the USA'. *Political Power and Social Theory*, Vol. 5:273–324.

Kjellberg, A. (1983) *Facklig Organisering i Tolv Länder.* Lund: Arkiv.

Korpi, W. (1983) *The Democratic Class Struggle,* London: Routledge & Kegan Paul.

Lash, S. (1985) 'The Breakdown of Neo-corporatism?: The Breakdown of Centralized Bargaining in Sweden', *British Journal of Industrial Relations,* 23, (2) July 1985.

Laudan, R. (ed.) (1984) *The Nature of Technological Knowledge.* Dordrecht: Reidel.

Layton, E.T. (1974) 'Technology as Knowledge'. *Technology and Culture,* 15:31–42.

Leach, G. et al. (1979) *A Low Energy Strategy for the UK.* London: International Institute for Environment and Development.

Leblebici, H. and G.R. Salancik (1982) 'Stability in Interorganizational Changes: Rule-making Processes of the Chicago Board of Trade'. *Administrative Science Quarterly,* 27:27–242.

Leontief, W. and F. Duchin (1985) *The Future Impact of Automation on Workers.* Oxford: Oxford University Press.

Levi-Strauss, C. (1963) *Structural Anthropology.* New York: Basic Books.

Levi-Strauss, C. (1972) 'History and Dialectic', in Richard and Fernande DeGeorge (eds.), *The Structuralists from Marx to Levi-Strauss.* New York: Doubleday & Company.

Lilja, J. (1984) 'Läkemedelskontrollen: ett mångtydigt begrepp', *Svensk Farmaceutisk Tidskrift,* 88:26–31. bib.

Lilja, J. (1984) 'The Nationalization of the Swedish Pharmacies'. ms. Department of Social Pharmacy, Uppsala University.

Lindblom, C.E. (1977) *Politics and Markets.* New York: Basic Books.

Litterer, J.A. (1969) *Organizations: Structure and Behavior.* New York: Wiley.

Luce, R.D. and H. Raiffa (1957) *Games and Decisions.* New York: Wiley.

McGinn, R.E. (1978) 'What is Technology? in P.T. Durbin (ed.)

de Man, R. (1986) *The Organization and Politics of Forecasting.* PhD dissertation, University of Amsterdam.

de Man, R. and H. van Rossum (1984) *Barriers against Energy Savings in New Home Construction* (in Dutch). Leiden: University Report.

Mansfield, E. (1975) *Micro-economics.* New York: Norton.

March, J.G. and J.P. Olsen (1976) *Ambiguity and Choice in Organizations.* Oslo: Universitetsforlaget.

Margolis, J. (1978) 'Culture and Technology', in P.T. Durbin (ed.) (op. cit.).

Marin, Bernnd (1985) 'Generalized Political Exchange'. Paper presented at the XIIIth World Congress of the International Political Science Association (IPSA), Paris, July, 1985. EUI Working Paper No. 85/190. Florence: European University Institute.

Martin, A. (1984) 'Trade Unions in Sweden: Strategic Responses to Change and Crisis', in P. Gourevitch et al., *Unions and Economic Crisis: Britain, West Germany and Sweden.* London: George Allen & Unwin.

Martino, J.P. (1972) *Technological Forecasting for Decision-making.* New York: American Elsevier.

Matthews, D.R. (1960) *U.S. Senators and Their World.* Chapel Hill: University of North Carolina Press.

Matthews, D. R. (1968) 'Rules of the Game'. *International Encyclopedia of Social Science.* New York: Free Press, pp. 571–6.

Maynard, D.W. (1985) 'On the Function of Social Conflict among Children'. *American Sociological Review,* 50:207–23.

Merton, R. (1976) *Sociological Ambivalence.* New York: Free Press.

Merton, R. (1957) *Social Theory and Social Structure.* Glencoe, Illinois: Free Press.

Midttun, A. (1986) *The Structuring and Restructuring of the Norwegian Hydro-power Segment.* Ph.D. dissertation. Uppsala: Institute of Sociology.

Miller, G.A., E. Galanter, and K. H. Pribram (1960) *Plans and the Structure of Behavior.* New York: Holt, Rinehart and Winston.

Mitcham, Carl (1978) 'Types of Technology', in P.T. Durbin (ed.) (op. cit.).

Moore, Jr. B. (1966) *Social Origins of Dictatorship and Democracy.* Boston: Beacon Press.

Mouzelis, N.P. (1967) *Organization and Bureaucracy.* Chicago: Aldine.

von Neumann, J. and O. Morgenstern (1953) *Theory of Games and Economic Behavior,* 3rd edition. Princeton, N.J.: Princeton University Press.

North, D.C. (1981) *Structure and Change in Economic History.* New York: Norton.

Norwegian Social Power Study (Maktutredningen) (1982) *Final Report.* (see Hernes, 1982).

Offe, C. (1983) 'Legitimation Problems in Nuclear Conflict'. Paper presented at the Somso Meeting in the Nuclear Energy Debate, Utrecht, Netherlands, 24 June, 1983.

Olsson, A. (1986) *The Transformation of a Collective Bargaining System: The Case of Sweden,* dissertation manuscript, Uppsala: Department of Sociology, Uppsala University.

Pagels, E.H. (1983) 'Born Again'. (Review of W.A. Meeks, *The First Urban Christians: The Social World of the Apostle Paul), New York Review of Books,* 30, 12:41–3.

Parsons, T. (1951) *The Social System.* Glencoe, Ill.: Free Press.

Parsons, T. (1960) *Structure and Process in Modern Societies.* Glencoe, Ill.: Free Press.

Perrow, C. (1979) *Complex Organizations.* Glenview, Ill.: Scott, Foresman and Company. 2nd edition (1st edition, 1972).

Pfeffer, J. and G.R. Salancik (1978) *The External Control of Organizations.* New York: Harper and Row.

Polanyi, K., C. Arensberg, and H. Pearson (1957) *Trade and Market in the Early Empires.* New York: Free Press.

Powers, W.T. (1973) *Behaviour: The Control of Perception.* Chicago: Aldine.

Rapoport, A. (1960) *Fights, Games and Debates.* Ann Arbor: University of Michigan Press.

Rawles, J. (1955) 'Two Concepts of Rules'. *Philosophical Review,* 64:3–32.

Reichenbach, H. (1982) *Modern Philosophy of Science.* New York: Greenwood.

Roethlisberger, F.J. and W.J. Dickson (1939) *Management and the Worker.* Cambridge: Harvard University Press.

Rosenberg, N. (1982) *Inside the Black Box: Technology and Economics.* Cambridge: Cambridge University Press.

Rossi, P. et al. (1974) 'The Seriousness of Crimes: Normative Structure and Individual Differences'. *American Sociological Review,* 39:224–237.

Roy, D. (1964) 'Efficiency and "The Fix": Informal Intergroup Relations in a Piece-work Machine Shop'. *American Journal of Sociology,* 60:155–266.

Salaman, G. (1980) 'Roles and Rules,' in G. Salaman and K. Thompson (eds.).

Salaman, G. and K. Thompson (eds.) (1973) *People and Organizations.* London: Longman.

Salaman, G. and K. Thompson (eds.) (1980) *Control and Ideology in Organizations.* Milton Keynes, England: Open University Press.

Samuelson, P.A. (1958) *Economics: An Introduction.* New York: McGraw-Hill

Schadewaldt, W. (1979) 'The Concepts of Nature and Technique According to the Greeks', in P.T. Durbin (ed.) (op. cit.).

Schmitter, P.C. (1979a) 'Still the Century of Corporatism', in P.C. Schmitter and G. Lehmbruch (eds.), *Trends Toward Corporatist Intermediation*. London: Sage Publications.

Schmitter, P.C. (1979b) 'Modes of Interest Mediation and Models of Societal Change in Western Europe', in Schmitter and Lehmbruch (eds.).

Schon, D.R. (1969) 'Managing Technological Innovation'. *Harvard Business Review*, 47:156–72.

Scott, P.B. (1985) *The Robotics Revolution: The Complete Guide for Managers and Engineers*.

Scott, W.R. (1981) *Organizations: Rational, Natural, and Open Systems*. Englewood Cliffs, N.J.: Prentice-Hall.

Searle, J. (1965) 'What is a Speech Act?', in M. Black (ed.), *Philosophy in America*. Ithaca: Cornell University Press.

Segerstedt, T. (1970) *Socialt system för samfärdsel*. Uppsala: Acta Universitatis Upsaliensis.

Selvik, A. and G. Hernes (1977) *Dynamikk i borehullene, om kraftutbygging og lokalsamfunn*. Bergen: Universitetsforlaget.

Selznick, P. (1953) *TVA and Grass Roots*. Berkeley: University of California Press.

Shaiken, H. (1985) *Work Transformed: Automation and Labor in the Computer Age*. New York: Holt, Rinehart and Winston.

Sherby, O.D. and J. Wadsworth (1985) 'Medieval Forging Methods May Make Possible the Mass Production of Ultra-high-carbon Steels'. *Scientific American*, 252.

Simon, H.A. (1977) *Models of Discovery and Other Topics in the Methods of Science*. Dordrecht, Holland: Reidel.

Simon, H.A. (1981) *The Sciences of the Artificial*. Cambridge: MIT Press.

Sjöstrand, S-E. (1985) *Samhällsorganization*. Lund: Doxa.

Smelser, N.J. (1963) *The Sociology of Economic Life*. Englewood Cliffs, N.J.: Prentice-Hall.

Sonnedecker, G. et al. (1974) *History of Pharmacy*. Madison, Wisconsin: American Institute of the History of Pharmacy.

Strauss, A., L. Schatzmann, D. Ehrlich, R. Bucher and M. Sabshin (1963) 'The Hospital and its Negotiated Order', in E. Friedson (ed.), *The Hospital in Modern Society*. New York: Macmillan.

Streeck, W. and P.C. Schmitter (1984) 'Community, Market, State, and Associations. The Prospective Contribution of Interest Governance to Social Order', EUI Working Paper No. 94. Florence: European University Institute.

Suarez, P. and G. Golborne (1986) 'The Electoral Consequences of the Enfranchisement of Women: Problems, hypotheses and methodological approaches'. Paper presented at the 28th World Congress of the International Institute of Sociology, Albufeira, Portugal, June, 1986.

Swidler, A. (1986) 'Culture in Action: Symbols and Strategies', *American Sociological Review*, 51:273–86.

Teulings, A.W. M. (1985) 'The Rise of Organized Capitalism: Tri-Partite Networks and Neo-corporative Policy-making in the Netherlands'. Report of the Sociology of Organizations Research Unit. Amsterdam: University of Amsterdam.

Thompson, J.D. (1967) *Organizations in Action*. New York: McGraw-Hill.

Thompson, K. (1980) 'The Organizational Society', in Salaman and Thompson (eds.), 1980.

Tichy, N. (1973) 'An Analysis of Clique Formation and Structure in Organizations', *Administrative Science Quarterly*, 194–208.

Tumin, J. (1982) 'The Theory of Democratic Development', *Theory and Society*, 11:143–64.

Turner, S. (1985) *Strong Trade Unions, Corporatism and Economic Performance: A Critical Review of the Literature*. Stockholm: IUI and Harvard University.

Twining, W. and D. Miers (1982) *How To Do Things with Rules*. 2nd ed. London: Weidenfeld and Nicolson.

Ullenhag, J. (1971) *Den Solidariska Lönepolitiken i Sverige*. Stockholm: Läromedelsförlagen.

Wagner, P. (1985) 'De la "scientification" de la politique a la pluralisation de l'expertise: Expertise en sciences sociales et regulation des conflits sociaux en RFA'. Report of the Science Center Berlin, Report P.85–5. Berlin: Wissenschaftszentrum.

Wahlke, J. et al. (1962) *The Legislative System: Explorations in Legislative Behavior*. New York: Wiley.

Wallace, W.L. (1969) *Sociological Theory*. London: Heinemann.

Wardell, M.L. and J.K. Benson (1979) 'A Dialectical View: Foundations for an Alternative Sociological Method', in S.G. McNall (ed.), *Theoretical Perspectives in Sociology*. New York: St Martin's Press.

Weber, M. (1946) *From Max Weber: Essays in Sociology*. Gerth, H.H. and C.W. Mills (eds.) New York: Oxford University Press.

Weber, M. (1968) *Economy and Society*. New York: Bedminister Press.

Weber, M. (1977) *Critique of Stammler*. New York: Free Press.

Weingart, P. (1984) 'The Structure of Technological Change: Reflections on a Sociological Analysis of Technology', in R. Laudan (ed.) 1984.

Weiss W. (1982) 'The Historical and Political Perspective on Organizations of Lucien Karpik', in M. Zey-Ferrell and M. Aiken. Glenview, Illinois: Scott, Foresman and Company.

Westerståhl, J. (1945) *Svensk Fackföreningsrörelse*. Stockholm: Tidens förlag.

White, H.C. (1981) 'Where do markets come from', *American Journal of Sociology*, 87:517–47.

Whyte, W.F., Jr. (1956) *Money and Motivation: An Analysis of Incentives in Industry*. New York: Harper and Row.

Wildavsky and Tannenbaum (1981) *The Politics of Mistrust: Estimating American Oil and Gas Resources*. Beverly Hills, California: Sage Publications.

Wiley, N. (1983) 'The Congruence of Weber and Keynes', *Sociological Theory*, 1:30–57.

Wiley, N. (1985) 'The Current Interregnum in American Sociology', *Social Research*, 52:179–207.

Willer, D. and B. Anderson (1981) *Networks, Exchange and Coercion*. New York: Elsevier.

Williamson, O. (1975) *Markets and Hierarchies*. New York: Free Press.

Winner, L. (1977) *Autonomous Technology*. Cambridge, Mass.: MIT Press.

Winner, L. (1983) 'Technolcgies as Forms of Life', in R.S. Cohen and M.W. Wartofsky (eds.), *Epistemology, Methodology and the Social Sciences*. Holland: Reidel.

Wittrock, B. (1984) 'Useful Science and Scientific Openness: Baconian Vision or Faustian Bargain', in M. Gibbons and B. Wittrock (eds.), *Science as a Commodity: Threats to the Open Community of Scholars*. London: Longman.

Wittrock, B. (1986) 'Social Knowledge and Public Policy: Eight Models of Interaction', in C. Weiss and H. Wollman (eds.), *Social Science and Governmental Institutions*. London: Sage Publications.

Zaltman, G. and M. Wallendorf (1979) *Consumer Behavior.* New York: Wiley.

Zelizer, V.A. (1981) 'The Price and Value of Children: The Case of Children's Insurance', *American Journal of Sociology*, 86.

Zelizer, V.A. (1978) 'Human Values and the Market: The Case of Life Insurance and Death in 19th Century America', *American Journal of Sociology* 84.

Zetterberg, H. (1983) 'The Victory of Reason — Max Weber Revisited', contribution to Festschrift for Professor Georg Karlsson. Sifo/Safo Skriftserie No. 2. Vällingby: Sifo.

Zey-Ferrell, M. (1982) 'The Dominant Perspective on Organizations', in P.O. Berg and P. Daudi (eds.), *Traditions and Trends in Organization Theory.* Lund: Studentlitteratur, pp. 156–200.

Zimmerman, D. (1973) 'The Practicalities of Rule Use', in G. Salaman and K. Thompson (eds.), pp. 250–63.

Other sources

Arbetsmarknadsstatistisk Årsbok, 1973–1983, Stockholm: SCB.

Fakta om Sveriges Ekonomi, 1983–1985, Stockholm: SAF.

Förlikningsmannaexpeditionen Statistics over conflicts, Various years, Stockholm.

Nationalräkenskaperna, Various years, Stockholm: Finansdepartementet?. *Statistiska Meddelanden,* SmP 1984, Stockholm: SCB.

Statistisk Årsbok, 1950–1984, Stockholm: SCB.

Index

About the authors and contributors

Tom R. Burns is Professor in the Department of Sociology, University of Uppsala. He is also Program Co-Director, Social Science Theory and Methodology Program, The Swedish Collegium for Advanced Studies in the Social Sciences.

Helena Flam is Research Associate, Social Science Theory and Methodology Program, The Swedish Collegium for Advanced Studies in the Social Sciences, and Research Associate in the Department of Sociology, University of Lund.

Reinier de Man is Research Associate, Technology and Society Program, Erasmus University, Rotterdam.

Tormod Lunde is Assistant Professor at Columbia University, New York.

Atle Midttun is Research Associate, Norwegian School of Business, Oslo.

Anders Olsson is Fellow in the Department of Sociology, University of Uppsala.